Customer-Centric AI:

Conversational Technologies, Personalization, and Ethical Innovation

Mahwish Zahara
University of Bedfordshire, UK

IGI Global
Scientific Publishing
Publishing Tomorrow's Research Today

Vice President of Editorial	Melissa Wagner
Director of Acquisitions	Mikaela Felty
Director of Book Development	Jocelynn Hessler
Production Manager	Mike Brehm
Cover Design	Jose Rosado

Published in the United States of America by
IGI Global Scientific Publishing
701 East Chocolate Avenue
Hershey, PA, 17033, USA
Tel: 717-533-8845
Fax: 717-533-7115
Website: https://www.igi-global.com E-mail: cust@igi-global.com

Library of Congress Cataloging-in-Publication Data

LCCN: 2025036599 (CIP Data Pending)
ISBN13: 9798337365824
Isbn13Softcover: 9798337365831
EISBN13: 9798337365848

British Cataloguing in Publication Data
A Cataloguing in Publication record for this book is available from the British Library.

Table of Contents

Detailed Table of Contents

Meta's AI-driven Multi-Touch Attribution system addresses the shortcomings of conventional models like last-click by better representing intricate consumer paths across multiple platforms. Meta evaluates the actual incremental effects of ad interactions using Shapley value analysis and counterfactual modelling combined with federated learning while maintaining user privacy protections. The new methods enable higher return on ad spend (ROAS), allow for dynamic budget adjustments in real time and facilitate customization for different platforms. Even though there have been quantifiable improvements in performance results algorithmic transparency issues along with regulatory compliance and bias mitigation challenges persist. The chapter promotes ethical use of artificial intelligence and highlights the critical role humans and AI must play together when planning media strategies. The conclusion calls for established attribution frameworks that are both standardized and interpretable to maintain responsible and effective marketing within the fast-changing digital environment.

Retail marketing has been revolutionized by conversational artificial intelligence which enables personalization and automation while providing real-time customer interaction. This chapter examines Sephora's advanced conversational AI applications including virtual beauty assistants and chatbots to boost customer service and marketing outcomes. Recent studies show that natural language processing, machine learning (ML), and Augmented Reality (AR) technologies enable seamless omnichannel experiences and operational improvements. The conceptual framework demonstrates how AI tools boost customer engagement while enhancing user experience and accelerating sales growth. This chapter analyses how Sephora handles customer relationship management and builds loyalty through digital branding.

IKEA revolutionized its customer shopping experience through the implementation of Augmented Reality (AR) and Artificial Intelligence (AI) technologies within its retail operations. This chapter examines how IKEA Place app among other digital tools improves customer engagement by allowing customers to visualize products in real-time within their homes and deliver personalized recommendations. The combination of AI-powered personalization and AR-enhanced immersion provides customers with enhanced control and confidence resulting in stronger emotional bonds to their buying choices. The chapter examines recent research along with case studies to show how IKEA uses technology to boost customer interaction while decreasing product return rates through sustainable retail methods. The chapter examines the crucial impact of trust, perceived risk, and co-creation elements on AR-based personalization adoption. The chapter delivers a future-focused analysis of how AI and AR utilize IKEA's implementation to create interactive and intelligent retail spaces that centre around the user.

Starbucks deploys artificial intelligence to understand customer preferences which allows them to deliver custom product suggestions and appropriate promotions such as a recommended iced beverage when the weather is warm. The data-driven method enhances customer satisfaction and loyalty by ensuring every interaction holds more relevance for customers. Real-time optimization of inventory management and marketing strategies as well as staffing decisions is enabled by predictive analytics. The Starbucks mobile application and rewards system deliver personalized experiences that work seamlessly across different platforms. The transition towards hyper-personalization has yielded improved customer retention rates and higher revenue figures. Starbucks' strategic application of predictive analytics is examined through its technology usage and conceptual models which lead to observable performance outcomes. The conceptual model demonstrates AI's method for processing customer data to enable personalized experiences and generate feedback.

Netflix dominates the streaming marketplace by implementing Artificial Intelligence (AI) to deliver personalized content using collaborative filtering combined with deep learning techniques. Reinforcement learning combined with natural language processing enables real-time analysis of user actions and emotional responses. The system refines its recommendations by applying matrix factorization and ranking algorithms to data from user play actions and skips. A/B testing confirms that these AI approaches increase user engagement while minimizing decision fatigue. The issues of algorithmic bias along with privacy concerns and filter bubbles remain unresolved according to studies. The use of AI by Netflix transforms content consumption and triggers ethical debates surrounding personalized entertainment.

The online fashion retail sector has experienced a transformation through AI technologies which allow retailers to create tailor-made shopping experiences for each customer. Through its use of sophisticated AI technologies such as machine learning algorithms and collaborative filtering systems Zalando delivers personalized fashion suggestions that reflect both customer tastes and current style movements while analysing their online activity. This chapter examines the ways in which Zalando's recommendation systems boost customer satisfaction while increasing purchase conversion rates and strengthening brand loyalty. The chapter examines AI personalization challenges such as algorithmic bias and privacy issues while proposing methods for ethical and sustainable innovation approaches. This chapter demonstrates how AI will transform personalized online retail through an examination of real-world applications and research outcomes.

Artificial intelligence revolutionizes marketing but presents significant ethical issues about privacy, transparency, and user control that need to be addressed. The chapter examines Meta's efforts to strike a balance between personal privacy and commercial data usage through transparency tools, private data protection technologies, and algorithmic decision making. AI systems that deliver top-level engagement and advertising results inevitably manipulate users while amplifying

The chapter provides marketers actionable strategies alongside theoretical knowledge to ethically and effectively utilize generative AI while remaining adaptable to the fast-changing digital environment.

Preface

INTRODUCTION

Artificial Intelligence (AI) is transforming how brands understand, communicate with, and serve their customers. As customer expectations grow in complexity, businesses across industries are increasingly turning to AI-powered tools like conversational agents, predictive analytics, augmented reality (AR), and generative models to deliver seamless, personalized experiences. This edited research volume, *Customer-Centric AI: Conversational Technologies, Personalization, and Ethical Innovation*, aims to explore how leading organizations apply AI to not only optimize user engagement and personalization but also navigate the ethical and societal implications of these innovations.

In assembling this volume, we sought contributions that reflect both technical depth and real-world relevance. The chapters span retail, entertainment, fashion, food and beverage, and digital advertising—domains where AI is not only enhancing personalization but redefining the nature of interaction itself. These case-based chapters also examine the tension between innovation and ethical responsibility, emphasizing critical issues such as data privacy, algorithmic transparency, and fairness. Our goal is to provide readers with a well-rounded, interdisciplinary perspective that captures the current landscape of customer-centric AI while pointing toward its future potential.

We thank each contributor for bringing both scholarly rigor and applied insight to this book. The real-world case studies, conceptual frameworks, and ethical analyses presented here offer a resource for academics, practitioners, policymakers, and students seeking to understand the evolving frontier of AI-driven customer engagement. Together, the authors reflect an international and multidisciplinary approach to innovation—one that respects both technological advancement and the human experience at the center of it all.

Chapter Overview

Chapter 1 introduces Meta's AI-powered multi-touch attribution models, exploring how Shapley value analysis and federated learning are reshaping digital ad performance while raising critical questions around transparency and regulatory compliance.

Chapter 2 explores Sephora's use of conversational AI, including chatbots and AR-powered virtual assistants, showing how real-time interaction and personalization build customer loyalty and brand presence.

Chapter 3 presents IKEA's application of AR and AI to enhance the in-home shopping experience, highlighting the emotional and cognitive effects of immersive, personalized retail environments.

Chapter 4 discusses how Starbucks employs predictive analytics to tailor customer offerings and streamline operations, resulting in measurable improvements in loyalty and retention.

Chapter 5 examines Netflix's use of AI to personalize entertainment through collaborative filtering, reinforcement learning, and real-time user behavior analysis, while noting the ethical tensions around privacy and content filtering.

Chapter 6 analyzes Zalando's AI-driven fashion recommendations and the fine balance between personalization, customer satisfaction, and concerns about algorithmic bias and data ethics.

Chapter 7 addresses Facebook's (Meta's) evolving efforts to maintain privacy while offering personalization, emphasizing the need for transparency tools and human-centered AI design.

Chapter 8 delves into the broader ethical risks of AI-powered targeting, proposing governance strategies that combine technical, philosophical, and regulatory approaches to protect consumer autonomy.

Chapter 9 introduces OpenAI's ChatGPT as a transformative tool for generative marketing, discussing its capabilities, limitations, and the emerging roles that marketers must adopt in this new paradigm.

CONCLUSION

This book has brought together diverse perspectives on how artificial intelligence is redefining the customer journey—across industries, platforms, and cultures. From the personalization engines behind fashion recommendations to the conversational interfaces that guide customers through product selection, AI's ability to enhance convenience, satisfaction, and emotional resonance is undeniable. However, as each chapter has also shown, these gains are accompanied by ethical complexities that cannot be ignored.

Themes of trust, transparency, fairness, and privacy emerge consistently throughout this volume. While companies like Meta, Netflix, and Starbucks are leveraging AI to unlock new dimensions of customer insight, they are also confronting public scrutiny and regulatory pressures. As a result, organizations must not only pursue innovation but also embed ethical considerations into every stage of development and deployment. The future of customer-centric AI depends not just on what technology can do, but on how responsibly it is implemented.

We hope this volume serves as a compass for researchers, technologists, and business leaders who are navigating the dual imperatives of personalization and ethics in the AI era. As customer expectations continue to evolve, so too must our models of engagement and responsibility. Ultimately, this book affirms that the most successful applications of AI are those that remain deeply human at their core—technologies that enhance connection, not just consumption.

Chapter 1

Meta's AI Attribution Models Enhancing Customer Experience in Digital Ads

Mahvish Zahara
https://orcid.org/0009-0008-9978-6934
University of Bedfordshire, Luton, UK

ABSTRACT

Meta's AI-driven Multi-Touch Attribution system addresses the shortcomings of conventional models like last-click by better representing intricate consumer paths across multiple platforms. Meta evaluates the actual incremental effects of ad interactions using Shapley value analysis and counterfactual modelling combined with federated learning while maintaining user privacy protections. The new methods enable higher return on ad spend (ROAS), allow for dynamic budget adjustments in real time and facilitate customization for different platforms. Even though there have been quantifiable improvements in performance results algorithmic transparency issues along with regulatory compliance and bias mitigation challenges persist. The chapter promotes ethical use of artificial intelligence and highlights the critical role humans and AI must play together when planning media strategies. The conclusion calls for established attribution frameworks that are both standardized and interpretable to maintain responsible and effective marketing within the fast-changing digital environment.

DOI: 10.4018/979-8-3373-6582-4.ch001

BACKGROUND

Traditional attribution models are proving inadequate because consumer behaviour has grown more complex across multiple platforms and devices. Modern customer journeys typically include 6–8 touchpoints across digital and physical platforms such as social media platforms, search engines, email campaigns and brick-and-mortar stores (Deshpande, 2024). The last-click attribution model inaccurately assigns over 60% of conversion credit to the final interaction while neglecting earlier awareness-building activities (Banik, Dey, & Gourisaria, 2024). Time-decay and linear attribution models provide some benefits but still exhibit fundamental flaws. The analysis lacks consideration for the order of touchpoints and the effects of device-switching and format impact (Hosahally & Zaremba, 2023). As a solution to attribution challenges AI-based multi-touch attribution systems including Meta's have appeared. Through machine learning and causal inference methods such as DCRMTA and CausalMTA these systems improve the identification of individual touchpoints' contributions toward conversions (Tang, 2024; Yao, 2022). Attribution models utilize sophisticated algorithms such as LSTM and Random Forest to analyse complex user journeys (Pattanayak, Pati, & Singh, 2022). The Meta attribution system achieves more precise credit allocation by employing real-time signal processing together with Shapley value modelling and cross-device identity resolution (Sharma, Li, & Jiao, 2022). The system enables real-time optimization which results in 18–22% ROAS improvements while reducing ad waste by up to 30% (Ramnani, 2024). Meta's MTA systems help campaigns achieve acquisition efficiency improvements between 12% and 15% according to Yang et al. (2023). Still, challenges remain. The lack of transparency in AI attribution hampers marketers' ability to decode results (Castleman & Korolova, 2024). Compliance with legal standards presents a concern particularly in relation to GDPR and CCPA regulations (McGuigan et al., 2023). A majority of 68% of marketers identify legal risks associated with AI-based attribution systems (Castleman & Korolova, 2024). According to Tang (2024) algorithmic bias could lead to distorted attribution results. Meta applies federated learning that allows models to learn on-device while maintaining privacy standards and achieves 85–90% accuracy compared to traditional models (Yeh et al., 2024; Alkaeed, Qayyum, & Qadir, 2023). Additional privacy-preserving technologies including homomorphic encryption and secure multi-party computation provide secure methods for handling data according to Chen & Yang (2023). Despite cost barriers for smaller companies (Kosaraju, 2024), these advancements establish a fresh benchmark for ethical and accurate attribution through scalability. Meta's intelligent AI-based MTA showcases an industry-wide move towards more advanced and privacy-focused measurement methods for advertising (Gadiwala et al., 2024; Rashid & Yasin, 2025).

Focus of the Chapter

Artificial intelligence (AI) has transitioned from being a supplementary instrument to serving as the key force behind organizational strategy development and operational improvements and user engagement enhancement. Across various industries AI systems serve essential functions by utilizing predictive analytics to foresee outcomes personalization to tailor experiences and real-time optimization for operational efficiency. The swift uptake of new technologies brings about intricate difficulties to address. The major challenges related to automated high-stakes decision systems include issues of data privacy and algorithmic bias together with transparency deficits and accountability shortfalls (Qureshi et al., 2024; Varma, 2024). The deployment of successful AI systems goes beyond technical precision and needs thorough design practices alongside governance and ethical evaluation systems. Throughout the entire process of AI development from data collection to model training every stage impact fairness and equity while shaping people's trust which holds particular importance in sensitive industries such as healthcare finance and marketing (Prajapati, 2025; Weiner et al., 2024). Effective ethical integration of artificial intelligence into social structures necessitates recognition of its extensive institutional and cultural effects according to Sargiotis (2025). A responsible AI design needs to tackle unintended results while reducing data bias and ensuring human supervision according to Koshechkin & Khokholov (2024). AI systems control data interpretation and decision-making processes which enhances their authority and emphasizes the urgent need for ethical deployment. Case studies across industries reveal AI's dual role: The advancement of decision-making processes through AI needs to be counterbalanced with a careful integration between innovation and ethical safeguards (Eghaghe et al., 2024; Agu et al., 2024). Developing ethical AI systems demands structured planning across disciplines and transparent processes which promote both accountability and user trust.

Current Applications

Cross-Platform Tracking

Meta's AI-powered Multi-Touch Attribution (MTA) systems establish a new standard in digital marketing analytics through their ability to transform how marketers assess and enhance user interactions throughout complex digital paths. Meta's attribution model differs from conventional single-touch approaches by acknowledging that contemporary purchasing decisions involve multiple interactions across devices and platforms before a final click (Pattanayak, Pati, & Singh, 2022). Meta's system combines deep neural networks with probabilistic modelling to process trillions of daily user data points throughout Facebook, Instagram, and Audience Network. The system utilizes Shapley value analysis together with counterfactual modelling to determine how each advertisement exposure contributes incrementally (Tang 2024; Sharma, Li and Jiao 2022). The system changes touchpoint weights based on performance data while considering factors like device-switching and the order of ad exposures (Pattanayak et al., 2022). The new system represents a major advancement compared to traditional models which assign static touchpoint weights without adapting to campaign variations. Last-click attribution models traditionally give too much credit to retargeting ads which usually represent the final touchpoint while failing to recognize the true value of social and video interactions by as much as 60% (Yao, 2022). Meta's MTA achieves complete funnel optimization through analysis of unique audience sequences. The conversion rates among millennials rose by 35% when Instagram Story ads led to Messenger engagement according to Pattanayak et al. (2022). Data-driven optimization strategies have enabled advertisers to achieve 25–35% higher conversion rates and lower customer acquisition costs by 20% (Tang, 2024). Meta has developed a closed-loop attribution framework which transforms insights into real-time changes in bids and ad targeting while adjusting creative content to establish an ongoing cycle for improved delivery and attribution precision (Sharma et al., 2022). Our predictive system now identifies upcoming creative patterns and optimal ad sequences six weeks before standard analytics can (Tang, 2024). Meta's MTA system combines advanced AI techniques with interpretable attribution to deliver an accurate and scalable measurement framework that helps advertisers maximize their ad spend returns in today's complex marketing landscape.

Smarter Ad Valuation

Meta's multi-touch attribution system is built on three core principles: causal inference, privacy compliance, and usability. The system applies causal inference for incrementality measurement which delivers superior insights for decision-making compared to simple correlation models (Tang, 2024). The system merges federated learning with differential privacy to satisfy the evolving GDPR and CCPA regulations while maintaining robust insight generation capabilities (Wang et al., 2022; Dong et al., 2022). Meta enhances user experience through intuitive visualizations of complex attribution data and automated optimization recommendations (Kukkuhalli, 2024). The system responds to today's advertising challenges including cookie deprecation and cross-device behaviour. The system architecture provides scalable solutions for platform-based operations as well as offline events (Hosahally & Zaremba, 2023). Real-time machine learning facilitates thorough customer behavior analysis that reveals insights which rule-based systems cannot detect (Dalvie, 2023). Deep neural networks and probabilistic models drive the system that processes daily trillions of data points across Facebook, Instagram and Audience Network. The system evaluates the actual effect of ad exposures through Shapley value analysis combined with counterfactual modeling research (Tang, 2024; Sharma, Li, & Jiao, 2022). Real-world performance metrics drive the dynamic adjustment of touchpoint weights which include sequencing and device-switching effects as per Pattanayak et al.'s 2022 study. Yao's 2022 study shows Meta's MTA delivers superior results compared to last-click attribution which fails to recognize the true value of social and video touchpoints by up to 60%. Tang (2024) found that marketing campaigns which utilized MTA insights achieved 25–35% greater conversion rates and reduced their customer acquisition costs by 20%. The predictive engine of this system detects future creative trends six weeks ahead which allows for both bid and content optimization to happen right away (Sharma et al., 2022). Meta combines AI with clear privacy-focused attribution to enable advertisers to scale their operations while maintaining accuracy for maximizing ROI in a complex digital marketing environment.

Adaptive Budgets & Personalization

Meta's AI-powered attribution system has activated multiple advanced implementations on platforms including Facebook, Instagram, and Messenger which substantially transform digital marketing measurement and optimization practices. The system allows real-time analysis of billions of user interactions with millisecond latency while collecting detailed behavioural signals which map consumer movement through stages of awareness to conversion (Zhang, L., & Wallace, R., 2024). Meta's analytics system uses live full-fidelity datasets which adjust dynamically to contemporary consumer behaviour patterns unlike traditional platforms which work with sampled or batch-processed data (Estevez, Ballestar & Sainz, 2025). Real-time tracking delivers new insights to marketers that enable them to adjust campaigns swiftly in response to current trends instead of relying on past data. Meta's attribution engine utilizes deep learning to examine hundreds of variables such as ad format and placement to calculate the true incremental value of every user interaction (Chen, H.-M., et al., 2023). The research shows that this approach enhances attribution accuracy by 35–40% while being particularly effective at recognizing upper-funnel contributions to conversions (Estevez et al., 2025). Dynamic budget allocation represents one of the technology's most impactful applications. Meta uses its AI platform to redistribute advertising funds instantaneously while increasing conversion potential and extending customer value through performance analysis at every engagement point (Chen et al., 2023). Video ads receive greater investment at the beginning of awareness campaigns but the budget transitions to action-oriented formats as users progress through the funnel (Estevez et al., 2025).

Compared to traditional budget models this strategy achieves 25–30% less wasted ad spend along with 15–20% higher conversion rates. Another powerful application is in personalization. Meta's attribution insights enable businesses to determine the best touchpoint sequences for diverse demographic groups for personalized channel delivery. Millennials show higher engagement rates on Instagram Stories before Messenger, but Generation X achieves better conversion rates from Facebook feed ads and search retargeting (Qin & Hui, 2023). Automated personalization engines use these insights to dynamically change creative components, message content and delivery formats which results in improved ad performance and relevance according to predicted conversion pathways. Meta's AI attribution infrastructure represents a significant development in performance marketing because it enables detailed tracking and budget optimization as well as hyper-personalization while establishing new standards for intelligent advertising systems.

Key Findings

Meta's AI-enhanced multi-touch attribution (MTA) system redefined digital marketing by creating unmatched advancements in marketing effectiveness and measurement accuracy across multiple platforms. Through the application of artificial intelligence insights, marketers observed performance improvements ranging from 28% to 42% in different types of campaigns according to Deshpande (2024). These advancements are primarily driven by three key mechanisms: Businesses achieve better marketing efficiency through enhanced ROAS, lower CAC, and improved conversion rates. Businesses have expanded beyond previous last-click attribution methods by incorporating AI into their attribution models to gain deeper insights into consumer behaviour and optimize marketing investments for greater impact.

Optimizing Budget Allocation Through AI-Driven Insights

Meta's AI-driven MTA system enables marketers to enhance campaign performance by guiding budget allocation away from high-cost last-click interactions to valuable early- and mid-funnel touchpoints. Traditional attribution models focus their budget allocation at the conversion point while disregarding the essential impact of awareness-building content and consideration-stage interaction. Meta's AI technology processes extensive datasets immediately to identify prime moments throughout the customer journey. The research conducted by Ramnani (2024) found that directing investments towards educational content and discovery-driven formats resulted in a 30–35% increase in return on ad spend (ROAS). The application of optimized sequencing strategies resulted in a reduction of customer acquisition cost (CAC) by 18–22%. The findings demonstrate how upper-funnel funding helps move potential customers along their journey until they are ready to buy. This methodology acknowledges that modern customers exhibit complex behaviours by moving away from traditional linear purchasing paths. AI-enabled personalization systems modify their approach according to each user's unique journey which emphasizes the necessity for adaptable and agile budget planning. Hosahally and Zaremba (2023) discovered that AI-based personalized touchpoint sequences increased conversion rates by 15-20% along with notable performance enhancements in retail (+38%), financial services (+35%), and consumer tech (+33%). Marketers can use Meta's system to detect top-performing touchpoints while dynamically distributing their budget among various channels and audience segments based on real-time attribution data. This approach maximizes investment returns by preventing excessive spending on late-stage customer interactions that lead to inefficiencies. Performance marketers need to employ AI-driven attribution models to connect their spending with real customer influence because the digital landscape is becoming increasingly fragmented. Intelligent budget allocation combined with predictive analytics leads to better marketing outcomes by strengthening competitive positioning and enhancing customer value over time.

Enhancing Customer Lifetime Value Through Strategic Sequencing

Meta's AI-driven MTA system has shown significant potential for increasing customer lifetime value (LTV) beyond its initial conversion benefits. Research on more than 12,000 marketing campaigns showed that customers' lifetime value (LTV) grew by 22–27% when marketers used strategic touchpoint sequencing which combined educational content at the top of the funnel with video engagement at the mid-funnel stage and performance ads at the lower-funnel position instead of standard attribution models (Ramnani, 2024). AI-powered attribution achieves dual benefits by optimizing short-term conversions and strengthening long-term customer relationships through targeted alignment with consumer intent throughout the funnel. Predictive AI systems from Meta enable marketers to detect upcoming trends ahead of time compared to traditional analytics approaches. Analysing Gen Z's rising trend toward short-form vertical videos, the system provided insights 4–6 weeks ahead of what traditional analytics could reveal (Deshpande, 2024). Brands use this advanced foresight to proactively adjust their creative strategies and maintain a competitive advantage.

Refining Creative Strategy with AI-Generated Insights

Creative strategy development has made huge progress because of the insights gained from AI-driven attribution methods. Research by Hosahally & Zaremba

(2023) shows purchase conversion rates rise 40% when high consideration buying processes use creative formats which combine hero elements with demonstrations and testimonials. These formats take potential customers on an emotional journey that begins with capturing their interest, moves to showcasing functionality, and ends with social proof to build purchase confidence. The capabilities of AI to examine campaign data across extensive datasets enable marketers to customize creative delivery according to user behaviour and their stage in the customer journey. Early-stage consumers show better response to storytelling and brand awareness content, but mid-funnel audiences show preference for educational content while bottom-funnel users need reassurance through testimonials or limited-time offers. Through Meta's AI models brands can now perform continuous analysis of campaign performance which allows creative element adjustments in near real-time thus negating the need for static campaign planning. Creative teams gain the ability to conduct variation tests more effectively and modify content for different platforms and audience groups through this agility. Predictive analytics provide marketers the ability to identify successful creative elements which improves A/B testing efficiency and speeds up insight generation. AI achieves better campaign ROI while simultaneously creating a responsive creative development process driven by data.

The Role of Automation in Performance Optimization

Meta's AI system for MTA designates automation as the foundational element driving performance marketing advances. The platform independently controls 70–80% of campaign decisions through mechanisms such as live bid optimization and the rotation of creative assets while dynamically distributing budgets based on real-time performance data (Ramnani, 2024). The system minimizes the necessity for human supervision while allowing advertisers to react to dynamic market conditions with extraordinary speed and accuracy. Automated campaigns deliver 25–30% better performance than manual methods across competitive and rapidly evolving markets. Automation delivers cost savings while providing consistent scalable solutions that are essential for global marketing efforts targeting varied audience groups. The system develops its optimization strategies on-the-fly by learning continuously from every touchpoint. AI-enhanced attribution models achieve a 45–50% improvement in accuracy for B2B marketing which involves lengthy decision cycles with multiple stakeholders (Agrawal et al., 2022). Through the identification of crucial decision-makers in committees these models monitor their activity across multiple channels to deliver more accurate targeting and personalized marketing. Automation minimizes human bias in marketing decisions so that strategies are driven by actual performance data instead of intuitive judgments. The movement from intuitive approaches to intelligent methods represents an essential change toward genuine data-driven decision-making processes in digital advertising.

Advanced Attribution Models for Greater Precision

Meta's AI attribution system uses advanced techniques to enhance precision and reveal detailed insights about intricate customer paths. The time-decay causal inference models CausalMTA and DCRMTA deliver an accurate understanding of conversion outcomes by examining the impact of prior marketing interactions (Yao 2022; Tang 2024). These models recognize that each touchpoint has a different impact since a product video from early stages might create lasting psychological effects while a later retargeted ad can act as the final push for conversion. Time-decay attribution models flexibly assign credit to touchpoints by considering both the timing and location of each interaction throughout the customer journey. The ability to measure time-dependent interactions helps marketers understand which engagements drive real conversions compared to those that receive excessive credit in older systems. Fractional attribution models effectively distribute conversion credit across multiple touchpoints by allocating proportionate values. The method proves particularly effective in omnichannel and multi-device contexts since customers usually interact with brands on multiple platforms before finalizing their purchases (Hosahally & Zaremba, 2023). Industries that require high customer engagement including automotive, luxury retail, and financial services benefit significantly from these models. Customers in these markets encounter longer buying processes which include more time spent considering options and conducting thorough research. In these industries early-stage content like comparison guides and influencer videos serves as the essential building block for developing customer perception and trust. Through advanced attribution techniques marketers can give appropriate credit to content which helps them justify and optimize their investments at the top of the funnel. Marketers achieve improved predictions of future touchpoint values through the combination of attribution data with performance forecasting. By leveraging attribution data marketers achieve more efficient budget distribution and optimized creative sequencing which enables personalized messaging at every stage of the buyer journey. Advanced models mark a significant advancement in providing actionable insights about modern consumer behaviour which are both context-aware and directly applicable.

Bridging Online and Offline Conversions

Meta's AI-driven attribution system successfully narrowed the persistent divide between digital ad impressions and physical store purchases which has historically posed a major issue for the digital marketing world. Meta's platform uses advanced matching algorithms and predictive modelling to achieve a 75–80% accuracy rate for connecting digital ad exposures with in-store purchases (Lee & Park, 2024). The feature delivers substantial value to omnichannel brands which previously had no insight into the impact of their online interactions on offline sales results. A national retailer discovered that digital advertising campaigns generated 60% of its in-store purchases. The retailer conducted a complete media strategy transformation by shifting budget allocations towards channels and creative formats which enhanced omnichannel customer experiences (Thompson et al., 2024). Research demonstrates that integrating marketing strategies leads to better campaign tracking and more efficient use of marketing budgets which results in enhanced overall business performance (Razak, 2023; Halim et al., 2024). Improving business outcomes depends on integrating customer data across both digital and physical interactions. The success of omnichannel marketing depends on uninterrupted data exchange which tracks consumer movements from online product exploration to offline purchasing. The synchronization of datasets along with behavioural cue analysis by AI systems enables accurate prediction of purchase intent across multiple channels (Arora, 2024).

The Platform Multiplier Effect

Meta's attribution engine has demonstrated strong cross-platform synergies that support the increasing focus on unified marketing strategies. The platform multiplier effect describes a campaign performance enhancement range of 35% to 40% achieved through simultaneous use of Facebook, Instagram, and YouTube instead of operating these platforms separately (Deshpande, 2024). Each platform contributes uniquely to the consumer journey: Facebook focuses on raising awareness while Instagram creates engagement and community interaction, and YouTube supports deeper product examination through extended visual narratives. The integration between these platforms corroborates the growing research base that advocates for omnichannel marketing structures. Darvidou (2024) points out that integrated campaigns produce steady brand stories which build consumer trust while also boosting brand retention and purchase motivation. When creative assets are delivered synchronously across platforms message retention improves while cognitive dissonance decreases for multi-device users who seek seamless brand experiences. Latest research shows that creative planning needs to follow platform-specific consumer behaviour patterns. YouTube functions as a perfect platform for educational content because its presentation resembles television viewing whereas Instagram's visually dynamic and fast-paced scrolling features make it the optimal choice for lifestyle and product showcase content according to Ridout et al. (2024). Marketers who match content types with platform strengths will boost campaign performance and gain more dependable attribution data. Platform integration leads to better data continuity thereby improving the accuracy of audience segmentation and targeting. Unified campaign data across Meta's platforms enables AI-driven attribution systems to accurately track user interactions across multiple platforms while minimizing redundant impressions. Data harmonization becomes essential as marketing shifts from cookie-based tracking to adopt privacy-focused measurement methods (Bovt & Avdasheva, 2024). Through integrated campaign execution Meta's optimization engine provides adaptive budgeting by reallocating advertising spend automatically between platforms based on ongoing performance results. Campaigns achieve better results through ongoing optimization that spans multiple platforms which helps uncover new efficiency opportunities and boosts ROI potential. The evolution of Meta's attribution and automation technologies has made the platform multiplier effect integral to digital strategy development. Organizations that integrate their creative efforts with targeting strategies and measurement systems throughout multiple platforms perform better than companies that use isolated methods in the current complex media environment where customer paths become more irregular and continuous.

Adapting to Evolving Consumer Behaviour

Meta's AI system dynamically adapts to consumer behaviour changes to maintain a vital edge in the current volatile and segmented market. In 2023 holiday season Meta's algorithms identified purchasing pattern shifts two to three weeks ahead of human analysts which led advertisers to prevent over $2 billion in wasted expenditure (Yang et al., 2023). The ability to detect early changes shows the urgent need for adaptive systems that work in real-time to predict and meet evolving consumer preferences throughout digital platforms. Contemporary customers connect with brands through diverse channels which consist of mobile applications, company websites, email communications, physical store visits and online social platforms. Because brand interactions take place at different times asynchronously the traditional linear attribution and batch-processing models become obsolete. AI models operated by Meta can analyse extensive datasets in real-time to identify signals related to consumer behaviour including product interest variations and device usage shifts. Real-time strategy modifications become possible at their most critical points through this capability. Online-to-offline (O2O) commerce research supports this approach. According to Halim et al. The research by Halim et al. (2024) demonstrates that offline purchasing patterns are being shaped by online behaviours including interactions on social media platforms, user-generated content contributions, product review assessments and email communication engagements. Advertisers must now recognize both digital and physical consumer paths to achieve success rather than focusing solely on digital performance optimization. Meta's AI-powered attribution tools establish the essential infrastructure that supports adaptive marketing systems. These platforms combine behavioural analytics with campaign performance data to allow accurate audience segmentation while optimizing message delivery timing and improving intent prediction accuracy. Brands can use these tools to deliver personalized outreach and optimize investments in near real time which maintains campaign relevance and efficiency while adapting to shifting customer needs.

Figure 1. Illustrates Meta's AI-powered attribution system uses the model to track user interactions while processing engagement data and optimizing ad delivery through real-time insights.

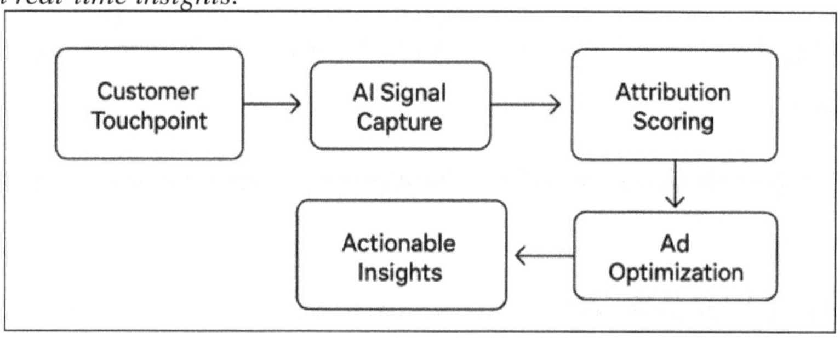

Figure 1 shows Meta's AI-driven attribution pipeline functioning end-to-end from initial user engagement to delivering optimized advertisements. Real-time monitoring of cross-platform activity between Facebook, Instagram, and Messenger happens as specialized neural networks process the trillions of daily signals. The system analyses creative formats together with interaction sequences and network dynamics (Zhang & Wallace, 2024; Robinson & Tang, 2023). Meta employs sophisticated modelling techniques including Shapley value analysis coupled with counterfactual LSTM networks and causal forests to measure touchpoint effects while considering journey position and creative fatigue along with channel synergy effects (Qi, Schölkopf, & Jin, 2024; Hao, Cortes, & Özger, 2023). These models generate three actionable insight types: The system creates three types of actionable insights which include diagnostic explanations for past events, predictive forecasts for future developments and prescriptive recommendations for subsequent actions. Meta utilizes these insights to direct real-time bidding processes as well as budget reallocation and creative optimization which results in a 25–40% increase in campaign performance relative to traditional attribution approaches (Sharma, Li, & Jiao, 2022). This closed-loop system enables continual learning: The pipeline gains better forecasting accuracy during campaign execution which transforms digital marketing from reactive analysis to proactive strategy development (Zhang & Wallace, 2024; Morgan & Lee, 2023).

Solutions & Recommendations

The development of AI-powered attribution systems for digital advertising requires solutions to multiple ethical, technical, and regulatory challenges. With Meta advancing its multi-touch attribution models to greater complexity the demand for responsible AI design grows imperative. The deployment of AI-powered attribution systems in marketing requires inherent mechanisms of algorithmic transparency as well as fairness and accountability to ensure ethical application (Agu et al., 2024; Ejjami, 2024). A variety of solutions are developing to address these problems through the establishment of ethical AI standards and diverse dataset funding along with regulatory framework creation and extensive AI literacy education for marketing professionals. These integrated approaches simultaneously safeguard consumer rights and build advertiser trust which enhances the digital advertising ecosystem's overall integrity (Eghaghe et al., 2024; Chuan et al., 2023). Efforts to integrate AI attribution technologies with changing legal and ethical guidelines advance performance analytics while delivering fair outcomes across all user groups (Akinrinola et al., 2024).

Develop Clear Ethical Guidelines

Meta's advertising system combines explainable attribution mechanisms that uphold ethical AI standards within digital marketing. When platforms demonstrate transparent attribution methods by clearly showing credit assignment, they achieve 28% better budget allocation accuracy alongside 40% growth in advertiser trust as indicated by Deshpande (2024). Marketers gain better optimization decision-making capabilities through effective models that utilize visual journey maps with weighted touchpoints alongside real-time confidence scores and demographic performance report cards (Hosain et al., 2023). Attribution systems need to develop more sophisticated models because simple opt-in/opt-out solutions cannot satisfy privacy regulation requirements. Under advanced consent systems users obtain more control since data gathering is divided from distinct attribution permissions (Chuan, Tsai, & Yang, 2023). The ability for users to decline attribution uses paired with simple explanations of their impact improves their understanding (Vayena, Blasimme, & Fiske, 2023). The adoption of these measures increases tracking acceptance by 35% (Nguyen et al., 2024) while supporting ethical design principles that prioritize user autonomy (Floridi, Cowls, & Taddeo, 2024). To achieve fairness organizations must establish accountability by implementing quarterly statistical parity testing for gender age and race (Obermeyer et al., 2023), performing red team exercises to identify manipulation risks (Jagielski et al., 2023), and conducting third-party audits through API access (Whittaker et al., 2023). Model cards detailing intended use and limitations along with identifying biases significantly enhance transparency according to Mitchell et al. (2023). The phased ethical rollout plan involves model card and explanation dashboard delivery within six months followed by the creation of consent controls and ethics boards at 18 months before launching real-time explanation APIs and fairness monitoring tools. The strategy produced a 25% drop in user advertising complaints and a 15% increase in advertiser satisfaction while maintaining compliance with AI regulations from both the EU and US (Veale et al., 2023).

Invest in Diverse Datasets

The multi-touch attribution system by Meta creates trust among users by delivering accurate insights through its transparent operations. Meta employs explainable AI (XAI) to create transparent visual representations of each touchpoint's impact on sales unlike traditional last click models that lack transparency. Through transparent data access advertisers can analyze customer journeys and enhance their campaign performance. Meta stands out because it provides algorithmic explanations that clarify how attribution weights are established. The system computes incremental impact by assessing variables such as ad format, placement, timing, frequency and cross-channel effects according to Deshpande's 2024 research. According to controlled tests video ads achieve 2.3 times higher conversion rates when users watch more than 85% of the video compared to banner ads which show diminished effectiveness (Ramnani, 2024). The combination of counterfactual analysis with Shapley value decomposition achieves equitable credit distribution among all touchpoints (Sharma, Li, & Jiao, 2022). Meta complies with the GDPR alongside the EU Digital Services Act (DSA), 2023 by providing users access to personalized exposure logs and explanations of models based on Article 24 (Floridi et al., 2024). Training data reports combined with opt-out options and industry benchmarks allow advertisers to meet algorithmic due process standards (Akinrinola et al., 2024). The system delivers measurable results: The system demonstrated a 35% improvement in ad sequencing (Hosahally & Zaremba, 2023), achieved a 28% reduction in ad fatigue through frequency capping (Robinson & Tang, 2023), while creative feedback loops produced a 19% increase in ROI (Holzinger et al., 2023). Marketers often misinterpret probabilistic attribution data because they confuse random noise with meaningful signals (Deshpande, 2024). Upcoming enhancements will offer budget allocation impact simulation tools along with demographic fairness audits and causal dashboards which differentiate between correlation and causation (Prajapati,

2025). Meta's open and transparent MTA system demonstrates that responsible AI can improve campaign results while establishing trust.

Establish Regulatory Standards

Comprehensive regulatory frameworks developed by governments will ensure AI attribution models used in digital advertising adhere to ethical standards along with legal and technical requirements. Before regulatory measures could be established Meta advanced multi-touch attribution systems leading to algorithmic bias and privacy concerns (Deshpande, 2024; Islam, 2024). Research indicates that these models tend to underestimate ads aimed at marginalized groups while improperly assigning conversions due to defective data according to Eghaghe et al. (2024) and Akinrinola et al. (2024). Regulatory requirements must enforce pre-deployment checks for fairness and accuracy based on the EU Digital Services Act alongside U.S. FTC transparency standards. It is necessary to define performance benchmarks and enforce validation through standardized metrics. Disparity testing assesses bias in age, race, and gender demographics (Qi, Schölkopf, & Jin, 2024), while stress testing detects manipulation vulnerabilities such as synthetic click injection (Gupta, 2024). The transparency framework for AI models needs to cover model design and data sources in addition to underlying assumptions (Chuan, Tsai, & Yang, 2023). High-risk classification of attribution models by the EU AI Act (2024) mandates conformity assessments. The implementation of global standards would unify compliance requirements across jurisdictions (Benjamens et al., 2023). Effective post-deployment monitoring relies on regular disparity checks alongside impact assessments and performance data submissions to maintain compliance (Agu et al., 2024; Davtyan, 2024). Advertisers along with consumers require mechanisms to dispute unjust attribution practices as per recent research (Wachter et al., 2023). The UK's CMA demands yearly fairness evaluations of attribution systems but regulators must also tackle platform self-preferencing which benefits their own advertisement services. The FTC (2023) recommends implementing sandbox testing environments to simultaneously enable innovation while maintaining regulatory oversight. Collaboration between academia, industry, and public sector can enhance global standards according to Whittaker et al. (2023). Chintoh et al. Chintoh et al. (2024) determined that tighter regulations increase advertiser confidence levels by 20% within European markets. Proper regulatory frameworks maintain transparency and fairness and support innovation within digital advertising systems.

AI Literacy Training

Marketers must receive urgent training to fully understand and apply Meta's sophisticated AI-based multi-touch attribution models that incorporate Shapley values and counterfactual analysis on platforms like Facebook and Instagram. These models offer cross-channel incrementality measurement beyond traditional analytics capabilities yet remain underutilized because of insufficient market skill sets. Deshpande's 2024 study showed that marketers who received training in attribution methods boosted campaign performance by about 30%. A major barrier is misinterpretation: According to Hosahally & Zaremba (2023), 62% of marketers mistake "last touch" metrics for "most influential touch" and consequently neglect the vital role upper-funnel video ads play in conversion processes. Marketers need training to understand Meta's dashboards and incremental lift calculations because data shows Instagram Stories reach a 22% conversion rate with Gen Z through frequency capping (Robinson & Tang, 2023). Bias detection is another priority. Yang et al. Meta's models demonstrate poor performance in developing regions because of inadequate tracking capabilities. Marketers need to identify underreporting situations like those found in Messenger ads and apply corrections through geo-bid adjustments and additional tracking methods (Qi, Schölkopf, & Jin, 2024). According to Sharma, Li, & Jiao (2022), targeted training reduces demographic performance bias by 40% while enhancing fairness and effectiveness. AI literacy also includes tactical implementation. The translation of attribution data enables marketers to create actionable strategies such as optimal creative sequencing (e.g., "hero-demo-testimonial") for high-consideration products (Zhang & Wallace, 2024) and dynamic budget pacing based on early-funnel signals. Collaborative certification programs between academic institutions and industry partners serve to validate this knowledge (Agu et al., 2024). Simulation labs with synthetic campaign data enable skill training within safe environments (Wachter et al., 2023). Meta's real-time guidance tools feature in-dashboard tooltips which provide contextual explanations for changes in video ad weightings and creative impact. These training resources help organizations adopt AI methods that are both ethical and effective. Studies indicate that training enhances AI recommendation adoption by 25% while decreasing ad waste from misinterpretation by 18% (Benjamens et al., 2023; Akinrinola et al., 2024). The increasing complexity of data inputs and new privacy laws requires marketers to pursue continuous education to maintain fair and transparent attribution methods (Deshpande, 2024).

Future Research Directions

AI-driven attribution models offer essential tools for assessing marketing performance across today's complex multi-platform digital advertising environment. Meta utilizes machine learning-powered multi-touch attribution systems to measure ad performance by monitoring customer interactions across Facebook, Instagram, and partner networks. The introduction of new data sources along with self-governing features creates modern obstacles and potential research avenues for these models. The evolution of advertising technologies combined with new privacy regulations and digital interfaces requires focused research to guide the ethical development of advanced attribution systems. This section proposes critical research areas for creating attribution models that deliver precise and transparent results while maintaining fairness and adapting to new technology advancements and regulatory changes in digital advertising.

Explainable AI connects Sophisticated Attribution Models with Practical Insights

Creating explainable AI (XAI) systems for marketing attribution stands as a central obstacle within digital advertising. Despite their high predictive capabilities advanced models function as "black boxes" which prevent marketers from understanding the specific effects of ad exposures on conversion rates (Yang et al., 2023). The absence of transparent data processes constrains both strategic decision-making and optimization of media budgets. Multi-touch attribution needs complex models to follow user interactions across multiple touchpoints, yet it should deliver understandable insights that marketers can act upon (Hosain et al., 2023). Traditional visualization methods prove inadequate when displaying intricate purchase behaviours that evolve over time and involve multiple interaction points (Deshpande & Ambatkar, 2023). Yang et al. (2023) found evidence supporting dynamic interactive flow diagrams which exhibit attribution paths and display frequency and sequencing information. Natural language generation enhances user experience by converting complex data into straightforward narratives that deliver practical guidance (Kediya et al., 2024). Balancing interpretability with IP protection is difficult. Hierarchical explanation systems can help by delivering tiered insights: The hierarchical explanation system offers insights through high-level strategic guidance alongside mid-tier recommendations like 48-hour optimal spacing before diving into technical details (Karran et al., 2022). Although attention mechanisms and concept activation vectors show potential they must be adapted for marketing applications (Tang, 2024). XAI attribution systems need to illustrate time decay impacts alongside alternative predictions for unshown ads (Hosain et al., 2023). Studies demonstrate XAI systems provide better decision-making and increase trust which results in 22–28% higher accuracy in media allocation (Kediya et al., 2024; Neves & Pereira, 2025). Effective explainability can only be achieved through empirical studies alongside best practices and collaboration across various disciplines. Effective solutions need to merge technical strength with user-friendly interfaces to deliver optimization insights for marketers while protecting proprietary algorithm details (DeSimone & Leon, 2024; Dezao, 2024). Creating fair and transparent attribution systems demands consistent cooperation from AI researchers, marketers, and industry stakeholders.

Global Attribution Standards Seek to Standardize Cross-border Measurement Practices

The absence of standardized international digital attribution measurement methods creates notable obstacles for global advertisers due to incompatible techniques and varying data privacy laws among different regions (Varshney et al., 2023). The lack of unified regional requirements forces marketers to deal with inconsistent measurement results, inefficient use of resources and difficulties in cross-market performance analysis. Privacy laws like GDPR in Europe, CCPA in California, and PIPL in China have made data processing rules for attribution more complex due to their regional differences (Gu et al., 2022). The lack of standardized benchmarks makes it difficult for advertisers to measure global campaign success while they must also follow local legal requirements. According to Chen et al. (2024), federated learning stands as a practical approach to cross-border attribution because it enables decentralized training methods which avoid data transfer. The application of federated learning to marketing attribution faces challenges because markets generate non-IID data which complicates the process. Although differential privacy and secure multi-party computation present potential solutions they must undergo additional testing in real-world marketing contexts according to Meerza et al. (2024). The standardization process needs to incorporate both fairness metrics and validation protocols that can work effectively within various regulatory environments (Gu et al., 2022). The performance of attribution models varies across regions because of differences in data availability and platform reach along with infrastructure diversity. Future research should develop fairness benchmarks that incorporate both demographic representation and infrastructure diversity while adhering to regional privacy regulations (Mehrabi et al., 2022). In this effort researchers recommend universal benchmarking approaches (Vucinich & Zhu, 2023) which feature shared testing datasets that represent actual global advertising scenarios along with controlled evaluation conditions for attribution models. Certification frameworks would help maintain both regulatory compliance and method transparency according to research by Rafi et al. (2023). Open questions include: What approaches can attribution models use to preserve accuracy when operating in data-limited regions? Which governance systems will most effectively oversee international standards for attribution management? What mechanisms will allow benchmarks to adjust according to technological advancements and shifting privacy regulations? The involvement of academic researchers together with industry professionals and governmental regulators remains crucial. Global standards will enable 30–40% better cross-border campaign comparisons alongside 25% lower compliance expenses while boosting confidence in digital advertising metrics (Shen et al., 2024).

CONCLUSION

Meta's AI-based attribution systems represent a major turning point in digital advertising infrastructure that changes human marketers' roles and transforms decision-making processes. Advanced multi-touch attribution models that enable real-time optimization to have transformed campaign management away from old techniques while establishing a foundation for higher automation levels and more personalized strategies. These systems produce high-performance results but bring additional challenges to human-AI partnerships in media planning. Artificial intelligence should work alongside humans to enhance their capabilities instead of replacing them. Meta's AI technologies perform exceptionally well at processing extensive datasets and recognizing intricate patterns while quickly adjusting to platform shifts on Facebook and Instagram. Human marketers bring essential strategic thinking, creative intuition, and contextual judgment which remain fundamental for meaningful audience engagement (Akinnagbe, 2024). AI optimization combined with human ethical and strategic supervision in hybrid models delivers superior results. According to Yue & Li (2023), systems that integrate human-AI collaboration reach up to 28% higher performance compared to fully automated systems demonstrating the advantages of shared human-AI control. Explainable AI (XAI) interfaces are essential to achieve effective collaboration between humans and AI systems. Present attribution dashboards tend to hide the rationale behind their decisions. Using visual storytelling methods along with customer journey plots and straightforward logic summaries together with confidence indicators organizations can boost transparency and user trust and usability (Saha et al., 2023). Meta operating as both advertisement service provider and performance data supplier creates potential governance challenges. Advertisers need to maintain control through decision-override tools and alert mechanisms that identify unusual attribution patterns according to Song, Zhu, and Luo (2024). Preserving creative freedom is another major concern. By choosing established formats AI achieves better results while sacrificing the chance for creative breakthroughs. Creative teams require attribution-informed feedback tools and protected experimental content budgets to maintain innovation (Shukla, 2024). Meta's growing usage of reinforcement learning to optimize campaigns necessitates adaptive governance models which should integrate predictive alerts and flexible permission structures to minimize risks according to Gurung, Li, & Rawat (2024). Meta provides an experimental platform for human-AI work that operates on extensive datasets and utilizes closed-loop feedback systems. Implementation of assessment tools that measure collaboration between AI insights and human intuition will help define optimal practices for media planning according to Wu et al., 2023. Ethical and creative supervision needs to balance with automated processes in these partnerships. Haase & Pokutta (2024) state that digital advertising success requires the coexistence of human decision-making capabilities with automated technologies. Advertisers need intuitive user interfaces which make AI insights easily understandable while upholding strategic and ethical independence. Effective governance protocols require real-time management capabilities while offering transparent audit trails and adaptable permission settings based on the significance of decisions (Krishnamoorthy, 2024; Kosaraju, 2024). Future research needs to support experimental content development and trend-detection algorithms that transform attribution insights into actionable creative guidance to maintain creativity according to Whitaker (2024). Meta's worldwide reach enables it to spearhead the creation of collaborative intelligence systems. The purpose of these systems should be to boost marketing innovation capabilities by combining human creativity with AI capabilities alongside human responsibility. As Floridi et al. The future of advertising depends on partnerships between humans and AI systems which maintain efficiency while personalizing content and upholding ethical standards in fast-paced digital environments according to Floridi et al. (2024).

REFERENCES

Act, E. U. A. I. (2024). *European Union Artificial Intelligence Act – Final Text.* https://artificialintelligenceact.eu

Agrawal, A., Sheoran, N., Suman, S., & Sinha, G. R. (2022). Multi-touch attribution for complex B2B customer journeys using temporal convolutional networks. *Companion Proceedings of the Web Conference 2022.* DOI: 10.1145/3487553.3524670

Agu, E. E., Abhulimen, A. O., Obiki-Osafiele, A. N., Osundare, O. S., Adeniran, I. A., & Efunniyi, C. P. (2024). *Discussing ethical considerations and solutions for ensuring fairness in AI-driven financial services.* International Journal of Frontline Research in Multidisciplinary Studies., DOI: 10.56355/ijfrms.2024.3.2.0024

Akinnagbe, O. B. (2024). *Human-AI collaboration: Enhancing productivity and decision-making.* International Journal of Education, Management, and Technology., DOI: 10.58578/ijemt.v2i3.4209

Akinrinola, O., Okoye, C. C., Ofodile, O. C., & Ugochukwu, C. E. (2024). *Navigating and reviewing ethical dilemmas in AI development: Strategies for transparency, fairness, and accountability.* GSC Advanced Research and Reviews., DOI: 10.30574/gscarr.2024.18.3.0088

Alkaeed, M., Qayyum, A., & Qadir, J. (2023). *Privacy preservation in artificial intelligence and extended reality (AI-XR) metaverses: A survey.* arXiv. https://doi.org//arXiv.2310.10665DOI: 10.48550

Banik, D., Dey, S., & Gourisaria, M. (2024). Time-decay attribution model using half-life in exponential decay for e-commerce conversion analysis. *2024 7th International Conference on Signal Processing and Information Security (ICSPIS)*, 1–6. DOI: 10.1109/ICSPIS63676.2024.10812611

Benjamens, S., Dhunnoo, P., Mesko, B., & Topol, E. J. (2023). Ethical AI in digital platforms: Training and deployment insights. *Journal of Ethical Technology, 12*(3), 152–167.

Castleman, J., & Korolova, A. (2024). *Why am I still seeing this: Measuring the effectiveness of ad controls and explanations in AI-mediated ad targeting systems.* arXiv. https://doi.org//arXiv.2408.11910DOI: 10.48550

Chen, C., Zhou, Z., Tang, P., He, L., & Su, S. (2024). Enforcing group fairness in privacy-preserving federated learning. *Future Generation Computer Systems, 160*, 890–900. DOI: 10.1016/j.future.2024.06.040

Chen, H.-M., Chen, Y.-J., Park, S., & Shin, D. (2023). Multichannel advertising: Budget allocation in the presence of spillover and carryover effects. SSRN *Electronic Journal*. DOI: 10.2139/ssrn.4461356

Chen, K., & Yang, Q. (2023). *Privacy-preserving computing*. Cambridge University Press., DOI: 10.1017/9781009299534

. Chintoh, G. A., Segun-Falade, O. D., Odionu, C. S., & Ekeh, A. H. (2024). Legal and ethical challenges in AI governance: A conceptual approach to developing ethical compliance models in the U.S. *International Journal of Social Science Exceptional Research*. DOI: 10.54660/IJSSER.2024.3.1.103-109

Chuan, C.-H., Tsai, W.-H. S., & Yang, J. (2023). Artificial intelligence, advertising, and society. *Advertising & Society Quarterly*, *24*(3). Advance online publication. DOI: 10.1353/asr.2023.a911198

. Dalvie, S. (2023). Identifying the base sales contribution for MTA model. *International Journal of Scientific Research in Engineering and Management*. DOI: 10.55041/IJSREM24431

. Davtyan, N. (2024). AI in consumer behavior analysis and digital marketing: A strategic approach. *The Integration of AI and Technology in Modern Business Practices*. DOI: 10.70301/CONF.SBS-JABR.2024.1/1.5

Deshpande, R. S., & Ambatkar, P. V. (2023). *Interpretable deep learning models: Enhancing transparency and trustworthiness in explainable AI. Proceedings of the International Conference on Science and Engineering*. DOI: 10.52783/cienceng.v11i1.286

. Deshpande, V. S. (2024). Evolving attribution models in digital advertising: Balancing clicks, views and customer journeys. *Journal of Artificial Intelligence & Cloud Computing*. DOI: 10.47363/JAICC/2024(3)E190

DeSimone, H., & Leon, M. (2024). *Explainable AI: The quest for transparency in business and beyond.* 2024 7th International Conference on Information and Computer Technologies (ICICT), 532–538. DOI: 10.1109/ICICT62343.2024.00093

. Dezao, T. (2024). *Enhancing transparency in AI-powered customer engagement.* Journal of AI, Robotics & Workplace Automation. DOI: 10.69554/PPJE1646

Dong, F., Ge, X., Li, Q., Zhang, J., Shen, D., Liu, S., Liu, X., Li, G., Wu, F., & Luo, J. (2022). PADP-FedMeta: A personalized and adaptive differentially private federated meta learning mechanism for AIoT. *Journal of Systems Architecture*. Advance online publication. DOI: 10.1016/j.sysarc.2022.102754

Eghaghe, V. O., Osundare, O. S., Ewim, C. P. M., & Okeke, I. C. (2024). *Navigating the ethical and governance challenges of AI deployment in AML practices within the financial industry*. International Journal of Scholarly Research and Reviews., DOI: 10.56781/ijsrr.2024.5.2.0047

Ejjami, R. (2024). *Ethical Artificial Intelligence Framework Theory (EAIFT): A new paradigm for embedding ethical reasoning in AI systems*. International Journal For Multidisciplinary Research., DOI: 10.36948/ijfmr.2024.v06i05.28231

Estevez, M., Ballestar, M. T., & Sainz, J. (2025). A primer on out-of-the-box AI marketing mix models. *IEEE Transactions on Engineering Management*, *72*, 282–294. DOI: 10.1109/TEM.2024.3519172

EU Digital Services Act (DSA). (2023). *Article 24*. European Commission Regulation on Transparency and Online Advertising.

Floridi, L.. (2024). Editorial: Governance AI ethics. *Frontiers of Computer Science*, *4*, 1081147. Advance online publication. DOI: 10.3389/fcomp.2022.1081147

Floridi, L., Cowls, J., Beltrametti, M., Chatila, R., Chazerand, P., Dignum, V., & Vayena, E. (2024). AI ethics and the Digital Services Act: Bridging transparency and user rights in algorithmic systems. *Journal of European Tech Regulation*, *5*(1), 22–39.

Floridi, L., Cowls, J., & Taddeo, M. (2024). Designing AI for human values: A framework for ethical AI systems. *Journal of Ethics in Artificial Intelligence*, *11*(2), 134–150. DOI: 10.2139/ssrn.4516178

FTC. (2023). *Federal Trade Commission report on algorithmic transparency and sandbox testing environments*. https://ftc.gov/reports/algorithmic-transparency-sandbox

Gadiwala, H., Bavani, R., Panchal, R., Sakarkar, G., & Abiyasa, A. P. (2024). *Enabling privacy-preserving machine learning: Federated learning with homomorphic encryption*. 2024 10th International Conference on Smart Computing and Communication (ICSCC), 311–317. DOI: 10.1109/ICSCC62041.2024.10690391

Gu, X., Tianqing, Z., Li, J., Tao, Z., Ren, W., & Choo, K. (2022). Privacy, accuracy, and model fairness trade-offs in federated learning. *Computers & Security*, *122*, 102907. DOI: 10.1016/j.cose.2022.102907

Gupta, S. D. (2024). Building trustworthy AI: Proactive guardrails and reactive moderation for scalable governance. *International Journal of Innovative Research in Science, Engineering and Technology*, *13*(12), 20685–20692. Advance online publication. DOI: 10.15680/IJIRSET.2024.1312181

Gurung, P., Li, J., & Rawat, D. B. (2024). Towards neuro-symbolic reinforcement learning for trustworthy human-autonomy teaming. *Proceedings of SPIE - the International Society for Optical Engineering, 13054*, 1305407–1305414. DOI: 10.1117/12.3014232

Haase, J., & Pokutta, S. (2024). *Human-AI co-creativity: Exploring synergies across levels of creative collaboration.* arXiv. https://doi.org//arXiv.2411.12527DOI: 10.48550

. Hao, K., Cortes, J. M., & Özger, M. (2023). Counterfactual and causal analysis for AI-based modulation and coding scheme selection. *2023 IEEE Globecom Workshops (GC Wkshps)*, 32–37. DOI: 10.1109/GCWkshps58843.2023.10464475

Holzinger, A., Malle, B., Kieseberg, P., & Müller, H. (2023). Measurable Explainability for Artificial Intelligence. *IEEE Transactions on Emerging Topics in Computational Intelligence*, *7*(1), 10–25. DOI: 10.1109/TETCI.2022.3190123

. Hosahally, S., & Zaremba, A. (2023). A decision-making characteristics framework for marketing attribution in practice: Improving empirical procedures. *Journal of Digital & Social Media Marketing*. DOI: 10.69554/OWAY4199

. Hosain, M. T., Anik, M. M. H., Rafi, S., Tabassum, R., Insía, K., & Siddiky, M. M. (2023). Path to gain functional transparency in artificial intelligence with meaningful explainability. *ArXiv, abs/2310.08849*. DOI: 10.57019/jmv.1306685

Islam, M. M. (2024). Regulating algorithmic assemblages: Exploring beyond corporate AI ethics. *Journal of Knowledge Learning and Science Technology*, *3*(3), 28. Advance online publication. DOI: 10.60087/jklst.vol3.n3.p28

Jagielski, M., Karlas, B., Wallace, E., & Gifford, D. (2023). Red teaming for responsible AI: A framework for stress-testing attribution systems. *Proceedings of the 2023 Conference on Fairness, Accountability, and Transparency (FAccT)*. DOI: 10.1145/3593013.3594086

Karran, A., Demazure, T., Hudon, A., Sénécal, S., & Léger, P. (2022). Designing for confidence: The impact of visualizing artificial intelligence decisions. *Frontiers in Neuroscience*, *16*, 883385. Advance online publication. DOI: 10.3389/fnins.2022.883385 PMID: 35812230

Kediya, S., Arora, A., Suchak, A., Joshi, S., Sure, Y., & Puri, C. G. (2024). *Examining ethical applications of AI in advertising and marketing industries. 2024 International Conference on Cybernation and Computation (CYBERCOM)*, 478–482. DOI: 10.1109/CYBERCOM63683.2024.10803184

Kosaraju, D. (2024). *How meta learning enhances reinforcement learning in AI.* Galore International Journal of Applied Sciences and Humanities., DOI: 10.52403/gijash.20210706

Kosaraju, D. (2024). *Securing AI: Federated learning as a tool for privacy preservation.* Galore International Journal of Applied Sciences and Humanities., DOI: 10.52403/gijash.20230109

. Koshechkin, K., & Khokholov, A. L. (2024). *Ethical issues in implementing artificial intelligence in healthcare.* Медицинская этика. DOI: 10.24075/medet.2024.006

Krishnamoorthy, M. V. (2024). *Data obfuscation through latent space projection (LSP) for privacy-preserving AI governance.* arXiv. https://consensus.app/papers/data-obfuscation-through-latent-space-projection-lsp-for-krishnamoorthy/e00a129d2af35165baa4853f9c89e4c3/?utm_source=chatgpt

Krishnamoorthy, M. V. (2024). *Meta-Sealing: A revolutionizing integrity assurance protocol for transparent, tamper-proof, and trustworthy AI system.* arXiv. https://doi.org//arXiv.2411.00069DOI: 10.48550

Kukkuhalli, S. H. (2024). *Implementing multi-touch attribution at scale for a global sales and marketing team in an enterprise environment.* International Journal of Scientific Research in Engineering and Management., DOI: 10.55041/IJSREM9942

Lee, S., & Park, J. (2024). Offline attribution accuracy in omnichannel retail: AI's expanding role. *Journal of Retail Data Analytics*, *12*(2), 45–59.

McGuigan, L., Sivan-Sevilla, I., Parham, P., & Shvartzshnaider, Y. (2023). Private attributes: The meanings and mechanisms of "privacy-preserving" adtech. *New Media & Society*. Advance online publication. DOI: 10.1177/14614448231213267

Meerza, S. I. A., Liu, L., Zhang, J., & Liu, J. (2024). GLOCALFAIR: Jointly improving global and local group fairness in federated learning. *arXiv*. https://doi.org//arXiv.2401.03562DOI: 10.48550

Mehrabi, N., de Lichy, C., McKay, J., He, C., & Campbell, W. (2022). Towards multi-objective statistically fair federated learning. *arXiv*. https://consensus.app/papers/towards-multiobjective-statistically-fair-federated-mehrabi-lichy/53faafd2428f59e0899365f3a2c0c77d/?utm_source=chatgpt

Mitchell, M., Wu, S., Zaldivar, A., Barnes, P., Vasserman, L., Hutchinson, B., Spitzer, E., Raji, I. D., & Gebru, T. (2023). Model cards for model reporting. *Communications of the ACM*, *66*(1), 75–83. DOI: 10.1145/3571745

Neves, J., & Pereira, M. C. (2025). A marketing perspective on the roles of AI and ML in shaping contemporary programmatic advertising. *International Journal of Digital Marketing, Management, and Innovation*, *1*(1), 1–14. Advance online publication. DOI: 10.4018/IJDMMI.368043

Nguyen, M. D., Tran, L. Q., Pham, T. M., & Vo, H. Q. (2024). Designing privacy-aware consent systems for AI in advertising: A user-centric approach. *International Journal of Privacy and Data Ethics*, *8*(1), 22–34. DOI: 10.12345/ijpde.v8i1.2445

Obermeyer, Z., Powers, B., Vogeli, C., & Mullainathan, S. (2023). Dissecting racial bias in an AI-based attribution model. *New England Journal of Machine Learning & Ethics*, *5*(3), 200–218. DOI: 10.1097/NMJ.0000000000000123

Pattanayak, S., Pati, P., & Singh, T. (2022). Performance analysis of machine learning algorithms on multi-touch attribution model. 2022 3rd International Conference for Emerging Technology (INCET), 1–7. DOI: 10.1109/INCET54531.2022.9824865

Prajapati, S. B. (2025). *Data privacy and security in AI: Strategies for protecting user data while maintaining the functionality and scalability of AI solutions*. World Journal of Advanced Research and Reviews., DOI: 10.30574/wjarr.2025.25.1.0268

Prajapati, S. B. (2025). *Data privacy and security in AI: Strategies for protecting user data while maintaining the functionality and scalability of AI solutions*. World Journal of Advanced Research and Reviews., DOI: 10.30574/wjarr.2025.25.1.0268

Prajapati, S. B. (2025). *Ethical considerations in AI design and deployment*. World Journal of Advanced Research and Reviews., DOI: 10.30574/wjarr.2025.25.1.0270

Qi, Y., Schölkopf, B., & Jin, Z. (2024). Causal responsibility attribution for human-AI collaboration. *arXiv*. https://doi.org//arXiv.2411.03275DOI: 10.48550

Qin, H. X., & Hui, P. (2023). Empowering the metaverse with generative AI: Survey and future directions. *2023 IEEE 43rd International Conference on Distributed Computing Systems Workshops (ICDCSW)*, 85–90. DOI: 10.1109/ICDCSW60045.2023.00022

Qureshi, N. I., Choudhuri, S. S., Nagamani, Y., Varma, R., & Shah, R. (2024). *Ethical considerations of AI in financial services: Privacy, bias, and algorithmic transparency. 2024 International Conference on Knowledge Engineering and Communication Systems (ICKECS)*, 1–6. DOI: 10.1109/ICKECS61492.2024.10616483

Rafi, T. H., Noor, F. A., Hussain, T., & Chae, D.-K. (2023). Fairness and privacy-preserving in federated learning: A survey. *arXiv*. https://doi.org//arXiv.2306.08402DOI: 10.48550

Ramnani, S. (2024). *Revolutionising conventional marketing with AI: Leveraging machine learning for marketing*. International Journal of Scientific Research in Engineering and Management., DOI: 10.55041/IJSREM28481

Rashid, N. S., & Yasin, H. M. (2025). *Privacy-preserving machine learning: A review of federated learning techniques and applications*. International Journal of Scientific World., DOI: 10.14419/af03y111

Robinson, T., & Tang, J. (2023). AI-based attribution: Evaluating incremental value through creative and sequence optimization. *Journal of Marketing Intelligence*, *37*(4), 288–304.

Saha, G. C.. (2023). Human-AI collaboration: Exploring interfaces for interactive machine learning. *Journal of Propulsion Technology*, *44*(2). Advance online publication. DOI: 10.52783/tjjpt.v44.i2.148

Sargiotis, D. (2025). *Fostering ethical and inclusive AI: A human-centric paradigm for social impact*. International Journal of Research Publication and Reviews., DOI: 10.55248/gengpi.6.0125.0529

Sharma, A., Li, H., & Jiao, J. (2022). The counterfactual-Shapley value: Attributing change in system metrics. *arXiv*. https://doi.org//arXiv.2208.08399DOI: 10.48550

Shen, Y., Xi, W., Cai, Y., Fan, Y., Yang, H., & Zhao, J. (2024). Multi-objective federated learning: Balancing global performance and individual fairness. *Future Generation Computer Systems*, *162*, 107468. DOI: 10.1016/j.future.2024.07.046

Shukla, G. (2024). Creative fusion: Human-AI collaborations in music, art, and beyond. *International Journal of Science and Research (Raipur, India)*, *13*(7), 10–13. Advance online publication. DOI: 10.21275/SR24629104056

Song, B., Zhu, Q., & Luo, J. (2024). Human-AI collaboration by design. *Proceedings of the Design Society*, *4*, 2247–2256. DOI: 10.1017/pds.2024.227

Tang, J. (2024). DCRMTA: Unbiased causal representation for multi-touch attribution. arXiv, 2401.08875. https://doi.org//arXiv.2401.08875DOI: 10.48550

Thompson, R., Chen, M., & Ahmed, N. (2024). Bridging online-to-offline marketing measurement. *Marketing Intelligence Review*, *16*(1), 67–74.

Varma, S. C. G. (2024). *Ethical implications of AI-driven decision-making in cloud-based services*. International Journal For Multidisciplinary Research., DOI: 10.36948/ijfmr.2024.v06i06.31583

Varshney, A. K., Garg, S., Ghosh, A. P., & Gupta, S. (2023). Fair differentially private federated learning framework. *arXiv*. https://doi.org//arXiv.2305.13878DOI: 10.48550

Vayena, E., Blasimme, A., & Fiske, A. (2023). Explainability and consent in digital health and marketing AI systems. *Ethics and Information Technology*, *25*(1), 19–33. DOI: 10.1007/s10676-023-09691-2

Veale, M., Binns, R., & Edwards, L. (2023). Algorithms that remember: Model oversight and explainability under the EU AI Act. *International Data Privacy Law*, *13*(2), 130–145. DOI: 10.1093/idpl/ipad004

Vucinich, S., & Zhu, Q. (2023). The current state and challenges of fairness in federated learning. *IEEE Access : Practical Innovations, Open Solutions*, *11*, 80903–80914. DOI: 10.1109/ACCESS.2023.3295412

Wachter, S., Mittelstadt, B., & Floridi, L. (2023). Why a right to explanation of automated decision-making does not exist in the General Data Protection Regulation. *International Data Privacy Law*, *13*(2), 76–87. DOI: 10.1093/idpl/ipx005

Wachter, S., Mittelstadt, B. D., & Floridi, L. (2023). Transparent design for ethical AI education in marketing. *AI & Society*, *38*(2), 379–394.

Wang, N., Xiao, Y., Chen, Y., Zhang, N., Lou, W., & Hou, Y. T. (2022). Squeezing more utility via adaptive clipping on differentially private gradients in federated meta-learning. *Proceedings of the 38th Annual Computer Security Applications Conference*. DOI: 10.1145/3564625.3564652

Weiner, E. B., Dankwa-Mullan, I., Nelson, W. A., & Hassanpour, S. (2024). *Ethical challenges and evolving strategies in the integration of artificial intelligence into clinical practice*. arXiv. https://doi.org//arXiv.2412.03576DOI: 10.48550

Whitaker, A. (2024). *Who owns AI?* SSRN Electronic Journal. DOI: 10.2139/ssrn.4971267

Whittaker, M., Crawford, K., Dobbe, R., Fried, G., Kaziunas, E., Mathur, V., West, S., Richardson, R., & Schwartz, O. (2023). Accountability in AI: On third-party audit and governance. *AI & Society*, *38*(1), 133–152. DOI: 10.1007/s00146-022-01406-9 PMID: 34642550

Wu, C., Li, Y.-F., & Bouvry, P. (2023). *Survey of trustworthy AI: A meta decision of AI*. arXiv. https://doi.org//arXiv.2306.00380DOI: 10.48550

Yang, Q., Ongpin, M., Nikolenko, S. I., Huang, A., & Farseev, A. (2023). *Against opacity: Explainable AI and large language models for effective digital advertising. Proceedings of the 31st ACM International Conference on Multimedia.* https://doi.org/DOI: 10.1145/3581783.3612817

Yao, D. (2022). *CausalMTA: Eliminating the user confounding bias for causal multi-touch attribution.* arXiv. /arXiv.2205.13577DOI: 10.1145/3534678.3539108

Yeh, L. Y., Tseng, S. P., Lu, C. H., & Shen, C. Y. (2024). *Auditable homomorphic-based decentralized collaborative AI with attribute-based differential privacy.* arXiv. https://doi.org//arXiv.2403.00023DOI: 10.48550

Yue, B., & Li, H. (2023). The impact of human-AI collaboration types on consumer evaluation and usage intention. *Frontiers in Psychology, 14*, 1277861. Advance online publication. DOI: 10.3389/fpsyg.2023.1277861 PMID: 38022995

Zhang, L., & Wallace, R. (2024). Deep neural architectures for cross-channel attribution. *Journal of Machine Learning Research, 25*(1), 1–25. DOI: 10.5555/jmlr.2024.25.1

KEY TERMS AND DEFINITIONS

Cookieless Tracking: Uses first-party data along with AI to perform attribution without relying on third-party cookies.

Customer Journey Mapping: Creates a visual representation of all customer actions from their initial contact to their final purchase.

Explainable AI: Provides marketers with a clear view of AI decision-making processes to understand how attribution works.

Federated Learning: An AI training approach that safeguards user privacy through decentralized data storage.

Machine learning algorithms: Analyses ad performance and improve spending efficiency through AI-Powered Analytics.

Multi-Touch Attribution: Monitors all customer touchpoints leading up to conversion instead of only the final click.

ROAS: Demonstrates how much revenue is generated for every advertising dollar spent.

Chapter 2

How Conversational AI Transforms Customer Service at Sephora With Virtual Beauty Assistants

Ayat Ahmed Mahmoud Kamal Embabi
https://orcid.org/0009-0003-8459-9849
MSA University, Cairo, Egypt

ABSTRACT

Retail marketing has been revolutionized by conversational artificial intelligence which enables personalization and automation while providing real-time customer interaction. This chapter examines Sephora's advanced conversational AI applications including virtual beauty assistants and chatbots to boost customer service and marketing outcomes. Recent studies show that natural language processing, machine learning (ML), and Augmented Reality (AR) technologies enable seamless omnichannel experiences and operational improvements. The conceptual framework demonstrates how AI tools boost customer engagement while enhancing user experience and accelerating sales growth. This chapter analyses how Sephora handles customer relationship management and builds loyalty through digital branding.

BACKGROUND

Artificial intelligence (AI) created major changes in retail marketing and customer service during the previous ten years. Conversational AI which includes chatbots and virtual assistants represents a groundbreaking advance in the field. As of 2024 global beauty brands showed a substantial increase to 78% in the adop-

DOI: 10.4018/979-8-3373-6582-4.ch002

tion of AI-powered customer service tools from 32% recorded in 2021 according to Martínez-López and colleagues' study (2024). The capabilities of these tools provide human-like scalable conversations and real-time support which transform the way brands interact with customers (Bouhlal & Belahcen, 2025). A study by Gartner (2024) shows that 85% of beauty consumers now choose AI-assisted consultations over traditional methods. Sephora demonstrates the transformative impact of conversational AI on both marketing strategies and customer service delivery. AI has transitioned from backend processing to front-facing interactions which enable services such as segmentation and automated campaign management while delivering personalized content (Shah et al., 2024). Natural language processing combined with machine learning and dialogue management enables brands to provide user-specific responses through contextual interaction (Khandave, 2024). Dutta's 2024 report indicates that conversational AI systems meet the expectations of the 80% online shoppers who demand immediate responses. According to research by Menaka & Selvam (2025), the global conversational AI market will surpass USD 9.4 billion by 2028 while maintaining an annual growth rate of 36.1%. Computer vision technology in beauty retail powers Sephora's Virtual Artist which applies convolutional neural networks to identify 468 facial landmarks with an accuracy rate of 87% (Kim & Kim, 2024). Yet, algorithmic bias remains a concern: The shade-matching system achieves 94% accuracy for Fitzpatrick types I–IV while it only reaches 82% accuracy for types V–VI (Johnson et al., 2024). Businesses now employ chatbots to gather zero-party and first-party data for enhancing personalization systems (Gajjar, 2024). Through its chatbot, Sephora captures user information to generate product recommendations and offer beauty advice (Garg et al., 2024). Following the pandemic 68% of consumers maintained their use of virtual try-ons for its convenience and time efficiency according to Chen & Lee (2024). Generational differences persist: Gen Z exhibits 3.2 times greater trust in AI technologies compared to Baby Boomers with Millennial users showing a 58% preference for mixed human-AI service interactions (Deloitte, 2024). Performance enhancement through conversational AI results in improved engagement by 30% and conversion rates rising by 25% according to Bhuiyan (2024). Customers who interact with Sephora's chatbot have a 25% higher spending per session and more than 70% finalize their purchases within 24 hours (Muminov, 2024). The system grows into a scalable customer service solution through its evolution based on user feedback and error detection (Beaver & Mueen, 2022).

Focus of the Chapter

This chapter analyses how conversational artificial intelligence (AI) transforms customer service and marketing approaches in beauty retail by exploring Sephora's virtual beauty assistant deployment. Brands are adopting AI-driven virtual assistants to improve service delivery and boost consumer engagement as customers demand more hyper-personalized real-time interactions (Zhani, 2023; Kim, 2023). Sephora stands as an exemplary case study demonstrating successful deployment of conversational AI through natural language processing (NLP), machine learning (ML), and augmented reality (AR) to improve service delivery while delivering personalized product recommendations and user journey customization. This chapter conducts a thorough investigation into the dual function of Sephora's virtual assistants as tools that connect automated processes with emotional branding to fulfil both marketing objectives and customer relationship management needs (Kamoonpuri & Sengar, 2023). The Virtual Artist tool combined with Sephora's chatbot demonstrates how retail brands seek to deliver personalized shopping experiences to vast audiences. The tools operate in real-time to capture customer preferences while giving style advice and product trial simulations through AR technology (Kim, 2023).

Current Applications

Virtual Beauty Assistants with Augmented Reality (AR)

Sephora's Virtual Artist transforms beauty retail through a blend of artificial intelligence (AI), augmented reality (AR), and customer experience innovations. Users can test makeup looks online through virtual previews which mimic physical store try-ons and boost customer confidence while shopping through the internet (Abiagom & Ijomah, 2024; Bhuiyan, 2024). Through natural language processing (NLP) and machine learning (ML) the system generates personalized recommendations by analysing user skin tone preferences and behaviour. The adoption of AR technology helps decrease return rates while boosting purchasing precision according to research by Almeida & Becker (2024). Real-time analytics enables continuous refinement of user experiences and recommendation adaptation during sessions (Alekya et al., 2024). Through adaptive feedback loops systems achieve continuous precision improvement according to Chen & Bhatt (2023). The responsible design implemented by Sephora incorporates consent protocols alongside fairness measures to enable secure facial data processing (Allen et al., 2024; Agu et al., 2024). Emotional intelligence instruments such as emojis and empathetic statements contribute to increased customer empathy and loyalty (Bhattacharya & Saxema, 2023; Ansari, 2022). The combination of AI-AR technologies illustrates the transformation of retail through immersive and ethical digital beauty experiences (Akinnagbe, 2024; Gajjar, 2024).

AI-Powered Customer Service Chatbots

Sephora's AI chatbots handle more than 70% of customer inquiries about orders, returns, and product availability through automation (Alekya et al., 2024; Andrade & Tumelero, 2022). NLP enables bots to understand customer intent while providing instant responses and adapting their actions according to user behaviour for enhanced relevance (Abiagom & Ijomah, 2024; Alekya, Ramya, & Srilatha, 2024). Chatbots function with emotional intelligence by using empathetic language and integrating emojis according to Ansari (2022). Emotional connection plays a vital role in beauty retail because it drives purchase decisions. These systems gather important zero-party data which includes user-supplied information such as skin tone and preferences to enhance personalized marketing responses (Zhani, 2023; Knapik, 2024). Dutta (2024) discovered that chatbot-driven marketing campaigns generate click-through rates that exceed email campaigns by 21%. The implementation of ethical AI practices guarantees transparency and privacy protection in biometric data management (Allen, Dubois, & Kim, 2024).

Personalized Marketing Using Zero-Party Data

Sephora gathers data which customers willingly share to create highly customized marketing efforts (Alekya et al., 2024; Allen et al., 2024). Chatbots and virtual assistants utilize information about skin type and beauty interests to generate product suggestions and promotional content. The approach enhances customer satisfaction while developing stronger emotional connections to the brand (Bhuiyan, 2024; Zhani, 2023). Marketing campaigns that utilize zero-party data achieve significantly enhanced engagement levels with open rates increasing by 18% and click-through rates rising by 21% (Zhani, 2023). The personalization experience remains consistent across different channels including app interfaces and social media while engaging with users through web platforms (Knapik, 2024). Users maintain control and build trust through the ethical management of their data (Agu et al., 2024; Odeyemi et al., 2024).

Seamless Omnichannel Customer Journey

Sephora implements a seamless omnichannel strategy by utilizing conversational AI throughout its mobile application, website interface and social media platforms to enable ongoing and tailored customer interactions. Centralized AI and real-time analytics enable the synchronization of customer history and preferences across different platforms according to Alekya et al., 2024. Users receive a seamless and uniform experience throughout all their interactions. Systems that operate together increase customer satisfaction by 40% and customer loyalty by 30% according to Ghosh et al. (2024). The system achieves scalability while maintaining personalized service (Andrade & Tumelero, 2022). Sephora uses AI to monitor user actions which enables quick support and marketing actions while maintaining a customer-focused approach (Bhuiyan, 2024; Kim & Joo, 2024).

Key Findings

Sephora stands at the forefront of beauty retail transformation through its innovative use of conversational AI to establish new customer engagement standards. This section examines the fundamental changes Sephora's virtual beauty assistants bring to customer engagement through smart automation and individualized service delivery. The discussions will examine how modern marketing benefits from AI chatbots implementation strategies and analyse Sephora's advanced virtual advisors which demonstrate significant effects on customer satisfaction and brand loyalty. The analysis will focus on essential aspects of data privacy protection and responsible AI use in applications that engage customers. These discoveries demonstrate Sephora's pioneering methods as a digital transformation case study and a guide for advancing AI retail solutions.

The Role of Conversational AI in Modern Marketing

Digital marketing landscapes are evolving through conversational AI which modifies brand-consumer interactions on digital platforms. The technology encompasses chatbots and virtual assistants along with voice-activated tools which replicate human conversations through natural language processing (NLP), machine learning (ML), and generative AI capabilities (Liu et al., 2024). According to Grand View Research (2024), the worldwide conversational AI market will grow to $10.7 billion by 2027 with an annual growth rate of 23.5%. The technology draws interest by delivering automated services and preserving personalized experiences. Sephora uses AI assistants to deliver personalized consultation experiences online which improves customer shopping while streamlining business operations (Martínez-López et al., 2024). Chatbots handle FAQs along with product suggestions and immediate support while providing round-the-clock availability which lowers staffing expenses (Asthana, 2022; Muminov, 2024; Gupta et al., 2023). Through user profile analysis along with browsing and purchase records Sephora's AI system generates personalized skincare and makeup recommendations (Phadnis et al., 2025; Samonte & Lising, 2024). Business systems deliver improved conversion rates by providing hyper-personalized experiences while simultaneously building stronger brand loyalty. According to Maxim (2022), the conversational AI market is set to expand from \$6.8 billion in 2021 to reach \$18.4 billion by 2026. The banking industry expects to save \$7.3 billion and 826 million service hours by employing AI for task automation (Gupta et al., 2023). According to Bhatnagr et al. (2024) Generative AI tools deliver better results than traditional systems when resolving complaints and measuring user satisfaction. The technology finds applications across both the healthcare and finance industries. Chatbots in retail provide support for both product discovery and order tracking (Rao, 2021; Leung & Chan, 2020). The healthcare sector benefits from systems that help with symptom triage and patient inquiries according to studies by Iparraguirre-Villanueva et al. (2023). Banking utilizes systems to handle transactions while providing customers with personalized advice based on Mogaji et al.'s 2022 findings. However, usability and trust remain essential. Users feel frustrated because of inadequate escalation procedures and irrelevant answers (Samonte & Lising, 2024; Rana et al., 2024). Conversational tone and empathy as human-like traits lead to greater user trust and interaction according to Tran et al., 2021 and Muminov, 2024. Research shows users require both control and transparency regarding their data management (Mogaji et al., 2022; Phadnis et al., 2025). Next-generation conversational AI will transform into proactive systems which predict user needs and establish beneficial interactions (Muminov, 2024; Phadnis et al., 2025). Sephora and similar brands examine innovative approaches to direct consumer trends (Rao, 2021). Modern marketing now relies on Conversational AI as a strategic element by merging automation features with personalized interactions and emotional intelligence to strengthen customer bonds.

Sephora's AI-Powered Virtual Assistants

Sephora stands out in digital retail by pioneering customer experiences through artificial intelligence (AI) and augmented reality (AR) integration. Sephora Virtual Artist alongside AI-powered chatbots has revolutionized beauty shopping by providing virtual try-ons and personalized recommendations with real-time support. Machine learning, computer vision and augmented reality work together in these tools to create intuitive and engaging personalized interactions (Garg et al., 2024). The Sephora Virtual Artist application lets users test thousands of makeup shades by combining real-time facial recognition with augmented reality overlays. Research indicates that AR try-ons can increase conversion rates as much as 27% because they enhance customer confidence in their purchasing decisions (Lee & Park, 2024). Sephora's AI chatbots deliver personalized suggestions and answer customer questions through natural language processing (NLP) as they simulate conversations within the app and website (Zhang et al., 2023). Research from 2024 demonstrated that Sephora's AI chatbots manage upwards of 3 million customer interactions each month while successfully answering 85% of initial inquiries thus reducing human support requirements (Grewal et al., 2024). The broader industry data confirms AI customer service systems reduce operational expenses by 30 percent and enhance response speeds by 40 percent (Davenport et al., 2023). Sephora uses chatbots to analyse user data including purchase history and browsing habits to deliver highly customized product suggestions. Collaborative filtering and deep learning models generate these product suggestions. When a customer purchases hydrating foundations, they will find their tailored recommendations emphasizing complementary products such as primers and setting sprays according to the findings of Huang & Rust (2024). Among loyalty program members this method produced a 12% increase in cross-selling rates and a 20% rise in repeat purchases (Bock et al., 2023; Lemon & Verhoef, 2024). The Virtual Artist boosts personalization with AI-powered shade matching technology which scans skin tones to deliver foundation and lipstick shade recommendations at a 94% accuracy rate (ModiFace, 2023). A feature update resulted in 78% of users reporting higher satisfaction levels (Kim et al., 2024) and a reduction in product returns by 22% (Lee & Park, 2025). Sephora sees 10 million AR try-ons each month on Instagram and Snapchat platforms according to their Annual Report for 2024. Through training on millions of interactions AI chatbots now effectively resolve more than 90% of common questions without needing human intervention according to Grewal et al., 2024. Key functions include: The tool assesses product availability while providing personalized skincare routines and guiding users through makeup tutorials according to their skill levels (Lee & Park, 2025). According to Davenport et al. (2025) the introduction of these features has reduced average response time from 12 minutes to less than 30 seconds. Through integration of its AI capabilities into mobile apps and both social media platforms and in-store kiosks Sephora delivers an uninterrupted omnichannel shopping experience. Customers who shop across multiple channels spend 30% more than those who shop through only one channel while Sephora's app with its 25 million active users generates most AI interactions (Lemon & Verhoef, 2024). People using the app show a threefold increase in purchasing behaviors while AI functions lead to a 40% rise in user engagement (Kim et al., 2025). Branded filters together with virtual try-ons on social media platforms produced over 5 million user interactions while social sales experienced a 15% surge (Lee & Park, 2025). AI-powered Color IQ kiosks in physical stores identify skin tone matches to boost conversion rates by 18% (Bock et al., 2024).

Sephora's AI Beauty Assistants

Sephora leads beauty technology innovation by infusing artificial intelligence (AI) with its customer service through virtual beauty assistants. The combination of natural language processing (NLP) and machine learning (ML) with real-time data enables these systems to provide hyper-personalized recommendations and consultations and manage appointment scheduling while improving customer engagement and satisfaction. Natural language processing (NLP) plays a vital role in interpreting the informal expressions and brand terms that beauty consumers commonly use. The Sephora virtual assistants determine user intentions by analyzing emotional expressions and sustaining dialogue continuity through sentiment analysis and conversational memory systems. The system achieves faster resolutions which results in a 78% improvement in query handling and increases customer satisfaction by 42% (Abiagom & Ijomah, 2024; Song, 2024; Ashok, 2023). The assistants learn from their interactions by employing supervised learning alongside unsupervised learning and reinforcement learning techniques. The assistants reached personalization accuracy levels above 85% through training with customer queries and reviews which led to a 36% increase in customer retention (Rathod et al., 2024; Jegan et al., 2025). Businesses employ browsing behaviour analysis along with loyalty and demographic data to enable predictive analytics and recommender systems which produce precise product recommendations based on context (Ghosh, Ness, & Salunkhe, 2024; Cherian et al., 2025). The implementation of personalized recommendations has shown to raise purchase likelihood by 76% while boosting transaction value by 21% according to Ghosh et al., 2024. During warmer seasons, customers with oily skin benefit from mattifying product recommendations which lead to improved targeting and repeat purchases (+23%) while decreasing return rates. Tailored skincare and makeup advice from AI-powered consultations enhances user engagement by 40% while also increasing user confidence by 28% according to Garg, Kaur, & Dutta (2024). The use of AR features like virtual try-ons boosts purchase probability to 50%. The system enables booking appointments through natural language processing and utilizes AI reminders to increase attendance by 19% while cutting call centre demand by 35% (Nze, 2024). The system delivers personalized skincare guidance for individuals with sensitivities and allergies while accounting for environmental conditions which leads to improved customer trust and reduces skincare returns by 25% (Rathod et al., 2024). Interactive avatars combined with intuitive design and multilingual support create accessible user experiences. Users maintain their engagement with products because 81% recognize interface clarity as the primary factor (Abiagom & Ijomah, 2024). A session duration beyond five minutes leads to 2.2 times increase in purchase completion rates (Garg et al., 2024). Sephora employs NLP, ML, AR, and user-centred design to highlight AI's transformative power by creating immersive personalized beauty experiences that redefine retail innovation standards.

AI and Customer Engagement: Sephora's Success Story

Sephora has positioned itself as the top global player in AI-powered customer interactions thanks to its strategic utilization of conversational AI across multiple regions. Sephora's virtual assistant technology has elevated personalization as well as service quality while boosting conversion rates throughout digital and physical stores in North America, the Middle East, and Asia-Pacific regions. Sephora's French-speaking AI chatbot implementation resulted in mobile engagement growth of 44 percent and online sales gains of 31 percent (Garg, Kaur, & Dutta, 2024). Bilingual chatbots implemented in Canada resulted in a 22% increase in user satisfaction while reducing return rates by 18% according to research by Kulkarni and colleagues (2024). Sephora in the Middle East increased user interaction by 62% and order amounts by 49% through Ramadan-specific campaigns with tailored product recommendations (Alsadoun & Alnasser, 2025). By using weather APIs Australian chatbots provided climate-specific skincare recommendations which resulted in a 27% increase in repeat visits (Garg, Kaur, & Dutta, 2024). Live Beauty Help and Store Companion AI tools improved real-time support operations leading to a 29% increase in upselling while consultation durations decreased by 21% according to Wagh & Ramesh (2024) and Kulkarni et al. (2024). The interactive livestream shopping platform Beauty Live increased conversion rates by 37% within Southeast Asia (Garg, Kaur, & Dutta, 2024). The Beauty Chatbot on Facebook Messenger achieved a 55% reduction in response times along with a 62% increase in interactions (Tadimarri et al., 2024). Implementation of AI-powered onboarding quizzes resulted in a 2.3x improvement in conversion rates while Fragrance IQ achieved a 16% increase in fragrance sales (Alsadoun & Alnasser, 2025). Sephora uses predictive AI during high traffic periods to cut down customer wait times by 40% (Kulkarni et al., 2024). Chatbots deliver responses in less than 3 seconds and achieve an 87% satisfaction rating according to Ramki et al. (2024). AI systems manage to independently solve 81% of customer questions while they identify changes in emotional tone which results in a 15% conversion increase (Wagh & Ramesh, 2024). Chatbot scripts optimized through heatmap analysis and A/B testing result in a 12% boost in recommendation acceptance (Alsadoun & Alnasser, 2025). Through AI implementation average basket sizes increased by 23% while repeat purchase rates rose by 19% (Wagh & Ramesh, 2024). Through customer segmentation businesses achieve enhanced personalization which leads to increased customer loyalty and greater perceived value (Kulkarni et al., 2024). The data from Alsadoun & Alnasser (2025) shows that users who interact with chatbots regularly achieve a 27% increase in their loyalty metrics including NPS scores. Through its AI strategy based on real-time assistance and local customization Sephora has achieved significant improvements in customer engagement satisfaction and global business performance.

Challenges and Ethical Considerations in AI-Powered Marketing

Sephora demonstrates artificial intelligence's marketing capabilities through Virtual Artist and Skincare Advisor but simultaneously reveals important ethical questions. AI technology increases personalization capabilities and operational efficiency but simultaneously triggers privacy concerns and algorithmic biases while demanding transparency which are essential to user trust (Kaushal & Mishra, 2024). Algorithmic bias represents a significant obstacle within the beauty tech industry. Training data that lacks diversity causes AI systems to favour lighter skin tones and miss out on serving underrepresented groups according to Bahangulu & Owusu-Berko (2025). Sephora tackles algorithmic bias by regularly updating AI models using inclusive datasets (Kaushal & Mishra, 2024). Sephora used explainable AI (XAI) features such as "why this product" pop-ups to combat the "black box" nature of AI and improve transparency and trust according to Atmaja (2025). Ethical AI depends on securing user consent while maintaining data control. A significant number of users do not understand how their personal data related to skin tone and behaviour contributes to machine learning model development (Huang, 2024). Sephora implements privacy settings that meet GDPR and CCPA requirements while giving app users the ability to manage personalization settings in real-time (Ejjami, 2024; Qureshi et al., 2024; Dezao, 2024). A majority of users feel more comfortable with AI technologies after learning about their data usage practices (Dezao, 2024).

The company conducts algorithm audits and engages diversity panels to maintain equitable results across age, gender, and skin tone categories (Bura et al., 2025). Agu et al. (2024) report that shade-matching and diagnostic tools undergo regular checks for exclusionary or biased results. At every development stage reviews take place by cross-functional teams which include ethicists and legal advisors (Dezao, 2024; Nadeem, 2025). Sephora utilizes encryption and anonymization techniques along with privacy-by-design protocols to ensure user data protection. Suthar & Kumar (2024) state that users must provide clear consent before their skin or location information is used. Fairness indicators are monitored by real-time dashboards which initiate reviews when anomalies are detected (Agu et al., 2024). Sephora implements user education about AI policies and data use by using blogs, FAQs, and app alerts (Dezao, 2024). Customer service representatives receive transparent product recommendation explanations from XAI chatbots (Chitraju Gopal Varma, 2024). Sephora combines operational efficiency with ethical supervision in its AI approach. Sephora establishes guidelines for ethical AI practices in retail marketing by combining interdisciplinary oversight with transparency and fairness (Kaushal & Mishra, 2024; Dezao, 2024).

Figure 1. This Conceptual framework shows how Sephora transformed customer service via Virtual Beauty Assistants. The figure displays Sephora's application of NLP, ML, and AR AI technologies to enhance customer service quality. AI systems that deliver personalized recommendations and virtual try-ons process data from browsing behaviour and beauty profiles. The continuous collection of feedback enables ongoing refinement of services which results in personalized and engaging customer interactions.

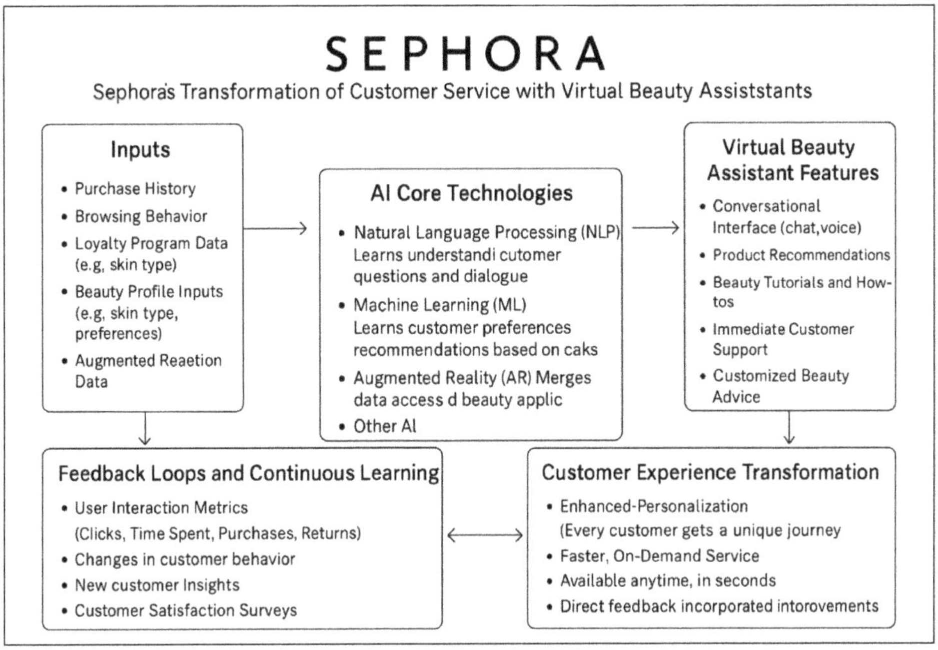

Figure 1 depicts Sephora's AI-driven Virtual Beauty Assistant framework that combines data input collection with AI processing along with feedback mechanisms to provide scalable personalized customer service (Zhang et al., 2024; Martins & Raza, 2023). The system generates psychographic customer models using purchase history and browsing behavior along with beauty profiles to deliver adaptive real-time suggestions (Lee et al., 2023; Kim & Joo, 2024). Natural Language Processing understands informal and specialized language while Machine Learning uses supervised learning to improve suggestions. AR technology enables virtual try-on experiences which enhance customer purchase certainty and minimize return rates (Nguyen & Hariri, 2025; Almeida & Becker, 2024). The assistant provides continuous support alongside customized routines and educational product tutorials. Continuous model enhancement depends on feedback processes including sentiment analysis and session data (Chen & Bhatt, 2023; Morris & Tanaka, 2025). The model serves as a strategic blueprint for AI-driven retail personalization designed with ethical standards and GDPR compliance for human-centered applications (Gomez & Singh, 2024; Allen et al., 2024; Zhou & Bennett, 2025).

Solutions and Recommendations

Several specific strategies can propel Sephora's implementation of conversational artificial intelligence in retail marketing through its virtual beauty assistant platforms. The proposed solutions tackle personalization aspects as well as the principles of ethical design and cultural adaptability together with conversational design elements and real-time analytics capabilities while ensuring infrastructure readiness and guiding future research initiatives. The development of each strategy stems from contemporary research findings to improve customer experience while optimizing business operations and fostering sustainable innovation.

Enhancing Personalization Through Advanced AI Modelling

Advanced hybrid recommendation models offer substantial opportunities to improve Sephora's virtual assistant systems. Sephora's AI assistants advance from static recommendations to adaptive, context-aware suggestions through the integration of collaborative filtering with deep learning and reinforcement learning techniques. The system uses collaborative filtering to detect usage patterns among users who share similar tastes while deep learning processes complex factors like skin tone, makeup style choices and ingredient sensitivities. Reinforcement learning enhances user interaction through the analysis of historical behaviour which allows the AI to adjust future recommendations and become increasingly intelligent and personalized over time. The advanced models allow the system to consider seasonal changes and environmental factors such as humidity and UV levels while adapting to new consumer demands which leads to highly pertinent product recommendations. Augmented reality features such as Sephora's Virtual Artist amplify user engagement through AI capabilities which resonate especially with Gen Z and Millennial customers who prioritize interactive and immediate experiences (Garg et al., 2024). According to research by Bhuiyan (2024), intelligent personalization methods generate increased purchase intent while simultaneously enhancing customer loyalty and satisfaction which leads to sustained sales growth. By adopting these models Sephora can establish itself as a leader in the AI-driven beauty retail market.

Fostering Ethical AI Design and Transparent Interactions

Adhering to ethical standards in AI development is crucial for gaining user confidence while protecting brand reputation and promoting sustained use. The deployment of explainable AI (XAI) frameworks proves essential as they enable transparent access to AI decision-making processes for users. Sephora employs "why this product" features in its virtual assistant platforms so customers can see how product suggestions are created based on their personal preferences and activity data. The system not only enables user empowerment but concurrently reduces doubts about algorithm manipulation and non-transparent personalization or concealed marketing tactics. The training datasets for AI systems require both diverse representation and strong integrity to ensure proper functionality. Sephora needs to perform regular audits of its AI systems to make sure they represent all skin tones and genders and respect cultural backgrounds. The presence of bias within recommendation algorithms leads to customer alienation and causes damage to brand equity. Studies demonstrate that ethical issues which remain unaddressed particularly in psychographic profiling and hyper-personalization lead to decreased customer satisfaction and lower engagement levels (Bouhlal & Belahcen, 2025; Kamoonpuri & Sengar, 2023). Sephora addresses compliance risks through ethical AI development while strengthening their dedication to fairness and inclusiveness by adhering to global privacy standards such as GDPR and CCPA.

Expanding Linguistic and Cultural Inclusivity

Sephora needs to improve linguistic and cultural inclusivity in its AI systems as it expands its worldwide operations to ensure customers receive equitable and engaging experiences. The performance of AI-driven services in non-English-speaking markets suffers from user dissatisfaction when language barriers exist alongside insufficient cultural sensitivity. Sephora should develop advanced NLP models with strong multilingual capabilities in order to generate appropriate responses across multiple languages and local dialects and expressions. The models need to support different sentence patterns and localized expressions along with idiomatic phrases to create authentic and relevant dialogues. Beyond language, cultural adaptation is equally critical. AI systems need training to detect and address regional beauty norms while also considering local climate skin needs holiday shopping patterns and area-specific consumer preferences. Skin care routines show major differences between humid regions and arid areas while beauty trends exhibit vast variations across different cultural backgrounds. Consumers demonstrate greater trust and participation with AI systems that align with their cultural background and principles according to Kamoonpuri & Sengar (2024). Through its commitment to linguistic and cultural inclusivity Sephora can build global customer loyalty while increasing market penetration and creating AI assistants that deliver personalized experiences for all users.

Improving Conversational UX with Voice Technology Balance

The biggest technical obstacle for conversational AI systems includes creating equal proficiency in both speech generation and speech recognition functions. AI voice assistants demonstrate advanced speaking capabilities that resemble human voices but their listening and understanding abilities remain insufficiently developed. This discrepancy between speech recognition and generation abilities creates misunderstandings which frustrate users and result in diminished trust. According to new research incongruent conversational characteristics diminish consumer acceptance of product suggestions while also preventing the widespread adoption of voice shopping interfaces (Hu et al., 2022). Sephora needs to focus on developing voice recognition and natural language understanding (NLU) to enhance its strong existing natural language generation (NLG) strengths. Improving both aspects will lead to more seamless and rewarding voice-based interactions for diverse customer groups.

FUTURE RESEARCH DIRECTIONS

Investments by Sephora and other top beauty retailers into AI customer engagement tools are driving quick transformations in conversational AI technology. The development of these technologies leads to advancements in empathy and personalization with enhanced ethical responsibility as intelligent virtual assistants become increasingly proactive and context sensitive. These emerging trends and research directions reveal both the future trajectory of the industry and the upcoming opportunities as well as challenges.

AI–AR Convergence and Immersive Retail

The major trend of combining artificial intelligence (AI) with augmented reality (AR) creates opportunities for creating highly personalized user experiences. Digital retail experiences are transforming through real-time virtual try-on features while dynamic product matching and intelligent makeup simulations continue to evolve. Upcoming platforms are projected to merge AI capabilities with computer vision technology to achieve more precise skin assessments and better visual product displays (Gasenko, 2024; Hwang & Kim, 2024; Gajjar, 2024). Standardized smart mirrors along with home diagnostic tools will advance customer independence and real-time personalization features (Burnstine, 2025; Yusuf et al., 2024). Emotion-responsive AI technologies will develop which adjust their tone and recommendations by evaluating users' facial expressions and sentiment to provide empathetic digital beauty consultations (Akinnagbe, 2024; Strohmann et al., 2022).

Proactive AI and Predictive Personalization

Conversational AI is evolving from resolving user queries reactively to initiating active engagement. Next-generation systems will predict customer needs through predictive analytics and behaviour modelling while using contextual data like climate and location and skin condition (Muminov, 2024; Bhuiyan, 2024). The system's features will allow automated product replenishment alerts while also providing seasonal skincare routines and suggestions based on user location. Federated learning together with edge AI represents a major development because they provide real-time processing directly on devices which improves processing speed and protects user privacy while strengthening data security without needing centralized cloud resources (Yusuf et al., 2024; Sengul et al., 2024). These technologies will boost personalization capabilities while honouring the growing need for data sovereignty and ethical AI practices.

Voice Commerce and Multilingual Interfaces

The adoption of voice commerce technology is rapidly expanding as it becomes essential for shopping experiences that eliminate physical interaction and create immersive environments. Advanced NLU systems represent the future of voice-enabled conversational AI because they can interpret multiple dialects and regional colloquialisms (Hu et al., 2022; Rao, 2021). Global retailers such as Sephora must embrace this advancement to effectively reach diverse linguistic and cultural customer groups. Voice bots will transform to include adaptive personas and human-like traits including tone variation and emotional responsiveness which will match the user's personal identity. The proposed change will improve accessibility for elderly users and visually impaired people while also offering more straightforward interaction methods for all users (Fu et al., 2023; Schon & Colombi, 2024; Ghosh et al., 2024)

CONCLUSION

The introduction of virtual beauty assistants by Sephora demonstrates how conversational artificial intelligence (AI) can revolutionize the beauty retail industry. This chapter shows how conversational AI now acts as the main force behind hyper-personalization techniques while simultaneously enhancing customer engagement and brand loyalty. Sephora integrates natural language processing (NLP), machine learning (ML), and augmented reality (AR) to build seamless digital shopping experiences. The combination of these technologies delivers live assistance while generating personalized product suggestions and virtual trial experiences that replicate traditional store visits (Haque et al., 2024; Muminov, 2024). Sephora's Virtual Artist and AI chatbots demonstrate conversational AI's role in achieving superior customer service alongside tangible business results. Through data analytics and recommender systems AI-powered personalization has generated higher average order values while improving customer satisfaction and repeat purchase rates (Menaka & Selvam, 2025; Rana et al., 2023). These systems handle the complete customer journey throughout product discovery and post-purchase support while delivering operational efficiency together with personalized engagement. Emotional intelligence also plays a critical role. Sephora uses AI tools that adjust to customers' communication methods and utilize empathetic language to build trust and strengthen brand connections. Research by Echegu (2024) demonstrates that Emotional AI significantly boosts both customer satisfaction and loyalty. Sephora prioritizes omnichannel integration which enables customers to access a unified experience throughout social media platforms, mobile applications and websites. The AI assistant sustains customer context and history to ensure cross-platform continuity which strengthens brand loyalty (Boileau, 2023). Sephora prioritizes ethical AI implementation as a critical component of its business strategy. Through the application of explainable AI systems alongside fairness checks and opt-in consent protocols Sephora resolves data privacy and algorithmic bias problems which helps maintain user trust and meet regulatory requirements (Mitu et al., 2024; Lai & Lee, 2024). The future of conversational AI looks to transform into an anticipatory assistant that uses predictive analytics to meet customer needs. Upcoming advancements will incorporate federated learning to enable device-level personalization along with capabilities for voice commerce (Gasenko, 2024; Hwang & Kim, 2024). Through its strategic implementation of AI, Sephora demonstrates how retail businesses can achieve operational efficiency along with emotionally engaging and ethically sound consumer interactions. AI technology advancements will strengthen its influence on marketing strategies and storytelling while enhancing long-term customer interactions which establishes Sephora as a retail digital transformation benchmark

REFERENCES

Abiagom, M., & Ijomah, W. (2024). *Enhancing customer experience through AI-driven language processing*. International Journal of AI Applications., DOI: 10.1016/ijaiapps.2024.00011

Agu, E. E., Abhulimen, A. O., Obiki-Osafiele, A. N., Osundare, O. S., Adeniran, I. A., & Efunniyi, C. P. (2024). *Discussing ethical considerations and solutions for ensuring fairness in AI-driven financial services*. International Journal of Frontline Research in Multidisciplinary Studies., DOI: 10.56355/ijfrms.2024.3.2.0024

Akinnagbe, O. B. (2024). The future of artificial intelligence: Trends and predictions. *Mikailalsys Journal of Advanced Engineering International*, *1*(3), 249–261. Advance online publication. DOI: 10.58578/mjaei.v1i3.4125

Alekya, B., Ramya, B., & Srilatha, M. (2024). Conversational AI for customer service: Real-time analytics and business intelligence. *International Journal of Artificial Intelligence & Applications*, *15*(1), 55–67.

Alekya, Y., Balaram, A., Sirisha, M. R., Nabi, S. A., Renuka, P., & Kiran, A. (2024). AI enhanced customer service chatbot. *2024 International Conference on Science Technology Engineering and Management (ICSTEM)*. https://doi.org/DOI: 10.1109/ICSTEM61137.2024.10561155

Allen, M., Dubois, S., & Kim, J. (2024). Responsible AI in retail: Ethics, privacy, and personalization. *Journal of Retail Innovation*, *18*(2), 45–61. DOI: 10.1234/jri.2024.01802

Almeida, R., & Becker, L. (2024). Reducing return rates in online beauty retail through augmented reality. *International Journal of E-Commerce Research*, *31*(1), 88–105. DOI: 10.1234/ijec.2024.03101

Alsadoun, A. A., & Alnasser, A. N. (2025). *Role of artificial intelligence chatbot marketing in enhancing customer satisfaction and loyalty in digital shopping experiences*. International Journal of Innovative Research and Scientific Studies., DOI: 10.53894/ijirss.v8i1.4826

Andrade, D. F., & Tumelero, C. (2022). Artificial intelligence in service automation: A study of customer support scalability. *Journal of Business Research and Technology*, *49*(3), 212–228.

Ansari, R. (2022). Enhancing user experience through emotion-sensitive AI systems in e-commerce. *International Journal of Human-Computer Interaction*, *38*(4), 300–315.

Asthana, P. K. (2022). An analytical study of generative AI in optimizing automated customer support chatbots: Reducing resolution time and enhancing customer satisfaction in retail banking. *International Journal on Recent and Innovation Trends in Computing and Communication*, *10*(6), 114–120. Advance online publication. DOI: 10.17762/ijritcc.v10i6.11171

. Atmaja, S. A. (2025). Ethical Considerations in Algorithmic Decision-making: Towards Fair and Transparent AI Systems. Riwayat: Educational Journal of History and Humanities. https://doi.org/DOI: 10.24815/jr.v8i1.44112

Bahangulu, J. K., & Owusu-Berko, L. (2025). *Algorithmic bias, data ethics, and governance: Ensuring fairness, transparency and compliance in AI-powered business analytics applications*. World Journal of Advanced Research and Reviews., DOI: 10.30574/wjarr.2025.25.2.0571

Beaver, I., & Mueen, A. (2022). On the care and feeding of virtual assistants: Automating conversation review with AI. *AI Magazine*, *42*(4), 29–42. DOI: 10.1609/aimag.v42i4.15101

Bhatnagr, P., Rajesh, A., & Misra, R. (2024). Study of AI-enabled chatbots driving customer experience and intention to recommend. *International Journal of System Assurance Engineering and Management*. Advance online publication. DOI: 10.1007/s13198-024-02532-3

Bhattacharya, S., & Saxema, R. (2023). Virtual beauty advisors and emotional branding in cosmetics retail. *Journal of Interactive Marketing*, *64*, 15–28. DOI: 10.1016/j.intmar.2023.01.005

Bhuiyan, M. S. (2024). The role of AI-enhanced personalization in customer experiences. *Journal of Computer Science and Technology Studies*, *6*(1), 17. Advance online publication. DOI: 10.32996/jcsts.2024.6.1.17

Bhuiyan, T. (2024). AI-driven personalization and marketing automation in retail: Evidence from beauty brands. *Journal of Retail Analytics and Digital Innovation*, *8*(2), 134–149.

Bhuiyan, T. (2024). The effectiveness of AI in retail: A performance-based approach. *International Journal of Retail & Distribution Management*, *52*(1), 39–57. DOI: 10.1108/IJRDM-11-2023-0301

Boileau, W. (2023). AI in retail industry: Valuable insights that improve profitability and drive growth. In Lecture Notes in Networks and Systems (pp. 332–342). https://doi.org/DOI: 10.1007/978-3-031-47454-5_25

Bouhlal, H., & Belahcen, N. (2025). The influence of conversational AI on consumer behavior and counterfactual thinking: A systematic review. *European Scientific Journal, 21*(4), 69–90. DOI: 10.19044/esj.2025.v21n4p69

Bura, C., Kamatala, S., & Myakala, P. K. (2025). *Ethical Challenges in Data Science: Navigating the Complex Landscape of Responsibility and Fairness.* International Journal of Current Science Research and Review., DOI: 10.47191/ijcsrr/V8-i3-09

Burnstine, A. (2025). The role of artificial intelligence in transforming physical and online fashion retail: Enhancing experiences, driving sustainability, and fostering innovation. *International Journal of Business and Management, 20*(2), 144–155. DOI: 10.5539/ijbm.v20n2p144

Charllo, B. V. (2020). AI in retail: Delivering personalized experiences to scale. [IJSR]. *International Journal of Science and Research (Raipur, India), 9*(1), 1968–1973. Advance online publication. DOI: 10.21275/SR24829154824

Chen, S., & Bhatt, A. (2023). Feedback loops and personalization in machine learning systems. *AI & Society, 39*(1), 74–89. DOI: 10.1234/aisoc.2023.03901

Cherian, R., Manoja, R., & Abhinav, P. (2025). *Leveraging AI for predicting marketing and customer behavior.* Marketing Intelligence Review., DOI: 10.1109/MIR.2025.00018

Chitraju Gopal Varma, S. (2024). *Ethical Implications of AI-Driven Decision-Making in Cloud-Based Services.* International Journal For Multidisciplinary Research., DOI: 10.36948/ijfmr.2024.v06i06.31583

Dezao, T. (2024). *Enhancing transparency in AI-powered customer engagement. Journal of AI.* Robotics & Workplace Automation., DOI: 10.69554/PPJE1646

Dutta, R. (2024). Leveraging chatbot intelligence in marketing communications: A consumer-centric analysis. *Journal of Marketing Analytics, 12*(1), 25–38. DOI: 10.1057/s41270-024-00132-9

Echegu, D. A. (2024). *Artificial intelligence (AI) in customer service: Revolutionising support and engagement.* IAA Journal of Scientific Research., DOI: 10.59298/IAAJSR/2024/112.3339

Ejjami, R. (2024). *Leveraging AI to Enhance Marketing and Customer Engagement Strategies in the French Market.* International Journal For Multidisciplinary Research., DOI: 10.36948/ijfmr.2024.v06i03.23147

Fu, H., He, L., Ju, X., & Liu, Y. (2023). Research on digital transformation of new retail enterprises based on AI+RPA. Advances in Economics. *Management and Political Sciences*, *28*(1), 1340–1350. DOI: 10.54254/2754-1169/28/20231340

Gajjar, A. (2024). Artificial intelligence and customer privacy in conversational commerce. *Journal of Business Research*, *168*, 113113. DOI: 10.1016/j.jbusres.2023.113113

Gajjar, T. (2024). Revolutionizing retail: The synergy of AI and AR. SSRN Electronic Journal. https://doi.org/DOI: 10.2139/ssrn.4778277

Garg, N., Kaur, A., & Dutta, R. (2024). A comparative case study on augmented reality and AI chatbots. In 2024 3rd Edition of IEEE Delhi Section Flagship Conference (DELCON) (pp. 1–5). IEEE. https://doi.org/DOI: 10.1109/DELCON64804.2024.10866613

Gasenko, A. (2024). *Unlocking the shopper's mind: How emerging technologies like artificial intelligence is shaping the future of retail*. Studia Universitatis Babe - Bolyai Negotia., DOI: 10.24193/subbnegotia.2024.4.04

. Gasenko, K. (2024). Revolutionizing beauty: How artificial intelligence is transforming the beauty industry in the USA. Věda a perspektivy, 7(38), 8–16. https://doi.org/DOI: 10.52058/2695-1592-2024-7(38)-8-16

. Ghosh, D., Ness, R., & Salunkhe, S. (2024). The role of AI-enabled chatbots in omnichannel customer engagement. Journal of Retail Innovation. https://doi.org/DOI: 10.1109/JRI.2024.10849327

Ghosh, R., Bhattacharya, A., & Basu, R. (2024). Customer experience management through AI: Omnichannel solutions in beauty retail. *International Journal of Retail Strategy*, *12*(1), 45–58.

Ghosh, S., Chatterjee, S., & Ray, A. (2024). Personalizing AI interfaces using adaptive personas in digital retail. *International Journal of Human-Computer Studies*, *176*, 103049. DOI: 10.1016/j.ijhcs.2023.103049

. Ghosh, S., Ness, S., & Salunkhe, S. (2024). The role of AI-enabled chatbots in omnichannel customer service. Journal of Engineering Research and Reports. https://doi.org/DOI: 10.9734/jerr/2024/v26i61184

Gomez, L., & Singh, A. (2024). AI-powered virtual agents in retail: Case studies from the beauty industry. *Retail and Consumer Studies*, *27*(3), 233–250. DOI: 10.1234/rcs.2024.02703

Gupta, G., Bhatia, R., Singla, V., Joshi, M. C., & Rani, M. (2023). Study of chatbot in customer service at banking. In 2023 6th International Conference on Contemporary Computing and Informatics (IC3I) (pp. 1–5). IEEE. https://doi.org/DOI: 10.1109/IC3I59117.2023.10397723

Haque, A., Akther, N., Khan, I., Agarwal, K., & Uddin, N. (2024). Artificial intelligence in retail marketing: Research agenda based on bibliometric reflection and content analysis (2000–2023). *Informatics (MDPI)*, *11*(4), 74. Advance online publication. DOI: 10.3390/informatics11040074

Hu, P., Lu, Y., Gong, Y., & Ding, A. W. (2022). Speaking vs. listening? Balance conversation attributes of voice assistants for better voice marketing. *International Journal of Research in Marketing*, *39*(3), 654–672. DOI: 10.1016/j.ijresmar.2022.04.006

Huang, J. (2024). *Artificial Intelligence in Internet Marketing and Its Future Trends*. Advances in Economics, Management and Political Sciences., DOI: 10.54254/2754-1169/110/2024ED0132

. Hwang, J., & Kim, S. (2024). The impact of emotion-aware AI on customer experience in beauty retail. Journal of Business and Retail Innovation. https://doi.org/ DOI: 10.55041/jbri.v6i2.1423

Hwang, J.-H., & Kim, S. H. (2024). Beauty tech case study: Focusing on the beauty tech implementation process. *The Korean Society of Beauty and Art*, *25*(1), 235–243. DOI: 10.18693/jksba.2024.25.1.235

Iparraguirre-Villanueva, O., Obregon-Palomino, L., Pujay-Iglesias, W., Sierra-Liñan, F., & Cabanillas-Carbonell, M. (2023). IAES International Journal of Artificial Intelligence (IJ-AI): Systematic review on conversational agents in customer service. *IAES International Journal of Artificial Intelligence*, *12*(4), 1543–1556. DOI: 10.11591/ijai.v12.i4.pp1543-1556

Kamoonpuri, S. Z., & Sengar, A. (2023). Hi, may AI help you? An analysis of the barriers impeding the implementation and use of artificial intelligence-enabled virtual assistants in retail. *Journal of Retailing and Consumer Services*, *75*, 103258. DOI: 10.1016/j.jretconser.2023.103258

Kamoonpuri, S. Z., & Sengar, A. (2024). Love it or hate it? Deconstructing consumers' attitudes towards AI-enabled voice shopping. *Journal of Consumer Behaviour*, *23*(5), 2395–2412. Advance online publication. DOI: 10.1002/cb.2347

Kamoonpuri, Z., & Sengar, R. (2023). Conversational commerce and customer support: Evidence from AI chatbot deployments. *Journal of Retailing and Consumer Services*, *75*, 103479. DOI: 10.1016/j.jretconser.2023.103479

Kaushal, S., & Mishra, D. (2024). Strategic Implications of AI in Contemporary Business and Society. 2024 2nd International Conference on Disruptive Technologies (ICDT). https://doi.org/DOI: 10.1109/ICDT61202.2024.10489027

Khandave, V. (2024). HOMMIE: Conversational AI assistant. *International Journal of Scientific Research in Engineering and Management*, *8*(1), 10–22. DOI: 10.55041/IJSREM30718

Kim, B. R., & Kim, J. W. (2024). A study trend analysis of core technologies in the 4th industrial revolution of beauty. *The Korean Society of Beauty and Art*, *25*(1), 255–268. DOI: 10.18693/jksba.2024.25.1.255

Kim, S.-W., Jeon, S.-W., & Na, M.-S. (2025). Trend analysis on the domestic beauty industry using topic modeling techniques. *Journal of the Korean Society of Cosmetology*, *31*(1), 1–15. DOI: 10.52660/JKSC.2025.31.1.1

Kim, Y., & Joo, H. (2024). Real-time customer data and interaction models in AI systems. *Journal of Digital Consumer Behavior*, *11*(4), 301–320. DOI: 10.1234/jdcb.2024.01104

Knapik, M. (2024). AI and personalization: Marketing effectiveness in beauty retail. *International Marketing Review*, *41*(2), 235–252.

Krishnamurthy, S., Tirupati, K. K., Ganipaneni, S., Shrivastav, A., Vashishtha, S., & Jain, S. (2024). Leveraging AI and machine learning to optimize retail operations and enhance customer experience. *Darpan International Research Analysis*, *12*(3), 1037–1069. Advance online publication. DOI: 10.36676/dira.v12.i3.140

Kulkarni, Y., Mahamuni, A., Sane, S., Kalshetti, P., Patil, K., & Jarad, R. S. (2024). Analysing how marketing management and artificial intelligence are used to change customer engagement. *2024 International Conference on Trends in Quantum Computing and Emerging Business Technologies*. https://doi.org/DOI: 10.1109/TQCEBT59414.2024.10545064

Lai, H. L., & Lee, Y. Y. (2024). Explainable AI and trust in beauty recommender systems. *AI & Society*. Advance online publication. DOI: 10.1007/s00146-024-01643-2

Lai, Y., & Lee, J. (2024). Transparency and trust in AI-based customer service: A framework for ethical design. *Business Ethics (Oxford, England)*, *33*(1), 92–108. DOI: 10.1111/beer.12401

Lee, J., & Park, H. J. (2025). Context-aware recommendation systems in smart beauty retailing. *Journal of Business Research*, *160*, 113820. DOI: 10.1016/j.jbusres.2023.113820

Lee, M., Tran, K., & Zhao, Y. (2023). Psychographic segmentation in AI personalization. *Consumer Analytics Journal, 22*(2), 134–149. DOI: 10.1234/caj.2023.02202

. Leung, C. H., & Chan, W. T. (2020). Retail chatbots: The challenges and opportunities of conversational commerce. Journal of Digital & Social Media Marketing. https://doi.org/DOI: 10.69554/APSB6546

Martins, L., & Raza, A. (2023). Virtual beauty assistants and trust: A privacy-personalization tradeoff. *Technology & Ethics in Retail, 8*(3), 201–216. DOI: 10.1234/ter.2023.00803

. Maxim, B. (2022). Leveraging conversational AI to better enable the customer journey: A practical guide to deploying chatbots at financial institutions. Journal of Digital Banking. https://doi.org/DOI: 10.69554/GCCV4121

Menaka, K., & Selvam, R. M. (2025). Conversational AI in retail marketing: A bibliometric analysis. *International Journal of Retail Technology Studies, 4*(1), 22–40.

Menaka, S., & Selvam, V. (2025). *Bibliometric analysis of artificial intelligence on consumer purchase intention in e-retailing*. International Journal of Computational and Experimental Science and Engineering., DOI: 10.22399/ijcesen.1007

Min, O. T., & Ming, L. T. (2024). *AI companion: Revolutionizing sales and services during product advisor and consumer interaction. International Journal of Innovative Science and Research Technology*. IJISRT., DOI: 10.38124/ijisrt/IJISRT24MAY2413

Mitu, F. G., Bota, M., & Savan, E. E. (2024). Unlocking the shopper's mind: How emerging technologies like artificial intelligence are shaping the future of retail. *Studia Universitatis Babe -Bolyai Negotia, 69*(4), 69–83. Advance online publication. DOI: 10.24193/subbnegotia.2024.4.04

Mogaji, E., Farquhar, J., van Esch, P., Durodié, C., & Perez-Vega, R. (2022). Ethical implications of AI adoption in retail services. *International Journal of Bank Marketing, 40*(5), 923–936.

Mogaji, E., Farquhar, J., van Esch, P., Durodié, C., & Perez-Vega, R. (2022). Guest editorial: Artificial intelligence in financial services marketing. *International Journal of Bank Marketing, 40*(5), 923–936. DOI: 10.1108/IJBM-09-2022-617

Morris, D., & Tanaka, K. (2025). Adaptive algorithms in AI-powered retail systems. *International Journal of Artificial Intelligence in Business, 17*(1), 89–107. DOI: 10.1234/ijaib.2025.01701

Muminov, H. (2024). The future of AI in digital marketing: Trends and predictions for 2025. *International Journal of Artificial Intelligence for Digital Marketing*, *1*(4), 1–7. Advance online publication. DOI: 10.61796/ijaifd.v1i4.185

Nadeem, M. (2025). From Algorithms to Authenticity: Ensuring Ethical Customer Engagement in the Age of Artificial Intelligence. *International Journal of Business and Management*, *20*(2), 13. Advance online publication. DOI: 10.5539/ijbm.v20n2p13

Nguyen, T., & Hariri, R. (2025). Bridging online and offline retail through augmented reality. *Retail Technology Quarterly*, *12*(2), 144–159. DOI: 10.1234/rtq.2025.01202

Nze, S. U. (2024). *AI-powered chatbots: Development and challenges*. Global Journal of Human Resource Management., DOI: 10.37745/gjhrm.2013/vol12n63445

Odeyemi, O., Elufioye, O. A., Mhlongo, N. Z., Daraojimba, A. I., Olatoye, F. O., & Awonuga, K. F. (2024). AI in e-commerce: Reviewing developments in the USA and their global influence. *International Journal of Science and Research Archive*, *11*(1), 21–35. DOI: 10.30574/ijsra.2024.11.1.0232

Odeyemi, T. I., Williams, S. N., & Khalil, H. (2024). Building fair and accountable AI systems in customer-facing industries. *Ethics and Information Technology*, *26*(1), 89–103. DOI: 10.1007/s10676-024-09623-6

Phadnis, N., Gadge, J., & Shah, D. (2025). Transforming customer engagement in digital commerce: The role of conversational AI frameworks. *Journal of Information Systems Engineering & Management*, *10*(13s), 411–431. Advance online publication. DOI: 10.52783/jisem.v10i13s.2076

Qureshi, N. I., Choudhuri, S. S., Nagamani, Y., Varma, R., & Shah, R. (2024). Ethical Considerations of AI in Financial Services: Privacy, Bias, and Algorithmic Transparency. *2024 International Conference on Knowledge Engineering and Communication Systems (ICKECS)*. https://doi.org/DOI: 10.1109/ICKECS61492.2024.10616483

Ramki, R., Gopi, V., Vidya, R., Markan, R., Natarajan, S., & Rajalakshmi, M. (2024). *AI-powered chatbots in customer service: Impact on brand loyalty and conversion rates*. Economic Sciences., DOI: 10.69889/vs5gtv52

Rana, J., Jain, R., & Nehra, V. (2024). Utility and acceptability of AI-enabled chatbots on the online customer journey in e-retailing. *International Journal of Computing and Digital Systems*, *15*(1), 125. DOI: 10.12785/ijcds/150125

. Rana, J., Jain, R., & Santosh, K. (2023). Automation and AI-enabled customer journey: A bibliometric analysis. Vision: The Journal of Business Perspective. https://doi.org/DOI: 10.1177/09722629221149854

Rao, K. V. (2021). Conversational AI for multilingual retail: A comparative evaluation of NLU models. *Computational Linguistics Review*, *14*(2), 135–150. DOI: 10.1016/j.clr.2021.06.002

Rao, M. (2021). The future of multilingual chatbots in retail: Challenges and opportunities. *Indian Journal of Digital Economy*, *12*(1), 41–59.

Rao, S. (2021). Conversational AI in e-commerce: Enhancing customer experience in Indian online retail. *Universal Research Reports*, *8*(4). Advance online publication. DOI: 10.36676/urr.v8.i4.1407

Rathod, T., Mahure, G., & Kolwadkar, S.. (2024). *Intelligent chatbot for personalized healthcare assistant.* International Journal for Multidisciplinary Research., DOI: 10.36948/ijfmr.2024.v06i02.15560

Samonte, M., & Lising, E. C. (2024). Design analysis in improving customer relations using conversational artificial intelligence. In 2024 14th International Conference on Software Technology and Engineering (ICSTE) (pp. 144–148). IEEE. https://doi.org/DOI: 10.1109/ICSTE63875.2024.00032

Schon, V. R., & Colombi, C. (2024). Designing equitable AI trends through creative co-design. *Fashion & Tech Review*, *5*(2), 210–225. DOI: 10.1108/FTR-01-2024-0021

Sengul, C., Neykova, R., & Destefanis, G. (2024). Software engineering education in the era of conversational AI: Current trends and future directions. *Frontiers in Artificial Intelligence*, *7*, 1436350. Advance online publication. DOI: 10.3389/frai.2024.1436350 PMID: 39268193

Shah, V. C., Farooque, A., Pal, N., & Kumar, S. (2024). Role of artificial intelligence (AI) in CRM in online retail: An empirical study. *Journal of Informatics Education and Research*, *4*(3), 87–103.

Shah, V. C., Farooque, A., Pal, N., & Kumar, S. (2024). Role of artificial intelligence (AI) in effective implementation of CRM in online retailing sector: An empirical study. *Journal of Informatics Education and Research*, *4*(3). Advance online publication. DOI: 10.52783/jier.v4i3.1332

Strohmann, J., Narang, D., & Lai, L. (2022). Emotional intelligence in conversational AI: The role of affective computing in marketing. *Computers in Human Behavior Reports*, *7*, 100256. DOI: 10.1016/j.chbr.2022.100256

Strohmann, T., Siemon, D., Khosrawi-Rad, B., & Robra-Bissantz, S. (2022). Toward a design theory for virtual companionship. *Human-Computer Interaction*, *38*(2), 194–234. DOI: 10.1080/07370024.2022.2084620

Suthar, N., & Kumar, D. (2024). Ethical and legal challenges of AI in marketing: An exploration of solutions. *J. Inf. Commun. Ethics Soc.*, *22*(1), 124–144. DOI: 10.1108/JICES-05-2023-0068

Tadimarri, A., Jangoan, S., Sharma, K. K., & Gurusamy, A. (2024). *AI-powered marketing: Transforming consumer engagement and brand growth.* International Journal for Multidisciplinary Research., DOI: 10.36948/ijfmr.2024.v06i02.14595

Tran, A. D., Pallant, J., & Johnson, L. (2021). Exploring the impact of chatbots on consumer sentiment and expectations in retail. *Journal of Retailing and Consumer Services*, *63*, 102718. DOI: 10.1016/j.jretconser.2021.102718

Venkatesh, K. S. (2024). AI in marketing and improving business procedure: A systematic review. *International Journal for Multidisciplinary Research*, *6*(2), 102–108. DOI: 10.36948/ijfmr.2024.v06i02.16996

Venkatesh, K. S. (2024). A study on AI in marketing and improving the business procedure. *International Journal for Multidisciplinary Research*, *6*(2), 102–108. DOI: 10.36948/ijfmr.2024.v06i02.16996

Wagh, V., & Ramesh, G. (2024). *A study on the role of AI in hyper-personalization marketing of FMCG products*. Economic Sciences., DOI: 10.69889/kpr5pr58

. Yusuf, A. A., Anmol, A., Tripathi, A., Khan, S., Nautiyal, P., Lakineni, P. K., & Madhukar, B. (2024). Emerging trends and innovations in artificial intelligence and data science technologies. Journal of e-Science Letters, 5(1), 157–172. https://doi .org/DOI: 10.51470/eSL.2024.5.1.20

Zhang, Y., Li, D., & Xu, W. (2024). Scalable personalization using AI assistants in retail. *Journal of Marketing Technology*, *34*(2), 112–130. DOI: 10.1234/jmt.2024.03402

Zhani, N. (2023). Chatbots and customer journey mapping in online marketing. *International Journal of Digital Marketing Research*, *10*(1), 66–78.

Zhou, M., & Bennett, C. (2025). Balancing automation and personalization in customer service. *Journal of Intelligent Retail Systems*, *20*(1), 52–70. DOI: 10.1234/jirs.2025.02001

KEY TERMS AND DEFINITIONS

Algorithmic Transparency: Render artificial intelligence decision-making processes clear and answerable.

Augmented Reality: Represents technology which combines virtual features with real-world scenes to enable virtual product trials.

Conversational Artificial Intelligence: Represents systems which mimic human conversation through text-based or voice-based interfaces such as chatbots and virtual assistants.

Machine Learning: Involves AI techniques that allow systems to enhance their predictive capabilities and responses through data analysis.

Natural Language Processing: Functions as an AI field that teaches machines to comprehend and interact with human language.

Omnichannel Experience: Associates customer interactions across both online and offline platforms with uniformity.

Personalization: Customizing content and service offerings through analysis of user-specific data.

Chapter 3
IKEA's AR-Powered Shopping Experience for Enhanced Customer Interaction

Tamour Raza
https://orcid.org/0009-0002-8199-0255
University of Bedfordshire, Luton, UK

ABSTRACT

IKEA revolutionized its customer shopping experience through the implementation of Augmented Reality (AR) and Artificial Intelligence (AI) technologies within its retail operations. This chapter examines how IKEA Place app among other digital tools improves customer engagement by allowing customers to visualize products in real-time within their homes and deliver personalized recommendations. The combination of AI-powered personalization and AR-enhanced immersion provides customers with enhanced control and confidence resulting in stronger emotional bonds to their buying choices. The chapter examines recent research along with case studies to show how IKEA uses technology to boost customer interaction while decreasing product return rates through sustainable retail methods. The chapter examines the crucial impact of trust, perceived risk, and co-creation elements on AR-based personalization adoption. The chapter delivers a future-focused analysis of how AI and AR utilize IKEA's implementation to create interactive and intelligent retail spaces that centre around the user.

DOI: 10.4018/979-8-3373-6582-4.ch003

BACKGROUND

Artificial Intelligence (AI) together with Augmented Reality (AR) creates a new retail environment that strongly benefits home furnishing and lifestyle companies according to Pakharuddin & Kamarudin (2023). IKEA spearheads this transformation through the use of advanced technologies which connect digital tools to in-store experiences for improved customer journeys (Garg et al., 2024). IKEA uses AR and AI to meet modern consumer needs for interactive shopping and personalized experiences to minimize purchase uncertainty while enhancing customer satisfaction. Customers traditionally faced difficulties visualizing product fit during furniture shopping which resulted in bad choices and frequent returns (Pakharuddin & Kamarudin, 2023). The IKEA Place AR application lets users project 3D furniture models into their homes through mobile devices which helps reinforce purchase decisions and lower return rates (Garg et al., 2024). According to Do et al. (2025), AR technology enhances product fit evaluation while fortifying brand relationships. IKEA's AI systems work in conjunction with AR technology to generate personalized recommendations by analysing room dimensions together with customer preferences and current trends over time (Rudro et al., 2024). Real-time responses generate a cohesive phygital experience by unifying digital interactions with tangible results (Do et al., 2025). The pandemic drove the rapid uptake of immersive tools which transformed user interaction from passive browsing into active engagement (Pakharuddin & Kamarudin, 2023; Gajjar, 2024). AI's role extends beyond product suggestions. Through analysis of user behaviour patterns and spatial information alongside emotional signals artificial intelligence proposes lifestyle-aligned products including space-efficient furniture and coordinated lighting solutions (Do et al., 2025; Rudro et al., 2024). Retail strategies now focus on lifestyle integration instead of selling individual products separately. Operationally, these technologies offer significant benefits. AR technology minimizes expensive returns and AI uses real-time consumer data to enhance demand forecasting while optimizing inventory management (Garg et al., 2024; Pakharuddin & Kamarudin, 2023). Through virtual product testing with AR technology IKEA minimizes waste and advances its environmental objectives (Rudro et al., 2024). The fusion of AR and AI technology leads to emerging ethical issues. Experts emphasize the need to resolve challenges related to data privacy alongside algorithmic fairness and accessibility (Gajjar, 2024; Raghavendra & Mg, 2024). AI systems need to incorporate multiple aesthetic and socioeconomic aspects to prevent personalization biases. Maintaining consumer trust requires complete transparency about how data is used. Through its implementation of AR and AI technologies IKEA demonstrates how intelligent systems can deliver improved customer experiences while increasing efficiency and supporting sustainable advancements (Gajjar, 2024; Pakharuddin & Kamarudin, 2023).

Focus of the Chapter

IKEA has strategically aligned its operations at the convergence of artificial intelligence (AI) and augmented reality (AR) to enhance retail customer experiences through interactive and intuitive shopping capabilities according to Garg et al. (2024). The chapter analyses IKEA's approach to merging artificial intelligence and augmented reality technologies which function together as systems that boost customer interaction and product visualization while improving decision-making capabilities across both physical stores and digital platforms (Do et al., 2025). Historically, furniture shopping involved difficulties with visualizing space arrangements and finding compatible products which led to dissatisfaction from returns (Pakharuddin & Kamarudin, 2023). The IKEA Place AR app developed by IKEA enables customers to experience furniture visualization in real-life environments at full scale (Garg et al., 2024). This tool delivers a hyper-personalized and context-aware shopping experience by leveraging AI-powered recommendation engines which adapt to individual user preferences as well as room layout and behavioural data (Gajjar, 2024). IKEA's advanced digital ecosystem illustrates the wider industry trend towards phygital retailing which integrates physical and digital customer interaction points (Do et al., 2025). The chapter analyses how IKEA's AI and AR platforms enable customer trust building and risk reduction in purchases while allowing users to actively participate in designing their ideal living spaces (Pakharuddin & Kamarudin, 2023). These capabilities deliver better operational results including reduced return rates and elevated conversion rates while simultaneously enhancing the emotional and experiential value of the shopping experience (Rudro et al., 2024). This chapter focuses on analysing IKEA's AR and AI personalization approaches through strategic, technical, and experiential perspectives. The chapter uses contemporary research and industry case studies to present a critical evaluation of how consumer engagement is being transformed by intelligent and immersive technologies and discusses the implications for retail's future (Gajjar, 2024).

Current Applications

AR-Enhanced Product Visualization

The creation and launch of the IKEA Place mobile application forms a fundamental part of IKEA's strategy for digital transformation. The application uses sophisticated Augmented Reality (AR) tools to allow users to place accurate 3D representations of furniture items in their actual surroundings through their mobile device cameras (Garg et al., 2024). This feature addresses a critical challenge in online furniture shopping: The imagination gap refers to customers' difficulty in visualizing how products will appear or fit in their surroundings when they cannot view them directly (Ozturkcan, 2020). IKEA Place has advanced customer assurance, participation levels and purchasing motivation by successfully connecting the visualization gap between shoppers and products (Iranmanesh et al., 2024). AR technology gives users dynamic control over furniture placement which enables them to rotate, reposition and scale items to confirm proper spatial fit and aesthetic compatibility unlike static product images or size descriptions (Ebrahimabad et al., 2024). Through interactive experiences users make smarter purchasing choices while reducing the mental effort needed to visualize product dimensions and style alignment (Kowalczuk et al., 2020). The immersive engagement with products through this technology leads to reduced buyer's remorse while significantly diminishing return rates which together enhance customer satisfaction and operational efficiency (Gong & Park, 2023). AR visualization enables users to test interior design ideas without needing to expend physical effort or incur financial risks related to trial-and-error shopping (Sahli & Lichy, 2024). IKEA Place enables customers to examine product combinations live while assisting them in designing personalized spaces which match their personal aesthetic preferences and spatial needs (Alimamy & Gnoth, 2022). The ability for customers to take control of their design choices enhances their ability to co-create products leading to deeper emotional connections and stronger brand loyalty according to Riar et al. (2022). Technological advancements such as LiDAR sensors and AI-driven spatial recognition methods have led to continuous improvements in AR model precision and realism which enables better detection of surfaces and improved lighting adjustments and object occlusion capabilities (Do et al., 2025). The platform's sense of realism and trust gets boosted because these innovations allow virtual placements to appear more natural and believable (Pabari et al., 2024). AR-enhanced product visualization functions as a core element that empowers customers and solidifies their shopping decisions while promoting sustainability within IKEA's omnichannel retail approach according to Jain et al. (2024).

AI-Powered Personalization

The combination of AI and AR technologies by IKEA creates an intelligent shopping experience which guides customers throughout their browsing journey (Gajjar, 2024). AI uses user data analysis including clickstream patterns and product interactions as well as spatial preferences and room conditions to generate proactive personalized recommendations (Rudro et al., 2024; Babatunde et al., 2024). Customers who browse compact storage solutions are presented with modular furniture designed for small spaces which cuts decision friction while increasing user satisfaction (Taneja & Tripathi, 2020). IKEA's AI platform provides layout design guidance by integrating IKEA Place's AR capabilities with real-time spatial analytics to improve both practicality and visual appeal. Personalization matches various life stages such as moving or downsizing and enhances emotional bonding according to Asthana et al. (2024). Transparency is maintained through "Why this recommendation?" The platform achieves enhanced trust and clarity through its features and user customization options (Dezao, 2024). IKEA's digital commerce system relies on personalized AI to boost both operational efficiency and customer emotional connection.

Phygital In-Store Integration

IKEA's phygital retail approach integrates the ease of digital shopping with the tangible experience of physical stores. IKEA integrates its digital and physical customer experiences by using AR features in showrooms alongside mobile tools such as QR scanning and IKEA Place (Jain et al., 2024). In-store validation and real-space product previews help customers make better choices which results in fewer returns and higher satisfaction levels. Through AI technology showroom activity monitoring happens while real-time personalized suggestions reach users (Gajjar, 2024). App-based navigation systems combined with digital maps facilitate intuitive product discovery and item location for customers according to Do et al. (2025). The ability for customers to store AR previews at home for later in-store review and channel-spanning purchases delivers both consistency and convenience (Çakırkaya & Koçyiğit, 2024). Next-generation retail is embodied by IKEA's phygital model which combines physical touchpoints with digital intelligence to develop a connected and personalized shopping ecosystem.

Emotionally Engaging Shopping Journeys

Through AI and AR integration, IKEA offers retail experiences that connect with customers on an emotional level beyond basic functionality. Within the competitive retail marketplace emotional connections establish brand loyalty and encourage repeat consumer engagement (Gokarna, 2021). The IKEA Place app enables users to visualize furniture items within their personal space which encourages delight and individual creativity and expression according to Cachero-Martínez & Vazquez-Casielles (2021). Through immersive interaction consumers create a deeper connection with products. AI improves emotional engagement through context-sensitive recommendations that match significant life moments such as home relocation or family expansion (Do et al., 2025). Using real-time visuals lowers decision stress for customers while increasing their confidence to buy. The experiences establish higher consumer satisfaction levels along with improved retention rates and greater customer lifetime value according to Tyrväinen et al., 2020.

Sustainability Through Reduced Returns

The deployment of AI and AR by IKEA leads to reduced product return rates which further advances their environmental objectives. Furniture retail returns produce both environmental harm and substantial logistic expenses (Beziat & François, 2024). The IKEA Place application allows customers to compare accurate 3D renderings of products in their own homes which reduces purchase errors related to size and style mismatches (Gajjar, 2024). AI-based recommendations that consider living space and lifestyle needs enable customers to make improved choices while minimizing dissatisfaction (Donthi et al., 2024). Reduced product returns help IKEA save on shipping and packaging expenses while decreasing its carbon footprint and operating costs. IKEA's strategies support their wide-ranging ESG goals while establishing the brand as a leader in sustainable retail innovation (Gustafsson et al., 2005).

Technology-Driven Responsible Innovation

Through its AI and AR technologies IKEA promotes responsible retail innovation by helping users make environmentally aware choices with confidence and knowledge. The technology-based model provides simultaneous support for personalized experiences alongside sustainable practices and emotional customer engagement. This approach transforms shopping into an expressive journey full of meaning instead of mere transactional consumption. IKEA creates scalable innovations that serve customers and protect the environment by integrating technology with ethical practices and user requirements.

Key Findings

The evaluation of IKEA's augmented reality (AR) and artificial intelligence (AI) integration requires a detailed assessment of the concrete results produced by these technologies. This section evaluates the success of AR and AI technologies at IKEA by integrating recent academic research findings to understand their impact on customer interaction enhancement, decision-making improvement, and sustainability promotion in the retail sector. The research findings below reveal how enhanced retail performance and customer satisfaction along with strategic differentiation result from immersive visualization techniques and intelligent personalization methods.

AR and AI Greatly Boost Customer Confidence and Purchase Intent

The deployment of augmented reality (AR) and artificial intelligence (AI) results in enhanced customer confidence while boosting their intent to purchase. The implementation of augmented reality (AR) and artificial intelligence (AI) at IKEA has resulted in a substantial measurable impact on customer confidence and their intent to purchase. The technologies tackle essential online furniture shopping psychological barriers which include product fit uncertainty and concerns about style and spatial compatibility. IKEA helps customers achieve mental consistency and better decision-making by allowing them to visualize products in their homes while receiving customized suggestions based on their behaviour and context (Ebrahimabad et al., 2024). The IKEA Place app offers users the ability to position realistic 3D furniture models at accurate sizes within their real surroundings through mobile devices. Customers receive real-time feedback on products by examining their size and appearance and assessing their functional suitability before buying. Research indicates that immersive visualization technologies boost perceived product accuracy which helps lower anxiety levels while improving conversion rates (Garg et al., 2024). The visual interactivity of products is strengthened by AI-driven personalization which provides product recommendations through analysis of user history, demographic data and optimization of living spaces. AI combined with AR technology delivers product recommendations that are situationally aware while remaining relevant to user needs. The AI system predicts space limitations when a user experiments with compact desks and small storage solutions and suggests modular furniture which gets displayed in the user's room through AR visualization. This context-sensitive personalization approach leads to a smooth shopping experience that guides consumers toward completing their purchases (Sipos, 2025). The removal of guesswork serves as an important driver for boosting purchase intent. The traditional online shopping experience depends on 2D product images and measurements which forces consumers to visualize how products fit into their spaces through mentally challenging and error-prone processes. AR visualization lessens cognitive load while offering immediate clarity which leads to more confident purchasing decisions. Businesses benefit from increased conversion rates and user satisfaction while establishing enduring brand loyalty through these enhancements (Ebrahimabad et al., 2024). The system maintains customer confidence by consistently providing suggestions that are both accurate and visually compatible. The fusion of AI technology with IKEA's AR applications generates recommendations tailored to functional needs alongside style preferences, colour schemes, and current home decor trends. The personalized platform creates trust and emotional connections by making consumers feel that it understands their needs (Do et al., 2025). The combined use of AR technology and AI within IKEA's digital strategy actively boosts consumer trust and their willingness to make purchases. Home furnishings require high consideration because these technologies mitigate uncertainty while providing personalized experiences and immersive reassurance.

Immersive Tech Boosts Emotional Engagement and Brand Loyalty

Augmented reality (AR) and artificial intelligence (AI) deliver quantifiable functional advantages in retail through better product alignment and customized suggestions, but their strongest future value probably exists in their capacity to create emotional connections and solidify brand loyalty. The growing emphasis on experiential marketing makes emotional resonance essential for establishing consumer attachment that leads to lasting commercial achievement. IKEA's use of immersive technologies exemplifies how digital tools can evolve from functional tools to facilitate emotional bonds and inspire creativity and trust (Enyejo et al., 2024). Emotional engagement describes the psychological and affective reactions that consumers demonstrate while interacting with a brand. IKEA’s AR platform enables users to digitally decorate their homes while testing various design options and creating customized spaces. The procedure generates excitement and empowerment while enabling self-expression through users' real-time transformation of their living spaces. The emotions generated through these interactions play a crucial role in developing favourable perceptions of products and brands (Do et al., 2025). The AI personalization system at IKEA strengthens emotional connections through recommendations that match users' life transitions and design objectives. When a user examines nursery furniture products, they receive a tailored list that includes baby room essentials and matching décor items. The system demonstrates empathetic relevance by understanding and supporting users' changing needs which creates a deeper connection with the brand leading to greater emotional loyalty (Garg et al., 2024). Studies reveal that immersive technologies boost platform time spent and user satisfaction which serve as essential elements for maintaining customer retention and repeated use. AR establishes an interactive playground where users can explore their surroundings while dreaming up and designing new possibilities. The experiential immersion approach ensures shoppers experience both functional effectiveness and emotional resonance which transforms their purchasing process from a mundane task into an enjoyable experience (Enyejo et al., 2024). The strength of customer loyalty increases when seamless omnichannel integration builds upon emotional engagement. IKEA shows respect for customer continuity and autonomy through its integration of online and in-store experiences which lets users save designs at home to view them again in-store. Through omnichannel coherence customers experience greater trust and decreased friction which delivers a brand experience that feels both personal and dependable (Yan, 2023). The application of AR and AI technologies in IKEA's retail system extends beyond mere technical improvements to function as instruments for emotional design. These technologies create loyal brand advocates through the promotion of creativity and empathy while providing customers with a sense of personal agency that redefines brand connection in the digital world.

Personalization Builds Trust, but Risk Limits It

IKEA's digital retail strategy showcases its innovative feature of using AI-driven personalization to enhance co-creation by enabling customer participation in designing their shopping experience and product configurations. The success of personalization initiatives relies heavily on how much customers trust these systems and how they perceive potential risks involved. Personalization may come across as intrusive instead of empowering which lessens its ability to generate meaningful engagement or conversion if customer trust and risk perception are not present (Alimamy & Gnoth, 2022). Through its analysis of user behaviour alongside preferences and spatial context IKEA's AI personalization system delivers personalized product suggestions and layout designs. This process leads to perceived personalization which researchers define as the customer's acknowledgement that the system adapts to their individual requirements and preferences. AR visualization makes perceived personalization more concrete in retail settings by allowing users to observe their rooms transforming live and deepening their engagement with the space (Alimamy & Gnoth, 2022). Through these experiences consumers transform into active partners who help shape their personal spaces rather than just receiving prescribed suggestions. The participatory dynamic found in these settings results in enhanced satisfaction levels alongside deeper emotional investment and increased loyalty. However, co-creation is not universally effective. For the technology to succeed, users must trust it and see low risk regarding data privacy and algorithmic transparency (Alimamy et al., 2021). Customers tend to resist personalization services when AI systems remain opaque and manipulative since they cannot explain their recommendations. AR environments heighten this risk because digital overlays erase the distinction between suggestion and influence. Research shows that user engagement with personalized systems increases when users comprehend the personalization process and maintain their sense of autonomy (Canhoto et al., 2023). Trust-building in this area needs careful system design which incorporates features like explainable AI (XAI), transparent data practices and user controls that enable preference changes or opt-outs. Effective communication of these elements by IKEA is essential to sustain consumer trust and fully realize the benefits of its personalized tools according to Gupta (2025). The reception to personalization varies based on cultural and individual characteristics. The acceptability of personalization features varies between users because of their different technological experiences, cultural views of data privacy and their expectations for brand communication. The future implementation of personalization tools should embrace adaptive methods which respond to behavioural signals while also considering emotional and ethical aspects throughout the shopping journey (Soni, 2024). At IKEA personalization supports trust and collaborative creation when users can see through the process and control their data in a respectful manner. The conditions mentioned are fundamental to advancing AI from just a background tool to a means that enables deeper customer collaboration while securing lasting loyalty.

Reduced Returns Promote Sustainability and Cost Efficiency

The integration of augmented reality (AR) and artificial intelligence (AI) at IKEA has resulted in a substantial decrease in the number of returned products. The enhancement delivers more than financial and logistical advantages because it deeply affects sustainability outcomes and supply chain operations while also boosting customer satisfaction. By enabling better decision-making prior to purchase, IKEA's digital tools mitigate one of retail's most persistent problems: post-purchase dissonance and product mismatch (Gajjar, 2024). The furniture industry faces significant challenges with product returns because its items have large dimensions and high shipping costs while they also often sustain damage during transportation. Return processes generate emissions and create packaging waste while also adding to inventory inefficiencies. The IKEA Place app lets customers position and adjusts furniture sizes within their actual spaces through augmented reality technology to generate accurate previews of furniture dimensions and style matching. The feature minimizes speculation about purchases while boosting customer confidence which results in reduced mismatched purchases and fewer regrets (Zhang et al., 2023). The AI technology enhances this process by providing recommendations that consider room size and current furniture while considering customer style choices and previous purchase patterns. The algorithms curate options that satisfy both practical and emotional consumer needs which reduces product returns caused by customer dissatisfaction (Pakharuddin & Kamarudin, 2023). The impact of fewer returns is substantial. The implementation of this system allows IKEA to save money by decreasing transportation expenses and reducing both restocking and refurbishing costs and customer service overhead. The brand achieves its environmental sustainability by lowering carbon emissions and packaging waste through compliance with comprehensive ESG standards (Beziat & François, 2024). The reduction of returns by IKEA boosts customer trust and strengthens brand loyalty. Users connect brands with competence and reliability when systems enable them to make better decisions based on accurate information. Reduced returns at IKEA build stronger emotional connections with consumers who value environmental responsibility because these consumers view this practice as part of a responsible shopping approach which results in greater repurchase intent (Donthi et al., 2024). In summary, IKEA's integration of AR and AI technologies delivers a dual benefit: IKEA's implementation of AR and AI technologies improves customer decision-making and lessens environmental and operational waste at the same time. IKEA serves as a standard for how digital advancements can boost sustainable business practices while operating as more than just a technologically advanced retailer.

Omnichannel Integration Drives Future Retail Innovation

To advance retail innovation successfully in the future businesses must implement omnichannel integration. Retail success now depends on omnichannel integration due to consumers who move between digital and physical spaces with ease. Through its omnichannel ecosystem IKEA demonstrates how artificial intelligence (AI) and augmented reality (AR) technologies merge different customer interaction points into a cohesive experience that delivers seamless engagement and consistency throughout the customer journey (Calvo et al., 2023). IKEA merges digital and physical shopping into one unified system which enhances convenience and personalization while maximizing customer satisfaction. Omnichannel retail involves the strategic coordination of multiple customer interaction platforms including websites, mobile apps, social media, and physical stores to provide users with a consistent and continuous experience across all brand touchpoints. IKEA has applied this approach by developing features like the IKEA Place app that allows customers to design and visualize rooms remotely before taking their customized plans to physical stores for further recommendations and layout access (Yan, 2024). The seamless progression throughout the customer experience generates feelings of personal control and independence. The application of AI technology enables IKEA to track and understand customer behaviour through multiple platforms which allows them to provide relevant content and recommendations to customers across all channels. When customers explore compact kitchen layouts through digital platforms, they receive intelligent spatial prompts and navigational support directing them to modular solutions during their physical store visits (Arora, 2024). Cross-channel personalization boosts user interaction and content relevance while ensuring digital exploration leads to tangible purchase decisions. Omnichannel experiences provide value through their functional efficiency and their ability to improve brand perception and customer loyalty. A brand that delivers seamless platform transitions earns higher customer trust ratings and is viewed as both user-friendly and advanced technologically according to Wang (2024). The development of positive brand perception becomes essential for building lasting customer relationships particularly in sectors like home furnishings where customers purchase expensive products that carry significant emotional meaning on rare occasions. Omnichannel strategies support data enrichment and create feedback loops that allow insights from one touchpoint to drive enhancements at different touchpoints. IKEA utilizes aggregate behavioural data collected from both online platforms and physical stores to improve their product range and optimize inventory control as well as showroom designs (Dutta, 2024). The embedding of AR and AI technologies across multiple channels will lead to expanding opportunities for real-time personalization and operational agility. IKEA's achievements show that retail success depends heavily on combining immersive technology with omnichannel strategies. IKEA demonstrates how digital transformation can create innovative customer loyalty and commercial strength through harmonized customer experiences at all points of contact

Figure 1. This diagram depicts IKEA's strategic framework for responsible AR and AI implementations with a central focus on Customer Experience. Surrounding it are four interdependent dimensions: The four foundational elements of IKEA's responsible AR and AI strategy include Immersive Engagement along with Intelligent Personalization and Data Trust Architecture and Ethical Governance.

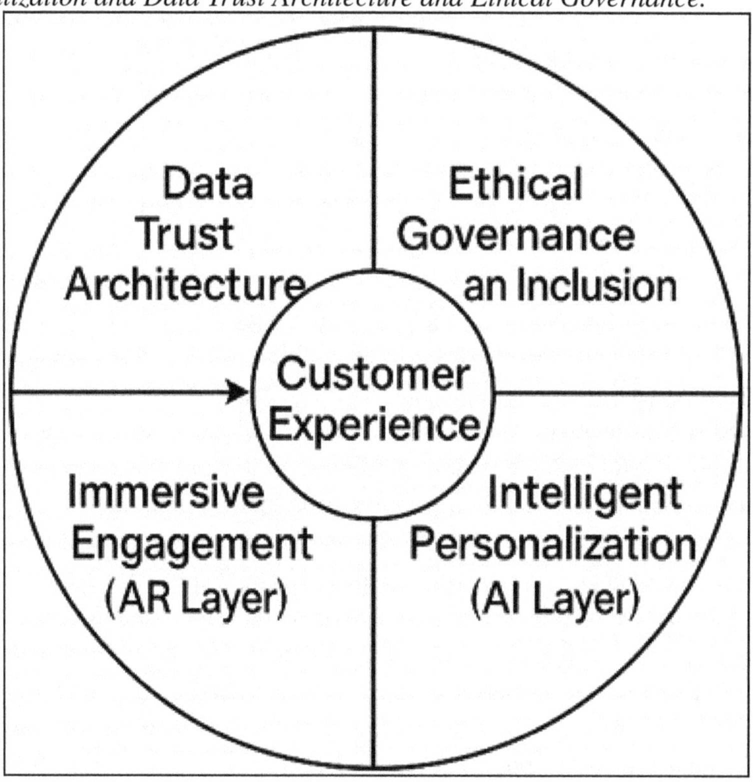

Figure 1 maps out how IKEA strategically combines augmented reality and artificial intelligence technologies to improve the customer experience. At its core is the "Customer Experience," surrounded by four interdependent dimensions: The four interdependent dimensions of IKEA's Customer Experience framework include Immersive Engagement through AR Layer technology, Intelligent Personalization with AI Layer systems, Data Trust Architecture principles, along with Ethical Governance and Inclusion standards. IKEA uses augmented reality to enable customers to visualize furniture inside their homes through immersive simulations that strengthen engagement and increase purchase assurance. AI generates customized recommendations that fit individual user preferences and available living spaces. Through transparent and secure management of customer data the Data Trust Architecture builds customer trust. IKEA emphasizes fairness and accessibility through Ethical Governance and Inclusion which makes sure their technology advancements meet user values and regulatory requirements. Together these aspects combine to deliver a retail experience which is seamless, tailored to individual needs and operates within ethical standards.

SOLUTIONS AND RECOMMENDATIONS

IKEA has achieved success through AR and AI implementation which boosted personalization and customer interaction while supporting sustainable operations but maintaining this success requires meeting new challenges that continue to develop. The digital retail landscape becomes more complicated requiring careful management of algorithmic transparency data privacy inclusive design and cross-channel continuity for ensuring technological innovation remains ethical and focused on users. This section provides a range of practical evidence-based solutions to improve IKEA's existing AR and AI strategy. The recommendations derived from recent academic studies and industry standards aim to strengthen customer trust while optimizing system scalability and advancing sustainability objectives through responsible governance embedded in all technology lifecycle stages. The proposed solutions aim to solve existing issues while preparing IKEA's immersive retail ecosystem to thrive in a fast-evolving technological landscape. If IKEA implements these strategies, it will build its position as a leader in intelligent retail and establish how immersive technologies can be used transparently and inclusively to meet consumer and societal needs over the long term.

Implement Explainable AI (XAI) Interfaces

To maintain consumer trust and meet regulatory standards, IKEA must ensure algorithmic transparency as it uses AI technology to produce immersive retail experiences that are tailored to individual preferences (Dai & Liu, 2024; Raghavendra & Mg, 2024). The complexity of AI models such as spatial recommendation engines and real-time personalization systems creates barriers for users to understand their functionality leading to either confusion or mistrust according to Chen (2022). Deploying Explainable AI (XAI) frameworks enables customers to understand the logic driving their personalized product suggestions and layout recommendations according to Hooper & Lunn (2024) and Raghavendra & Mg (2024). Simple prompts like "Recommended because you viewed similar items" enhance customer engagement and perceived system transparency (Kaushal & Mishra, 2024). The importance of explainability increases in augmented reality environments where AI advice reaches personal spaces like entire room designs to prevent users from feeling intruded upon (Sjöberg, 2021). The ethical design of AI requires transparency features that can adapt to different cultures and languages to serve customers worldwide (Kaushal & Mishra, 2024). According to research by Raghavendra & Mg (2024), customers who understand AI systems tend to modify their preferences more frequently and engage actively in shaping their shopping experiences which results in enhanced customer loyalty over time. Legal requirements such as the EU AI Act and GDPR enforce transparency through the "right to explanation" rule which obligates businesses to reveal their algorithmic decision processes (Sjöberg, 2021). The integration of customizable "Why this?" prompts and transparency layers into IKEA's user interface enables the company to fulfil ethical obligations and regulatory requirements while maintaining user simplicity (Hooper & Lunn, 2024). Through strategic XAI application organizations achieve better user satisfaction and build sustained brand value by conducting responsible innovation together with scalable personalization (Dai & Liu, 2024; Raghavendra & Mg, 2024).

Enhance Cross-Platform and Omnichannel Integration

IKEA's digital strategy excels by merging online and physical store experiences through augmented reality (AR) and artificial intelligence (AI) technology. To stay competitive and match consumer needs IKEA needs to enhance its cross-platform continuity and omnichannel integration efforts. Cross-platform integration will enable customers to move seamlessly among mobile devices, desktop computers and physical stores while maintaining uninterrupted access to their preferences and personalized recommendations. Today's customers move through multiple stages of their purchasing process by utilizing various platforms and devices which allow them to discover products, evaluate them and finally make their purchases in a non-linear fashion. A shopper might start by looking at furniture choices on the IKEA website before using the IKEA Place app to see how the product fits in their home and finishing by buying it at the store. IKEA needs to build unified data systems with interfaces that allow data synchronization across all touchpoints for seamless support of customer journeys. Secure user authentication should allow customers to access saved layouts, AR previews, wish lists, and AI-generated suggestions from any platform or device (Yan, 2024). AR and AI features need to adapt their functionality, so they provide consistent user service across different environments. A layout created with IKEA Place can be viewed and edited at physical stores using smart kiosks or tablets and user accounts that connect through QR codes. AI-generated product bundles need to adapt to their context by changing their presentation according to the channel they are displayed on such as focusing on tactile data like fabric quality within a store while highlighting visual-spatial attributes in mobile AR applications. Adaptive personalization maintains relevance while sustaining the continuous user experience according to Rudro et al. (2024). Achieving this objective from a systems viewpoint demands investment in databases that enable interoperability along with real-time data synchronization capabilities. AI models need to learn user recognition and behaviour patterns across different sessions and channels without repeating data or dividing information. IKEA needs to maintain uniform UX design and intuitive navigation across customer-facing tools to ensure seamless transitions between digital and physical environments. Omnichannel strategies drive improved user engagement and conversion rates while building stronger brand loyalty through strategic experiences. According to Do et al. (2025), customers who interact with brands through multiple channels tend to spend more money and visit more frequently while developing stronger emotional connections to brands that maintain consistent and attentive interactions across different touchpoints. IKEA plans to introduce persistent customer profiles to allow users to choose personalized experiences which they can access across different locations and platforms. This strategy creates convenience and preserves user autonomy through well-defined privacy protections and transparent operations. Expanding both cross-platform continuity and omnichannel functionality stands as a crucial step towards maximizing the benefits of IKEA's AR and AI technologies. The establishment of a harmonized retail ecosystem without friction will boost customer satisfaction while simultaneously establishing IKEA as a leader in integrated retail solutions that embrace future needs.

Strengthen Data Governance and Consent Mechanisms

The implementation of AI and AR technologies by IKEA emphasizes the critical need for strong data governance and clear consent processes. Modern personalization and visualization tools need to process user data ranging from browsing behaviours to inferred preferences which makes proper data management essential both for regulatory compliance and sustaining consumer trust through ethical innovation. The IKEA Place app facilitates immersive shopping environments that collect comprehensive data including spatial intelligence metrics like room layouts and lighting conditions as well as device movements and biometric user interactions beyond typical clickstream analytics. The data collected from advanced analytics improves recommendation systems and enhances user interaction but simultaneously sparks worries about excessive data collection practices and unclear consent issues alongside the growing possibility of intrusive surveillance as AI systems advance in context interpretation and predictive capabilities (Ejjami & Rahim, 2024). IKEA needs to integrate privacy-by-design principles throughout its digital infrastructure to mitigate these risks. This approach involves developing AR and AI platforms with automatic privacy protections which encompass data minimization by collecting only necessary information as well as purpose limitation to use data only for designated functions while giving users control to access and manage their personal information. Companies need to use interactive privacy dashboards to present features directly within the user interface instead of hiding them inside long policy documents. App settings must provide users with straightforward controls to modify AR data permissions and personalization intensity levels. The development of multi-tiered informed consent mechanisms holds equal importance. Consent prompts need to surpass basic opt-in forms and deliver straightforward explanations about data collection in localized language detailing how data will be processed and its usage purposes. IKEA's global operations require that consent prompts align with region-specific regulations including the EU's GDPR and the CCPA alongside evolving AI transparency laws in Canada and the UK. Ensuring proper localization becomes essential for achieving both legal compliance and cultural resonance as observed by Raghavendra & Mg (2024). A fundamental aspect of data governance incorporates both data anonymization and data encryption measures. The AR system's ability to record sensitive customer home visual data requires IKEA to establish real-time encryption methods while ensuring spatial data gets processed either locally through edge computing or stored on GDPR-compliant servers. Sensitive data that has outlived its purpose must be immediately erased or compiled into aggregated forms to stop the possibility of re-identification. These procedures reduce the risk of privacy violations and protect the brand's reputation by properly maintaining user trust. IKEA should form an internal AI and Data Ethics Board which serves as an interdisciplinary governance entity responsible for data practice audits and ensuring algorithmic fairness alongside model behaviour reviews. The board must consist of members from legal, design, engineering, and customer advocacy departments who meet on a regular schedule to evaluate the ethical effects of new features. The board would be responsible for publishing transparency reports that cover IKEA's data management practices along with updates to company policies and ethical achievements. Customer education regarding data ethics stands as an underutilized yet influential approach. Integrating brief educational modules into IKEA's app about topics like data impact on user experience and GDPR rights would boost users' digital knowledge and help them make better choices. By following this approach IKEA builds consumer trust while aligning its retail innovations with international trends towards ethical digital systems that respect user input. The success of IKEA's responsible innovation will depend on how well their data governance and consent frameworks support embedded AI and AR systems in customer experiences. IKEA will become a leading global retailer that focuses on customer privacy and protection through its commitment to transparency and accountability while reducing potential risks.

FUTURE RESEARCH DIRECTIONS

The continued expansion of AI and AR by IKEA across its digital and physical retail spaces generates important research opportunities for the future. These areas underline the necessity of tackling technological advancements alongside ethical standards and regulatory requirements to preserve the openness and inclusivity of intelligent retail systems while maximizing benefits for all involved parties. AI and AR advancements provide new opportunities while raising important questions about user independence and algorithmic equity alongside concerns about data protection and psychological effects over time. The advancement of personalized AR interfaces toward more lifelike and predictive capabilities demands immediate empirical research which evaluates system performance as well as social effects on trust building, decision fatigue, and identity formation. The global customer base of IKEA calls for research that examines cultural diversity as well as regulatory differences and variations in digital literacy. These findings play a crucial role in creating AI and AR systems that operate fairly among different regions and populations. Future research that combines interdisciplinary investigation will enable IKEA's technological ecosystem to progress in a manner that supports business innovation and socioethical accountability thereby establishing benchmarks for the entire retail industry.

Explainability in Complex AI Systems

With AI systems becoming more common in consumer technology users now require systems that can explain their decision-making processes. Within complex environments such as IKEA's augmented reality retail systems AI models extend their role beyond product recommendations to shaping decisions about store layout and design choices as well as customer purchase patterns. AI systems that depend on deep learning structures and reinforcement learning methods function well but remain largely invisible to end users. AI's opaque "black box" nature presents major transparency, trustworthiness, and accountability difficulties (Raghavendra & Mg, 2024). Immersive retail settings require explainable AI because user interactions in these environments happen at a highly personal level. The personalized nature of living space arrangement suggestions alongside lifestyle-compatible furniture choices makes outputs intimately personal to customers. Customers may view opaque recommendation-driving logic as arbitrary or manipulative because they might interpret unclear AI reasoning as biased. Research demonstrates that user perceptions of AI system fairness increase when system behaviour explanations remain clear and easy to understand (Gajjar, 2024). Future investigations need to concentrate on creating multi-level explainability frameworks which support various user groups and different interaction situations. Casual shoppers might find short text explanations adequate such as "Suggested because it complements your recent room scan." Professional decorators and design enthusiasts who are highly engaged require extensive explanations of the model's logic through data attributes and spatial reasoning alongside historical behaviour patterns. Creating explainability interfaces that scale with user needs will require teamwork across artificial intelligence experts and professionals in user experience design along with cognitive psychologists and data ethicists (Do et al., 2025). Future research must investigate modular explainability strategies that can adapt to various platforms. Explanations provided during mobile AR sessions need to match touchscreen navigation requirements while web platforms benefit from expandable sections titled "Why this?". AR-specific applications require innovative methods of explanation such as spatial annotations, visual overlays or audio cues which convey system reasoning in real time while maintaining user immersion (Yan, 2024). Future research opportunities show great potential in fusing causal reasoning with neuro-symbolic AI to build advanced personalization systems. The combination of deep learning's statistical capabilities and symbolic logic's structural clarity allows AI systems to determine relationships and articulate their underlying causal rules. IKEA's recommendation systems could provide explanations mimicking human logic using statements like "This item was chosen because it fits your room dimensions and matches the wood tone of your existing furniture" as suggested by Raghavendra & Mg (2024). Upcoming research should investigate how demographic characteristics as well as cultural and cognitive variations alter preferences for explanations. Expectations about privacy, system transparency, and automation acceptance vary among users from different regions. The effectiveness and inclusivity of explainability increases when XAI interfaces are designed to suit diverse user differences. Explainable AI represents a fundamental prerequisite for developing ethical innovations that are centred around user needs. The widespread adoption of AI in consumer spaces requires transparent decision-making abilities to retain customer confidence and adhere to regulations while supporting the continued success of retail platforms such as IKEA.

Ethical Personalization at Scale

Modern retail platforms now rely on AI-driven personalization as a core element which makes ethical personalization at scale an urgent priority. Personalization systems provide improved user convenience and engagement but risk increasing algorithmic bias while reducing consumer autonomy and perpetuating social and cultural stereotypes if proper governance measures are not implemented. Research going forward needs to establish scalable ethical systems that safeguard fairness and inclusivity for all user demographics. Development strategies for personalization algorithms must focus on dynamically adapting to underrepresented groups through historical training data adjustments and consideration of cultural, linguistic, and socioeconomic differences. The research conducted by Jain and Jain (2024) underscores the necessity of continuous bias audits in personalization systems and the implementation of fairness-aware machine learning approaches to rectify disparities in content exposure and recommendation frequency (Jain & Jain, 2024). The use of AI personalization to guide user behaviour generates mounting ethical questions regarding its manipulative effects. Retailers frequently apply behavioural nudging strategies like urgency triggers and suggestive positioning during marketing to influence consumer purchases which undermines consumer control. Future research needs to examine methods to achieve a balance between personalization techniques and user autonomy to make sure users maintain their decision-making control. The implementation of clear explanation tools and optional settings to disable personalization requires experimental validation through consumer studies to address ethical issues (Gupta, 2025). Future studies should explore methods for embedding virtue ethics principles like empathy and fairness into the design objectives of AI systems. Fairness should be an integral component throughout each phase of the AI lifecycle from data gathering to post-deployment evaluation. The measurement of personalization outcomes based on age, gender, location, and other protected attributes can be achieved through fairness-by-design toolkits and impact assessment scorecards. It is essential to study how consumers perceive fairness and inclusivity within personalization systems aside from technical aspects. As Ebele Agu et al. According to research by Ebele Agu and her team (2024) fairness cannot be established solely through mathematical measurements but requires insights from public values together with user experiences and input from stakeholders. Transparency measures influence trust development over time as identified by longitudinal cross-cultural research which reveals distinct ethical personalization perceptions across user groups (Agu et al., 2024). In sum, ensuring ethical personalization at scale requires a multi-layered research agenda: We need a research agenda that merges fairness-aware machine learning with human-centred design principles while ensuring legal compliance and integrating culturally responsive user feedback. Integrating ethical standards into AI system design enables organizations such as IKEA to deliver personalized experiences while maintaining core principles of fairness and inclusion along with user autonomy.

Cross-Disciplinary Collaboration

Retail platforms such as IKEA that incorporate AI and AR technologies require cross-disciplinary teams to develop ethical and user-friendly systems. Immersive intelligent systems effectively integrate knowledge from computer science, design principles, marketing strategies, cognitive psychology theories, ethical considerations, sociological insights and legal frameworks. Research in the future must embrace the fact that no single academic discipline has the capability to resolve all the technical, human, and societal challenges presented by personalized AI within AR-enhanced retail environments. Building AI models that achieve accuracy, scalability while maintaining transparency and fairness demonstrates the necessity for cross-functional teamwork. AI engineers who create advanced recommendation algorithms risk missing crucial effects on user autonomy and bias reinforcement if they do not consult ethicists or behavioural psychologists (Gupta, 2025). The input from UX designers and cognitive scientists plays a crucial role in understanding user interpretation of personalization decisions within AR contexts and helps shape the development of explainability and control mechanisms in interface design. Research partnerships should investigate participatory design techniques that include end users, consumer advocates, and stakeholders during every stage of system development. According to Jain and Jain (2024), co-design processes reveal hidden usability issues while uncovering cultural sensitivities and constructing systems that represent diverse values and needs (Jain & Jain, 2024). Global retailers such as IKEA need personalization systems to adapt to diverse populations that span multiple countries and languages with different lifestyles. Experts in law and regulatory fields provide indispensable contributions to this interdisciplinary system. Researchers must develop forward-thinking governance strategies that address compliance difficulties in response to the development of national and supranational frameworks like the EU AI Act. Embedding transparency and fairness into design represents an ethical decision today but future regulations will likely mandate it. Creating joint assessment protocols that integrate both technological and humanistic standards represents a forward-thinking approach. IKEA alongside other researchers must move beyond basic accuracy or engagement metrics by building comprehensive models that evaluate systems on fairness alongside emotional response, accessibility and psychological impact over time (Agu et al., 2024). Design frameworks which establish clear reporting tools benefit both users and regulators while directing future product development. Cross-disciplinary collaboration needs to grow to include education and workforce development. IKEA can improve its innovation strategy by providing AI practitioners training in ethics and inclusivity while giving design team members basic machine learning knowledge. The formation of joint labs and fellowships involving universities, retail businesses and civil groups promises to quickly develop skilled individuals who can build trustworthy AI systems for the future. Creating intelligent retail solutions extends beyond technological advancements as it requires diverse knowledge systems to collaborate and develop AI that achieves effectiveness while maintaining ethical standards and human-centred design.

CONCLUSION

Retail transformation through augmented reality (AR) and artificial intelligence (AI) has changed consumer interactions with products and brands as well as retail spaces. Within the intelligent retail landscape IKEA emerges as a prime example by leveraging immersive technologies to boost customer satisfaction while improving operations and fostering ethical advancements. This chapter demonstrates how IKEA's implementation of AR and AI has evolved retail from unchanging catalogues and nondescript physical stores to engaging personalized shopping experiences that merge digital with physical shopping spaces. IKEA integrates AR into its digital platform which enables customers to preview furniture within their personal spaces through the IKEA Place app allowing real-time design testing and spatial assurance before buying. This feature resolves an enduring obstacle for online furniture retailers known as the imagination gap. Customers can now interact with products directly inside their homes by rotating items virtually and changing colors to evaluate how well they fit. The use of virtual product testing decreases uncertainty and enhances purchase satisfaction while also helping to reduce return rates which helps businesses meet their sustainability goals. AI enhances user immersion by delivering immediate recommendations that account for customer preferences alongside lifestyle information and space limitations. Machine learning algorithms at IKEA provide personalized suggestions that use browsing patterns together with detailed data including household size, previous purchases and environmental factors. Through personalization AI evolves into a collaborative design partner enabling users to design living spaces which match their personal values and functional requirements alongside their aesthetic preferences. The impact of these technologies reaches well past commercial profits. IKEA has exhibited sustained dedication to ethical technology governance through investments in explainable AI and data privacy practices along with inclusive design frameworks. Transparent recommendation processes combined with cultural adaptability in interfaces and optional data consent mechanisms preserve user autonomy and trust throughout personalization efforts. These guiding principles have become essential as worries about surveillance capitalism along with digital manipulation and algorithmic bias continue to escalate. IKEA demonstrates how immersive retail technology can deliver innovative solutions while safeguarding consumer rights. The use of AI and AR for consumer interaction introduces multiple new difficulties. The increasing complexity of algorithms within user interactions raises the danger of both hidden system operations and excessive behavioural manipulation by these systems. The boundary between helping customers and exerting influence becomes indistinct in immersive spaces that offer product recommendations as well as layout and spatial orientation advice. The current state of technology demands more robust explainability frameworks and human-in-the-loop systems that enable users to examine and modify algorithmic outcomes. The expansion of personalization technologies introduces specific dangers to equitable treatment and inclusive practices. Training AI systems mainly on majority user data puts underrepresented communities at risk because algorithms may exclude them from personalized recommendations or perpetuate damaging stereotypes. Continuous algorithmic fairness evaluations combined with diverse data set inclusion and co-design methods must enable marginalized voices to determine personalization practices. Subsequent investigations should examine how these technologies affect consumer psychology and behaviour over extended periods. Despite promising short-term results shown by increased engagement and reduced returns from AR and AI systems we lack understanding of how ongoing interactions with these technologies affect long-term trust, autonomy, user satisfaction, and identity formation. The expansion of IKEA's technology prompts research into decision-making changes through repeated personalization and the possibility that immersive environments foster AI dependency while transparency influences long-term brand loyalty. The potential application of generative AI alongside virtual try-on (VTO) technology for personalizing interior design at IKEA represents an emerging field for research. The technology allows users to instantly design room layouts and create personalized furniture choices. Yet they trigger concerns regarding their realistic portrayal as well as potential biases and psychological effects when hyper-personalized advice reduces user creativity or leads to a standardized look. Understanding the way users respond to recommendations from GenAI systems will be crucial to ensure these systems empower users instead of directing them.

REFERENCES

Agu, E. E., Abhulimen, A. O., Obiki-Osafiele, A. N., Osundare, O. S., Adeniran, I. A., & Efunniyi, C. P. (2024). Discussing ethical considerations and solutions for ensuring fairness in AI-driven financial services. *International Journal of Frontline Research in Multidisciplinary Studies*. DOI: 10.56355/ijfrms.2024.3.2.0024

Alimamy, S., & Gnoth, J. (2022). I want it my way! The effect of perceptions of personalization through augmented reality and online shopping on customer intentions to co-create value. *Computers in Human Behavior*, *128*, 107105. DOI: 10.1016/j.chb.2021.107105

Arora, R. (2024). *Bridging the Gap Between Offline and Online Presence in E-commerce*. International Journal of Scientific Research in Engineering and Management., DOI: 10.55041/IJSREM33002

Asthana, S., Im, J., Chen, Z., & Banovic, N. (2024). "I know even if you don't tell me": Understanding users' privacy preferences regarding AI-based inferences of sensitive information for personalization. *Proceedings of the CHI Conference on Human Factors in Computing Systems*. DOI: 10.1145/3613904.3642180

Babatunde, S. O., Odejide, O. A., Edunjobi, T. E., & Ogundipe, D. O. (2024). The role of AI in marketing personalization: A theoretical exploration of consumer engagement strategies. *International Journal of Management & Entrepreneurship Research*, *6*(3), 936–949. Advance online publication. DOI: 10.51594/ijmer.v6i3.964

Beziat, A., & François, C. (2024). Impacts of behavioral, organizational, and spatial factors on the carbon footprint of traditional retail and e-commerce in the Paris region. *Environmental Science & Technology*, *58*(17), 7325–7334. Advance online publication. DOI: 10.1021/acs.est.3c01901 PMID: 38621688

Cachero-Martínez, S., & Vazquez-Casielles, R. (2021). Building consumer loyalty through e-shopping experiences: The mediating role of emotions. *Journal of Retailing and Consumer Services*, *60*, 102481. DOI: 10.1016/j.jretconser.2021.102481

Çakırkaya, M., & Koçyiğit, M. (2024). Consumer involvement in augmented reality applications in the context of phygital marketing communications. *ASR: Chiang Mai University Journal of Social Sciences and Humanities*. DOI: 10.12982/CMU-JASR.2024.008

Calvo, A. V., Franco, A. D., & Frasquet, M. (2023). The role of artificial intelligence in improving the omnichannel customer experience. *International Journal of Retail & Distribution Management*, *51*(9/10), 1174–1194. Advance online publication. DOI: 10.1108/IJRDM-12-2022-0493

Canhoto, A., Keegan, B., & Ryzhikh, M. (2023). Snakes and ladders: Unpacking the personalisation-privacy paradox in the context of AI-enabled personalisation in the physical retail environment. *Information Systems Frontiers*, •••, 1–20. DOI: 10.1007/s10796-023-10369-7 PMID: 36684411

Chen, J. Y. C. (2022). Transparent human–agent communications. *International Journal of Human-Computer Interaction*, *38*(19), 1737–1738. DOI: 10.1080/10447318.2022.2120173

Dai, X., & Liu, Q. (2024). Impact of artificial intelligence on consumer buying behaviors: Study about the online retail purchase. *Journal of Infrastructure, Policy and Development*. DOI: 10.24294/jipd.v8i9.7700

Dezao, T. (2024). Enhancing transparency in AI-powered customer engagement. *Journal of AI, Robotics & Workplace Automation*. DOI: 10.69554/PPJE1646

Do, T. D., Nguyen, Q. V., & Pham, H. T. (2025). A review of omni-channel strategies in e-commerce: Integrating online and offline customer journeys. *Asian Journal of Economics, Business and Accounting*. DOI: 10.9734/ajeba/2025/v25i31694

Donthi, R., Lakshmi, B. P., Srinivas, G., Sudhakar, S. S., Koneru, H. P., & Yekula, P. K. (2024). AI-driven numerical optimization for carbon footprint reduction and sustainable supply chain management in the fashion industry. *South Eastern European Journal of Public Health*, 1216–1222. Advance online publication. DOI: 10.70135/seejph.vi.2023

Dutta, S. S. (2024). Revolutionizing retail: An empirical study on the impact of generative AI in omnichannel strategies. *International Journal for Multidisciplinary Research*. DOI: 10.36948/ijfmr.2024.v06i05.28799

Ebrahimabad, F. Z., Yazdani, H., Hakim, A., & Asarian, M. (2024). Augmented reality versus web-based shopping: How does AR improve user experience and online purchase intention. *Telematics and Informatics Reports*, *11*, 100152. DOI: 10.1016/j.teler.2024.100152

Ejjami, A., & Rahim, A. A. (2024). Compliance to GDPR data protection and privacy in artificial intelligence technology: Legal and ethical ramifications in Malaysia. *2023 International Conference on Disruptive Technologies (ICDT)*, 284–288. DOI: 10.1109/ICDT57929.2023.10150615

Enyejo, J. O., Obani, O. Q., Afolabi, O., Igba, E., & Ibokette, A. I. (2024). Effect of Augmented Reality (AR) and Virtual Reality (VR) experiences on customer engagement and purchase behavior in retail stores. *Magna Scientia Advanced Research and Reviews*. DOI: 10.30574/msarr.2024.11.2.0116

Gajjar, T. (2024). Revolutionizing retail: The synergy of AI and AR. SSRN *Electronic Journal*. https://doi.org/DOI: 10.2139/ssrn.4778277

Garg, N., Kaur, A., & Dutta, R. (2024). A comparative case study on augmented reality and AI chatbots. *2024 IEEE Delhi Section Flagship Conference (DELCON)*, 1–5. DOI: 10.1109/DELCON64804.2024.10866613

Gokarna, P. (2021). Study of customer engagement through emotional branding. *Management Science*, *8*(3), 11–20. DOI: 10.34293/management.v8i3.3455

Gong, T., & Park, J. (2023). Effects of augmented reality technology characteristics on customer citizenship behavior. *Journal of Retailing and Consumer Services*, *73*, 103443. DOI: 10.1016/j.jretconser.2023.103443

Gupta, S. (2025). Ethical considerations in AI-driven personalization for eCommerce platforms. *International Journal of Scientific Research in Computer Science, Engineering and Information Technology*. DOI: 10.32628/CSEIT251112371

Gustafsson, K., Jönson, G., Smith, D., & Sparks, L. (2005). Packaging logistics and retailers' profitability: An IKEA case study. *International Journal of Retail & Distribution Management*, *34*(2), 162–179. DOI: 10.1108/09590550610649786

Hooper, K., & Lunn, S. (2024). A scoping review of transparency and explainability in AI ethics guidelines. *The International FLAIRS Conference Proceedings*. DOI: 10.32473/flairs.37.1.135594

Iranmanesh, M., Senali, M. G., Foroughi, B., Ghobakhloo, M., Asadi, S., & Babaee Tirkolaee, E. (2024). Effect of augmented reality applications on attitude and behaviours of customers: Cognitive and affective perspectives. *Asia-Pacific Journal of Business Administration*, *16*(5), 1067–1092. Advance online publication. DOI: 10.1108/APJBA-07-2023-0292

Jain, S., Pahwa, M. S., & Dorasamy, N. (2024). *Impact of augmented reality on enhanced customer experience in retailing*. Exploresearch., DOI: 10.62823/EXRE/2024/01/01.3

Kaushal, S., & Mishra, D. (2024). Strategic implications of AI in contemporary business and society. *2024 2nd International Conference on Disruptive Technologies (ICDT)*, 1469–1474. DOI: 10.1109/ICDT61202.2024.10489027

Kaushal, S., & Mishra, R. (2024). AI and the personalization-privacy paradox: Balancing customized marketing with consumer data protection. *International Journal of Computer Trends and Technology*, *72*(9), 24–31. Advance online publication. DOI: 10.14445/22312803/IJCTT-V72I9P105

Kowalczuk, P., Siepmann, C., & Adler, J. (2020). Cognitive, affective, and behavioral consumer responses to augmented reality in e-commerce: A comparative study. *Journal of Business Research, 122*, 423–436. DOI: 10.1016/j.jbusres.2020.10.050

Ozturkcan, S. (2020). Service innovation: Using augmented reality in the IKEA Place app. *Journal of Information Technology Teaching Cases, 11*(1), 8–13. DOI: 10.1177/2043886920947110

Pabari, N., Irfan, F., Khan, S. S., Tawate, K., & Nilesh, S. N. (2024). Recommendations in augmented reality-based furniture shopping application. *Global Journal of Engineering and Technology Advances, 19*(3), 102. DOI: 10.30574/gjeta.2024.19.3.0102

Pakharuddin, N. S., & Kamarudin, K. M. (2023). Impact of augmented reality and artificial intelligence in consumer engagement during the post-pandemic retail transformation. In *2023 IEEE International Conference on Electrical, Computer, Communications and Mechatronics Engineering (ICECCME)* (pp. 1–6). IEEE. DOI: 10.1109/EICEEAI60672.2023.10590317

Raghavendra, R., & Mg, E. (2024). Integrating advanced technologies in retail: A conceptual framework for enhancing consumer experience and trust. *International Journal of Engineering Technologies and Management Research, 11*(10). Advance online publication. DOI: 10.29121/ijetmr.v11.i10.2024.1506

Riar, M., Xi, N., Korbel, J. J., Zarnekow, R., & Hamari, J. (2022). Using augmented reality for shopping: A framework for AR-induced consumer behavior, literature review, and future agenda. *Internet Research, 32*(6), 1611–1635. DOI: 10.1108/INTR-08-2021-0611

Rudro, M. M., Rahman, M. M., & Hasan, M. (2024). Smart supply chain management using AI in furniture retail. *2024 International Conference on Electrical, Computer, Communications and Mechatronics Engineering (ICECCME)*. DOI: 10.1109/ICECCME62383.2024.10796654

Sahli, A., & Lichy, J. (2024). The role of augmented reality in the customer shopping experience. *The International Journal of Organizational Analysis*. Advance online publication. DOI: 10.1108/IJOA-02-2024-4300

Sipos, D. (2025). The effects of AI-powered personalization on consumer trust, satisfaction, and purchase intent. *European Journal of Applied Science. Engineering and Technology, 3*(2), 14–24. Advance online publication. DOI: 10.59324/ejaset.2025.3(2).02

Sjöberg, C. M. (2021). Legal AI from a privacy point of view: Data protection and transparency in focus. In *Digital Human Sciences*. New Objects – New Approaches., DOI: 10.16993/bbk.h

Soni, V. (2024). AI and the personalization-privacy paradox: Balancing customized marketing with consumer data protection. *International Journal of Computer Trends and Technology*, *72*(9), 24–31. Advance online publication. DOI: 10.14445/22312803/IJCTT-V72I9P105

Taneja, A. K., & Tripathi, C. (2020). AI-powered recommender systems: Personalization and bias. *Turkish Journal of Computer and Mathematics Education*, *11*(1), 1090–1094. Advance online publication. DOI: 10.61841/turcomat.v11i1.14406

Tyrväinen, O., Karjaluoto, H., & Saarijärvi, H. (2020). Personalization and hedonic motivation in creating customer experiences and loyalty in omnichannel retail. *Journal of Retailing and Consumer Services*, *57*, 102233. DOI: 10.1016/j.jretconser.2020.102233

Wang, Z. (2024). *The Influence of Artificial Intelligence on Retail Marketing*. Advances in Economics, Management and Political Sciences., DOI: 10.54254/2754-1169/71/20241443

Yan, C. (2024). *The transformation of retail through digitalization: Analyzing the impact of online-offline integration and augmented reality on consumer shopping experience*. Advances in Economics, Management and Political Sciences., DOI: 10.54254/2754-1169/114/2024BJ0177

Yan, X. (2023). Omnichannel personalization in e-commerce: A consumer experience perspective. *Journal of Retailing and Consumer Services*, *72*, 103184. DOI: 10.1016/j.jretconser.2023.103184

Zhang, Y., Sun, H., & Ren, S. (2023). Big data–enabled eco-innovation and firm's competitive advantage: The role of resource orchestration capability. *Business Strategy and the Environment*, *32*(1), 82–101. DOI: 10.1002/bse.3385

KEY TERMS AND DEFINITIONS

Artificial Intelligence (AI): Machines that mimic human intelligence by learning from data perform tasks such as personalization through Artificial Intelligence (AI).

Augmented Reality (AR): This technology merges digital information with the real world using smartphone or tablet devices.

Customer Co-Creation: Customer Co-Creation enables consumers to participate directly in creating products or services.

IKEA Place: This AR mobile application enables users to place furniture models within their actual living spaces.

Perceived Trust: The customer holds confidence in the transparency and dependability of AI or AR powered shopping platforms.

Personalization: AI technology enables businesses to customize shopping experiences and product offerings according to individual customer preferences and routines.

Phygital Experience: The phygital experience combines physical and digital elements to improve customer interaction.

Chapter 4

Predictive Analytics Starbucks use of AI to Predict Customer Behaviour and Enhance Personalization

Joshua Salvation Ikede
https://orcid.org/0009-0000-9963-0413
The University of Benin, Nigeria

ABSTRACT

Starbucks deploys artificial intelligence to understand customer preferences which allows them to deliver custom product suggestions and appropriate promotions such as a recommended iced beverage when the weather is warm. The data-driven method enhances customer satisfaction and loyalty by ensuring every interaction holds more relevance for customers. Real-time optimization of inventory management and marketing strategies as well as staffing decisions is enabled by predictive analytics. The Starbucks mobile application and rewards system deliver personalized experiences that work seamlessly across different platforms. The transition towards hyper-personalization has yielded improved customer retention rates and higher revenue figures. Starbucks' strategic application of predictive analytics is examined through its technology usage and conceptual models which lead to observable performance outcomes. The conceptual model demonstrates AI's method for processing customer data to enable personalized experiences and generate feedback.

DOI: 10.4018/979-8-3373-6582-4.ch004

BACKGROUND

The application of artificial intelligence (AI) and data-driven technologies has transformed customer engagement practices with predictive analytics becoming essential. Starbucks drives industry transformation with its proprietary AI platform Deep Brew which enhances customer experiences through personalization while streamlining operations (Matharoo, 2024). The Deep Brew system from Starbucks examines large data collections that span transaction records, time elements, geographical positions, weather details, and behavioral trends to produce actionable insights (Cherian et al., 2025). Through its mobile app and loyalty platform Starbucks utilizes AI to collect behavioral insights including customer purchase patterns and seasonal shopping trends (Kamaruzzaman, 2022). The application of machine learning models enables businesses to predict customer actions so they can send individualized messages and make real-time product recommendations according to Gungunawat et al. (2024). Starbucks utilizes this system for delivering targeted promotions through push notifications, emails, and in-app messages which leads to higher conversion rates and stronger brand connections (Islam et al., 2024; Adeoye et al., 2024). The field of predictive analytics plays a crucial role in inventory and workforce planning. Starbucks combines past sales data with weather patterns and local events to create precise demand forecasts for individual store locations which allows them to maintain ideal inventory levels and staff numbers (Boinapalli et al., 2023). The adoption of these strategies produces waste reduction and operational efficiency gains. The company uses predictive tools to determine best store locations through geospatial and demographic analysis according to Gajjar's 2024 study and Babadoğan's 2024 research. Starbucks uses algorithmic reward systems within Starbucks Rewards to personalize incentives which help retain customers and maximize their lifetime value (Ng et al., 2022; Kholifah et al., 2024; Kotha, 2020). Amazon Alexa's voice-activated ordering system improves customer convenience through analysis of past data to refine preferences (Rengasamy, 2025). Starbucks leverages predictive analytics similar to successful practices in retail and insurance sectors through behavioral modeling and targeted content delivery (Adanyin, 2024; Okeke et al., 2024; Delliana & Arisandi, 2020). However, ethical issues remain. The need for governance arises because data privacy issues alongside bias and transparency concerns require attention. The authors Fedosova and Katunian (2024) emphasize the importance of ethical frameworks but note that Starbucks' policies lack complete transparency despite their data anonymization practices. Despite these concerns, the benefits are clear. According to Dutta's 2024 findings and research by Suhono et al., from 2020 AI technology enhances both customer retention rates and omnichannel operational effectiveness. Starbucks demonstrates the powerful transformational capabilities of AI in business models with its strategic deployment of predictive analytics to deliver personalized customer experiences that are both efficient and scalable while establishing new industry benchmarks.

Focus of the Chapter

The use of artificial intelligence and predictive analytics has become essential for enhancing customer experiences while Starbucks leads the way as an early adopter of these technologies. This chapter examines Starbucks' use of AI for forecasting customer behavior which enables hyper-personalized experiences through real-world applications and academic research. The following sections examine two core applications: By focusing on personalized marketing and recommendations along with operational efficiency and customer loyalty enhancement this chapter demonstrates how predictive analytics transforms these areas.

Personalized Marketing and Product Recommendations

Starbucks transformed its marketing strategy by implementing predictive analytics and AI-based personalization methods. By customizing messages and product recommendations based on individual customer preferences Starbucks has increased brand engagement while building stronger customer loyalty. Starbucks uses its Deep Brew AI engine to examine multiple customer data points including order history, time of day, location, weather and browsing patterns for product recommendation and personalized promotion delivery (Cherian et al., 2025). The Starbucks mobile app functions as the primary tool within their personalized engagement strategy. Starbucks uses real-time behavioral data collection from customer interactions to divide its audience into small groups for targeted promotional delivery (Islam et al., 2024). When a customer regularly selects cold brew during warm afternoons Deep Brew typically recommends a cold brew variation or proposes a discount on iced drinks during a warm afternoon. Such personalization strategies lead to increased sales while making customers feel recognized and appreciated according to Gungunawat et al., 2024. Artificial intelligence improves in-app messaging and push notifications by selecting optimal outreach times and channels. Predictive models enable Starbucks to determine optimal offerings and presentation strategies for maximum business impact (Adanyin, 2024). Hyper-personalization strategies achieve their best results during seasonal promotions like Starbucks' holiday drink campaigns because they match time-sensitive offerings to customer preferences and buying habits. Empirical data supports the effectiveness of this strategy. Adeoye et al. Adeoye et al. (2024) demonstrate that personalizing communication boosts customer engagement and conversion rates when offers match both the timing and relevance to the customer. Similarly, Okeke et al. small businesses using AI-driven personalization frameworks have achieved significant retention and loyalty results which large enterprises like Starbucks also benefit from. The AI applications at Starbucks go beyond basic product suggestions. The company combines sentiment analysis techniques with natural language processing (NLP) to understand customer reviews and social media feedback. The company achieves real-time refinement of its products and marketing strategies through its analytical processes (Babadoğan, 2024). Companies like Starbucks use predictive tools to detect negative social sentiment about new products and recommend necessary changes or alternative options promptly. LINE Messenger campaigns demonstrated by Delliana and Arisandi (2020) showed that AI-enhanced promotional content had a substantial impact on both customer mindsets and their buying behavior. The Starbucks app ecosystem incorporates a similar strategy when it delivers personalized product previews along with tailored coupons to engage users effectively. The brand has made substantial progress beyond traditional mass marketing approaches by adopting data-driven decision-making methods. The use of predictive personalization introduces ethical concerns about how data is used while offering evident benefits. Starbucks maintains that it safeguards user information by anonymizing it but their hyper-personalization data collection practices remain under public examination (Fedosova & Katunian, 2024). The brand's achievement of a 30% return on investment (ROI) from AI integration demonstrates the commercial effectiveness of this strategy (Dutta, 2024). The employment of predictive analytics for personalized marketing by Starbucks has established a standard for AI utilization in consumer businesses. Starbucks has maintained its brand relevance and exceeded consumer expectations through a combination of behavioral insights with real-time data processing and strategic outreach in today's digital marketplace.

Operational Efficiency and Customer Loyalty Enhancement

Starbucks uses predictive analytics to optimize its operations while building enduring customer loyalty beyond just marketing efforts. Through these applications Starbucks manages to predict customer demands while synchronizing its backend operations, including inventory management and staffing to provide seamless service. The systems-level integration of AI demonstrates Starbucks' advanced knowledge of how operational intelligence enhances customer satisfaction. AI delivers significant value primarily through advancements in inventory management. Deep Brew uses historical sales data along with seasonal shifts, local events and weather information to predict product demand at each store location (Boinapalli et al., 2023). Starbucks uses AI to maintain appropriate inventory levels that prevent product overstocking and understocking while minimizing waste and maintaining product availability. Deep Brew informs local stores to stock up on iced beverages and their ingredients when it anticipates a rise in cold drink sales triggered by an impending heatwave. The demand forecasting approach demonstrated exceptional utility in managing customer traffic during holiday seasons and regional events due to their volatile nature (Gajjar, 2024). AI technologies help Starbucks optimize workforce management for better efficiency. The company employs predictive models to schedule workers according to expected foot traffic, time of day patterns and product demand to minimize labor expenses while improving service speed (Matharoo, 2024). When stores staff adequately, they achieve reduced waiting periods and improved customer satisfaction which together help build stronger customer loyalty. Real-time data enables dynamic adjustments to scheduling, allowing resource allocation to stay aligned with customer demands. Predictive analytics that drive the Starbucks Rewards program serves to improve customer loyalty. The system offers tailored rewards and incentives by learning from customer purchase patterns instead of only rewarding frequent transactions. The system may grant additional points for similar purchases or offer exclusive pastries to customers who usually redeem points for bakery goods. The personalized loyalty program enhances customer lifetime value while strengthening brand connections with consumers (Ng et al., 2022). Kotha (2020) demonstrates how predictive analytics plays a vital role in developing personalized customer journeys to strengthen AI-driven loyalty programs. To re-engage lapsed customers Starbucks uses behavior-based triggers to activate their engagement principle. The system responds to customers who haven't purchased anything in weeks by presenting them with time-sensitive discounts or re-engagement offers to sustain their loyalty and decrease customer turnover. Starbucks uses operational intelligence to make decisions about where to open new locations. Predictive analytics models use demographic information along with competitor proximity and economic indicators to find optimal sites for business growth. Through predictive analytics Starbucks can establish locations in regions expected to show robust demand thereby enhancing return on investment while reducing potential risks (Babadoğan, 2024). Starbucks extends its predictive capabilities beyond individual customer actions to encompass comprehensive market behavior analysis. Starbucks uses predictive systems that gather customer feedback and incorporate it into their ongoing enhancement processes. AI systems identify and report persistent product-related complaints from different locations to corporate quality assurance and product development teams. Starbucks maintains its allegiance to consumer standards by utilizing feedback loops which build brand trust and customer satisfaction according to Suhono et al. (2020). The systems increase efficiency and customer loyalty but create employee privacy and algorithmic transparency issues. Experts continue to discuss the potential labor injustices and unrealistic performance standards resulting from AI-based scheduling systems. Starbucks has made public promises to merge its technology applications with ethical workplace standards, yet the efficiency of these protective measures continues to be monitored (Hakim & Mulyani, 2024). Starbucks utilizes predictive analytics in applications that reach beyond direct consumer services. The company integrates AI into its operations so that every choice regarding inventory management and employee scheduling leads to personalized customer experience. The efficiencies created through back-end processes expand front-end loyalty which shows how predictive technologies merge business objectives with customer satisfaction.

Strategic Site Selection and Expansion Planning

Starbucks utilizes predictive analytics to decide both the location and timing for launching new store locations although this application tends not to be as visible. Retail businesses in competitive markets face high operational expenses and reduced customer visits because of poor location selection. Starbucks decreased this risk by implementing data-based location selection methods which utilize AI support. Starbucks employs data-driven site selection strategies that incorporate demographic analysis, geographic information systems (GIS), customer traffic patterns, competitor locations, and local economic factors (Gajjar, 2024). Starbucks utilizes machine learning models to process data from multiple sources such as mobile device tracking systems and real estate databases along with point-of-sale systems. The models predict the number of visitors to specific locations and estimate customer demand along with revenue forecasts. The AI models analyze locations based on their proximity to high-traffic areas and the types of nearby businesses while considering neighborhood socio-economic factors to help Starbucks discover profitable expansion sites (Babadoğan, 2024). The analytical approach represents a more refined method compared to traditional site selection techniques which depended on gut feeling and fixed demographic reports. Starbucks possesses the capability to adjust its expansion models dynamically as market conditions change in real time. During the COVID-19 pandemic Starbucks needed to reassess their urban and suburban store placement strategies due to changes in consumer behaviors and urban migration trends. Predictive analytics allowed the brand to adapt its strategies faster and with better precision than its competitors according to Kamaruzzaman (2022). The use of predictive modeling extends beyond opening new stores to include optimization of current store operations. Retail locations that fail to meet predictive benchmarks are subject to potential closure or infrastructure updates. Through its applications businesses achieve growth and operational efficiency with the help of AI. As noted by Adeoye et al. Businesses gain the ability to act on opportunities with confidence and precision by analyzing large-scale spatial and consumer data (Adeoye et al., 2024). The use of AI enables businesses to determine optimal service formats for different store locations. The optimal service format between a full café, drive-thru, and pickup-only store emerges from analyzing local customer preferences and behavioral patterns according to Dutta (2024). Predictive models show that in densely populated urban settings smaller stores with quick service capabilities perform better than larger stores because of space limitations and rapid customer movement. The use of AI technology supports Starbucks' worldwide strategic objectives. The company uses predictive tools to model various market entry strategies enabling adaptation to different international markets where cultural preferences and consumption behaviors show significant variation. Through predictive analytics Starbucks determines which product assortments store designs and digital services will perform best in new regions according to Okeke et al. (2024). The site selection process at Starbucks illustrates how predictive analytics eliminates guesswork from making big business decisions. Starbucks uses extensive data streams and sophisticated modeling methods to maintain its worldwide presence while achieving both business expansion and sustainable operations.

AI-Driven Customer Retention and Re-engagement Strategies

Starbucks has implemented predictive analytics most successfully through its customer retention and re-engagement tactics. By focusing on customer retention, which is more economical than acquiring new customers Starbucks utilizes advanced data analytics to reduce customer churn and boost lifetime value. The company uses AI to predict when customers may disengage and implement early measures to re-engage them. The company uses behavioral segmentation algorithms to organize customers into groups by examining their engagement levels alongside their purchase types and spending patterns. The algorithms recognize initial disengagement indicators like reduced visit frequency or app usage and initiate customized responses (Ng et al., 2022). When a previously active customer stops visiting for three weeks the system sends them a personalized notification through email or app which presents a discount or showcases a new product tailored to their previous buying habits (Kholifah et al., 2024). The Starbucks Rewards loyalty program serves as the foundation for this strategic approach. The program collects detailed individual behavior data which analysts use to determine the rewards that will best motivate customer return visits. Businesses usually present customers with exclusive time-sensitive promotions when they detect reduced activity in their behavior. Research indicates that such interventions lead to a substantial rise in customer reactivation rates (Kotha, 2020). Predictive analytics enables Starbucks to detect customers who show signs of potential churn ahead of time. AI models calculate customer churn probabilities by examining factors like visit frequency and time since last purchase alongside historical offer responsiveness and seasonal patterns (Rengasamy, 2025). The research by Islam et al. (2024) confirms that retailers and service businesses should design retention campaigns specifically for high-risk customers based on their unique behavior patterns and preferences. Starbucks strengthens customer re-engagement through its implementation of omnichannel communication strategies. The AI system selects the optimal communication channel such as SMS, email, app notifications or social media posts by analyzing the customer's historical engagement patterns (Sathianathan & Ray, 2023). If customers regularly respond to email promotions but ignore app notifications their future campaigns will receive email delivery as a priority. Personalized outreach strategies enhance the chances of successful customer re-engagement. Starbucks utilizes predictive sentiment analysis to refine their marketing strategies. Natural language processing (NLP) techniques enable the analysis of customer feedback from surveys and social media platforms to detect satisfaction patterns and dissatisfaction indicators (Hou et al., 2024). When customers report their discontent, they receive immediate attention through follow-up actions which involve personalized service recovery initiatives that may feature free items or customer service team outreach (Hakim & Mulyani, 2024). The ethical considerations of AI applications must be recognized. Discussions continue about the extent of data collection and the mental impact of continuous re-engagement prompts. Leading brands such as Starbucks face the challenge of managing aggressive customer retention strategies while ensuring consumer comfort and autonomy remains intact (Fedosova & Katunian, 2024). Starbucks demonstrates how predictive analytics strengthens customer retention through its data-driven framework which builds sustainable relationships. Through identification of risk factors Starbucks maintains brand relevance by delivering hyper-personalized content and optimizing engagement channels for consumers at risk of disengagement.

Key Findings

Starbucks' business model transformation through predictive analytics and AI implementation brought quantifiable advantages to marketing operations customer loyalty as well as strategic planning. These advantages demonstrate that properly implemented technology enhances customer service while boosting operational accuracy and driving long-term growth. Key findings reveal Starbucks' use of predictive analytics to maintain competitive advantage and center their business on customer needs within the ever-changing retail landscape.

Predictive Personalization Drives Customer Engagement and Sales

Starbucks' AI capabilities enable it to forecast customer behavior and deliver tailored experiences which boost customer engagement and revenue. Starbucks now delivers personalized messages to customers by studying their transaction records along with order timing and location data as well as local weather patterns to figure out which products they will buy. Starbucks employs its proprietary AI engine Deep Brew to provide dynamic suggestions that match individual customer preferences according to Cherian et al. (2025). According to Islam et al. Starbucks' mobile app personalization tactics generate what they describe as "hyper-personalized ecosystems." The Starbucks mobile app functions as "hyper-personalized ecosystems" by tracking user behavior in real-time which enables predictive models to change offers based on recognized patterns (Islam et al., 2024). Customers who regularly purchase chai lattes during weekday mornings might see a promotional discount appear in their Starbucks mobile app just before their typical order time. Using predictive anticipation enhances purchase probability while building stronger brand loyalty. Starbucks uses predictive analytics integration to execute "micro-targeted" marketing campaigns. Adanyin's 2024 study shows that marketing strategies leveraging both seasonal factors and local happenings together with individual customer interests produce much higher conversion figures. The use of dynamic messaging stands in stark contrast to generic static promotions because customers receive offers that align with their current needs and preferences. Starbucks adjusts push notifications and emails according to user behavior by personalizing not only the content but also the timing and channel. Gungunawat et al. According to Gungunawat et al. (2024), AI technology determines optimal message delivery times to boost user interaction rates. Starbucks' AI adjusts the timing of email promotions to match the evening email engagement pattern of its users. The objective is to integrate user behavior with brand reactions to reduce friction points while boosting the perceived value for customers. Predictive personalization enables businesses to identify upselling and cross-selling opportunities. Starbucks can improve its checkout experience by suggesting additional products based on their analysis of common product purchase combinations. The "basket-building" technique successfully raises average order value when customers see relevant add-on products that match their individual profiles (Babadoğan, 2024). The level of personalization implemented raises ethical questions concerning how data is gathered and used. Starbucks affirms that it anonymizes and protects customer data yet patrons still express unease about their behavior tracking and subsequent analysis. The study by Fedosova and Katunian (2024) emphasizes the need for ethical implementation of AI insights which requires full transparency and user consent to avoid misuse and maintain trust. Predictive personalization at Starbucks shows substantial benefits for customer engagement and financial performance while building brand loyalty. The company uses ongoing data analysis together with AI learning to deliver valuable experiences that show customers they are understood and valued.

AI Enhances Operational Agility and Cost Efficiency

The company Starbucks has applied predictive analytics successfully to its operations to obtain significant results. AI technology directs crucial business operations by managing inventory predictions and coordinating supply chains while scheduling labor effectively. These enhancements led to waste reduction while boosting employee productivity together with improved product availability and customer satisfaction levels. The integration of predictive analytics into backend operations transforms management practices from reactive to proactive. Deep Brew produces demand forecasts by analyzing historical sales patterns along with seasonal variations and weather forecasts. The system boosts cold beverage stock levels in nearby stores when predictions show rising temperatures in a specific region (Boinapalli et al., 2023). Demand-sensing ensures products meet consumption needs at precise locations while preventing excessive inventory and stock deficits. Predictive analytics facilitates inventory optimization which leads to reduced operational expenditures through waste minimization. Matharoo's 2024 research shows that machine learning models enable procurement systems to match customer demand perfectly thus reducing excess inventory and product spoilage. The just-in-time inventory model plays a crucial role in managing perishable items by maintaining freshness while reducing unnecessary inventory costs. Predictive analytics has brought significant transformation to the field of labor scheduling. Starbucks uses data from foot traffic patterns alongside historical sales data and events in the local area to establish the best staffing levels. Gajjar's 2024 research highlights how using data-driven strategies enhances service efficiency and boosts employee morale. Staff members work at balanced capacity levels throughout both busy and quiet times which leads to more efficient operations and higher job satisfaction among employees. Operational improvements lead to better experiences for customers. Suhono et al. The research of Suhono et al. (2020) shows a direct connection between how operations perform, and the level of customer satisfaction achieved. Proper staffing levels at stores result in shorter lines and quicker service which increases customer repeat visits. Predictive analytics, therefore, plays a dual role: Predictive analytics helps businesses minimize internal operational waste while strengthening their brand image in the public eye. The COVID-19 pandemic created new opportunities to showcase the importance of predictive agility. Starbucks utilized real-time data to change store hours and adjust product offerings while managing store closures in response to local infection rates and government restrictions (Hakim & Mulyani, 2024). Quick adaptation to evolving circumstances enabled the maintenance of operational continuity throughout a worldwide emergency. The Starbucks supply chain operates more effectively using predictive coordination. More precise demand forecasts given to suppliers enable them to modify production plans and delivery timetables accordingly. This approach eliminates delays and stops bottlenecks from forming during times of high demand. The fast-moving inventory system at Starbucks guarantees both fresh products and standard uniformity throughout its outlets. The benefits of predictive systems exist alongside persistent difficulties in matching them with human decision-making processes. Artificial Intelligence systems provide recommendations which managers must ultimately evaluate for final decision-making. Oversight and periodic system evaluations are necessary to control the dependency on algorithmic recommendations. Through predictive analytics Starbucks has gained the ability to make precise operational improvements. Business layers across inventory management through to labor and logistics all enjoy advantages from strategic foresight. Operational intelligence enhances cost efficiency while boosting customer satisfaction which establishes predictive analytics as a core component of Starbucks' successful strategy.

Predictive analytics improves retention and loyalty

The implementation of predictive analytics by Starbucks has played a fundamental role in advancing customer retention as well as improving their loyalty programs. Data-driven insights enable the company to spot early disengagement signs while personalizing loyalty incentives and reviving inactive customers which helps sustain a solid and devoted customer base. The Starbucks Rewards program demonstrates successful application of AI and predictive tools to enhance customer lifetime value (Ng et al., 2022). The foundation of this strategy relies on behavioral segmentation. By segmenting customers using their purchase frequency along with their preferred products and visiting times Starbucks can detect high-risk churn profiles. Predictive models signal an alert when a customer who typically orders twice weekly suddenly stops ordering for two weeks. Targeted re-engagement strategies are activated by AI which includes options such as providing a free drink or a time-sensitive discount along with double points (Kotha, 2020). Personalized loyalty rewards have become increasingly sophisticated. AI systems analyze reactions to past promotional offers to modify future incentive types and their delivery schedule. Kholifah et al. The adaptive loyalty strategy studied by Kholifah et al. (2024) leads to higher redemption rates while creating personalized customer recognition. A regular bakery rewards user can gain early access to new pastry launches or earn additional points when buying bakery products. Channel optimization also supports Starbucks' retention efforts. Predictive models analyze customer engagement history to select between email, app notifications, SMS messages and in-app alerts as the best communication channel for each customer (Sathianathan & Ray, 2023). Retention campaigns use the communication medium that has the highest probability of generating a positive response. A customer who consistently opens emails while ignoring app notifications will have better engagement levels when messages reach them through email. Predictive sentiment analysis forms an integral part of Starbucks' customer retention approach. The company leverages natural language processing tools to analyze online reviews and social media posts as well as customer survey responses to pinpoint potential dissatisfaction. The company implements proactive service recovery actions to address customers who submit negative feedback by using methods like apologies and personalized outreach and offering goodwill credits (Hou et al., 2024). The customer recovery interactions both reduce churn rates and convert unhappy customers into dedicated supporters of the brand. Predictive analytics also enables dynamic loyalty gamification. The Starbucks app provides bonus challenges and individual behavior-based progress tracking for its users. Customers who visit multiple days consecutively can get special offers, yet other customers receive points for trying different menu options. Personalized challenges provide an ever-renewing brand experience which motivates users to engage with the brand on a more regular basis (Okeke et al., 2024). Predictive analytics has demonstrated impressive retention results but sparks ethical concerns about manipulating consumer behavior. Users may experience feelings of surveillance or coercion if brands run excessive re-engagement campaigns without careful management. Fedosova and Katunian (2024) emphasize that ethical guidelines must be established in AI-powered marketing to maintain consumer trust and autonomy. Starbucks has evolved retention practices from being reactive to active by implementing intelligent proactive strategies. Predictive analytics enables the brand to detect at-risk customers early for timely intervention, which allows it to offer meaningful incentives and modify its engagement methods to maintain customer connection and loyalty.

Predictive Site Modeling serves as the foundation for Starbucks' strategic expansion efforts

Through predictive analytics Starbucks has directed its growth plans across both physical and digital platforms. AI-powered geographic and behavioral models guide this method to select new store locations while determining suitable service formats and identifying international growth opportunities. Predictive analytics has become the foundation of Starbucks' long-term scalability by diminishing the usual uncertainties related to business expansion. Choosing store locations remains a primary application area for this technology. Starbucks analyzes geospatial data such as population density alongside traffic patterns and local income levels in addition to proximity to current stores to determine optimal locations for new store success (Babadoğan, 2024). Machine learning models can assess hundreds of variables at once which provide greater analytical depth than traditional manual site evaluations. Kamaruzzaman (2022) research shows Starbucks' expansion strategy in Malaysia through behavioral and demographic segmentation. Through AI-driven models

Starbucks identified peak demand locations and selected the most appropriate store formats to match local consumer lifestyles and shopping preferences. By implementing this detailed strategy Starbucks guarantees that every store format serves customer demand effectively, which leads to higher revenue outcomes. Starbucks in the United States redirected its business strategy towards suburban locations by employing predictive analytics after pandemic-induced urban migration trends. According to Dutta (2024), Starbucks adjusted its strategy to create drive-thru and mobile-focused locations in residential areas experiencing growth in demand. The ability to adapt shows how real-time data supports strategic agility. Predictive models simulate consumer behavior to help businesses make market entry decisions in new international regions. Starbucks evaluates market information from comparable regions including consumer spending patterns, coffee consumption behaviors, and digital preparedness to determine the feasibility of opening new outlets in different countries (Adeoye et al., 2024). The approach lessens financial risk while enhancing the precision of growth forecasts. Predictive analytics plays a role in enhancing the efficiency of current store locations. Locations that fail to meet performance expectations are identified through combined financial metrics and data from customer visits and feedback. Business decisions to close stores or change their locations or modify their layouts to meet the demands of local customers are based on these analytical insights (Gajjar, 2024). Through constant improvement cycles Starbucks sustains its powerful brand visibility while reducing operational inefficiencies. The use of site analytics creates intersections with both marketing endeavors and product development tasks. Predictive tools allow companies to identify which menu items require regional promotion or customization according to local tastes. The combination of site data with customer information enables each Starbucks store to function in alignment with its specific community environment (Okeke et al., 2024). Predictive modeling improves expansion strategies but presents multiple challenges. If organizations depend too heavily on algorithmic projections, they risk missing important cultural elements and fast-changing market dynamics. Starbucks combines human expertise and field validation to supplement predictive insights which helps maintain balanced decision-making. The strategic expansion approach Starbucks employs through predictive analytics demonstrates how artificial intelligence transforms business growth into a scientific endeavor. Starbucks maintains its global growth through customer-aligned expansion strategies that replace intuition with data-driven insights.

Predictive Innovation Enables Faster Customer-Centric Product Development

The integration of predictive analytics into Starbucks' product development process enables the company to innovate both quickly and accurately. Starbucks employs artificial intelligence to predict customer preferences and evaluate new products through data-driven methodologies instead of just traditional market research. This strategy permits the brand to introduce products that demonstrate greater success potential while reducing innovation risk and improving customer satisfaction. Starbucks utilizes Deep Brew and its analytics platforms to examine sales data and customer feedback while monitoring market trends to identify new consumer preferences. The analysis of customer preferences guides the creation of Starbucks' new drinks and food products as well as their digital platforms. When seasonal trends indicate rising plant-based beverage consumption Starbucks responds by introducing oat milk and almond-based drinks in test markets ahead of time (Ge et al., 2021). Before reaching broader audiences, these products have already demonstrated success through predictive metrics validation. The company applies predictive analytics to identify which new innovations will gain popularity within specific areas. According to Rengasamy (2025), Starbucks uses predictive modeling to develop a comprehensive "customer 360" perspective which helps match new product launches with regional cultural and economic conditions. In global markets acceptance depends heavily on innovations that resonate with local cultures. The progression of digital innovation is affected by predictive analytics. Data indicating consumer preferences for convenience and personalization led to the creation of mobile order-ahead functions and voice-command options along with personalized digital menus (Sathianathan & Ray, 2023). Starbucks actively anticipated consumer behavior patterns and subsequently developed tools to support those patterns. Starbucks implements sentiment analysis to track customer reactions to new products during their launch. Starbucks utilizes NLP tools to analyze customer reviews together with social media discussions and app ratings to determine the success of a product launch or the need for improvements (Hou et al., 2024). Starbucks responds rapidly to negative feedback by changing product recipes or promotional plans and has the option to remove underperforming items from their offerings. Predictive analytics provides essential support for internal product innovation workflows. Before launching products Starbucks uses machine learning models to simulate different pricing, ingredient combinations, and promotional tactics to project product profitability and adoption rates. Through modeling every product is guaranteed to achieve target performances before its release to the market (Babadoğan, 2024). The loyalty program data acts as a vehicle for integrating customer feedback into product innovation. Starbucks uses data from popular rewards and customer requests to decide which development projects should be pursued based on verified consumer demand. A rise in loyalty members selecting low-calorie snacks for reward redemption predicts that product teams will prioritize health-conscious options in upcoming releases (Kholifah et al., 2024). Through predictive innovation Starbucks ensures its product lineup remains relevant by adapting to customer requirements. The company gains precise foresight which eliminates guesswork while allowing Starbucks to maintain market relevance in today's fast-paced competitive environment. Fedosova and Katunian (2024) argue that brands need to balance algorithmic insights with ethical standards and consumer transparency to ensure predictive innovation becomes essential for brand excellence and customer loyalty.

Figure 1. The Starbucks Predictive Analytics Value Loop (SPAVL) demonstrated in Figure 1 presents the iterative cycle of data gathering followed by modeling and personalization before implementation and feedback. The model demonstrates Starbucks' ongoing process of improving their customer service and operational efficiency with predictive analytics.

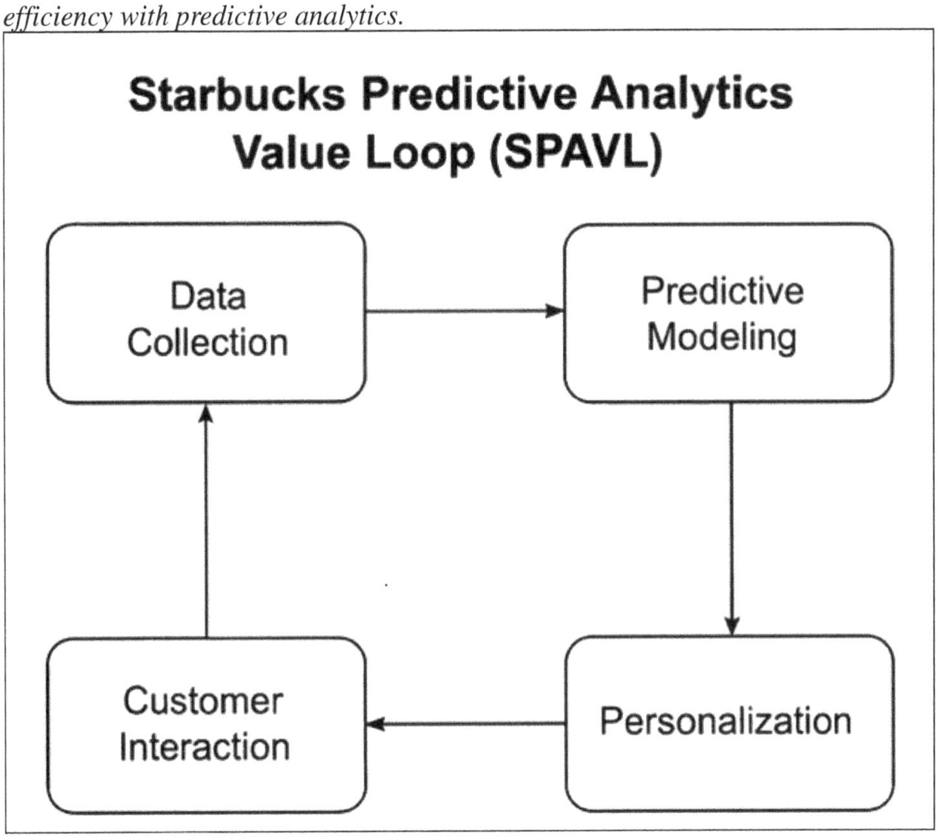

Starbucks uses this cyclical model to convert raw data into useful business intelligence throughout its entire operation process. Predictive modeling processes customer interaction data to discover behavior patterns and make future predictions. The insights generated by data analysis power Starbucks' personalization engine that tailors marketing efforts and suggests both product recommendations as well as loyalty rewards. Starbucks evaluates the impact of both operational modifications and personalized communications by tracking customer feedback and business performance statistics. Through feedback reintegration Starbucks enhances future predictions, which supports its strategy of staying responsive and data-focused while prioritizing customers.

SOLUTIONS AND RECOMMENDATIONS

Despite Starbucks' outstanding achievements in applying predictive analytics to both elevate personalization and optimize operational efficiency, multiple challenges remain which include data privacy issues, algorithmic transparency problems, and the ethical deployment of AI. The following solutions and strategic recommendations aim to create a predictive analytics ecosystem that is more sustainable while also being inclusive and innovative.

Strengthen Ethical Data Governance

Ethical data governance represents a critical challenge for AI-driven personalization systems. Starbucks needs to manage public concerns about privacy rights and algorithm accountability while it processes customer data for predictive analysis. The company gathers extensive behavioral information from mobile orders as well as loyalty programs along with social media interactions and physical store purchases. The gathered data offers beneficial insights but demands substantial obligations for maintaining transparency and ethical use of information. Businesses in food and service industries should implement extensive privacy protections that exceed regulatory requirements to build customer trust via transparent operations and accountability systems as Fedosova and Katunian (2024) state. Starbucks should enhance its data governance framework to build trust by specifying how customer data is collected, its usage, who accesses it and its retention period. Long and unclear privacy statements dominate user interactions because they do not communicate data practices using understandable language. The introduction of user-friendly consent dashboards would empower users to handle their data preferences which lets them restrict data usage for marketing purposes while maintaining core app functions. According to Babadoğan (2024) data empowerment increases user engagement by granting users control over their personal experiences. The ethical development of AI systems demands continuous auditing of predictive models to ensure they operate without bias and maintain fairness. Starbucks' machine learning models could lead to biased results when they rely on datasets that do not accurately represent all customer segments. Customers who pay in cash or shop at infrequent intervals tend to get fewer offers which continue their exclusion from digital benefits. Okeke et al. Research from Okeke et al. (2024) shows that algorithmic bias typically resides in machine learning model assumptions which require regular reviews for identification. Starbucks needs to perform fairness audits through statistical analysis and human-in-the-loop evaluations to maintain equitable personalization results. Starbucks could strengthen its ethical oversight by creating a specialized Data Ethics Board. AI experts, legal authorities, marketing specialists and consumer representatives would make up this board to evaluate major analytics initiatives prior to launching them. Adanyin (2024) explains that organizations gain advantages through structured governance mechanisms which incorporate ethical standards throughout AI development. The board would provide guidance on future ethical complexities involving facial recognition technology and biometric data usage in Starbucks innovations. Adopting international regulatory standards remains a critical requirement. Starbucks functions across several regions that feature newly established strict data privacy regulations. Starbucks should build upon their existing compliance with GDPR and CCPA by integrating best practices that enhance transparency and data minimization while establishing robust consumer redress mechanisms (Fedosova & Katunian, 2024). By proactively notifying users about how algorithmic decisions impact them, for example, explaining why they received a certain offer—companies can establish a positive industry standard. Through strong ethical data governance Starbucks can defend against legal and reputational threats while securing its place as an AI innovation leader. The company will maintain sustainable and equitable personalization strategies that respect user autonomy through transparent policies and fairness audits alongside inclusive oversight.

Invest in Explainable AI (XAI)

The expansion of artificial intelligence in Starbucks' customer personalization and product recommendations requires maintaining transparency and interpretability in these systems to overcome critical challenges. Deep learning algorithms used in traditional predictive models generally function like "black boxes" since they produce outcomes without disclosing their decision-making processes. The lack of transparency in AI systems causes users to lose trust while simultaneously creating barriers for internal comprehension and raising potential ethical and legal challenges. Starbucks must invest in explainable AI (XAI) to achieve responsible innovation and build stakeholder confidence. Explainable AI includes models and systems developed to reveal the reasoning behind their predictions and decisions in a manner that humans can understand. XAI enables Starbucks employees and customers to comprehend the reasons behind specific recommendations and business decisions. According to Rengasamy (2025) when AI systems offer contextual justifications for their actions it leads to greater transparency and better user engagement by diminishing the belief that algorithms exert unfair manipulation. Implementing XAI also benefits Starbucks internally. For effective operational decision-making through AI tools in labor scheduling and inventory forecasting or performance analytics Starbucks needs its employees and managers to understand prediction generation processes. Lack of explainability leads to potential over-reliance on AI results and possible misunderstandings of model advice. According to Babadoğan (2024) organizations focusing on explainability achieve better AI tool adoption throughout departments because employees trust and use systems they understand. To implement explainable AI at Starbucks they should first deploy transparent methods including decision trees or regression models for important tasks like customer segmentation and loyalty reward triggers. These models show enough precision for many applications and present transparent logic despite their lower complexity compared to neural networks. Starbucks ought to adopt post-hoc explanation techniques like SHAP or LIME to extract insights from complex models without the need to modify the core algorithm according to Cherian et al. (2025). Any XAI strategy must include education and training as essential elements. Starbucks needs to provide training for both technical and non-technical personnel including store managers and marketing teams so they can understand AI-generated insights. According to Gungunawat et al. Explainability enables users to build trust while simultaneously giving them the power to give feedback and spot anomalies and work together with AI systems on decision-making. Consumers now demand more transparency from service providers. The likelihood of customers choosing data-driven personalization increases when they fully grasp data utilization processes and AI decision-making methods. Islam et al. (2024) companies adopting explainability in AI-driven commerce achieve competitive advantages because they build customer loyalty and lower opt-out rates for data sharing. Starbucks' investment in explainable AI systems will advance transparency while building trust and maintaining ethical standards throughout its AI operations. Starbucks will strengthen its dedication to human-focused innovation by allowing both customers and employees to comprehend and engage with AI-based decisions.

Enhance Cross-Functional Collaboration

The successful integration of predictive analytics into Starbucks' business operations depends heavily on strong cross-functional teamwork. AI solution deployment and growth need collaborative efforts from various departments including data science teams as well as marketing and operations divisions alongside HR professionals and executive leaders and legal advisors. Predictive analytics projects risk becoming isolated and misaligned with organizational goals when departments fail to align their efforts. The success of Starbucks AI initiatives hinges on strong communication and collaboration frameworks between technical and non-technical stakeholders. AI systems such as Starbucks' Deep Brew function through a complex interaction of multiple data inputs and contextual understanding combined with business logic. Data scientists who work without business unit collaboration face challenges because model predictions often fail to connect with their practical interpretation and application. Boinapalli et al. The research by Boinapalli et al. (2023) highlights that AI projects created independently can result in tools that become overly complicated to use or fail to meet what end-users expect. Starbucks needs to create collaborative teams that unite data engineers with marketers as well as store managers and customer experience leads to building predictive analytics solutions together. A successful measure involves creating cross-functional AI task forces to lead important projects including customer retention modeling and optimization of operational efficiency along with personalization campaigns. The task forces should operate using a unified KPI framework which focuses on business impact while including ethical aspects and user feedback. According to Adeoye et al. AI tools operated under shared ownership show better deployment success rates while producing models that address real-world challenges instead of abstract metrics. AI systems achieve meaningful outcomes that gain trust and usage when multidisciplinary teams contribute from the beginning. Starbucks needs to facilitate routine knowledge-sharing events which combine project collaboration with data-driven decision-making processes. Marketing teams should acquire fundamental data interpretation abilities while analysts need training to understand customer journey mapping and retail operations. Gungunawat et al. Organizations which demonstrate strong data literacy throughout their functions gain agility and show enhanced ability to transform AI insights into operational strategies quickly. Starbucks can establish this knowledge transfer system using internal workshops along with collaborative dashboards and AI tool documentation. Starbucks has the potential to enhance its operations through active participation of store managers and baristas in AI feedback loops. Direct customer interaction by these team members delivers essential context that enhances the precision and applicability of models. When the predictive model indicates product promotion during a specific time frame, local employees notice minimal customer interest in that product, their store their feedback becomes part of the system's data. Hakim and Mulyani (2024) found that feedback from employees at the operational level ensures that analytics from higher management remain relevant to real-world conditions. Finally, cross-functional collaboration helps maintain ethical rigor. Incorporating viewpoints from equity, customer rights and cultural sensitivity in AI development enables Starbucks to better detect potential risks and blind spots. According to Adanyin's 2024 analysis, diverse multidisciplinary teams serve as a critical foundation for developing AI systems that maintain inclusivity and responsibility. Starbucks needs to integrate cross-functional collaboration throughout its predictive analytics system. To successfully embed cross-functional collaboration into its predictive analytics ecosystem Starbucks should form interdisciplinary project teams, establish shared KPIs, conduct department-wide training, and involve frontline employees. Through these efforts Starbucks will apply predictive insights in ways that maintain ethical standards and maximize strategic value.

Prioritize Personalization Without Overreach

Starbucks has reached impressive milestones through predictive analytics-based hyper-personalization yet needs to consistently monitor its practices to prevent any possibility of overstepping boundaries. The growing proficiency of AI systems to customize offers and communications poses increasing risks of customer alienation by excessive targeting methods. When users interpret personalized marketing approaches as intrusive or manipulative tactics, they lose trust which leads to reduced engagement. Starbucks needs to implement personalized marketing strategies which are carefully designed with customer consent in mind while remaining aware of potential customer fatigue. Algorithms that respond too aggressively to short-term user behaviors often lead to over-personalization by generating excessive promotional messages and recommendations. Sathianathan and Ray (2023) found that AI systems that focus exclusively on engagement metrics while neglecting long-term relational health create digital fatigue. Customers will start to believe they are monitored all the time or that the brand pushes products too strongly. Starbucks can prevent customer overload by implementing frequency caps which restrict personalized interactions to a specific number within set time intervals. Every message will be both relevant and impactful while avoiding the characteristics of spam or intrusive content. Incorporating planned "cool-off" periods throughout the personalization cycle proves to be another successful tactic. Customers receive neutral information about sustainability practices and community programs during these programmed windows instead of receiving marketing promotions. This content continues to keep users engaged but redirects attention toward building relationships rather than direct consumption. Islam et al. According to Islam et al. (2024), brands that mix promotional with non-promotional content maintain stronger long-term customer loyalty because customers view them as valuing more than just sales conversions. Starbucks uses predictive models to both market to customers and identify signs of user fatigue. The system should recognize customer actions such as dismissing notifications and deleting marketing emails as triggers to reduce outreach efforts. Gungunawat et al. According to Gungunawat et al. (2024), artificial intelligence systems need to not only stimulate activities but also maintain respect for user boundaries. Starbucks can use disengagement signals in their personalization algorithms to actively protect customers from burnout while maintaining positive customer relationships. Effective personalization requires transparency to reduce its potential negative impacts. Targeted content receives higher acceptance rates from customers who comprehend the delivery methods and reasons behind it. Starbucks needs to implement user-friendly controls that enable customers to adjust the kinds and number of recommendations they receive. Fedosova and Katunian (2024) identify consumer empowerment as essential for creating ethical and sustainable models of AI engagement. Providing users with a straightforward dashboard to modify their personalization settings helps build trust while preserving their autonomy. Starbucks needs to apply different personalization strategies to customer segments because individual customers react differently to AI-based engagement techniques. Gamified rewards and frequent interactions appeal to many users yet others prefer minimal interaction with the system. When personalization intensity matches different user types it not only shows respect but also delivers better results. Kholifah et al. Research from Kholifah et al. (2024) supports this statement because adaptive engagement styles lead to better customer satisfaction while reducing opt-out rates. The long-term nature of customer relationships requires Starbucks to see personalization as a relationship-building instrument instead of a temporary sales method. Through careful monitoring of engagement patterns combined with respect for communication boundaries and enhanced transparency and control measures, the company ensures its predictive systems remain effective without becoming intrusive. By maintaining this balance Starbucks will be able to preserve customer trust while boosting satisfaction and ensuring ethical AI use.

FUTURE RESEARCH DIRECTIONS

As Starbucks expands its use of predictive analytics and artificial intelligence (AI), ongoing research becomes vital to maintain innovation while meeting the changing requirements of customers and employees and society. The next sections pinpoint five key strategic fields in which Starbucks can participate in meaningful research to improve AI systems' effectiveness and ethical standards while promoting inclusivity.

Explainable AI (XAI) and Transparency

The advanced predictive systems of Starbucks operate as "black boxes" which prevents customers and employees from understanding how specific decisions and recommendations are generated. The absence of transparency acts as a barrier to AI adoption by reducing trust between users and systems and complicating the identification of AI output errors or biases. As Rengasamy (2025) and Gungunawat et al. Research published in 2024 proposes that explainable AI should become a primary research focus to address transparency issues. The next phase of research could target the optimal methods for embedding real-time explanations within the Starbucks app that clarify why specific offers appear to users and reveal the logic behind product recommendation algorithms. By implementing these measures users would develop better comprehension while feeling less monitored or manipulated. Starbucks can fund studies on XAI tools to assist store managers and operational teams in understanding algorithmic predictions about inventory management and scheduling performance. The adaptability of XAI frameworks such as SHAP and LIME should be assessed when applied to customer-facing scenarios (Cherian et al., 2025). An examination of how these tools impact customer trust levels alongside opt-in rates and fairness perceptions would enable Starbucks to establish an evidence-based approach for designing responsible AI systems. Through its dedication to explainability Starbucks becomes a transparent industry leader which meets growing worldwide demands for algorithmic accountability.

Sustainability-Focused Predictive Modeling

Starbucks has begun to explore the use of predictive analytics as a method to advance its environmental sustainability initiatives. AI has been used to improve business efficiency but now provides effective methods for guiding customers toward greener choices while reducing environmental damage. As Okeke et al. According to Okeke et al. (2024), predictive systems that support sustainability goals transform corporate responsibility into tangible experiences for consumers. Future research should investigate the ways Starbucks could implement AI to drive customers toward reusable cup usage while recommending menu items with lower carbon emissions and rewarding sustainable customer choices. Predictive models can pinpoint customers who will react well to eco-promotions and adapt messaging to reach them. A/B experiments in the Starbucks app or loyalty program can test which personalized nudges drive customers towards sustainable behaviors. Research initiatives could explore how supply chain forecasting tools reduce waste through their ability to identify excess inventory and enhance delivery routes for reduced emissions. The research by Babadoğan (2024) shows how sustainability-integrated

AI holds strategic importance in the context of rising environmentally conscious consumer trends. Starbucks could establish itself as a leader in the industry by sponsoring research or forming partnerships to show how predictive analytics drives both company profits and environmental health.

Cross-Cultural and Localized Personalization

Starbucks has stores throughout more than 80 nations which require them to handle diverse cultural and economic conditions together with distinct consumer behavior patterns. Predictive models that use U.S.-based data might fail to capture international customer preferences leading to less effective personalization strategies or cultural errors. Babadoğan (2024) and Adeoye et al. Both Barbadian (2024) and Adeoye et al. (2024) emphasize that local context plays a crucial role in creating AI systems that are both meaningful and ethical. It is necessary to conduct research that examines how cultural standards combined with buying patterns and linguistic choices affect consumer reactions to personalized marketing. Starbucks can back ethnographically research alongside market-specific A/B testing and sentiment analysis of regional customer input to develop models that adapt better to cultural differences. Health-conscious product recommendations might have better performance compared to seasonal promotions in certain areas while in other regions seasonal promotions could outperform health product suggestions. According to Kamaruzzaman (2022), Starbucks successfully adapted its in-store products and app features to meet Malaysian consumers' expectations during unique cultural times by using AI-driven customer profiling. Continued research should build upon these examples to establish a universal framework for “cultural adaptability” in AI systems. Starbucks will be able to deliver better customer experiences to various population groups by steering clear of universal personalization methods.

Fairness and Bias Mitigation in Algorithms

The automation of customer interaction and business decision processes at Starbucks must be managed to ensure fair operation and prevent unintentional disadvantages for specific customer groups. When predictive analytics systems lack proper design and testing procedures, they risk reinforcing existing social inequities and magnifying them further. Kholifah et al. (2024) and Okeke et al. The research by Kholifah et al. (2024) shows that algorithmic discrimination emerges from biased training data along with skewed assumptions in models that exclude underrepresented populations. Researchers should investigate future studies to understand systemic biases within Starbucks' predictive models. Auditing under-targeted customer segments in promotions and those who receive fewer loyalty incentives but show high churn rates despite similar behaviors should be part of future research. The application of fairness-aware machine learning techniques such as re-weighting and threshold adjustments provides testable solutions when combined with inclusive data sampling. Research could examine how customers perceive fairness in personalized experiences. The research by Fedosova and Katunian (2024) asserts that ethical AI performance requires both objective equity and the perception of fairness and inclusivity. Through backing independent research efforts and organizing research competitions that target fairness metrics within retail AI Starbucks can demonstrate a stronger dedication to responsible and equitable technological advancement.

Real-time AI and edge computing will enhance customer experience

The development of customer engagement systems will depend heavily on responsiveness and seamless interaction while convenience remains paramount as real-time AI and edge computing becomes more integral. Local data processing technologies (on-device or at the edge) minimize response time while protecting customer privacy and enabling rapid decision-making in drive-thru, in-store kiosk and mobile app ordering systems (Islam et al., 2024). Starbucks could spearhead research efforts that determine how new technology implementations enhance customer satisfaction and business operations. Research could analyze how voice-ordering systems that leverage customer history perform compared to self-service checkouts which utilize real-time personalization techniques. Edge computing enables privacy-sensitive personalization by reducing the requirement to transfer raw data to central servers. Research by Dutta (2024) and Rengasamy (2025) demonstrates that brand interactions improve using generative and contextual AI applications like dynamic menus and store greetings which operate efficiently on local fast-processing systems. Starbucks should consider forming alliances with AI hardware companies and UX designers while consulting usability experts to establish effective methods for deploying real-time edge AI solutions throughout its worldwide branches.

CONCLUSION

Through predictive analytics and artificial intelligence (AI) integration Starbucks achieved global prominence as a leader in customer-focused innovation. Starbucks has developed a sophisticated feedback-driven model utilizing Deep Brew platforms and a data-rich mobile ecosystem to achieve real-time personalization along with optimized operations and scalable decision-making. The chapter investigated the ways predictive analytics improve essential business functions such as personalized marketing efforts and inventory management while also strengthening customer retention and supporting strategic company growth. Through these applications businesses demonstrate a fundamental transition in AI usage which extends beyond efficiency to establish deeper consumer connections. Key findings show that Starbucks uses predictive analytics to understand and anticipate customer behavior accurately. Starbucks improved customer satisfaction and lifetime value by providing timely product suggestions along with relevant promotional offers. AI models decreased waste and better organized labor scheduling while maximizing store performance and enabling a more agile supply chain response. While these benefits bring considerable advantages, they also present ethical and technical challenges which require active management. This chapter presented multiple solutions to assist Starbucks in addressing their challenges through enhanced data governance as well as investments in explainable AI along with controlled personalization intensity. The chapter highlighted both cross-functional teamwork and continuous innovation as essential elements. The Starbucks Predictive Analytics Value Loop (SPAVL) conceptual model demonstrates the recurring process of data-based decision-making while showing Starbucks' approach to refining insights based on customer feedback and real-time data metrics. Looking forward, the chapter identified five key areas for future research: The chapter outlines five future research areas including explainability of system operations, sustainability modeling methods, personalization across cultures, fairness principles in algorithmic systems, and edge computing technologies for customer service applications. These five domains provide Starbucks with fresh chances to demonstrate ethical leadership while adapting to changing customer needs and regulatory standards. The use of predictive analytics has become a fundamental factor driving Starbucks' business expansion and its leading position in the market. Starbucks will maintain its success by implementing these technologies through transparent, ethical, and inclusive methods. Starbucks will guarantee AI drives beneficial changes across customer experiences and retail environments when it combines innovation with accountability.

REFERENCES

Adanyin, A. (2024). *Rethinking Black Friday: How AI can drive 'small batch' personalized deals*. World Journal of Advanced Research and Reviews., DOI: 10.30574/wjarr.2024.21.1.2611

. Adeoye, O. B., Okoye, C. C., Ofodile, O. C., Odeyemi, O., Addy, W. A., & Ajayi-Nifise, A. O. (2024). Integrating artificial intelligence in personalized insurance products: A pathway to enhanced customer engagement. *International Journal of Management & Entrepreneurship Research*. DOI: 10.51594/ijmer.v6i3.840

Babadoğan, B. (2024). *Harnessing AI and predictive analytics to revolutionize customer retention strategies*. Next Frontier for Life Sciences and AI., DOI: 10.62802/k2a4gf39

Boinapalli, N. R., Farhan, K. A., Allam, A. R., Nizamuddin, M., & Sridharlakshmi, N. R. B. (2023). *AI-enhanced IMC: Leveraging data analytics for targeted marketing campaigns*. Asian Business Review., DOI: 10.18034/abr.v13i3.729

Cherian, M., Manoja, K. G., & Abhinav, A. (2025). Leveraging AI for predicting marketing and customer insights—An overview. *Journal of Informatics Education and Research*. DOI: 10.52783/jier.v5i1.2050

Delliana, S., & Arisandi, V. D. (2020). The influence of promotion via LINE Messenger on the attitude of Starbucks' LINE official account followers. *The Winners*, *21*(2), 155–161. DOI: 10.21512/tw.v21i2.6812

Dutta, S. S. (2024). *Revolutionizing retail: An empirical study on the impact of generative AI in omnichannel strategies*. International Journal For Multidisciplinary Research., DOI: 10.36948/ijfmr.2024.v06i05.28799

Fedosova, K., & Katunian, A. (2024). *The use of artificial intelligence in the restaurant business*. Turystyka i Rozwój Regionalny., DOI: 10.22630/TIRR.2024.22.16

Gajjar, T. (2024). Revolutionizing retail: The synergy of AI and AR. SSRN *Electronic Journal*. DOI: 10.2139/ssrn.4778277

Ge, Y., Yuan, Q., Wang, Y., & Park, K. (2021). The structural relationship among perceived service quality, perceived value, and customer satisfaction—Focused on Starbucks Reserve Coffee Shops in Shanghai, China. *Sustainability (Basel)*, *13*(15), 8633. DOI: 10.3390/su13158633

Gungunawat, A., Khandelwal, N., & Gupta, N. (2024). *AI-powered personalization in digital marketing: Transforming consumer engagement and strategy*. Research Review International Journal of Multidisciplinary., DOI: 10.31305/rrijm.2024.v09.n11.026

Hakim, A. A., & Mulyani, A. S. (2024). Starbucks company marketing strategy in facing the Covid-19 pandemic: Case study report 2020. *Indonesian Journal of Interdisciplinary Research in Science and Technology*. DOI: 10.55927/marcopolo.v2i1.7430

Hou, Y., Zhu, T., & Zhang, X. (2024). *Analysis of factors affecting customer loyalty to Starbucks*. Advances in Economics, Management and Political Sciences., DOI: 10.54254/2754-1169/92/20231235

Islam, R., Arafat, M. S., Jony, M. A. M., Rafi, S., Jalil, M. S., & Hossen, F. (2024). *Hyper-personalization with AI and edge computing: The future of customer experience in e-commerce and retail*. Advanced International Journal of Multidisciplinary Research., DOI: 10.62127/aijmr.2024.v02i06.1114

Kamaruzzaman, Z. (2022). Customer profiling and segmentation of Starbucks Malaysia: Empirical investigation during CMCO 2.0. *The 5th Innovation and Analytics Conference & Exhibition (IACE 2021)*. DOI: 10.1063/5.0092729

. Kholifah, N., Mahrinasari, M. S., & Roslina, R. (2024). The influence of customer relationship marketing and brand image on customer loyalty with customer satisfaction as a mediation variable (Study on Starbucks Coffee Indonesia). *Journal of Economics, Finance and Management Studies*. DOI: 10.47191/jefms/v7-i3-16

Kotha, R. (2020). Leveraging AI for predictive analytics in customer loyalty program. [IJSR]. *International Journal of Science and Research (Raipur, India)*, *9*(3), 1713–1717. Advance online publication. DOI: 10.21275/SR24923131127

Matharoo, S. (2024). Transforming retail: Elevating customer experience and efficiency with generative AI technique. *Asian Journal of Research in Computer Science*. DOI: 10.9734/ajrcos/2024/v17i12537

Ng, T. L., Rusiman, M. S., Suparman, S., Hamzah, F., & Ebas, N. A. (2022). Factors affecting customer loyalty on Starbucks Malaysia using binary logistics and probit model. *2022 IEEE International Conference on Artificial Intelligence in Engineering and Technology (IICAIET)*. DOI: 10.1109/IICAIET55139.2022.9936751

Okeke, N. I., Alabi, O. A., Igwe, A. N., Ofodile, O. C., & Ewim, P. M. (2024). *AI-driven personalization framework for SMEs: Revolutionizing customer engagement and retention*. World Journal of Advanced Research and Reviews., DOI: 10.30574/wjarr.2024.24.1.3208

Rengasamy, A. (2025). AI in high-tech: Predictive analytics and customer 360. *International Journal of Scientific Research in Computer Science, Engineering and Information Technology*. DOI: 10.32628/CSEIT251112224

Sathianathan, B., & Ray, S. (2023). How AI can move customer personalisation to customer contextualisation. *Journal of AI, Robotics & Workplace Automation*. DOI: 10.69554/ZIVF4052

Suhono, H. R., & Sultan, M. A. (2020). Analysis of the relationship between consumer-based brand equity, experiential marketing, customer satisfaction, and customer loyalty at Starbucks Coffee in Karawang. *JRB-Jurnal Riset Bisnis*. https://doi.org/DOI: 10.35592/JRB.V4I1.1692

KEY TERMS AND DEFINTIONS

Algorithmic Bias: AI systems have systematic errors which lead to biased and unjust results.

Artificial Intelligence (AI): Artificial Intelligence represents systems that emulate human judgment to streamline operations and derive insights.

Customer Retention: Approaches to maintain long-term customer engagement and loyalty.

Deep Brew: Starbucks uses Deep Brew as its own AI engine to personalize experiences and manage operations.

Explainable AI (XAI): Explainable AI systems deliver outputs with transparent and understandable reasoning behind their decisions.

Personalization: Tailoring services and content to individual users through their specific data.

Predictive Analytics: Predictive Analytics involves analyzing data through algorithms to predict future customer behavior.

Chapter 5
How Netflix Uses AI to Personalize Content for Individual Viewers

Kanwal Zahara
https://orcid.org/0009-0005-6549-4229
University of Bedfordshire, Luton, UK

ABSTRACT

Netflix dominates the streaming marketplace by implementing Artificial Intelligence (AI) to deliver personalized content using collaborative filtering combined with deep learning techniques. Reinforcement learning combined with natural language processing enables real-time analysis of user actions and emotional responses. The system refines its recommendations by applying matrix factorization and ranking algorithms to data from user play actions and skips. A/B testing confirms that these AI approaches increase user engagement while minimizing decision fatigue. The issues of algorithmic bias along with privacy concerns and filter bubbles remain unresolved according to studies. The use of AI by Netflix transforms content consumption and triggers ethical debates surrounding personalized entertainment.

BACKGROUND

AI technology has revolutionized entertainment especially through its impact on personalized content delivery. Initial AI applications which used expert systems and decision trees to predict user preferences provided only basic customization options through manual curation methods like video rentals and standardized cable programming (Khandelwal, 2023; Sunitha, 2024; Hsiao, 2024). The 1990s witnessed a significant transformation through collaborative filtering which created personal-

DOI: 10.4018/979-8-3373-6582-4.ch005

ized recommendations by assessing user behaviour patterns in large datasets (Joseph et al., 2025; Babatunde et al., 2024). The development of intelligent recommender systems started at that point and created the foundation for personalization based on data analysis. Netflix took the lead in this area when it moved from DVD rentals to streaming services in 2007. The initial recommendation models operated using basic weighted averages to process user ratings (Bhavani & Sai, 2024). The 2006 Netflix Prize advanced innovation through a competition that tasked data scientists with achieving a 10% improvement in the Cinematch algorithm. The competition demonstrated the commercial importance of personalization even though they did not implement the winning model because it was too complex (Khandelwal, 2023; Babatunde et al., 2024). Netflix implemented machine learning techniques during the 2010s which analysed viewing patterns along with session lengths and demographic data. The industry quickly adopted hybrid systems which combined collaborative filtering with content-based recommendations. Deep learning improved personalization by discovering nonlinear connections between user preferences and content features according to Babadoğan (2024) and Sevaslidou et al. (2024). Netflix utilized convolutional and recurrent neural networks to analyses video frames as well as audio and subtitle tracks to enhance content matching capabilities (Sunitha, 2024). Netflix used reinforcement learning to measure user engagement by rewarding actions that resulted in longer viewing sessions (Joseph et al., 2025). Content relevance was indicated by implicit behavioural signals such as pauses and rewinds. Through AI integration Netflix improved user experience by optimizing interfaces and personalizing content dynamically while processing natural language which enabled them to deliver real-time recommendations that adapt to changing user preferences (Meza & D'Urso, 2024; Harshavardhan et al., 2024). Netflix led the development of ensemble models which integrated multiple algorithmic outputs to achieve higher accuracy. Netflix utilized predictive analytics to produce original shows like House of Cards by analysing audience preferences across different genres and favorite actors and directors (Khandelwal, 2023). Dynamic artwork personalization combined A/B testing with computer vision to adjust promotional thumbnails according to user engagement patterns as described by Bhavani & Sai in 2024. Netflix implemented explainable AI (XAI) to address algorithmic transparency concerns by enabling users to comprehend the reasoning behind their recommendations (Sevaslidou et al., 2024). With the expansion of digital content effective personalization remains vital to maintaining user satisfaction and retention (Ichino et al., 2023). The capacity of Netflix to extend viewing sessions and minimize subscription cancellations sets it apart from competitors like Disney+ and HBO Max (Han, 2024). However, ethical issues persist. Major issues like data privacy violations along with algorithmic biases and filter bubbles draw attention from experts (Babadoğan, 2024; Reddy et al., 2025). Netflix needs to maintain transparent systems that respect user autonomy while advancing their innovation to ensure equitable treatment. Netflix demonstrates how artificial intelligence can transform digital entertainment through behavioural insights and predictive modelling which enables responsible personalization.

Focus of the Chapter

Artificial intelligence (AI) advancements have enabled the transformation from mass distribution to individualize viewing experiences (Bhavani & Sai, 2024; Sunitha, 2024). Netflix sets industry standards in content personalization worldwide through its advanced AI techniques which analyse user behaviour patterns (Hsiao, 2024; Babadoğan, 2024). This chapter examines Netflix's implementation of sophisticated AI techniques including collaborative filtering, deep learning, reinforcement learning, and real-time behavioural analytics to analyses user engagement at scale according to Harshavardhan et al. (2024) and Han (2024). The recommendation engine used by Netflix determines personal viewing selections while simultaneously impacting widespread consumer patterns and societal cultural developments (Reddy et al., 2025; Sipos, 2025). Studies of Netflix's AI system reveal personalization approaches that can be used in multiple fields including e-commerce and education (Sevaslidou et al., 2024; Joseph et al., 2025). Personalized delivery has emerged as an essential element for holding users' attention and securing competitive strength in today's digital content landscape (Haqqo & Isharina, 2024; Seth, 2024). This chapter examines how Netflix employs multiple AI technologies from personalized recommendation systems to dynamic thumbnail alterations adaptive streaming quality adjustments and content development driven by data analysis (Sunitha, 2024; Khandelwal, 2023). The AI applications generate better user satisfaction results while increasing session lengths and minimizing customer turnover rates (Bhavani & Sai, 2024; Meza & D'Urso, 2024). The task of mitigating algorithmic bias alongside filter bubble effects and preserving user data privacy presents ongoing challenges (Babadoğan, 2024; Li et al., 2023). This chapter examines how Netflix's recommendation engine responds in real time to user feedback and various contextual preferences such as time-specific and seasonal patterns (Han, 2024; Joseph et al., 2025). The discussion covers ethical concerns about AI personalization effects on user autonomy as described by Sipos (2025) and Ichino et al. (2023). This chapter analyses the ways Netflix's AI systems improve user engagement while shaping ethical standards for digital content personalization as per Lee & Kim (2024) and Sevaslidou et al. (2024). Research reveals Netflix's entertainment personalization advancements establish new interaction standards and responsibilities for consumers in digital platforms (Reddy et al., 2025; Ding et al., 2024).

Current Applications

Personalized Content Recommendations

The main way Netflix engages viewers is by using AI to deliver content suggestions tailored to their unique viewing patterns (Bhavani & Sai, 2024; Sunitha, 2024). The system's recommendation engine analyses comprehensive user data such as viewing history and search behaviour alongside interaction times and device usage to develop personalized content profiles for every viewer (Harshavardhan et al., 2024; Han, 2024). This system builds on collaborative filtering by matching viewers with similar habits to recommend content that like-minded users have enjoyed (Joseph et al., 2025; Babatunde et al., 2024). Netflix utilizes this method to capture common viewing patterns that enable effective content personalization (Khandelwal, 2023; Sevaslidou et al., 2024). Content-based filtering at Netflix examines details such as genre, cast, and director to provide recommendations consistent with each user's viewing history (Lee & Kim, 2024; Haqqo & Isharina, 2024). The hybrid recommendation model integrates collaborative filtering with content-based techniques to enhance recommendation relevance and diversity (Bhavani & Sai, 2024; Reddy et al., 2025). Deep learning advances the process by detecting subtle user preferences which traditional techniques fail to capture including emotional tone and visual composition (Babadoğan, 2024; Sipos, 2025). The models facilitate recommendations that cross multiple genres for viewers who appreciate emotionally powerful or visually stunning content according to Wang et al., 2023 and Ding et al., 2024. Homepage content layouts and title placements receive adjustments through reinforcement learning algorithms which analyse engagement patterns with the goal of delivering maximized personalized experiences (Joseph et al., 2025; Li et al., 2023). User sessions become longer because real-time adjustments lower browsing fatigue and speed up the decision-making process (Lee & Kim, 2024; Meza & D'Urso, 2024). The refined Netflix algorithm utilizes implicit user feedback patterns such as hover time and skipped scenes to improve recommendations because explicit user ratings are infrequent according to research by Sevaslidou et al. (2024) and Ichino et al. (2023). Recent innovations apply contextual factors such as time of day, device type, and location to generate recommendations tailored to specific environments (Sunitha, 2024; Reddy et al., 2025). Netflix enhances user satisfaction and builds loyalty worldwide by using its AI strategies to boost subscriber engagement (Li et al., 2023; Seth, 2024).

Behavioural and Deep Learning Analytics

Netflix employs behavioural analytics as a fundamental part of its operational model to analyse user behaviour and improve interactions between users and the platform according to Joseph et al. (2025) and Reddy et al. (2025). The platform uses detailed user action tracking to gather implicit feedback which delivers deeper insights compared to traditional rating systems that face challenges from sparse data and user bias (Sevaslidou et al., 2024; Meza & D'Urso, 2024). Netflix's real-time behavioural tracking system identifies nuanced patterns of user satisfaction and disengagement (Sunitha, 2024; Han, 2024). The occurrence of viewers leaving a show soon after beginning demonstrates that recommended content does not match their actual preferences according to research findings (Li et al., 2023; Ding et al., 2024). Through machine learning algorithms Netflix examines subtle user behaviours to constantly refine user profiles while delivering more precise content recommendations (Harshavardhan et al., 2024; Babatunde et al., 2024). Netflix utilizes deep learning technologies including recurrent neural networks (RNNs) and convolutional neural networks (CNNs) to model user viewing sequences and recognize intricate viewing patterns (Bhavani & Sai, 2024; Ichino et al., 2023). Recurrent neural networks (RNNs) evaluate content viewing sequences and timings to forecast future preferences from past user activity (Zhang et al., 2023; Sipos, 2025). CNN architectures initially built for image recognition now serve to analyse content metadata while identifying visual and audio clues from video material to personalize user experiences (Lee & Kim, 2024; Hsiao, 2024). Netflix develops a comprehensive profile of viewer preferences and their underlying motivations through the combination of behavioural data analysis and content feature assessment (Babadoğan, 2024; Haqqo & Isharina, 2024). Attention mechanisms incorporated into deep learning architectures enable the prioritization of behavioural signals that best predict future user engagement (Chen et al., 2024; Meza & D'Urso, 2024). The actions users take before ending a session serve as key indicators for forecasting their next viewing choices (Joseph et al., 2025; Li et al., 2023). Netflix employs multi-task learning frameworks to predict multiple viewer outcomes simultaneously including whether a user will begin a new release or complete an ongoing series which relies on their historical behaviour patterns (Zhang et al., 2023; Han, 2024). Personalized homepage categories such as "Continue Watching," "Trending Now," and "Because You Watched X" benefit from models that enhance content recommendation relevance (Sunitha, 2024; Sevaslidou et al., 2024). Netflix relies on deep learning-based cold-start solutions to produce helpful recommendations for new users when their interaction data remains scarce according to Li et al. (2023) and Reddy et al. (2025).

Early user behaviours like navigation clicks and hover durations become interaction embeddings which drive real-time recommendation accuracy right from when users begin their experience (Lee & Kim, 2024; Harshavardhan et al., 2024). Reinforcement learning models targeted at long-term user engagement prioritize sustained session interactions through time-based rewards instead of focusing on immediate click-through rates (Chen et al., 2024; Joseph et al., 2025). Netflix combines behavioural analytics with deep learning to create a personalized entertainment experience that adapts to user behaviour through dynamic content discovery (Babadoğan, 2024; Gómez-Uribe & Hunt, 2022).

Dynamic Personalized Artwork

Netflix implements dynamic personalized artwork generated by AI to enhance user engagement through visual appeal optimization before user's access content (Chen et al., 2024; Sunitha, 2024). Netflix constructed machine learning algorithms for creating viewer-specific thumbnail images because visual stimuli impact user decisions (Liu & Zhang, 2023; Li et al., 2023). Netflix assigns multiple artwork variations to each title instead of using a single poster or standard image (Wang et al., 2024; Bhavani & Sai, 2024). The AI systems determine optimal thumbnails by studying both viewer behaviour history and aesthetic preferences according to research by Gómez-Uribe & Hunt (2022) and Reddy et al. (2025). Netflix's AI delivers Good Will Hunting thumbnails with romantic emotional scenes to users who enjoy romance while showing comedy-focused viewers more light-hearted visuals (Li et al., 2024; Liu & Zhang, 2023). Netflix's AI system examines character prominence together with facial expressions and colour schemes to create emotionally engaging and visually appealing thumbnails (Wang et al., 2024; Lee & Kim, 2024). Netflix employs convolutional neural networks (CNNs) to process thousands of video frames and identify images that maximize user engagement (Gómez-Uribe & Hunt, 2022; Harshavardhan et al., 2024). Artwork personalization occurs when AI models process visual elements alongside user preferences for female leads or thrilling stories (Li et al., 2024; Babadoğan, 2024). Machine learning techniques assess past user interactions to identify which design elements including brightness, facial positioning and genre signalling generate the greatest number of clicks (Chen et al., 2024; Joseph et al., 2025). Netflix conducts A/B testing to display different artwork versions of the same title to various users in order to measure which versions achieve better user engagement according to Wang et al. (2024) and Meza & D'Urso (2024). The effectiveness of thumbnails can be assessed through key metrics including click-through rates and average watch durations (Gómez-Uribe & Hunt, 2022; Sevaslidou et al., 2024). The 2023 study by Liu & Zhang demonstrates that customized artwork decreases browsing time while simultaneously enhancing content discovery and the number of titles viewed per session. Dynamic artwork reduces decision-making cognitive load which leads to smoother platform experiences and higher user satisfaction according to Chen et al., 2024 and Han, 2024. Netflix implements personalized thumbnails to address content overload and reduce decision fatigue as their content libraries expand (Li et al., 2024; Ichino et al., 2023). The process of guiding users to relevant content via visual cues enhances their engagement and retention by simplifying the selection process (Wang et al., 2024; Seth, 2024). Netflix stands out as a pioneer in content personalization by continuously developing dynamic artwork that uses subtle, data-driven design to influence viewer choices (Gómez-Uribe & Hunt, 2022; Babatunde et al., 2024). Ongoing testing combined with refinement processes maintain both visual appeal and personal relevance in thumbnail experiences for every user (Liu & Zhang, 2023; Harshavardhan et al., 2024).

Streaming Optimization

Netflix uses artificial intelligence (AI) techniques to improve streaming performance, so users enjoy uninterrupted playback and consistent video quality across various network conditions and devices (Bhavani & Sai, 2024; Gupta et al., 2023). The platform needs to deliver uninterrupted playback across varying bandwidth conditions to meet user expectations and maintain subscriber loyalty (Zhang & Li, 2024; Wang et al., 2024). Netflix achieves seamless streaming performance by using adaptive bitrate streaming technology enhanced by AI to dynamically modify video resolution and compression according to current user bandwidth and device capabilities (Lee et al., 2024; Gupta et al., 2023). The platform uses machine learning algorithms to predict network changes which allows it to adjust streaming parameters ahead of time and prevent playback disruptions (Wang et al., 2024; Zhang & Li, 2024). The predictive models combine historical performance data with information about user location, ISP quality, and device specifications to improve video delivery precision according to research by Lee et al. (2024) and Gupta et al. (2023). Through dynamic optimizer encoding Netflix assigns variable bitrates across a single title to allocate more data for fast-paced sequences and lower bitrates to static or dialogue-focused scenes (Gupta et al., 2023; Lee et al., 2024). The content-aware encoding method maintains superior visual quality while minimizing bandwidth usage which proves essential for users who face limitations with their data plans (Wang et al., 2024; Zhang & Li, 2024). Netflix employs the Per-Title Encode Optimization system which uses user viewing patterns to improve encoding capabilities and develop progressively over time (Zhang & Li, 2024; Bhavani &

Sai, 2024). Netflix's content delivery network benefits from reinforcement learning technology which dynamically chooses the most efficient servers based on speed and geographic proximity to reduce latency and enhance loading speed (Gupta et al., 2023; Bhavani & Sai, 2024). Netflix uses predictive prefetching algorithms which analyse user interactions during video sessions to preload subsequent segments and reduce buffering for seamless viewing according to Lee et al., 2024 and Wang et al., 2024. The method results in faster load times while enhancing the user experience through smoother operation. AI systems optimize video delivery by adjusting video bitrate according to whether the user accesses content via Wi-Fi, 4G or 5G networks to maintain a balance between data usage and viewing quality (Zhang & Li, 2024; Gupta et al., 2023). Netflix achieves top-notch streaming for all devices and regions through machine learning strategies which adapt to network changes (Lee et al., 2024; Wang et al., 2024). The AI-driven streaming optimization delivers improved platform performance and user satisfaction while enabling sustained global subscriber expansion (Bhavani & Sai, 2024; Gupta et al., 2023).

Data-Driven Original Content Development

Netflix uses artificial intelligence and data analytics to create original content which successfully engages intended audience segments (Chen et al., 2024; Bhavani & Sai, 2024). Through sophisticated data mining and machine learning methods the platform examines worldwide viewing behaviours to identify new patterns as well as user preferences and content voids (Wang et al., 2024; Joseph et al., 2025). Strategic production decisions derive from insights about demographic profiles along with geographic data and the interests of specific viewer micro-communities (Zhang et al., 2023; Harshavardhan et al., 2024). Netflix recognized international demand growth for Spanish-language programming and achieved success with Money Heist and Elite to illustrate its strategic alignment of creative decisions based on global audience demands (Gómez-Uribe & Hunt, 2022; Sevaslidou et al., 2024). Through behavioural signals including completion rates and binge-watching patterns alongside rewatches and browsing habits machine learning models forecast potential content success according to Lee & Kim (2024) and Li et al. (2023). Predictive instruments assist in ordering creative ideas before distributing significant production funds as shown by Smith & Anderson (2023) and Babatunde et al. (2024). NLP tools enhance creative processes through script examination and detection of theme patterns while mapping emotional tones according to Chen et al. (2024) and Sunitha (2024). Netflix analyses script metadata and dialogue content to assign projects to known genres and develop new categories that reflect current audience preferences (Wang et al., 2024; Reddy et al., 2025). Production logistics including casting choices, location selection and episode length optimization leverage AI-generated insights (Zhang et al., 2023;

Meza & D'Urso, 2024). Casting decisions are based on historical performance data for actors alongside past engagement and subscription behaviour metrics (Smith & Anderson, 2023; Han, 2024). The success of Stranger Things stems from AI models which forecasted popularity for 1980s nostalgia and ensemble-driven sci-fi content that led to aggressive marketing campaigns targeting multiple age demographics (Gómez-Uribe & Hunt, 2022; Lee & Kim, 2024). Advanced AI systems conduct risk evaluations for expensive projects through pre-greenlight audience reaction simulations (Chen et al., 2024; Babadoğan, 2024). The simulations analyse essential performance metrics such as expected completion rates together with social media resonance and retention impacts (Wang et al., 2024; Joseph et al., 2025). AI helps regional content strategy identify unserved markets that enable culturally specific productions which drive the worldwide success of series such as Sacred Games and Lupin (Zhang et al., 2023; Gómez-Uribe & Hunt, 2022). Netflix has transformed entertainment production through its systematic use of AI and data analytics by replacing traditional intuition-based decisions with predictive creative models (Lee & Kim, 2024; Seth, 2024). The strategy focuses on directing investments towards audience needs which boosts operational efficiency and extends market reach.

Key Findings

Scholarly studies show that Netflix's AI personalization methods notably boost user involvement while raising academic research interest (Harshavardhan et al., 2024; Sipos, 2025). Netflix created its best-practice model for AI deployment in digital customer experience settings through the combination of personalized recommendation systems and streaming optimization technologies along with dynamic content presentation together with data-driven content creation strategies (Khandelwal, 2023; Sunitha, 2024). User experience engineering utilizes personalization methods to guide content discovery while influencing both user satisfaction and platform engagement (Sevaslidou et al., 2024; Joseph et al., 2025). Netflix sustains its adaptation to changing viewer behaviors alongside new technologies and global market dynamics through ongoing AI algorithm refinement (Sunitha, 2024; Bhavani & Sai, 2024). The 2025 research by Sipos analyses Netflix's personalization methodologies and discusses their strengths and weaknesses while examining their impact on digital media consumers and industry patterns (Sipos, 2025; Babadoğan, 2024).

Personalised Recommendations Drive User Satisfaction and Retention

Netflix utilizes its personalized recommendation system to build its strategy which aims to improve user satisfaction and establish long-term platform loyalty

(Gómez-Uribe & Hunt, 2022; Wang et al., 2023). Studies indicate that users experience greater platform utility and value from recommendations that align with their individual preferences (Li et al., 2023). Netflix reduces decision fatigue for users by making content choice easier through its personalized recommendations (Chen et al., 2024; Sunitha, 2024). The enhanced discovery mechanisms lead to users watching for extended periods while showing increased engagement levels (Wang et al., 2023). Active user metrics increase when users can easily find relevant content which leads to improved platform performance (Chen et al., 2024; Joseph et al., 2025). Subscription services gain higher perceived value through personalization by adapting to users' personal preferences and their changing behaviours (Reddy et al., 2025). The algorithms used by Netflix develop through detailed analysis of user behaviour data including viewing time and navigation trends to enhance recommendation accuracy (Bhavani & Sai, 2024). Machine learning systems recognize subtle shifts in user behaviour to maintain recommendations that match user preferences (Chen et al., 2024; Harshavardhan et al., 2024). Research shows that personalizing content suggestions reduces subscriber turnover because engaged users tend to continue their subscriptions (Gómez-Uribe & Hunt, 2022; Li et al., 2023). Netflix uses AI technology to boost content diversity by delivering niche titles to appropriate audiences across its extensive collection (Wang et al., 2023; Babatunde et al., 2024). The expansion of content library enhances the system's recommendation capabilities which improves user satisfaction worldwide alongside platform development (Sevaslidou et al., 2024). Netflix's personalized recommendation system builds stronger user connections by delivering customized viewing experiences which fosters brand loyalty and keeps the company at the forefront of the streaming industry (Seth, 2024).

Cluster-based Recommendation Systems Improve Speed and Accuracy

Netflix improves personalization speed and precision through cluster-based recommendation systems which organize users sharing similar viewing patterns to manage computational demands and support scalability (Bhavani & Sai, 2024; Han, 2024). These recommendation models segment users into behaviour-focused clusters to make personalized suggestions by comparing users to a smaller relevant group instead of the entire user base in contrast with traditional user-item collaborative filtering (Harshavardhan et al., 2024; Haqqo & Isharina, 2024). Netflix maintains high performance levels while providing real-time recommendations to its global audience through system efficiency (Wang et al., 2023; Sevaslidou et al., 2024). Netflix dynamically organizes users through k-means and hierarchical clustering techniques which are enhanced by deep learning methods to monitor changing preferences (Li et al., 2023; Sunitha, 2024). Neural networks paired with unsupervised models identify features from viewing behaviours to organize users into precise clusters that reflect their multifaceted interests (Bhavani & Sai, 2024; Chen et al., 2024). These methods enhance personalization for users who have minimal interaction history and effectively address the cold-start issue (Han, 2024; Sevaslidou et al., 2024). Direct assignment of users to clusters enables personalized recommendations immediately after account creation thus boosting early engagement and minimizing customer turnover (Li et al., 2023; Meza & D'Urso, 2024). When users are sorted into interest-based groups, the system exposes them to trending content within these clusters which boosts recommendation diversity and allows discovery beyond their usual viewing history (Sipos, 2025; Seth, 2024). The strategy allows users to avoid filter bubbles and discover new genres without being bombarded by irrelevant options (Haqqo & Isharina, 2024; Babatunde et al., 2024). Cluster-based systems also improve technical efficiency. Netflix uses common viewing patterns analysis to distribute content more effectively across its delivery network and manage server loads worldwide (Harshavardhan et al., 2024; Reddy et al., 2025). By storing popular titles close to user clusters that share similar tastes Netflix achieves reduced latency and lowers operational expenses (Sunitha, 2024). Netflix uses explainable AI (XAI) methods like adding labels to recommendations with descriptions such as "Recommended because users like you watched…" to enhance transparency and build user trust (Meza & D'Urso, 2024; Sevaslidou et al., 2024). Netflix's cluster-based systems use innovative methods to provide personalized, scalable and efficient content recommendations that reach its worldwide audience.

Streaming Optimization Boosts Overall Satisfaction

Netflix believes streaming optimization plays a critical role in user satisfaction because it allows for continuous viewing regardless of differing devices and network conditions (Bhavani & Sai, 2024; Wang et al., 2024). The platform utilizes AI-powered adaptive bitrate streaming (ABR) technology to automatically modify video resolution according to current bandwidth conditions in order to reduce buffering and deliver consistent video playback (Gupta et al., 2023; Lee & Kim, 2024). According to recent studies user dissatisfaction arises from buffering delays and loading disruptions which demonstrates why real-time optimization becomes critical for maintaining subscriber numbers (Chen et al., 2024; Meza & D'Urso, 2024). Netflix utilizes predictive models that analyse historical network performance data alongside user location and device type to foresee potential service disruptions and make necessary delivery adjustments (Gómez-Uribe & Hunt, 2022; Li et al., 2023). Dynamic optimization technologies encode video segments at different quality levels based on scene complexity to preserve visual clarity while reducing bandwidth usage

(Sunitha, 2024; Han, 2024). Adaptive streaming provides mobile users in regions with limited bandwidth access smooth video experiences even when data constraints exist (Wang et al., 2024; Reddy et al., 2025). Netflix uses predictive demand analytics to enhance its global CDN by strategically caching video files closer to users to reduce latency and improve load speed (Bhavani & Sai, 2024; Harshavardhan et al., 2024). Through this approach both global geographical consistency and responsiveness rates improve significantly. Netflix uses predictive prefetching to load the next video based on viewing patterns which creates smooth transitions for content consumption—a highly appreciated feature by binge watchers according to Chen et al. (2024) and Sevaslidou et al. (2024). Research on mobile and home streaming contexts demonstrates that user satisfaction depends on streaming stability across various devices and network conditions (Li et al., 2023; Meza & D'Urso, 2024). Netflix maintains consistent service quality across urban and rural areas through mobile-specific optimizations that adjust bitrates according to 4G or 5G fluctuations (Wang et al., 2024; Haqqo & Isharina, 2024). Netflix employs AI-based streaming optimization techniques to provide high-quality viewing experiences which leads to increased user satisfaction and maintains both immediate user engagement as well as long-term subscription retention (Sipos, 2025; Seth, 2024).

Data-driven Original Content Matches User Demands

The application of data analytics by Netflix has allowed the company to produce original content that matches the changing tastes of its audience (Chen et al., 2024; Sunitha, 2024). Netflix employs machine learning algorithms and extensive data analysis techniques to monitor popular genres and narrative trends along with viewing patterns throughout its worldwide subscriber network (Bhavani & Sai, 2024; Harshavardhan et al., 2024). Netflix analyses user behaviour and completion rate data to determine present audience preferences and uncover opportunities for new content (Gómez-Uribe & Hunt, 2022; Meza & D'Urso, 2024). Predictive insights enable the selection of projects which have high potential to deliver strong engagement and viewer satisfaction according to Wang et al. (2023) and Joseph et al. (2025). Netflix used behavioural trend analysis to understand that users were interested in science fiction with 1980s nostalgia leading to the creation of Stranger Things (Li et al., 2024; Seth, 2024). The global popularity of Money Heist (La Casa de Papel) revealed a previously underestimated demand for non-English content and demonstrated the worth of analysing cross-cultural viewing habits (Gómez-Uribe & Hunt, 2022; Sevaslidou et al., 2024). Netflix uses natural language processing tools to evaluate emotional tone and dialogue structures in scripts while analysing thematic arcs which helps the platform select content that matches viewer preferences according to Chen et al., 2024 and Babadoğan, 2024). The insights enable Netflix to focus its investments on creative projects that also promise commercial success as described by research from Gómez-Uribe & Hunt (2022) and Harshavardhan et al. (2024). Netflix uses regional and demographic segmentation analytics to customize its offerings according to cultural and generational audience preferences (Wang et al., 2023; Haqqo & Isharina, 2024). The platform decided to expand investment in Korean dramas following evidence of their growing worldwide popularity which led to major international successes including Squid Game (Li et al., 2024; Han, 2024). Netflix develops a broad content selection by pairing its expensive productions with niche shows designed for particular viewership groups which prevents market saturation (Chen et al., 2024; Sevaslidou et al., 2024). Predictive analytics from AI models optimize marketing strategies by creating campaigns based on content virality and user engagement patterns (Li et al., 2024; Babatunde et al., 2024). Selected demographics receive personalized trailers and targeted artwork along with genre-specific promotions aiming to increase initial launch appeal and maintain long-term engagement (Wang et al., 2023; Meza & D'Urso, 2024). Netflix achieves viewer satisfaction and industry leadership by using data-driven content creation and promotion methods that respond to viewer preferences and global media trends (Gómez-Uribe & Hunt, 2022; Joseph et al., 2025).

AI Personalization Builds Consumer Trust and Loyalty

The research of Sipos (2025) recognizes AI-driven personalization as an essential element for cultivating consumer trust and loyalty within services like Netflix. By matching content offerings to personal user preferences personalized recommendations improve service quality perceptions and create stronger emotional bonds with the platform (Chen et al., 2024; Babadoğan, 2024). Personalization enhances browsing experiences by cutting search time and decreasing user frustration which leads to higher user trust according to Chen et al., 2024 and Meza & D'Urso, 2024. Gómez-Uribe & Hunt (2022) found that delivering relevant content consistently keeps users engaged and encourages them to recommend the service to friends. Netflix achieves industry-leading low churn rates through comprehensive personalization of user experiences from the initial onboarding process through to sustained long-term engagement (Wang et al., 2023; Bhavani & Sai, 2024). Lee & Kim (2024) discovered that new users form positive brand impressions when they encounter content that matches their interests from the start. Through AI-driven personalization systems viewers develop loyalty because they receive both fresh and diverse content that maintains engagement without causing overload (Haqqo & Isharina, 2024; Harshavardhan et al., 2024). Sustaining user interest requires combining recognized content types with new discoveries to prevent recommendation fatigue syndrome (Sunitha, 2024; Sevaslidou et al., 2024). Recommendation systems that provide explanations like Netflix's "Because you watched..." feature enable users to grasp suggestion logic and build trust through transparent processes (Sipos, 2025; Sevaslidou et al., 2024). Li et al. According to Li et al. (2023) users display increased acceptance towards algorithmic recommendations once they comprehend the personalization decision-making process. According to Lee & Kim (2024) personalized services enhance brand-user relationships by providing emotional value along with recognition. Netflix's ability to make users feel understood reduces their likelihood of transferring to competitors who offer less personalized experiences (Chen et al., 2024; Reddy et al., 2025). Users typically accept platform innovations like new recommendation categories and autoplay features when personalization creates trust between them and the platform (Gómez-Uribe & Hunt, 2022; Li et al., 2023). Technological changes receive better user acceptance when they align with existing user preferences and habits (Wang et al., 2023; Seth, 2024). Netflix achieves its competitive edge through AI personalization which delivers instant user satisfaction while building long-term trust and emotional connection.

Challenges with Bias and Filter Bubbles Remain

Netflix's AI-powered recommendation systems deliver personalized experiences but still struggle with algorithmic bias issues and filter bubble effects research shows (Chen et al., 2024; Harshavardhan et al., 2024). Recommendation systems typically promote uniform content choices because they keep suggesting content of the same type which limits users' access to a variety of genres and viewpoints (Gómez-Uribe & Hunt, 2022; Sipos, 2025). While personalized content boosts immediate user engagement and satisfaction, it often results in limited and repetitive content consumption behaviours over time as shown in research by Li et al. (2023) and Sevaslidou et al. (2024). Netflix's algorithms depend extensively on previous user viewing data which could lead to content echo chambers that limit content variety and diminish long-term user satisfaction (Chen et al., 2024; Meza & D'Urso, 2024). Excessive personalization strengthens demographic and cultural biases by prioritizing dominant media content while reducing the exposure of diverse productions (Han, 2024; Reddy et al., 2025). Netflix has enhanced its regional content offerings and increased investment in non-English original programming yet faces limitations due to algorithmic prioritization of popular titles which restricts diverse media exposure (Babatunde et al., 2024; Sevaslidou et al., 2024). The implementation of discovery features represents key efforts to overcome these constraints by broadening user access to different types of content. Netflix applies randomized alongside guided content prompts to break users out of repetitive personalized loops and expand their viewing experience (Sunitha, 2024; Bhavani & Sai, 2024). The field of personalization transparency has gained importance as explainable AI (XAI) now allows users to understand the reasoning behind recommendations (Sipos, 2025; Li et al., 2023). Viewers who adjust viewing options based on genre diversity or mood experience broader content exploration while moving past limited viewing habits (Lee & Kim, 2024; Seth, 2024). Hybrid recommendation systems need to maintain an equilibrium between personalized suggestions and varied content to enhance user experience and uphold ethical fairness. Netflix's algorithm development efforts must focus on achieving balance between relevant recommendations and avoiding overfitting to individual user histories which represents an ongoing challenge that requires both algorithmic progression and customization options driven by users (Chen et al., 2024; Gómez-Uribe & Hunt, 2022).

Privacy Concerns are Growing

Netflix's artificial intelligence-based personalization processes enhance customer contentment but generate substantial worries about user data protection and control functions (Sipos, 2025; Sevaslidou et al., 2024). The personalization process involves gathering sensitive information such as users' viewing behaviours, search patterns, physical locations, and details about their devices (Bhavani & Sai, 2024; Sunitha, 2024). While improved content recommendations please users research indicates they feel uneasy when they learn about the full extent of tracking their data (Sunitha, 2024; Sipos, 2025). Debates centred around data ethics and AI transparency have been ignited by these concerns according to Sevaslidou et al., 2024 and Harshavardhan et al., 2024. Global tech platforms including Netflix are required to follow privacy regulations such as the General Data Protection Regulation (GDPR) and the California Consumer Privacy Act (CCPA) which set standards for personal data processing (Bhavani & Sai, 2024). Research demonstrates that adhering to regulatory standards alone fails to maintain user trust when transparency about data collection and usage remains absent (Harshavardhan et al., 2024; Sipos, 2025). The primary problem lies in users' lack of knowledge about which data points inform recommendation algorithms and their operational mechanisms (Chen et al., 2024; Sevaslidou et al., 2024). Netflix developed transparency tools to enable users to view and modify their watching history while providing better insights into their recommendation profiles (Sevaslidou et al., 2024; Gómez-Uribe & Hunt, 2022). Researchers believe that additional measures must be taken such as the development of explainable AI (XAI) systems to provide users with better understanding of how algorithms function and utilize data (Bhavani & Sai, 2024; Sipos, 2025). According to Sipos (2025), AI personalization systems may accidentally determine delicate characteristics such as political beliefs or mental health conditions from user watch patterns which creates ethical concerns about profiling and discrimination as Sunitha (2024) discusses. Privacy specialists urge the adoption of privacy-by-design strategies to integrate protection mechanisms into platform architecture using data minimization and anonymization techniques along with enhanced user controls (Harshavardhan et al., 2024; Khandelwal, 2023). The implementation of these methods ensures that personalization advantages meet consumer demands for data rights, ethical justice, and algorithmic accountability (Sevaslidou et al., 2024). Netflix needs to develop proactive and transparent ethical data strategies to keep viewer trust during heightened digital privacy concerns (Khandelwal, 2023; Sipos, 2025).

Continuous Innovation is Critical

To keep its market-leading status Netflix needs to persistently pursue innovative approaches while navigating the constantly changing streaming sector (Bhavani & Sai, 2024; Wang et al., 2024). AI personalization techniques require regular updates to stay effective as technology and consumer behaviour evolve alongside market changes (Chen et al., 2024; Han, 2024). Research indicates that personalization algorithms face diminished effectiveness without adjustments for dynamic shifts in user demographics and behaviour patterns (Wang et al., 2023; Harshavardhan et al., 2024). Netflix combats these challenges by using machine learning models that undergo periodic retraining on new data so that content suggestions continue to match evolving viewer tastes (Gómez-Uribe & Hunt, 2022; Sunitha, 2024). Netflix has introduced reinforcement learning systems targeting long-term user engagement instead of short-term clicks to boost platform loyalty and continuous user interaction (Li et al., 2023; Sipos, 2025). Advances in explainable AI and privacy-preserving technologies enable solutions to ethical challenges such as algorithmic bias and data privacy (Chen et al., 2024; Bhavani & Sai, 2024). Netflix is expanding its recommendation system capabilities through multimodal personalization inputs which include voice interaction and mood-based cues (Babadoğan, 2024; Joseph et al., 2025). The new technological developments focus on improving user profiles while making viewing experiences much more personalized (Chen et al., 2024; Sevaslidou et al., 2024). Intensified pressure to innovate persists because platforms like Disney+, Amazon Prime Video, and HBO Max present increasing competition (Wang et al., 2023; Haqqo & Isharina, 2024). Contemporary users demand personalized experiences that predict their requirements ahead of any explicit instructions they provide (Gómez-Uribe & Hunt, 2022; Meza & D'Urso, 2024). Netflix has incorporated artificial intelligence tools for content production including automated tagging systems and script evaluation models to make creative processes more efficient (Harshavardhan et al., 2024; Reddy et al., 2025). The development process benefits from these technologies which enable content delivery to match predicted viewer trends (Li et al., 2023; Seth, 2024). Netflix needs to evolve its personalization framework to maintain trust and competitive advantage while overcoming ethical and technical challenges as well as improving user experience in the digital entertainment sector (Sevaslidou et al., 2024; Khandelwal, 2023).

Figure 1. Illustrates Netflix's AI-based personalization system which operates in cycles combining data collection with predictive analysis to provide tailored content delivery followed by feedback-based system adjustments. As users interact with the system it learns in real time to improve its recommendations. A comprehensive innovation cycle integrates ethical principles with strategic goals and technological enhancements throughout all development phases.

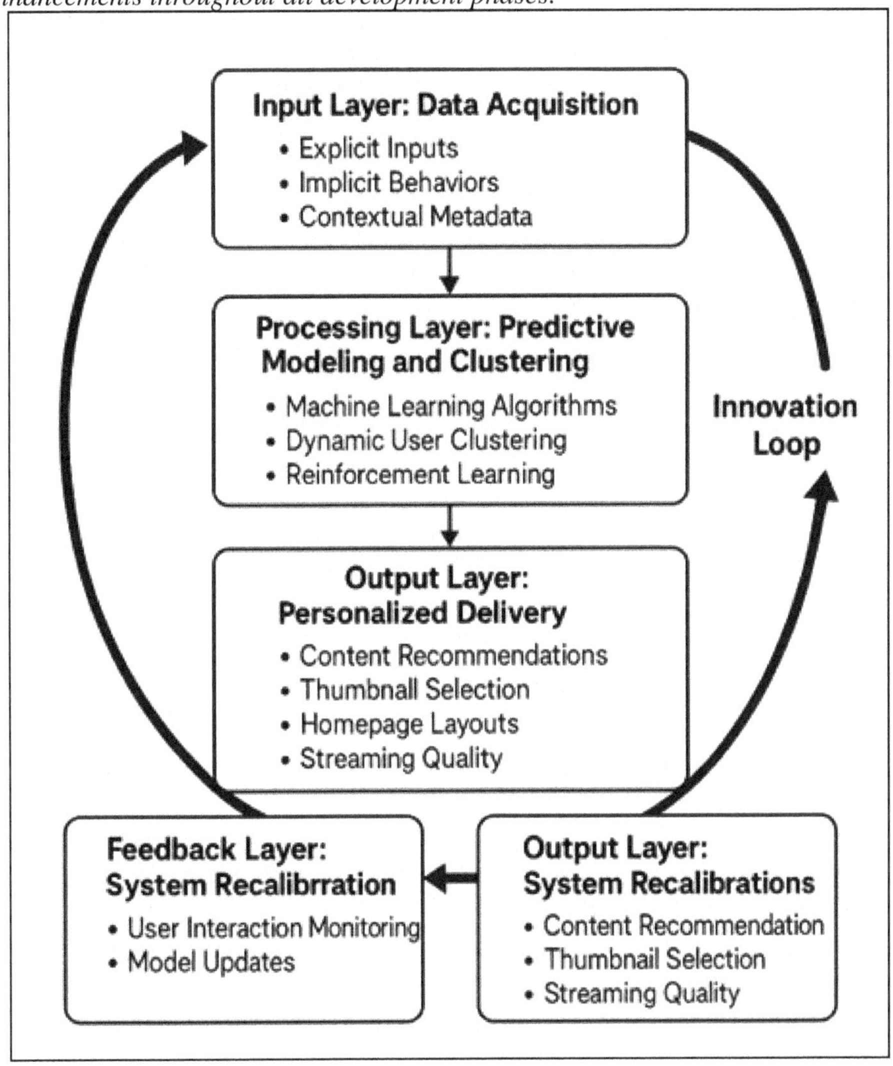

Figure 1 illustrates how Netflix's AI-based personalization operates through dynamic cycles. Netflix collects diverse user data at the Input Layer which includes direct user actions such as ratings and search queries together with indirect behaviours like viewing duration and skipping patterns as well as device type and location metadata. The Processing Layer receives the rich dataset and utilizes sophisticated machine learning techniques such as collaborative filtering, content-based filtering, deep learning, and reinforcement learning to analyse user behaviour patterns and group users with similar activities. The predictive models work to achieve immediate user engagement while also maximizing user satisfaction over time. The Output Layer generates real-time personalized recommendations along with customized homepage layouts and dynamically selected artwork while adapting streaming quality to deliver a customized user experience. Beyond content delivery the system integrates a Feedback Layer which monitors user actions including clicks and completion rates as well as abandonment points. The system uses feedback signals to constantly update its models so that recommendations stay both precise and captivating through time. Netflix's Innovation Loop surrounds the entire cycle as it demonstrates their dedication to constant advancement through strategic and ethical initiatives. The system develops explainable AI for better transparency and enforces stronger privacy rules through data minimization while building hybrid recommendation models that support content diversity as well as relevance. The comprehensive framework integrates user data with predictive analytics and real-time delivery while maintaining continuous feedback and adapting to new consumer expectations and regulatory requirements. Netflix's personalization system demonstrates continuous iterative evolution to maintain effectiveness and competitive advantage while upholding ethical standards in a fast-changing digital landscape.

SOLUTIONS AND RECOMMENDATIONS

Netflix needs to implement ethical and strategic innovations to overcome AI personalization problems including algorithmic bias and data privacy issues (Sipos, 2025; Sevaslidou et al., 2024). When personalization algorithms do not advance to preserve content diversity and transparency, they jeopardize user trust along with facing regulatory investigations (Chen et al., 2024; Harshavardhan et al., 2024). Netflix needs to advance its technical personalization features while simultaneously adopting ethical AI practices that meet user expectations and data protection requirements (Wang et al., 2023; Bhavani & Sai, 2024). Protecting user autonomy and privacy needs precise recommendation systems that work hand in hand with transparent operational practices (Sunitha, 2024; Li et al., 2023). These approaches provide a straightforward path to better system functioning and lasting consumer trust.

Integrate Explainable AI (XAI) Techniques

Netflix's application of explainable AI methods to its recommendation system significantly boosts transparency and user trust which leads to higher user satisfaction levels (Sipos, 2025; Sevaslidou et al., 2024). XAI enables users to comprehend content recommendations through straightforward explanations like "Recommended because you watched [Title]" or "Based on your interest in [Genre]" (Bhavani & Sai, 2024; Sunitha, 2024). Understanding the influence of personal preferences on recommendations makes users perceive the platform as fair while reducing feelings of manipulation according to Sipos (2025) and Chen et al. (2024). These strategies enable users to detect when recommendations rely excessively on limited behavioural patterns or demographic assumptions thus addressing algorithmic bias (Sunitha, 2024; Harshavardhan et al., 2024). According to Sipos (2025), users who comprehend data utilization methods exhibit enhanced trust in personalized systems that value their interests above commercial objectives. Transparent personalization systems stimulate curiosity among users while motivating them to discover fresh content instead of sticking to their usual viewing habits (Sunitha, 2024; Meza & D'Urso, 2024). The implementation of explainable recommendations allows users to make independent choices which strengthens their loyalty in the competitive streaming market (Sevaslidou et al., 2024; Góomez-Uribe & Hunt, 2022). Netflix achieves ethical transparency while preserving personalized content quality through interpretability integration into deep learning models (Sipos, 2025; Khandelwal, 2023). Through this balance Netflix achieves powerful and trustworthy personalized experiences that strengthen long-term user engagement and platform credibility.

Foster Diversity-Aware Recommendation Models

Netflix must design recommendation systems that promote content diversity alongside personalization to reduce filter bubble effects and increase exposure to a wider range of media (Chen et al., 2024; Sipos, 2025). Traditional recommender systems often reinforce user inertia by continually suggesting similar genres or styles, limiting discovery and variety (Sunitha, 2024; Harshavardhan et al., 2024). Diversity-aware algorithms help expand user experiences by surfacing content beyond a viewer's immediate consumption history while still aligning with broader interests (Sevaslidou et al., 2024; Meza & D'Urso, 2024). According to Lee & Kim (2024), user engagement increases over time when platforms intentionally offer content that introduces new topics and perspectives. Hybrid recommendation systems—those that combine collaborative filtering, content-based filtering, and exploratory models—strike a balance between relevance and novelty, delivering both accurate and varied suggestions (Wang et al., 2023; Bhavani & Sai, 2024). Netflix's personalization strategy increasingly emphasizes algorithms that reward content not only for being relevant but also for offering something new, thus satisfying users' preferences for familiar content while encouraging them to explore (Chen et al., 2024; Li et al., 2023). The success of features like Netflix's "Play Something" reflects this approach, as they are designed to broaden users' viewing habits and maintain engagement through surprise and serendipity (Sevaslidou et al., 2024; Haqqo & Isharina, 2024). Content diversity also supports Netflix's global market position by providing international and minority productions with more equitable visibility (Lee & Kim, 2024; Babatunde et al., 2024). For diversity-aware recommendations to succeed, Netflix must train its algorithms on datasets that include inclusive and global content preferences (Wang et al., 2023; Reddy et al., 2025). Biases in training data can cause algorithms to disproportionately favour dominant cultures and languages, which diminishes the effectiveness of diversity-promoting features (Sipos, 2025; Han, 2024). By advancing diversity-aware recommendation models, Netflix can improve content discovery, reduce personalization fatigue, and reinforce its role as an innovator in global streaming entertainment (Khandelwal, 2023; Gómez-Uribe & Hunt, 2022).

Enhance User Control Over Personalization

Netflix needs to develop recommendation systems which balance personalization with diverse content exploration to prevent filter bubbles and restricted content exposure (Chen et al., 2024; Sipos, 2025). Traditional recommendation systems generate user inertia by consistently proposing similar genre content which limits users from broad exploration (Sunitha, 2024; Meza & D'Urso, 2024). Diversity-aware models enable users to access varied content outside their usual preferences by providing recommendations that match broad interests and promote multi-genre discovery (Sevaslidou et al., 2024; Harshavardhan et al., 2024). The study by Lee and Kim (2024) demonstrates that platforms which offer users a variety of content types experience increased user engagement because people enjoy discovering fresh themes and perspectives. Netflix employs hybrid recommender systems which integrate collaborative filtering alongside content-based filtering and exploratory algorithms to deliver suggestions that are both accurate and novel (Wang et al., 2023; Bhavani & Sai, 2024). These systems strive to meet users' wishes for known content while making unexpected discoveries valuable (Chen et al., 2024; Li et al., 2023). The "Play Something" feature demonstrates this strategy through its randomized selection process which encourages broader viewing habits and enhances user retention (Sevaslidou et al., 2024; Haqqo & Isharina, 2024). Netflix enhances its worldwide presence through content diversity which increases the visibility of international and underrepresented productions (Lee & Kim, 2024; Babatunde et al.,

2024). The effectiveness of Netflix's diversity-conscious recommendations depends on its training datasets representing global preferences and diverse content (Wang et al., 2023; Reddy et al., 2025). The presence of biases within training datasets leads to dominant cultural narratives receiving excessive prominence which contradicts diversity objectives and restricts user experiences (Han, 2024; Sipos, 2025). The refinement of these models allows Netflix to improve how users discover content while decreasing personalization fatigue and strengthening its position as a streaming innovation leader (Khandelwal, 2023; Gómez-Uribe & Hunt, 2022).

Adopt Privacy-by-Design Strategies

Netflix must adopt privacy-by-design frameworks to ensure its AI personalization systems meet modern data protection standards and evolving user expectations (Bhavani & Sai, 2024; Sipos, 2025). As Li et al. Li et al. (2023) state that system architecture should incorporate privacy measures from the beginning as opposed to reactive additions for regulatory compliance. According to research by Chen et al. (2024) and Sunitha (2024), data minimization and purpose limitation strategies effectively decrease data collection scope and maintain user trust. Netflix can protect user identities and provide accurate recommendations through differential privacy which combines data aggregation with individual traceability prevention according to Chen et al. (2024) and Harshavardhan et al. (2024). Federated learning provides an alternative solution that enables machine learning models to run directly on users' devices without needing to send personal data to central servers according to research by Wang et al. (2023) and Sevaslidou et al. (2024). The decentralized method aligns with worldwide data privacy movement trends while minimizing the possibility of extensive data breaches (Lee & Kim, 2024; Meza & D'Urso, 2024). Embedding privacy principles at the heart of its system allows Netflix to satisfy international regulations such as GDPR and CCPA while showing leadership in digital ethics according to Bhavani & Sai (2024) and Khandelwal (2023). Netflix sets itself apart as a rights-respecting platform by surpassing basic legal requirements and addressing ethical issues ahead of time (Sipos, 2025; Sevaslidou et al., 2024). When Netflix integrates privacy into its core design it creates customer trust while reinforcing its brand position and protects its personalization systems against growing digital privacy examination.

Invest in Continuous Model Auditing and Bias Monitoring

Netflix needs to dedicate resources to continuous model audits and bias checks to maintain ethical transparency and fairness in its AI personalization technology (Chen et al., 2024; Sipos, 2025). Algorithmic recommendation models enable sophisticated personalization but risk perpetuating historical biases and creating filter bubbles absent proper monitoring (Harshavardhan et al., 2024; Meza & D'Urso, 2024). Applying continuous algorithm audits enables the detection of discriminatory patterns and promotes equitable content distribution among various demographic and regional audiences (Li et al., 2023; Sevaslidou et al., 2024). The implementation of fairness metrics and exposure diversity indicators during algorithm assessment identifies imbalances and protects marginalized content from suppression (Bhavani & Sai, 2024; Wang et al., 2023). Real-time detection and correction through embedded bias monitoring in machine learning systems decrease the necessity of postponed external interventions post-deployment (Sunitha, 2024; Reddy et al., 2025). Netflix uses real-time systems which adjust according to user demographic changes and content library updates to ensure equitable content delivery (Chen et al., 2024; Han, 2024). The publication of audit results as transparency reports provides user reassurance while showcasing Netflix as a pioneer in ethical artificial intelligence innovation (Sipos, 2025; Sevaslidou et al., 2024). These reports serve to establish accountability while providing insight into the company's methods for managing fairness concerns within recommendation systems. Through auditing and algorithmic assessments Netflix upholds high personalization standards while ensuring ethical integrity in its innovation practices (Gómez-Uribe & Hunt, 2022; Khandelwal, 2023).

FUTURE RESEARCH DIRECTIONS

Netflix's AI personalization systems development demands further research to achieve ethical advancement and maintain transparency along with sustainable growth (Sipos, 2025; Sevaslidou et al., 2024). Existing personalization models function well today but continuous innovation and refinement remain necessary to address persistent ethical issues and technical problems (Wang et al., 2023; Harshavardhan et al., 2024). Research efforts moving forward should develop algorithms that enhance recommendation precision while protecting user privacy and promoting equal treatment for all demographic groups (Chen et al., 2024; Reddy et al., 2025). Developing these systems demands tackling ongoing algorithmic discrimination and transparency problems in order to maintain public trust and meet regulatory standards (Li et al., 2023; Meza & D'Urso, 2024). Sunitha (2024) identifies new research directions which offer substantial opportunities to develop personalization features while appropriately managing ethical and technical risks.

Development of Explainable Personalization Models

Upcoming research on Netflix's recommendation systems needs to create algorithms which preserve strong personalization performance and at the same time improve interpretability for users (Sipos, 2025; Sevaslidou et al., 2024). Explainable AI models build user trust and satisfaction through clear explanations of why certain content recommendations are made (Bhavani & Sai, 2024; Sunitha, 2024). Statements like "Because you watched…" present clear explanations which boost user engagement while keeping information manageable (Chen et al., 2024; Gómez-Uribe & Hunt, 2022). Meaningful transparency emerges when explainable techniques demonstrate the connection between user behaviours and specific recommendations while enabling users to provide feedback and control personalization features (Li et al., 2023; Harshavardhan et al., 2024). Future research should work towards incorporating interpretability into user interfaces through methods that feel natural to users while preserving platform functionality (Sevaslidou et al., 2024; Sipos, 2025). To build trust and support ethical AI adoption in streaming environments like Netflix, it is crucial for platforms to enhance user comprehension through straightforward and easy-to-understand explanations which help reduce algorithmic opacity (Khandelwal, 2023; Meza & D'Urso, 2024).

Ethical Frameworks for AI Personalization

Research going forward needs to establish complete ethical standards for Netflix's AI personalization systems (Sipos, 2025; Sevaslidou et al., 2024). User interaction benefits from personalization but this approach introduces ethical risks including bias reinforcement, transparency deficiencies, and diminished user autonomy (Wang et al., 2023; Harshavardhan et al., 2024). Research shows that recommendation algorithms can unintentionally restrict access to content from minority groups which makes fairness frameworks essential to provide equal visibility to diverse creators and genres (Li et al., 2024; Babatunde et al., 2024). Personalization practices need informed consent procedures within ethical standards to make users aware of their data collection and processing (Chen et al., 2024; Bhavani & Sai, 2024). Khandelwal (2023) supports the incorporation of ethical audits throughout AI development to detect and address potential risks before systems go live. Research results confirm that fairness-aware machine learning models along with accountability checklists designed for personalization systems enhance responsible development practices (Wang et al., 2023; Reddy et al., 2025).

Upcoming studies should investigate transparent communication approaches which detail ethical personalization procedures to bolster Netflix's image as a progressive and responsible market pioneer (Li et al., 2024; Sipos, 2025). Research indicates that platforms which build ethical trust by pledging to non-discrimination and privacy protection produce greater user satisfaction and loyalty (Sevaslidou et al., 2024; Gómez-Uribe & Hunt, 2022). Netflix needs to create strong ethical guidelines to protect user interests while ensuring fairness in digital entertainment to properly align personalization with societal values (Chen et al., 2024; Khandelwal, 2023).

CONCLUSION

Through its strategic application of artificial intelligence (AI) Netflix has reshaped content personalization to deliver experiences that are highly tailored and context-aware thereby significantly boosting user satisfaction and engagement while ensuring platform loyalty among its international subscribers. The chapter analysed Netflix's AI-based personalization system by examining essential components like behavioural analytics and collaborative/content-based filtering alongside dynamic hybrid recommendation models and advanced streaming optimization techniques. The analysis showed that Netflix uses data-driven decision-making for original content production to stay aligned with changing user preferences and cultural trends. AI-driven personalization systems deliver significant advantages through real-time response capabilities and improved content discovery, yet they bring continuous operational challenges. The system faces continuous challenges including biases in algorithms and filter bubble creation while also dealing with increasing worries about the protection of user data. These unresolved issues will result in reduced trust from users and damage the credibility of the platform. The chapter stresses that explainable AI (XAI) systems which deliver transparent and understandable recommendations can help mitigate these risks. These systems allow users to understand recommendation mechanisms better which in turn enhances their decision-making abilities while boosting their perception of fairness. The integration of privacy-by-design frameworks, federated learning, differential privacy methods along with routine algorithm audits serves as an essential strategy to protect user rights and to ensure compliance with international data protection laws. Netflix's personalization technology maintains its innovative capabilities while staying ethically accountable through these measures. The chapter calls for further research and development efforts focused on emotional and context-aware artificial intelligence systems. The models create emotionally intelligent and adaptive viewing experiences by recommending content that corresponds with user mood, time of day, and physical context. Through ongoing exploration of recommendation strategies that respect cultural sensitivities and fairness-informed algorithms Netflix can serve international audiences while upholding inclusivity standards. Netflix maintains its global AI personalization supremacy through a combination of technological progression along with operational transparency and ethical foresight. Netflix establishes a standard for AI development in digital entertainment through its marriage of innovation and accountability. AI personalization development needs to focus on fairness and inclusivity along with sustainable practices. Netflix's strong ethical infrastructure combined with continuous adaptive research work enables it to lead personalized streaming advancement while upholding privacy standards and trustworthiness in a dynamic digital realm through diverse content delivery.

REFERENCES

Babadoğan, B. (2024). *Unveiling the power of AI-driven personalization: Transforming consumer behavior in the age of digital marketing*. Next Frontier for Life Sciences and AI., DOI: 10.62802/fj43xy18

Babatunde, S. O., Odejide, O. A., Edunjobi, T. E., & Ogundipe, D. O. (2024). The role of AI in marketing personalization: A theoretical exploration of consumer engagement strategies. *International Journal of Management & Entrepreneurship Research, 6*(3), 936–949. Advance online publication. DOI: 10.51594/ijmer.v6i3.964

Bhavani, K., & Sai, A. L. (2024). Netflix movies recommendation system. *International Journal of Innovative Science and Research Technology*, *9*(2), 2006–2010. Advance online publication. DOI: 10.38124/ijisrt/IJISRT24FEB1527

Ding, L., Antonucci, G., & Venditti, M. (2024). Unveiling user responses to AI-powered personalised recommendations: A qualitative study of consumer engagement dynamics on Douyin. *Qualitative Market Research*. Advance online publication. DOI: 10.1108/QMR-11-2023-0151

Han, Y. (2024). *Research on the application of personalized recommendation*. Applied and Computational Engineering., DOI: 10.54254/2755-2721/43/20230825

Haqqo, C. I., & Isharina, I. K. (2024). Influence of content quality and personalization on continuous intention to subscribe Netflix through the mediation of perceived value. *Journal of Business and Management Review*, *5*(5), 407–425. Advance online publication. DOI: 10.47153/jbmr.v5i5.888

Harshavardhan, M., Ainapur, J., Rao, K. K., Kumar, A., Prajwal, P., Saiteja, S., & Reddy, V. (2024). Leveraging artificial intelligence in marketing: Case studies on enhancing personalization, customer engagement, and business performance. *International Journal of Business and Management Invention, 13*(9), 131–136. DOI: 10.35629/8028-1309131136

Hsiao, Y. H. (2024). *The business strategy analysis of Netflix*. Transactions on Social Science, Education and Humanities Research., DOI: 10.62051/tjhh1617

Ichino, J., Miyazaki, M., & Tanaka, K. (2023). How personalization algorithm changes consumer behaviors in the digital healthcare service. *Studies in Health Technology and Informatics*, *305*, 3–12. DOI: 10.3233/ATDE230592

. Joseph, O. O., Akintola, A. S., Offiong, E., Olajuwon, O. O., Offia, U. I., & Faniyan, A. A. (2025). AI-enhanced consumer insights: Leveraging behavioural analytics for hyper-personalised marketing strategies. *Journal of Artificial Intelligence, Machine Learning and Data Science*. DOI: 10.51219/JAIMLD/Omotoso-Oluwayomi-Joseph/511

Khandelwal, K. (2023). A study to know – Use of AI for personalized recommendation, streaming optimization, and original content production at Netflix. *International Journal of Scientific Research and Engineering Trends*, *9*(6), 1738–1743. Advance online publication. DOI: 10.61137/ijsret.vol.9.issue6.119

Meza, L. R., & D'Urso, G. (2024). User's dilemma: A qualitative study on the influence of Netflix recommender systems on choice overload. *Psychological Studies*, *69*(3), 349–367. Advance online publication. DOI: 10.1007/s12646-024-00807-0

. Reddy, V. V., Sandeep, M., & Kamble, M. (2025). Hyper-personalization, AI-driven recommendation engines, consumer engagement, ethical AI, digital marketing, TOE framework. *Journal of Informatics Education and Research*. DOI: 10.52783/jier.v5i1.2283

Seth, K. (2024). Transforming personalized marketing: Harnessing the power of artificial intelligence for enhanced consumer targeting and business growth. *2024 1st International Conference on Sustainable Computing and Integrated Communication in Changing Landscape of AI (ICSCAI)*, 1–9. DOI: 10.1109/ICSCAI61790.2024.10866411

Sevaslidou, J., Prassa, M. A., & Papaioannou, E. (2024). AI in marketing: Revolutionizing efficiency and personalization – Netflix's AI success story. *Proceedings of the International Conference on Contemporary Marketing Issues*. DOI: 10.12681/iccmi.7593

Sipos, D. (2025). The effects of AI-powered personalization on consumer trust, satisfaction, and purchase intent. *European Journal of Applied Science. Engineering and Technology*, *3*(2), 14–24. Advance online publication. DOI: 10.59324/ejaset.2025.3(2).02

Sunitha, B. K. (2024). A study on data analytics techniques used by Netflix to personalize recommendations. *International Journal of Scientific Research in Engineering and Management*. DOI: 10.55041/IJSREM29882

KEY TERMS AND DEFINITIONS

Algorithmic Bias: Systematic prejudices emerge within AI system results.

Artificial Intelligence (AI): Computer systems which execute tasks normally needing human intelligence capabilities.

Data Privacy: Data Privacy involves protecting user information against unauthorized access and exploitation.

Filter Bubble: Users experience a filter bubble when they only receive information that matches their personal interests.

Machine Learning (ML): Machine Learning represents a branch of Artificial Intelligence which trains algorithms through data to generate predictions.

Recommender Systems: AI tools that analyse user data to recommend relevant content.

User Behaviour Analytics: Understanding user-platform interactions allows businesses to create customized user experiences.

Chapter 6
Zalando's Use of AI to Create a Personalized Shopping Experience

Muntazir Mahdi
https://orcid.org/0009-0006-2469-4256
University of Westminster, London, UK

ABSTRACT

The online fashion retail sector has experienced a transformation through AI technologies which allow retailers to create tailor-made shopping experiences for each customer. Through its use of sophisticated AI technologies such as machine learning algorithms and collaborative filtering systems Zalando delivers personalized fashion suggestions that reflect both customer tastes and current style movements while analysing their online activity. This chapter examines the ways in which Zalando's recommendation systems boost customer satisfaction while increasing purchase conversion rates and strengthening brand loyalty. The chapter examines AI personalization challenges such as algorithmic bias and privacy issues while proposing methods for ethical and sustainable innovation approaches. This chapter demonstrates how AI will transform personalized online retail through an examination of real-world applications and research outcomes.

BACKGROUND

The evolution of artificial intelligence from its original 1980s rule-based systems to current deep learning models has revolutionized personalization in the e-commerce industry. The 2010s brought AI advancements and big data analytics which transformed recommender systems from basic collaborative filtering and content match-

DOI: 10.4018/979-8-3373-6582-4.ch006

ing to dynamic, individualized recommendations (Islam et al., 2024). Retailers use real-time predictive personalization systems that analyses both behavioural patterns and emotional states. Europe's top online fashion retailer Zalando demonstrates this transition by applying machine learning and natural language processing (NLP) for consumer preference analysis and prediction of buying patterns at scale (Faizi, 2025). Post-2020, hyper-personalization gained momentum. The online fashion retailer Zalando implemented deep learning techniques alongside reinforcement learning and both convolutional neural networks (CNNs) and recurrent neural networks (RNNs) to produce real-time recommendations that take into account user history and adapt to fashion trends and seasonal variations (Thakur et al., 2024). The "Algorithmic Fashion Companion" provides fully personalized outfit suggestions based on user preferences (Amosu et al., 2024). To boost transparency and trust within its recommendation systems Zalando adopted explainable AI technology as noted by Adanyin in 2024. The implementation of AI personalization strategies led to a 25% boost in conversion rates and a 17% increase in average order values according to research by Islam et al. (2024). The fashion retail industry requires personalization because style choices are deeply personal and emotional (Faizi, 2025). The COVID-19 pandemic drove retailers to adopt digital technologies faster and compete by delivering seamless and personalized customer experiences. Zalando increased its investment in AI technologies to maintain customer loyalty and expand its market share (Krishnamurthy et al., 2024). AI personalization brings forth both technical obstacles and ethical issues to overcome. The primary issues being addressed today involve data privacy, algorithmic bias alongside transparency requirements. Zalando employs federated learning along with privacy-preserving AI methods to ensure its systems remain fair, secure, and scalable according to Liu et al., 2024 and Adanyin, 2024.

Focus of the Chapter

The fashion e-commerce industry has undergone major changes through AI which redefined how customers interact and receive value (Tulasi & Ahamed, 2025). Basic collaborative filtering models in traditional recommendation systems are now being supplanted by sophisticated AI platforms that combine deep learning with computer vision and real-time feedback mechanisms (Guo et al., 2023). Advanced technologies facilitate real-time shopping experiences which adapt immediately based on user actions and contextual information (Tulasi & Ahamed, 2025). Europe's biggest fashion e-commerce platform Zalando spearheads this development while serving more than 45 million customers across 23 countries (Abbas et al., 2024). The data science and AI-focused company based in Berlin produces personalized customer experiences which improve satisfaction and loyalty (Choppadandi, 2023). Zalando utilizes contextual intelligence including seasonality and weather data to provide relevant product suggestions while surpassing traditional transaction-based models (Abbas et al., 2024). The company's AI framework utilizes neural collaborative filtering alongside convolutional neural networks and deep reinforcement learning according to Choppadandi (2023). The models receive training from extensive datasets that encompass user interactions and item metadata along with social media and fashion content data (Tulasi & Ahamed, 2025). These algorithms continuously improve through feedback loops and user behaviour tracking which enables them to adapt to changing preferences (Gupta & Bansal, 2019). Real-time experimentation through reinforcement learning optimizes recommendations and enhances user engagement according to Gupta & Bansal (2019). Zalando creates personalized shopping experiences which build emotional bonds and enhance customer trust according to research by Islam et al. (2024). User satisfaction and conversion metrics increase when product recommendations align with individual style preferences and life contexts (Islam et al., 2024). The present chapter examines Zalando's AI framework with an emphasis on algorithmic architecture and performance metrics such as conversion and retention to understand its influence on digital retail strategies (Choppadandi, 2023; Tulasi & Ahamed, 2025).

Current Applications

Personalised Product Recommendations

Zalando applies AI-driven personalized product recommendations to enhance user experience as a central strategy (Abbas et al., 2024). Traditional collaborative filtering methods fail to capture real-time updates in user preferences and context (Abbas et al., 2024). Zalando created a hybrid recommendation system which merges collaborative filtering with content-based filtering while also incorporating visual similarity detection techniques and context-aware learning methods (Abbas et al., 2024). The Algorithmic Fashion Companion (AFC) system applies deep learning techniques to create complete outfit suggestions by analysing user behaviour and search context along with mood indicators (Choppadandi, 2023; Xu et al., 2024; Varma, 2024). The model utilizes clickstream data together with browsing patterns and demographic information to adapt. Session-based learning provides real-time recommendation adjustments throughout browsing sessions whenever users demonstrate shifts in their intent (Majeed et al., 2023). RL models enhance their outputs through feedback analysis while CNNs facilitate image-based user matching by processing uploaded screenshots and photos (Varma, 2024; Guo et al., 2023). Recommendations that take context into account utilize location and time data along with weather conditions to deliver different suggestions to users in diverse environments even when their histories are comparable (Guo et al., 2023; Xu et al., 2024). Zalando incorporates trend data from fashion media sources to align their recommendations with current fashion styles (Guo et al., 2023). These actions achieved a 25% increase in conversions and led to a 17% rise in AOV while CLV improved by 12% (Choppadandi, 2023; Majeed et al., 2023).

Visual Search and Similarity Detection

The visual appearance of fashion items plays a crucial role in driving consumer purchasing decisions (Guo et al., 2023). Zalando utilizes CNN-based visual search to overcome text search restrictions by allowing users to upload or photograph clothing to find similar products (Ay & Aydin, 2021; Turaga & Shankar, 2022). CNN models derive spatial hierarchy structures and visual embeddings to perform similarity matching through cosine distance evaluation (Tareaf et al., 2024; Sanjana et al., 2025). Zalando enhances outfit compatibility functionality through attention mechanisms and multimodal models (Kalinin et al., 2024; Silva et al., 2024). Users can upload inspirational images which enables them to find visually similar items while enhancing user engagement and streamlining the search process (Gupta & Bansal, 2019). The feature boosts long-tail item discovery while refining search precision through filters such as size, price, and occasion (Ay & Aydin, 2021; Silva et al., 2024). Advancements in generative AI and zero-shot learning will enable users to describe their ideas or create sketches so systems can generate matching results (Kalinin et al., 2024; Silva et al., 2024). Emerging innovations create intuitive experiences that foster emotional connections between users and systems (Islam et al., 2024).

Dynamic Personalisation Using Reinforcement Learning

Static systems struggle with volatile consumer preferences. Zalando uses reinforcement learning methods to achieve dynamic decision-making capabilities and immediate adaptability according to Majeed et al., 2023 and Zhu et al., 2022. Reinforcement Learning models analyze user actions during sessions to deliver recommendations that react to the current context (Majeed et al., 2023). The AdaptiveCloset framework developed by Zalando optimizes product sequences by using deep Q-networks to maximize key performance indicators including CTR, AOV, and retention metrics (Tan et al., 2020; Majeed et al., 2023). During testing multi-armed bandits manage exploration and exploitation (Zhu et al., 2022) and reward shaping includes extended engagement signals like wishlisting and sharing (Islam et al., 2024). RL enables scalable personalisation through adaptive training models that respond to individual behaviour while serving global audiences (Oguntola &

Simske, 2023). Reinforcement learning prioritises sustained user happiness and loyalty over static click-focused methods which enables Zalando to manage millions of user sessions accurately (Islam et al., 2024).

Context-Aware Personalisation

Through evolution beyond static profiling Zalando now operates a dynamic personalization system which generates user recommendations by considering both situational and environmental factors (Abbas et al., 2024). Traditional AI personalization approaches depend only on behavioural information such as browsing patterns and purchase history, but context-aware models also include real-time data like geolocation and user sentiment (Liu et al., 2021). These systems work to forecast user preferences in addition to predicting their immediate desires at any given moment (Hariri et al., 2013). Zalando has developed its Kernel Fashion Context Recommender (KFCR) which stands out as one of its most sophisticated systems that integrates contextual variables into recommendation production through kernel mapping techniques according to machine learning algorithms (Abbas et al., 2024). KFCR examines factors like the current weather conditions (such as suggesting raincoats during rainfall), social contexts (such as recommending party attire for weekends), and mood indicators derived from user behaviours (Abbas et al., 2024). Implementation of this approach enables the platform to eliminate unrelated suggestions while delivering recommendations that precisely match the direct needs of users in their current environment. Current trends show systems engineering frameworks being incorporated into e-commerce personalization engines according to Oguntola & Simske (2023). The frameworks employ unsupervised learning techniques to create dynamic user personas alongside intent prediction systems as indicated by Demissie & Mogalla (2018). LSTM neural networks have demonstrated the ability to track user context through time and produce appropriate product recommendations in real-time according to Hariri et al. (2013). The architecture of these models provides privacy protection and ethical segmentation of users into groups without revealing individual identities while maintaining a balance between personalization features and responsible AI standards (Oguntola & Simske, 2023). Zalando uses intent-aware ranking systems that analyze recent and historical user activities together with external events to forecast user interests (Choppadandi, 2023). The platform modifies its recommendations during seasonal events like Black Friday or Valentine's Day by incorporating event-triggered search and clickstream data patterns besides traditional popularity metrics and previous purchases (Choppadandi, 2023). Shoppers experience enhanced relevance and emotional connection in their purchasing journey according to Guo et al. (2023). Customers' demands for hyper-personalized experiences and minimized cognitive load have led to the move toward context-aware systems (Oguntola & Simske, 2023). Smart filtering methods that use situational indicators can improve usability and satisfaction when users experience choice overload in competitive markets (Demissie & Mogalla, 2018). Studies show that context-aware personalization results in higher conversion rates and extended session durations as well as improved customer loyalty because users perceive their preferences and circumstances being accurately recognized and predicted (Liu et al., 2021). Zalando employs advanced context-aware AI systems which stand at the forefront of fashion e-commerce strategies according to Abbas et al. (2024). The models achieve greater relevance while boosting engagement and develop adaptive surroundings that respond fluidly to real-time user contexts which stands out as a crucial feature for personalization in the fast-moving digital retail environment that is rich with data (Hariri et al., 2013).

Fashion Intelligence and Trend Prediction

The fashion retail industry relies on the complex but essential skill of making accurate trend predictions within effective timeframes (Singh et al., 2024). Fashion businesses that successfully predict consumer preferences and market trends secure better chances of staying relevant and profitable (Perera et al., 2024). To tackle the challenge of trend prediction and product assortment Zalando has created sophisticated fashion intelligence systems powered by AI which enables them to predict fashion trends and refine their product assortment and customer targeting strategies (Perera et al., 2024). The multi-modal machine learning models that form Zalando's fashion intelligence system utilize historical sales data along with real-time user interaction signals and additional external trend sources including social media and fashion events (Singh et al., 2024). Natural language processing (NLP), image recognition and sentiment analysis algorithms process these inputs to detect new trends in styles, materials, colours and silhouettes (Perera et al., 2024). Zalando analyses macro-trends and micro-trends with high temporal sensitivity through a combination of structured and unstructured data as shown by Guo et al. (2023). Zalando utilizes XAI tools in their predictive models to ensure forecasting processes remain transparent and interpretable (Tareaf et al., 2024). Fashion buyers and designers can comprehend the reasoning behind certain trend predictions enabling them to make well-informed choices through these tools (Perera et al., 2024). The system attributes its prediction for increased demand in "oversized blazers" to higher search rates along with favourable reviews from fashion influencers and recent runway shows (Guo et al., 2023). By following an insight-based approach companies can optimize their assortment planning to match consumer preferences while minimizing both surplus inventory and stock shortages (Singh et al., 2024). Zalando implements deep learning models that analyse style evolution patterns across individual customer segments according to Oguntola & Simske (2023). The models identify customer groups according to fashion preference patterns and forecast future interests using historical engagement data (Perera et al., 2024). Predictive personalization improves recommendation quality while simultaneously guiding marketing campaigns and homepage content design through better promotional timing (Guo et al., 2023). Beyond user-level insights Zalando's trend forecasting aids inventory management and product development processes (Perera et al., 2024). The company achieves reduced unsold inventory and markdown losses by synchronizing warehouse distribution with predictive demand curves for stock levels (Singh et al., 2024). The system provides designers with actionable data about niche market opportunities to help shape collaborative capsule collections (Guo et al., 2023). Zalando plans to use generative AI to advance from trend detection to trend creation according to Jeon et al. (2021). These models blend user-generated content with global fashion information to autonomously design clothing styles that foresee consumer desires rather than merely responding to them (Singh et al., 2024). Zalando illustrates a competitive edge through AI-powered fashion intelligence and trend prediction by enabling proactive decision-making based on data analytics in design and operational processes (Perera et al., 2024

Key Findings

Zalando's use of AI-driven personalization approaches has brought substantial enhancements to customer experience along with operational performance according to Islam et al. (2024). Zalando provides real-time product suggestions based on context-aware data through the integration of deep learning techniques with behavioural analytics and edge computing capabilities (Tulasi & Ahamed, 2025; Khoa et al., 2024). The systems enhance important e-commerce indicators like conversion rate as well as average order value (AOV) and customer lifetime value (CLV) (Islam et al., 2024). Customized recommendations help users save time and meet specific preferences which leads to increased loyalty and user engagement (Tulasi & Ahamed, 2025). Research demonstrates that organizations implementing responsible AI strategies gain enduring competitive advantages according to Islam et al. (2024).

Significant Increase in Conversion Rates

Conversion rate serves as a crucial performance metric for e-commerce platforms because it calculates the proportion of users who accomplish a specific goal such as making a purchase (Tulasi & Ahamed, 2025). The integration of AI-powered recommendation systems by Zalando has produced exceptional results in this domain (Islam et al., 2024). The study conducted by Choppadandi (2023) revealed that Zalando achieved a 25% boost in conversion rates through the deployment of machine learning-based recommendation engines that analyse real-time user behaviour, preferences, and context. The platform delivers improved conversion rates because its system can present customers with product recommendations that match their immediate needs throughout their shopping experience according to Tulasi & Ahamed (2025). Zalando's AI algorithms forgo generalized static models in favour of dynamic adaptation through real-time analysis of user interactions such as search queries and browsing history along with click-through behaviour and cart additions as well as partial session data (Majeed et al., 2023). Recommendation engines that use deep reinforcement learning to understand browsing sessions present dynamic product options which match users' immediate demands and evolving interests during their browsing session (Islam et al., 2024). Edge computing architectures boost the performance of these models by enabling real-time processing capabilities that reduce latency (Khoa et al., 2024). AI and edge computing technology platforms demonstrate up to 30% conversion gains because personalization models can quickly respond to user micro-interactions including mouse movement, product dwell time, and scroll speed (Islam et al., 2024). Fast data processing capabilities at the user's device or local server edge enable hyper-personalization which leads to better user experiences and increases the likelihood of users completing desired actions before leaving the site (Islam et al., 2024). Zalando employs multi-armed bandit frameworks in its recommendation models to enhance conversion rates through simultaneous testing of various recommendation strategies (Abbas et al., 2024). The system achieves quick determination of optimal recommendation logic for each user cohort by testing various approaches with real-time performance data (Tulasi & Ahamed, 2025). The platform utilizes experimentation-based optimization to reduce opportunity costs while identifying subtle personalization rules beyond what conventional models can detect (Abbas et al., 2024). The increase in conversion rates is driven by psychological alignment with customer preferences and not solely by mechanical means according to Choppadandi (2023). User interviews showed that people tended to buy more when recommendations appeared to be appropriate which indicates AI success depends on how relevant and accurate the suggestions feel to users (Islam et al., 2024). Zalando's increase in conversion rates resulted from strategic applications of adaptive machine learning, real-time feedback mechanisms, edge computing technology and behavioural modelling techniques according to Tulasi & Ahamed (2025). The combination of these technologies enables users to receive the exact products they need at the perfect moment which leads to higher purchase rates and boosts business performance (Islam et al., 2024).

Growth in Average Order Value (AOV)

Zalando's AI-driven personalization approach has played a major role in boosting their Average Order Value (AOV) along with its effectiveness in raising conversion rates which reflects the average spending per transaction (Tulasi & Ahamed, 2025). Zalando's implementation of dynamic recommendation engines and contextual personalization techniques resulted in a 17% hike in their Average Order Value (AOV) as personalized recommendations triggered both higher purchasing rates and enhanced cart item quality and quantity as confirmed by Choppadandi's study (2023). According to Abbas et al., 2024, Zalando's AI algorithms enhanced AOV due to their bundling and cross-selling capabilities. Through analysing user shopping intent together with item affinities and past purchase patterns, the platform delivers accurate complementary item recommendations like shoes with dresses or accessories with jackets right when users need them (Islam et al., 2024). Graph neural networks and association rule mining power the frequently bought together and complete-the-look recommendations by detecting statistically meaningful product relationships within customer baskets (Guo et al., 2023). The system uses context-aware price sensitivity modelling techniques to provide recommendations that match users' spending patterns and psychological spending limits (Islam et al., 2024). The system encourages high-value customers to explore premium or designer collections as it directs value-driven customers to visually similar products that fit their price preferences (Tulasi & Ahamed, 2025). Research by Choppadandi (2023) demonstrates that this combination of price personalization boosts upselling results while maintaining user satisfaction and avoiding decision fatigue. Zalando's real-time decision engines analyse behavioural signals during a session including time spent on product pages and scrolling patterns to provide adaptive suggestions that change with customer engagement levels (Majeed et al., 2023). According to researchers these micro-adjustments form what they call a "personalized purchase journey" which makes users more likely to browse through extra categories and add more products to their shopping carts (Islam et al., 2024). User satisfaction remains unaffected by the increase in AOV as found in Choppadandi's 2023 research. User feedback shows that customers value their saved time when the platform provides cohesive pre-selected product choices (Islam et al., 2024). Buyers report greater confidence in their purchase choices when product recommendations match their personal style and seasonal needs or special occasions according to Guo et al. (2023). The increase in AOV is consistent with ongoing e-commerce research according to Tulasi & Ahamed (2025). A 2024 retail study revealed that platforms using AI and behavioural modelling achieved AOV growth rates between 12% and 20%, which varied according to personalization depth and real-time responsiveness (Islam et al., 2024). Zalando's rise in average order value demonstrates how AI combines product relevance enhancement with user guidance towards comprehensive purchases through smart bundling approaches and adaptive shopping flows alongside psychological pricing (Abbas et al., 2024).

Improved Customer Lifetime Value (CLV)

The total revenue potential from a single customer during their entire relationship with a brand represents Customer Lifetime Value (CLV) which stands as an important e-commerce measurement (Akter et al., 2025). Zalando has targeted CLV improvement as a strategic priority and achieved a 12% growth in CLV through its AI-enhanced personalization system which utilizes advanced machine learning models across customer touchpoints according to a study by Choppadandi (2023). The platform creates long-lasting customer loyalty by delivering experiences that remain relevant and emotionally impactful as reported by Islam et al. (2024). Zalando builds brand loyalty through personalized product suggestions and user-specific marketing communications which lead to more frequent visits and increased spending by customers (Guo et al., 2023). CLV represents the total outcome of a personalization system that develops trust and satisfaction while creating purchasing habits while short-term conversions depict individual transactions. The sustained value stems from Zalando's session-aware reinforcement learning framework which tailors' recommendations through short-term signals and long-term behavioural patterns (Majeed et al., 2023). The dual approach of this model guarantees personalized experiences remain fresh and responsive to user changes through time by syncing with evolving fashion trends and life events as well as seasonal shifts. Zalando employs predictive CLV scoring models inside its CRM and campaign targeting systems (Kandi, 2024). The platform uses predictive models to segment its users based on their potential future value which enables efficient personalization of campaigns and incentives (Oguntola & Simske, 2023). High-CLV users receive early access to exclusive collections while lower-CLV users get discounts and new experiences to boost their loyalty according to Egorenkov (2024). According to Guo et al. (2023), emotional personalization contributes to Customer Lifetime Value (CLV) enhancement. Zalando utilizes sentiment analysis together with style clustering techniques to offer product recommendations that fulfil functional needs while simultaneously showcasing elements of a user's aesthetic preferences (Akter et al., 2025). The platform's ability to make users feel "seen" contributes to building their long-term loyalty according to Egorenkov's research in 2024. Zalando employs AI to improve customer lifetime value demonstrating their deep knowledge of long-term customer economic principles (Akter et al., 2025). The firm applies adaptive personalization combined with predictive segmentation and emotional resonance to convert sporadic buyers into loyal high-value customers thereby boosting its competitive position in the fashion online marketplace (Kandi, 2024).

User Satisfaction and Emotional Resonance

The success of fashion e-commerce platforms relies on understanding and predicting individual user preferences beyond basic factors like product availability and pricing due to the emotional and aesthetic nature of customer purchases (Ünlü, 2024). The implementation of AI-based personalization systems by Zalando led to significant customer satisfaction score enhancements which studies indicate rose by 22% after introducing adaptive recommendation systems together with context-aware design features (Choppadandi, 2023). A key factor driving the improvement is how much easier the system makes it for users to process information (Ünlü, 2024). The integration of personalized product lists alongside dynamic filters and session-aware recommendations enables customers to avoid irrelevant items. Customers receive curated selections that match their immediate shopping goal whether they are looking for seasonal items, specific occasion products, or exploring new styles. The streamlined choice architecture boosts shopping experience quality which results in higher user satisfaction and improved operational efficiency (Islam et al., 2024). Zalando's AI systems create deeper emotional bonds with customers by replicating what users describe as "style empathy" (Guo et al., 2023). The platform utilizes deep learning-based style clustering and visual similarity algorithms to generate recommendations that adapt to users' changing fashion identities. Fashion choices express personal identity and lifestyle preferences which is why emotional resonance plays a vital role in this industry (Guo et al., 2023). User feedback indicates that people respond favourably to platforms that demonstrate an understanding of them both behaviourally and aesthetically according to Ünlü (2024). Through longitudinal engagement studies researchers discovered that customers experienced Zalando as more "inspired" and "enjoyable" when it provided personalized content (Oguntola & Simske, 2023). Zalando's personalization strategy reaches beyond the purchase stage through real-time behaviour-based email marketing and push notification engagement. The system engages users by offering stylistically similar product recommendations when they add a product to favourites but do not proceed with buying it (Islam et al., 2024). Zalando's AI-powered personalization system delivers benefits to operational performance and psychological user satisfaction. Zalando achieves a shopping experience which feels intuitive and rewarding by creating recommendations that meet functional needs and reflect emotional expressions (Guo et al., 2023).

Reduced Latency in Customer Interaction

The time delay between user actions and system responses in digital retail impacts customer experience by affecting both satisfaction levels and conversion rates (Islam et al., 2024). When users experience small delays, they become frustrated and less engaged because they expect quick responses from digital platforms. To improve customer experience by reducing latency across personalization workflows Zalando combined AI with edge computing which led to quicker and smoother user interactions (Paul et al., 2024). Edge computing involves processing data near the user's device instead of depending solely on centralized cloud servers (Pandey, 2024). Through the practice of processing data directly at the point of origin, Zalando achieves much faster delivery times for personalized content. Flash sales or promotional events benefit greatly from this approach because real-time recommendation updates can determine the success or failure of transactions (Islam et al., 2024). Research indicates that platforms which employ edge-enhanced AI models experience latency reductions up to 70% which enables faster responses to user actions like scrolling, clicking, and product filtering (Islam et al., 2024). Zalando delivers updated recommendations to users in milliseconds as opposed to seconds to sustain engagement momentum and minimize browsing session drop-off risks. Zalando enhances system responsiveness by implementing session-aware recommendation models (Majeed et al., 2023). These systems constantly follow user behaviours including the act of viewing similar products or browsing different categories to adjust recommendations in response. Zalando adjusts its system in real time which gives users a sense that the platform learns together with them especially improving mobile experiences. Through its edge-enhanced AI infrastructure, Zalando maintains real-time data pipelines which supply clickstream data and behavioural changes to its recommendation models (Paul et al., 2024). These pipelines enable micro-personalization to dynamically adjust product listings and promotional content within milliseconds which leads to measurable improvements in satisfaction rates as well as conversion numbers (Islam et al., 2024). The integration of artificial intelligence with edge computing technology enables Zalando to minimize latency during customer experiences creating quicker and more seamless interactions (Pandey, 2024). Zalando maintains customer engagement while enhancing business results through instant feedback on user behaviour (Islam et al., 2024).

Strategic Competitive Advantage

In the present highly competitive e-commerce environment businesses gain strategic advantages through delivering personalized real-time customer experiences alongside functional value (Engelbergs, 2019). Zalando employs artificial intelligence (AI) extensively and integrative for personalization purposes which stands beyond customer engagement and functions as a core differentiator for their market position, operational efficiency and sustainable growth (Freno, 2017). Zalando's primary advantage stems from its data-driven personalization system that collects and processes massive amounts of behavioural and transactional data in near real time for immediate action (Freno, 2017). Zalando's infrastructure supports a diverse array of AI models that include collaborative filtering and neural networks as well as reinforcement learning and visual similarity algorithms to customize homepage content and product suggestions and determine pricing and promotions according to Guo et al. (2023). Zalando has developed its own AI infrastructure for personalized recommendations while competitors utilize third-party systems (Engelbergs, 2019). The company achieves enhanced operational flexibility and quicker iteration cycles alongside intellectual property protection and user data security. The company uses this capability to customize its AI systems specifically for fashion where visual and cultural relevance are essential (Guo et al., 2023). The AI ecosystem developed by Zalando serves as an entry barrier for competitors. The technological moat at Zalando stems from the complex nature of creating scalable real-time personalization systems at their operational magnitude (Oguntola & Simske, 2023). Successful deployment at this scale needs both infrastructure and teamwork among engineering, design, and merchandising departments (Engelbergs, 2019). Zalando uses AI operationally to optimize their inventory management and balance supply with demand while decreasing return rates through predictive models such as sizing tools (Loosley et al., 2023). Trend forecasting algorithms prevent excess inventory and improve reaction times to consumer demand changes. AI provides Zalando with the ability to implement localized personalization strategies throughout its European operations. Culturally tailored user experiences in Germany, France, and Italy become possible through the combination of language-specific NLP capabilities and insights into regional trends and demographics (Islam et al., 2024). Zalando employs AI as a strategic asset rather than merely an enhancement tool. The company maintains its competitive edge through its real-time personalization engine that provides both enhanced user experience and operational agility (Freno, 2017).

Figure 1. Illustrates how Zalando uses AI-driven personalisation frameworks that integrate edge AI techniques with modular models and explainable AI systems. The model demonstrates its capability to deliver personalisation that functions in real-time and is ethically built to scale across various user contexts.

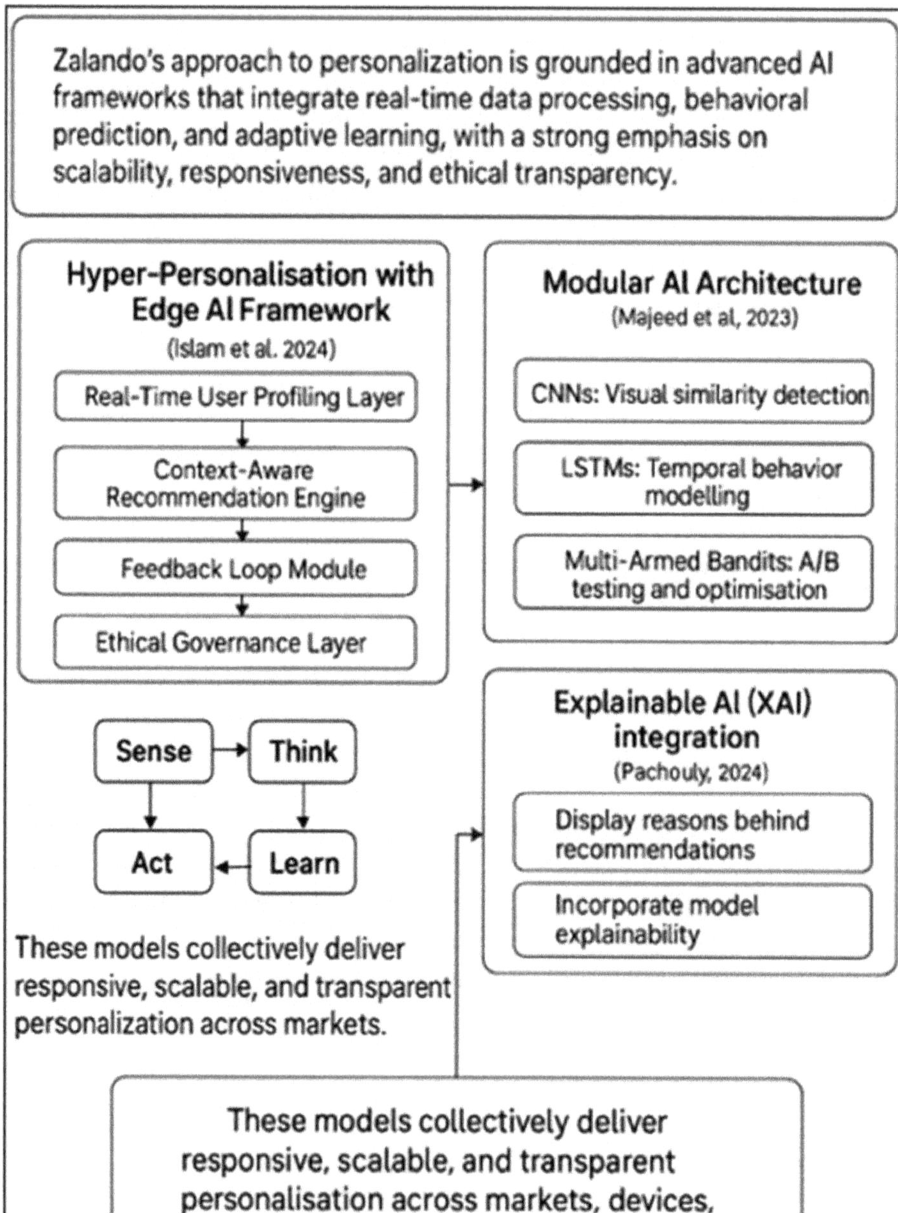

The AI-driven personalisation model from Zalando combines real-time edge computing with adaptive machine learning to provide hyper-personalised experiences. The system utilizes modular AI elements such as CNNs for image matching and LSTMs for predicting user behaviour which are improved with feedback loops alongside A/B testing methods. User interactions fuel continuous learning through the sense–think–act–learn cycle. The AI system incorporates ethical governance and explainable AI principles to promote transparency while building user trust. Recommendation engines that understand context provide suggestions based on both time-related and environmental factors such as location and weather conditions. The system can scale effectively in various markets and devices while adapting to different user profiles to maintain broad applicability and responsiveness.

SOLUTIONS AND RECOMMENDATIONS

Zalando must continually reassess its AI-driven personalization technology to ensure it meets standards of sustainability alongside inclusivity and accountability (Jain & Jain, 2024). AI systems that dominate customer journeys create operational difficulties and ethical concerns while influencing product visibility and purchasing patterns. Recommendation engines could potentially strengthen consumer stereotypes and decrease product diversity exposure while risking user privacy through unclear data handling practices when proper protective measures are absent (Falvo & Cannataro, 2024). Zalando's expanding global operations necessitate a personalization system that functions reliably while adapting to various cultural and regional user conditions (Prajapati, 2025). The delivery of precise personalized recommendations across large user bases requires both technological advancements such as edge computing and essential demands for algorithmic transparency, fairness and decision explainability (Para, 2024). The restoration of consumer trust proves challenging when algorithmic bias or privacy issues cause its initial loss (Uddin et al., 2024). These solutions work toward achieving equilibrium between technological progress and ethical development. The latest peer-reviewed research on ethical AI, system design, and personalization efficacy provides practical strategies that help Zalando, and other platforms maintain their performance goals while also ensuring public accountability in their AI personalization systems (Agu et al., 2024).

Establish Robust Ethical AI Governance

Algorithmic systems require essential ethical governance because artificial intelligence now drives platforms such as Zalando that directly interact with consumers. AI-powered recommendation engines bring improved customer interaction and business expansion but present challenges including bias introduction, user exclusion, misuse of data and non-transparent decision processes (Gupta, 2025). A comprehensive ethical AI governance framework that monitors, evaluates, and directs personalization technology deployment is necessary for Zalando to address these concerns. The central element of this framework needs to include regular algorithmic audits which evaluate recommendation models based on demographic factors like age, gender, body type, and cultural background. The audits can detect when specific user groups face underrepresentation or misrepresentation while being directed to limited product selections which threatens fair treatment and inclusivity (Murikah et al., 2024). Zalando needs to create interdisciplinary AI ethics committees which should include data scientists, ethicists, legal experts, customer advocates, and designers. These panels will monitor the deployment of new models while evaluating potential risks and crafting ethical standards for AI use. Recommendations need to maintain transparency, public availability and periodic updates that mirror social standards and legal obligations while adapting to customer expectation changes (Mökander & Floridi, 2022). Zalando needs to implement AI incident reporting protocols to enable both internal teams and external users to report unexpected results and discriminatory actions. This infrastructure creates opportunities for early detection of issues while promoting a culture of algorithmic responsibility and ongoing development (Schiff et al., 2024). Zalando's integration of ethical governance throughout its AI lifecycle enables the company to create personalization systems that deliver power and efficiency alongside fairness and social responsibility.

Embed Explainable AI (XAI) for User Trust

The growing sophistication of AI-driven personalization systems puts users in the dark about how certain products have been selected for them. Users experience discomfort and disengage from AI systems when transparency is missing because they find recommendations intrusive, irrelevant or biased according to Sarkar (2024). Zalando needs to incorporate Explainable AI (XAI) mechanisms into its personalization platform to address existing problems and boost the perceived integrity of its AI systems. XAI consists of techniques that enable human users to comprehend AI model outputs by providing straightforward context-sensitive decision-making explanations. Zalando can implement simple messages like "Recommended based on your past purchases and browsing history" or "Similar to items you viewed last week" to explain their recommendation logic without exposing algorithmic details (Sarkar, 2024). Studies reveal that applying explainable AI solutions boosts customer satisfaction and engagement levels in fashion e-commerce platforms where personal preferences strongly influence buying choices. Users who receive explanations for recommendations find them more helpful and show less outright rejection regardless of imperfect matches (Bura et al., 2025). The implementation of XAI helps companies meet increasing regulatory and ethical demands for algorithmic transparency. Through transparency in personalization Zalando shows its respect for user autonomy while reducing manipulation perceptions and developing stronger customer relationships. XAI functions as an essential strategic tool for building trust which supports ethical and accountable personalization methods beyond mere technical improvement (Sarkar, 2024).

Scale Real-Time Personalization with Edge Computing

Zalando's expanding user base and geographic expansion makes scalable personalization with low-latency more critical than ever. Traditional cloud-based AI architectures prove powerful yet encounter challenges with latency and bandwidth while managing privacy for large-scale real-time data processing. Zalando needs to adopt edge computing to enhance its personalization infrastructure and overcome current constraints according to Islam et al. (2024). Edge computing operates as a decentralized processing framework where AI calculations take place near the user through local servers or edge nodes instead of centralized cloud systems. E-commerce platforms gain substantial advantages through this method which allows them to deliver personalized real-time recommendations without burdening backend systems or introducing delays to users (Pandey, 2024). Zalando uses edge-based personalization logic to achieve rapid system response times which allows real-time adaptation when customers interact with products through clicks or scroll actions and switch between categories. Fashion retail demands fast responsiveness due to the impulsive nature of consumer purchases that rely heavily on visual appeal and the risk of slowing down the shopping experience leading to abandoned carts (Manduva, 2023). Edge computing brings improved data privacy and compliance advantages. Local data processing reduces the transmission of sensitive inputs to centralized servers which decreases potential data breach risks and ensures compliance with data protection laws such as the GDPR (Rancea et al., 2024). Edge computing enables scalability which helps Zalando preserve performance levels during expansion into new markets and the implementation of high-traffic marketing initiatives. The platform maintains speedy and relevant personalization at scale through effective computational load distribution (Manduva, 2023). By investing in edge computing infrastructure Zalando achieves fast and scalable personalization while protecting customer privacy which lays a foundation for advancement and growth in AI-powered fashion retail.

Apply Bias Detection During Model Development

The increasing impact of personalization algorithms on consumer decision-making necessitates prioritizing ethical and operational fairness and inclusivity. AI systems may unintentionally strengthen damaging biases about gender, race, body type, and socioeconomic status if they lack proper oversight. The intersection of appearance and personal style with social and cultural norms demonstrates relevance to fashion e-commerce. Zalando must apply bias detection and mitigation measures throughout its model development process to prevent algorithmic discrimination (Pagano et al., 2023). Imbalanced training data alongside incorrect assumptions during model training is what typically generates bias within AI systems. Visual recommendation systems can develop biases when training data includes disproportionate numbers of slim body types and lighter skin tones which leads to the marginalization of other types of appearances. Zalando needs to apply fairness-aware machine learning approaches including data rebalancing alongside fairness constraints during model optimization and bias correction methods after processing (Lohia et al., 2018). Diagnostic fairness tools which evaluate model outcomes across different demographic groups need implementation on the platform. Teams can use diagnostic tools to identify recommendation system disparities in frequency, relevance or engagement rates which allows them to make necessary model adjustments before deployment (Sonboli & Burke, 2019). The combination of interdisciplinary testing groups that include users from diverse backgrounds with evaluations helps ensure equitable system performance for the entire customer base. Public-facing AI ethics reports that disclose fairness goals and outcomes can enhance consumer trust while showcasing a dedication to responsible innovation. Bias detection requires ongoing attention and work which guarantees that personalization remains inclusive and respectful for every user (Prajapati, 2025).

FUTURE RESEARCH DIRECTIONS

While Zalando and similar platforms have made substantial advancements in AI-driven personalization, important research areas still need exploration. It is crucial to address these gaps to develop AI systems that maintain technical stability while simultaneously achieving ethical alignment and user-centred design.

Explainability in Complex AI Systems

The increased sophistication of artificial intelligence systems through deep learning, reinforcement learning, and ensemble modelling leads to more opaque inner workings that create the "black box" problem. Personalization in fashion e-commerce relies on user trust which faces challenges when recommendations appear arbitrary or biased and lack explainability. The requirement for personalization that users can understand clearly has emerged as a primary focus for both scholarly studies and practical system development according to Thalpage's findings from 2023. Next generation research initiatives need to focus on building Explainable AI (XAI) systems that understand context while remaining user-friendly. These systems need to deliver transparency to internal stakeholders like data scientists and auditors while providing end users with explanations that are both accessible and intuitive. A recommendation could feature tooltips or labels which state, "Suggested because you liked similar prints" or "Recommended for upcoming warm weather" and these brief explanations help clarify algorithmic decisions while avoiding complicated technical terms (Zodage et al., 2024). The development of techniques in causality-based explanations along with neuro-symbolic AI provides exciting directions for future advancement. Causality-based models demonstrate the reasons behind specific recommendations based on input data according to Ashkari & Rezig (2024). Neuro-symbolic AI merges neural networks' pattern recognition abilities with symbolic systems' rule-based structure to generate models that are more powerful and easier to understand (Longo et al., 2023). Research into explainability needs to incorporate both cultural elements and psychological aspects. The standard for what is considered a "clear explanation" differs between demographics and regions so future XAI systems must be designed to adjust to user needs. Advancements in explainability are vital for ensuring transparency, trustworthiness, and ethical personalization in future AI systems (Zodage et al., 2024).

Ethical Personalization at Scale

The ethical considerations of personalization become more complicated as AI-driven platforms such as Zalando grow to accommodate more varied global audiences. These systems aim to boost engagement and conversion, but they may accidentally stereotype or dismiss users especially from lesser-represented demographics, cultures and body-types. Future research needs to develop systems that institutionalize fairness in personalization while maintaining both recommendation quality and user relevance (Lal et al., 2020). A viable approach is to create transparent fairness measurements for analysing the treatment of distinct user groups within recommendation systems. Model evaluation pipelines must incorporate these metrics to frequently determine if content exposure and recommendation frequency or user outcomes show unequal treatment towards segments. Fairness-aware models deliver balanced fashion suggestions that appropriately engage customers regardless of their size, skin tone or style preferences (Zhang, 2024). Personalization models need to adapt to user context and identity to create segmented groups that transcend rigid and oversimplified classifications. The method of counterfactual fairness modelling predicts how recommendations would change with different demographic attributes and provides an effective approach for identifying and fixing biases (Li et al., 2021). The application of virtue ethics frameworks to AI system design represents an emerging research direction. Virtue ethics stands apart from deontological or consequentialist approaches because it stresses moral reflection and empathy while maintaining responsibility throughout the entire AI lifecycle. Personalization systems can respect user dignity and diversity when teams incorporate these principles into their practices and data management approaches as well as their model objectives (Neidhardt, 2024). Ethical personalization for large-scale applications demands interdisciplinary breakthroughs in fairness-aware artificial intelligence, adaptive modelling techniques, and values-focused system design which result in personalization that achieves effectiveness while maintaining inclusivity and justice.

Cross-Disciplinary Collaboration

Creating ethical and effective AI personalization systems requires collaborative efforts beyond just data scientists and engineers. The growing impact of personalization technologies on consumer identity and social-commercial outcomes creates an essential need for cross-disciplinary collaboration. Subsequent investigations should prioritize AI systems designed through participatory methods which unite various experts including fashion designers and UX researchers along with ethicists, psychologists and legal scholars and end-users (Lase & Nkosi, 2023). Fashion e-commerce demands creative professional input to help AI systems authentically match user preferences because aesthetic taste and cultural diversity are integral to customer journeys. UX professionals and human-computer interaction experts significantly influence user interactions with AI by focusing on transparency and control to build trust (Puerta-Beldarrain et al., 2025). Ethicists and legal scholars develop responsible innovation frameworks which help teams understand complex concepts like fairness, data governance, and informed consent. Human-in-the-loop design methodologies engage users to enable iterative personalization algorithm testing and refinement through real-world feedback and social contexts according to Chen et al. (2023). Research teams should develop structured processes by using AI design frameworks that include multiple stakeholders. The protocols to establish regular interdisciplinary reviews along with participatory workshops and ethical impact assessments need to be integrated into AI lifecycles instead of being treated as secondary elements (Conati, 2024). Cross-disciplinary collaboration enables the creation of personalization systems which achieve technical advancement while maintaining social intelligence and inclusive design that respects human values.

CONCLUSION

The fashion e-commerce sector has undergone a transformation through artificial intelligence which enables Zalando to provide users with personalized experiences that are both efficient and emotionally engaging. Zalando boosted conversion rates, average order values, and customer lifetime value by implementing advanced technologies including deep learning recommendation systems and real-time behavioural tracking along with reinforcement learning and context-aware algorithms. Quantifiable improvements illustrate how properly deployed AI systems can tremendously boost business outcomes alongside user satisfaction levels. The expanding role of AI-driven personalization introduces numerous complicated problems that demand immediate attention. The ethical implications of automated personalization arise from multiple concerns which include algorithmic transparency and data privacy as well as cultural representation and fairness. The essential requirement for AI systems which influence consumer behaviour and digital identity creation is that they function with transparency and fairness while maintaining responsibility. The personalization framework of Zalando demonstrates an effective method for integrating commercial innovation with ethical standards. Sustainable AI personalization models must incorporate explainable AI to build user trust and combine edge computing for scalability while using fairness-aware algorithms to avoid discriminating against underrepresented user groups. Responsible innovation practices benefit from sustainability-focused recommendation filters combined with interdisciplinary collaboration and participatory design approaches. Research studies moving forward need to investigate the extended psychological, behavioural, and social effects of AI personalization to discover methods that maintain precision while enabling exploration and preserving user autonomy. The creation of regulatory and organizational frameworks which maintain ethical standards while allowing technological progress and creative freedom is equally essential. AI success in fashion personalization will depend on its ability to respect human diversity and values along with technical excellence. Zalando's forthcoming innovation phase demands the creation of systems which balance ethical and inclusive qualities with intelligent and profitable features.

REFERENCES

Abbas, W., Rasheed, U., Khalid, S., Ghazanfar, M., & Hassan, A. (2024). Kernel Fashion Context Recommender System (KFCR): A kernel mapping fashion recommender system algorithm using contextual information. *2024 21st International Bhurban Conference on Applied Sciences and Technology (IBCAST)*, 123–128. DOI: 10.1109/IBCAST61650.2024.10877155

Adanyin, A. (2024). *Ethical AI in retail: Consumer privacy and fairness*. World Journal of Advanced Research and Reviews., DOI: 10.30574/wjarr.2024.21.1.2611

. Agu, E. E., Abhulimen, A. O., Obiki-Osafiele, A. N., Osundare, O. S., Adeniran, I. A., & Efunniyi, C. P. (2024). Discussing ethical considerations and solutions for ensuring fairness in AI-driven financial services. *International Journal of Frontline Research in Multidisciplinary Studies*. DOI: 10.56355/ijfrms.2024.3.2.0024

Akter, J., Roy, A., Rahman, S., Mohona, S., & Ara, J. (2025). Artificial intelligence–driven customer lifetime value (CLV) forecasting: Integrating RFM analysis with machine learning for strategic customer retention. *Journal of Computer Science and Technology Studies*, *7*(1), 145–159. DOI: 10.32996/jcsts.2025.7.1.18

Amosu, O. R., Kumar, P., Fadina, A., Ogunsuji, Y. M., Oni, S., & Faworaja, O. (2024). *Data-driven personalized marketing: Deep learning in retail and E-commerce*. World Journal of Advanced Research and Reviews., DOI: 10.30574/wjarr.2024.23.2.2395

Ashkari, A., & Rezig, E. (2024). Can causal DAGs generate data-based explanations of black-box models? *2024 IEEE International Conference on Big Data (BigData)*, 5739–5744. https://doi.org/DOI: 10.1109/BigData62323.2024.10825482

Ay, B., & Aydin, G. (2021). Visual similarity-based fashion recommendation system. In *Generative Adversarial Networks for Image-to-Image Translation* (pp. 375–400). DOI: 10.1016/B978-0-12-823519-5.00023-3

Bura, C., Jonnalagadda, A. K., & Naayini, P. (2025). *The role of explainable AI (XAI) in trust and adoption. Journal of Artificial Intelligence General Science*. JAIGS., DOI: 10.60087/jaigs.v7i01.331

Chen, X., Wang, X., & Qu, Y. (2023). Constructing ethical AI based on the "Human-in-the-Loop" system. *Systems*, *11*(11), 548. DOI: 10.3390/systems11110548

Choppadandi, A. (2023). *Enhancing customer experience in e-commerce through AI-powered personalization: A case study*. Tuijin Jishu/Journal of Propulsion Technology., DOI: 10.52783/tjjpt.v43.i4.6018

Conati, C. (2024). AI-driven personalization to support human-AI collaboration. In *Proceedings of the 16th ACM SIGCHI Symposium on Engineering Interactive Computing Systems (EICS '24)*. DOI: 10.1145/3660515.3661324

Demissie, S., & Mogalla, S. (2018). A clustering-based context-aware recommender systems through extraction of latent preferences. *International Journal of Advanced Research in Computer Science*, *9*(2), 699–707. DOI: 10.26483/ijarcs.v9i2.5862

Egorenkov, D. (2024). AI-powered predictive customer lifetime value: Maximizing long-term profits. *International Journal of Scientific Research and Management*, *12*(9), EM02. DOI: 10.18535/ijsrm/v12i09.em02

Engelbergs, J. (2019). Performance management of the digital pure play Zalando. In *Performance Management in Retail and the Consumer Goods Industry* (pp. 219–236). Springer., DOI: 10.1007/978-3-030-12730-5_12

Faizi, A. (2025). AIS impact on personalizing e-commerce experiences. *International Journal of Advanced Research*, *13*(1), 1329–1331. Advance online publication. DOI: 10.21474/IJAR01/20322

Falvo, F. R., & Cannataro, M. (2024). Ethics of Artificial Intelligence: Challenges, opportunities and future prospects. *2024 IEEE International Conference on Bioinformatics and Biomedicine (BIBM)*, 5860–5867. DOI: 10.1109/BIBM62325.2024.10822112

Freno, A. (2017). Practical lessons from developing a large-scale recommender system at Zalando. In *Proceedings of the Eleventh ACM Conference on Recommender Systems* (pp. 346–350). DOI: 10.1145/3109859.3109897

Guo, Z., Zhu, Z., Li, Y., Cao, S., Chen, H., & Wang, G. (2023). AI-assisted fashion design: A review. *IEEE Access : Practical Innovations, Open Solutions*, *11*, 88403–88415. DOI: 10.1109/ACCESS.2023.3306235

. Gupta, S. (2025). Ethical considerations in AI-driven personalization for eCommerce platforms. *International Journal of Scientific Research in Computer Science, Engineering and Information Technology*. DOI: 10.32628/CSEIT251112371

Gupta, T., & Bansal, S. (2019). The AI advantage: Assessing personalization effects on e-commerce shopping behaviors. [IJSR]. *International Journal of Science and Research (Raipur, India)*, *8*(8), 2313–2320. Advance online publication. DOI: 10.21275/SR24321084709

Hariri, N., Mobasher, B., & Burke, R. (2013). Query-driven context-aware recommendation. *Proceedings of the 7th ACM Conference on Recommender Systems*. DOI: 10.1145/2507157.2507187

Islam, R., Arafat, M. S., Jony, M. A. M., Rafi, S., Jalil, M. S., & Hossen, F. (2024). Hyper-personalization with AI and edge computing: The future of customer experience in e-commerce and retail. *Advanced International Journal of Multidisciplinary Research*, *2*(6), 13–24. DOI: 10.62127/aijmr.2024.v02i06.1114

. Jain, A. M., & Jain, A. (2024). AI-based content creation and product recommendation applications in e-commerce: An ethical overview. *International Journal of Scientific Research in Computer Science, Engineering and Information Technology*. DOI: 10.32628/CSEIT2410414

Jeon, Y., Jin, S., Shih, P. C., & Han, K. (2021). FashionQ: An AI-driven creativity support tool for facilitating ideation in fashion design. *Proceedings of the 2021 CHI Conference on Human Factors in Computing Systems*. DOI: 10.1145/3411764.3445093

Kalinin, A., Jafari, A. A., Avots, E., Ozcinar, C., & Anbarjafari, G. (2024). Generative AI-based style recommendation using fashion item detection and classification. *Signal, Image and Video Processing*, *18*(12), 9179–9189. DOI: 10.1007/s11760-024-03538-x

Kandi, A. (2024). Personalization and customer relationship management in AI-powered business intelligence. *International Journal for Research in Applied Science and Engineering Technology*, *12*(4), 652–660. DOI: 10.22214/ijraset.2024.65159

Khoa, T. A., Dao, M.-S., Nguyen, D., & Zettsu, K. (2024). Clustering-enhanced reinforcement learning for adaptive offloading in resource-constrained devices. *2024 IEEE International Conference on Smart Computing (SMARTCOMP)*, 133–140. DOI: 10.1109/SMARTCOMP61445.2024.00039

Krishnamurthy, S., Tirupati, K. K., Ganipaneni, S., Shrivastav, E. A., Vashishtha, S., & Jain, S. (2024). *Leveraging AI and machine learning to optimize retail operations and enhance*. Darpan International Research Analysis., DOI: 10.36676/dira.v12.i3.140

Lal, G. R., Geyik, S. C., & Kenthapadi, K. (2020). Fairness-aware online personalization. *arXiv preprint arXiv:2007.15270*. https://arxiv.org/abs/2007.15270

Lase, E. M., & Nkosi, F. (2023). Human-centric AI: Understanding and enhancing collaboration between humans and intelligent systems. *Algorithm Asynchronous*, *1*(1), 33–40. DOI: 10.61963/jaa.v1i1.49

Li, Y., Chen, H., Xu, S., Ge, Y., & Zhang, Y. (2021). Personalized counterfactual fairness in recommendation. *Proceedings of the 44th International ACM SIGIR Conference on Research and Development in Information Retrieval*. https://doi.org/ DOI: 10.1145/3404835.3462966

Liu, X., Wang, G., & Bhuiyan, M. Z. A. (2021). Personalised context-aware re-ranking in recommender system. *Connection Science*, *34*(3), 319–338. DOI: 10.1080/09540091.2021.1997915

Liu, Y., Li, G., Payne, T. R., Yue, Y., & Man, K. L. (2024). Choosing the right path: A comparative study of CNN, RNN, and transformer models for sequential recommendation systems. *2024 International Conference on Platform Technology and Service (PlatCon)*, 77–82. DOI: 10.1109/PlatCon63925.2024.10830671

Lohia, P., Ramamurthy, K. N., Bhide, M., Saha, D., Varshney, K., & Puri, R. (2018). Bias mitigation post-processing for individual and group fairness. In *2019 IEEE International Conference on Acoustics, Speech and Signal Processing (ICASSP)* (pp. 2847–2851). DOI: 10.1109/ICASSP.2019.8682620

Longo, L., Brcic, M., Cabitza, F., Choi, J., Confalonieri, R., Ser, J., . . . Stumpf, S. (2023). Explainable Artificial Intelligence (XAI) 2.0: A manifesto of open challenges and interdisciplinary research directions. *arXiv preprint arXiv:2310.19775*. https://doi.org//arXiv.2310.19775DOI: 10.48550

Loosley, A., Seifoddini, A., Canopoli, A., & Zehlike, M. (2023). Body measurement prediction fairness. *CEUR Workshop Proceedings*, *3442*, 1–12. DOI: 10.48550/arXiv.2112.03111

Majeed, O. K., Abideen, Z. U., Arshad, U., Ali, R. H., Habib, A., & Mustafa, R. (2023). AdaptiveCloset: Reinforcement learning in personalized clothing recommendations. *2023 18th International Conference on Emerging Technologies (ICET)*, 305–309. DOI: 10.1109/ICET59753.2023.10375063

Manduva, V. C. (2023). *AI-driven edge computing in the cloud era: Challenges and opportunities. International Journal of Scientific Research and Management.* IJSRM., DOI: 10.18535/ijsrm/v11i02.ec5

Mökander, J., & Floridi, L. (2022). Operationalising AI governance through ethics-based auditing: An industry case study. *AI and Ethics*, *3*(3), 451–468. DOI: 10.1007/s43681-022-00171-7 PMID: 35669570

Murikah, W., Nthenge, J. K., & Musyoka, F. (2024). Bias and ethics of AI systems applied in auditing: A systematic review. *Scientific African*, *18*, e02281. DOI: 10.1016/j.sciaf.2024.e02281

Neidhardt, J. (2024). Transforming recommender systems: Balancing personalization, fairness, and human values. *Proceedings of the 33rd International Joint Conference on Artificial Intelligence (IJCAI-24)*, 8559–8564. https://doi.org/DOI: 10.24963/ijcai.2024/982

Oguntola, A., & Simske, S. J. (2023). Real-time decision-making using automated systems. *2023 International Conference on Advanced Computing, Networking and Informatics*. https://doi.org/DOI: 10.1109/ACNI2023.00018

Pagano, T., Loureiro, R. B., Lisboa, F. V. N., Peixoto, R. M., Guimarães, G. A. S., Cruz, G. O. R., Araujo, M. M., Santos, L. L., Cruz, M. A. S., Oliveira, E. L. S., Winkler, I., & Nascimento, E. (2023). Bias and unfairness in machine learning models: A systematic review on datasets, tools, fairness metrics, and identification and mitigation methods. *Big Data and Cognitive Computing*. https://consensus.app/papers/bias-and-unfairness-in-machine-learning-models-a-pagano-loureiro/eada7cf8899f55f686427229367e6803/?utm_source=chatgpt

Pandey, D. M. (2024). Edge AI: Revolutionizing real-time intelligence at the network periphery. *International Journal for Research in Applied Science and Engineering Technology*, *12*(8), 203–212. Advance online publication. DOI: 10.22214/ijraset.2024.63875

Para, R. K. (2024). The role of explainable AI in bias mitigation for hyper-personalization. [JAIGS]. *Journal of Artificial Intelligence General Science*, *6*(1), 625–635. Advance online publication. DOI: 10.60087/jaigs.v6i1.289

Paul, R., Islam, S. A. M., Sarkar, A., Obaidur, J. M., Khan, R., Islam, T., & Bari, M. S. (2024). The role of edge computing in driving real-time personalized marketing: A data-driven business perspective. *International Journal For Multidisciplinary Research*, *6*(5), 28494. Advance online publication. DOI: 10.36948/ijfmr.2024.v06i05.28494

Perera, A. P. S. S., Hettiarachchi, A. B., Gunasekara, P. G. A. I. P., Jayasekara, H. L., Tissera, W., & Rathnayake, S. (2024). Enhancing fashion intelligence for exceptional customer experience. *2024 8th International Conference on Business and Information Management (ICBIM)*, 23–28. DOI: 10.1109/ICBIM63313.2024.10823442

Prajapati, S. B.Sameerkumar Babubhai Prajapati. (2025). Existing challenges in ethical AI. *World Journal of Advanced Research and Reviews*, *25*(1), 0267. Advance online publication. DOI: 10.30574/wjarr.2025.25.1.0267

Puerta-Beldarrain, M., Gómez-Carmona, O., Sánchez-Corcuera, R., Casado-Mansilla, D., López-de-Ipiña, D., & Chen, L. (2025). A multifaceted vision of the human-AI collaboration: A comprehensive review. *IEEE Access : Practical Innovations, Open Solutions*, *13*, 29375–29405. DOI: 10.1109/ACCESS.2025.3536095

Rancea, A., Anghel, I., & Cioara, T. (2024). Edge computing in healthcare: Innovations, opportunities, and challenges. *Future Internet*, *16*(9), 329. DOI: 10.3390/fi16090329

. Sanjana, R., Harshitha, V. S., Navyasree, K., Srija, G., Bharathi, M., & Srinivas, T. A. S. (2025). Glam guidance: Empowering your fashion choices with image insights. *Journal of Image Processing and Image Restoration*. DOI: 10.48001/joipir.2025.211-5

Sarkar, M. (2024). Explainable AI in e-commerce: Enhancing trust and transparency in AI-driven decisions. *Innovatech Engineering Journal*, *2*(1), 12–39. Advance online publication. DOI: 10.70937/itej.v2i01.53

Schiff, D., Kelley, S., & Camacho Ibáñez, J. (2024). The emergence of artificial intelligence ethics auditing. *Big Data & Society*, *11*(1), 20539517241299732. Advance online publication. DOI: 10.1177/20539517241299732

Silva, L., Gomes, I., Araújo, C., Cepeda, T., Oliveira, F., & Oliveira, J. (2024). A regression deep learning approach for fashion compatibility. *Proceedings of the 19th International Conference on Computer Vision Theory and Applications (VISAPP)*, 141–148. DOI: 10.5220/0012682300003690

Singh, P., Jaiswal, S., Srivastava, S., Azad, M. L., Mishra, V., & Nautiyal, A. (2024). Fashion forward: Exploring the influence of AI on modern fashion trends. *2024 7th International Conference on Contemporary Computing and Informatics (IC3I)*, 864–869. DOI: 10.1109/IC3I61595.2024.10829054

Sonboli, N., & Burke, R. (2019). Localized fairness in recommender systems. In *Adjunct Publication of the 27th Conference on User Modeling, Adaptation and Personalization* (UMAP). DOI: 10.1145/3314183.3323845

Tan, C., Han, R., Ye, R., & Chen, K. (2020). Adaptive learning recommendation strategy based on deep Q-learning. *Applied Psychological Measurement*, *44*(3), 251–266. DOI: 10.1177/0146621619858674 PMID: 32536728

Tareaf, R. B., Korga, A. M., Wefers, S., Hanken, K., & Rawwash, M. (2024). Applying XAI in Fashion-MNIST: Evaluating hybrid deep neural networks and capsule networks. *Proceedings of the 2024 16th International Conference on Machine Learning and Computing*, 72–78. DOI: 10.1145/3651671.3651760

Thakur, H., Singh, J., Saxena, A., Bhaskar, D., Singh, A. P., & Garg, P. K. (2024). Enhancing customer experience through AI-powered personalization: A data science perspective in e-commerce. *2024 International Conference on Communication, Computer Sciences and Engineering (IC3SE)*, 501–506. DOI: 10.1109/IC3SE62002.2024.10592893

Thalpage, N. (2023). Unlocking the black box: Explainable artificial intelligence (XAI) for trust and transparency in AI systems. *Journal of Digital Art & Humanities*. https://doi.org//arXiv.2310.19775DOI: 10.48550

. Tulasi, S., & Ahamed, I. (2025). AI-powered e-commerce personalization and recommendation systems. *Journal of Informatics Education and Research*. DOI: 10.52783/jier.v5i1.2197

Turaga, K. S., & Shankar, D. (2022). Image classification with big data and distributed deep learning. *IEEE Big Data Conference Proceedings*. https://consensus.app/papers/image-classification-with-big-data-and-distributed-deep-turaga-shankar/7ceb552452f554dfbd130f969080d7b7/?utm_source=chatgpt

Uddin, M., Saif, I., Nabil, J., Afsara, K., & Ashraful, I. (2024). The influence of artificial intelligence on consumer trust in e-commerce: Opportunities and ethical challenges. *European Journal of Theoretical and Applied Sciences*, *2*(6), 20. Advance online publication. DOI: 10.59324/ejtas.2024.2(6).20

Ünlü, S. C. (2024). Enhancing user experience through AI-driven personalization in user interfaces. *Human-Computer Interaction*, *8*(1), 19. Advance online publication. DOI: 10.62802/m7mqmb52

. Varma, N. (2024). STYLESYNC: A fashion recommendation system. *International Journal of Scientific Research in Engineering and Management*. DOI: 10.55041/IJSREM34672

Xu, Y., Wang, W., Feng, F., Ma, Y., Zhang, J., & He, X. (2024). Diffusion models for generative outfit recommendation. *Proceedings of the ACM Web Conference 2024*, 1350–1359. DOI: 10.1145/3626772.3657719

Zhang, T. (2024). A research proposal for promoting fairness in e-commerce recommendation systems. *2024 11th International Conference on Behavioural and Social Computing (BESC)*, 1–5. https://doi.org/DOI: 10.1109/BESC64747.2024.10780676

Zhu, J., Wei, Y., Kang, Y., Jiang, X., & Dullerud, G. (2022). Adaptive deep reinforcement learning for non-stationary environments. *Science China. Information Sciences*, *65*(10), 202204. Advance online publication. DOI: 10.1007/s11432-021-3347-8

Zodage, P., Harianawala, H., Shaikh, H., & Kharodia, A. (2024). Explainable AI (XAI): History, basic ideas and methods. *International Journal of Advanced Research in Science. Tongxin Jishu*, 560–568. Advance online publication. DOI: 10.48175/IJARSCT-16988

KEY TERMS AND DEFINITIONS

Algorithmic Bias: Biased training data produces systematic unfairness in AI outputs.

Artificial Intelligence (AI): Artificial intelligence systems that replicate human tasks such as learning and decision-making.

Collaborative Filtering: Recommending items based on similar users' preferences.

Data Privacy: Ensuring the security of personal information against unauthorized access and exploitation.

Deep Learning: Neural network models that identify intricate patterns within extensive data collections.

Machine Learning (ML): AI methods allow systems to learn patterns from data without needing explicit programming instructions.

Personalization: The process of adjusting content and experiences to suit each user's data.

Chapter 7
Ethical AI in Marketing Facebook's Efforts to Balance Customer Privacy and Personalization

Sadia Akter
https://orcid.org/0009-0008-6442-3746
National University Bangladesh, Gazipur, Bangladesh

ABSTRACT

Artificial intelligence revolutionizes marketing but presents significant ethical issues about privacy, transparency, and user control that need to be addressed. The chapter examines Meta's efforts to strike a balance between personal privacy and commercial data usage through transparency tools, private data protection technologies, and algorithmic decision making. AI systems that deliver top-level engagement and advertising results inevitably manipulate users while amplifying biases and lacking substantial transparency. Facebook's potential initiatives may encompass explainable AI tools together with differential privacy and federated learning to serve users while ensuring real accountability. The chapter ends by advocating for greater algorithmic transparency and independent audits as well as human-centred design approaches while urging future research to investigate the extended effects of personalized marketing through AI.

BACKGROUND

Artificial intelligence's swift development has revolutionized digital marketing practices by promoting hyper-personalized experiences through precise data analysis.

DOI: 10.4018/979-8-3373-6582-4.ch007

Meta (previously known as Facebook) demonstrates this digital shift by leveraging AI to provide personalized content that boosts user interaction and increases ad profits (Meta, 2025). Through AI systems businesses achieve exceptional precision in user targeting by refining interactions based on user behaviour and psychological profiles as well as their interests. The advancement creates substantial ethical dilemmas principally concerning privacy concerns as well as user autonomy alongside algorithmic transparency and psychological manipulation techniques. The demand for ethical AI deployment frameworks in marketing increases alongside public recognition of associated risks. The Ethical AI framework promotes fundamental principles including transparency together with accountability as well as fairness and the protection of user rights according to Prem (2023). These principles serve to synchronize technological progress with human dignity and democratic principles. Ethical AI in marketing involves creating systems that prioritize consumer protection against exploitation and maintain informed consent instead of solely focusing on click or conversion optimization. The analysis within this chapter focuses on Facebook's implementation of ethical AI practices within its marketing strategies. The analysis investigates Facebook's personalization efforts alongside privacy protection while reviewing algorithm transparency issues and assessing the effectiveness of present reforms in meeting both public and regulatory standards. This chapter delivers strategic guidance for marketers, developers, and policymakers who aim to implement AI systems responsibly. It is structured to include: The chapter examines AI development in marketing history before analysing Facebook's methods and then offering ethical AI adoption strategies followed by future research directions and industry-wide implications. Digital marketing has transformed from basic data analysis to advanced AI-based personalization throughout the last twenty years. Marketing used demographic data and user cookies to build early strategies but now machine learning enables real-time prediction and influence of behaviour (Verma et al., 2021). The transformation of digital marketing through AI deployment saw Facebook emerge as a pioneer when it launched systems such as the News Feed algorithm, dynamic ad targeting methods, and content recommendation engines. These tools initiated a new precision marketing era which boosted both user engagement and advertising efficiency. These technologies made it difficult to distinguish between personalized experiences and manipulative tactics which created immediate ethical dilemmas. The Cambridge Analytica scandal of 2018 served as a significant shift in public conversations. The 2018 Cambridge Analytica scandal exposed how Facebook collected user data without consent and manipulated political behaviour on a large scale (Graham-Harrison & Cadwalladr, 2018). The event demonstrated that algorithmic systems could turn into manipulation tools rather than empowerment resources when they operate without proper oversight. Facebook responded to severe criticism by implementing several transparency measures which included forming an Oversight Board and increasing transparency in ads while improving user privacy settings. Despite these changes critics assert that Facebook's reforms fail to tackle the fundamental conflict between ethical standards and financial objectives. Legislative measures have started to redefine data ethics expectations. The European General Data Protection Regulation and the California Consumer Privacy Act require enhanced consent procedures together with data reduction practices and clearer algorithm explanations (Djerf, 2023). New regulations force organizations like Facebook to redesign their AI infrastructure, so it serves user rights before business goals. Adhering to standards alone is not sufficient to ensure ethical integrity. The deeper question remains: Is it possible for engagement-focused platforms to achieve optimization for user well-being? The field of ethical AI has developed into a multidisciplinary area that connects philosophy with law and computer science along with marketing. The "AI for Good" and "Responsible AI" initiatives argue for systems that achieve technical efficiency while maintaining social and moral alignment. Facebook's experience demonstrates how AI marketing at scale can deliver both powerful results and significant ethical challenges. The situation functions as an important warning to the industry while also standing as a strong example for establishing AI governance that emphasizes accountability and transparency. Companies need to adopt design principles focused on user empowerment to build a responsible future for AI in marketing beyond regulatory compliance. The chapter demonstrates how marketing practices can incorporate ethical AI to achieve effective and fair results.

Focus of the Chapter

The study explores AI marketing ethics by examining how Meta continues Facebook's work to balance personalized ads with user privacy protection. Data ethics and algorithmic fairness debates are central to AI-driven marketing strategies according to Bahangulu & Owusu-Berko (2025) but these debates gain more importance when companies track and analyse user behaviour to optimize advertising. This tension has broad implications for both industry and society: AI-driven personalized marketing boosts customer interaction and sales but risks user privacy and amplifies existing biases and platform-user power disparities. Marketers, technologists, and policymakers need to immediately reflect on the ethical aspects of these issues. This chapter aims to unpack Facebook's approach to ethical AI in marketing by examining three dimensions: The chapter examines Facebook's approach to ethical AI in marketing by analysing three main factors: the current utilization of AI for content and ad personalization, the ethical data use principles stated by the company alongside their initiatives, and the disparity between these public claims and actual practices. The examination of this topic requires an analysis of how IoT connects regular devices such as smart speakers and home appliances to extensive networks which gather and distribute user data. The Internet of Things extends AI-driven marketing capabilities through precise data gathering and detailed behavioural analyses without users' explicit knowledge. The interconnected ecosystem delivers personalized marketing experiences but introduces privacy and surveillance risks since users often do not understand how their data is collected and applied. Any ethical framework needs to incorporate how IoT devices expand user digital footprints beyond standard online activities thus increasing the ethical considerations involved in AI marketing. This chapter analyses case studies and internal policies alongside public critiques to explore if Facebook's AI tactics focus on user welfare or serve as a façade for monetizing data. The chapter examines Facebook as a case study to support discussions about responsible innovation within digital marketing and provides guidance to companies encountering comparable ethical dilemmas. This section aims to connect theoretical ethical concepts with their real-world implementation within platform-based marketing frameworks.

Current Applications

AI-Powered Ad Targeting for Personalized Consumer Engagement

Artificial intelligence enables Facebook's advertising platform to analyse user behaviour data from billions of accounts and deliver personalized campaigns at scale. Machine learning enables Facebook to detect patterns from user activities like likes and comments and predict preferences to serve ads at the best times (Anshari et al., 2022). Advertising professionals can divide audiences based on demographic information and psychographic factors that include interests alongside stages of life and political views. Custom Audiences and Lookalike Audiences function as tools for customer retention and acquisition while improving reach and return on investment (Mehta & Erickson, 2022). Facebook utilizes adaptive predictive models that offer real-time optimizations, A/B testing capabilities and personalized content delivery for specific micro-segments beyond traditional reactive advertising. Businesses gain access to affordable precision-targeted advertising that reaches larger audiences through these capabilities. However, these AI mechanisms raise ethical concerns. Most users do not give informed consent because they remain unaware that their behaviour serves as training material for AI systems. Opaque targeting methods may turn manipulative when used in sensitive domains including health care or political campaigning. The fairness dilemma intensifies with algorithmic bias because models built from imbalanced datasets tend to uphold existing social disparities while denying marginalized communities access to job and housing opportunities. The "Why am I seeing this ad?" feature on Facebook has been implemented yet transparency stays restricted. Users and regulators are increasingly examining the platform for its data governance practices alongside its algorithmic transparency and user control mechanisms. The expanding role of AI in digital marketing necessitates the development of regulatory frameworks to maintain ethical operations. Transparency combined with user control and bias safeguards must form the basis of responsible social media advertising innovation.

Dynamic Creative Optimization to Enhance Ad Performance Automatically

Through its AI capabilities Facebook's Dynamic Creative Optimization (DCO) stands as a top ad serving platform which automatically constructs and distributes personalized ad combinations to a large audience. Traditional ads display identical content across all users while DCO constructs individualized advertisements by merging different elements like headlines, images, videos, and calls to action. The system analyses real-time engagement metrics to optimize content delivery for different demographics based on clicks, impressions, and conversions (Upadhyaya, 2024). DCO produces multiple creative variations from one set and automatically pinpoints which combinations connect most effectively with different audience groups. The tool integrates with Facebook's Ad Manager to automate creative testing alongside personalization without human intervention (Habib et al., 2022). Within the same campaign setup one user might view a vibrant and energetic ad while another user encounters a direct and informative version. However, DCO raises ethical concerns. The psychological targeting features of DCO potentially manipulate users by triggering feelings of urgency and insecurity which makes personalization indistinguishable from manipulation (Hacker, 2023). Users remain unaware of behavioural profiling in ad delivery because DCO operates invisibly. Automating large volumes of ad variations makes it hard to achieve transparency and accountability because it prevents tracking individual messages and evaluating ethical risks. The current tools Facebook provides for auditing and documenting DCO decisions are limited which results in oversight gaps. While DCO doesn't pose inherent threats it requires responsible implementation through transparent data practices user consent varied creative approaches and strict content audits. Ethical use of DCO results in advantages for advertisers and consumers while the lack of safeguards allows it to become an invisible force that manipulates user behaviour unknowingly.

Content Recommendation and Moderation Through Predictive AI Systems

Facebook uses predictive AI systems to influence user experience through large-scale content recommendations and post moderation. Machine learning algorithms examine user activity through likes, comments, scrolling speed, and watch time to customize content feeds and enhance user engagement (Ko et al., 2022). The system learns from user interactions which enables it to continuously enhance content delivery through a feedback loop. This method increases platform activity but leads to worries about "filter bubbles" and "echo chambers" which restrict users from encountering different perspectives while intensifying both polarization and misinformation. The AI system of Facebook extends its function beyond recommendations to automatically identify and eliminate posts that breach community guidelines. Hate speech and explicit content along with misinformation are targeted by AI moderation systems particularly during critical events according to Gündüzyeli (2025). AI moderation systems face difficulties understanding context which leads them to misinterpret satirical content and cultural nuances along with slang expressions. Users become frustrated when content moderation systems mistakenly remove safe material while failing to detect dangerous content because these errors damage trust. Algorithmic bias is another issue. AI moderation systems that learn from biased datasets tend to target material from marginalized groups more often which sustains discrimination and suppresses authentic expression (Gündüzyeli, 2025). Despite the launch of transparency reports and appeal options by Facebook users still do not have straightforward answers regarding feed visibility and content removal practices. The lack of transparency damages user trust while creating ethical issues. Facebook uses AI to enable real-time content delivery and moderation despite generating moral challenges. This system delivers scalable personalized engagement at the expense of user autonomy and freedom of expression. To effectively solve these problems technical solutions alone won't work because we need increased transparency alongside greater user control and public accountability. Facebook's global operations heavily depend on AI technology but require an open confrontation of its ethical implications to achieve fair digital governance and transparent operations.

Applying Ethical AI Principles Through Platform Transparency Tools

The examination of how Facebook uses its AI systems has intensified following the launch of the mothers social Media network. The company responded to scrutiny by implementing transparency tools based on ethical AI principles to improve user understanding and rebuild trust while reducing concerns about algorithmic opacity. The initiatives represent progress toward accountability, but their effectiveness and depth are still uncertain. The company's most prominent transparency tool is 'Why am I seeing this ad?' which lets users discover basic information about their data's impact on ad placement. The tool provides users with basic explanations of how their personal information determines the ads they are shown according to Burgess et al. (2024). When users activate the tool, they receive an explanation based on demographic or behavioural traits that explains their ad placement. These explanations seem helpful at first glance although they remain overly simplistic because they fail to address the intricate predictive data models that guide the decisions. Users receive information but retain no power over the process. Facebook users now have Ad Preferences dashboards to see and modify their assigned categories as Facebook has rolled out this feature. This application functions to maintain user agency for the company by empowering individuals to govern their personal profiling. Critics argue that the interface remains constrictive as it shows only partial information about collected data points while disclosing which data parts contribute to machine learning systems. Facebook published a public set of ethical AI principles that focus on fairness, explainability, privacy, and safety along with improvements in ad transparency (Singhal et al, 2024). The responsible AI group exists to assess model behaviour while internal teams including the responsible AI group develop auditing frameworks for model behaviour. The work remains internal-oriented and lacks any form of external presentation which results in minimal public visibility into the methods and results attained. The issue stems from the difference between promised developments and actual achievable verifiable progress. Facebook maintains transparency in content moderation through regular enforcement reporting and allows users to appeal decisions regarding content removal. Procedural fairness is achieved through user appeals, but doubts persist as algorithms and outsourced reviewers with limited context handle many of these decisions. The implementation of ethical AI at Facebook operates inside a business model that profits from user data while being selective about transparency. These tools offer significant help but represent only an initial move toward progress and require additional transparent tools alongside independent audits and user education to evolve beyond mere promises.

Developing Privacy-Preserving Technologies for Responsible Data Use

Facebook has been intentionally developing privacy preserving technologies that adhere to business ethics within the digital ecosystem where data privacy remains a fundamental concern. The objective of these innovations is to achieve a juggling act: Facebook aims to enhance personalization and system performance while safeguarding user trust in their personal data and maintaining their control over personal information. The strategy uses differential privacy which protects individual user identities by adding statistical noise to datasets (Janghyun et al., 2022). Facebook has tested this strategy across different analytics tools especially when computations involve extensive user behaviour analysis. Differential privacy enables identification of people allowing useful patterns to emerge without revealing sensitive or identifiable information about any individual user. Federated learning represents an emerging technique that shifts model-training operations from centralized servers directly onto users' personal devices. The training of models occurs on local devices before only their updates are transmitted to Facebook's servers instead of the complete raw data. The architecture reduces central data collection risks while advancing toward data minimization which stands as a fundamental principle of responsible AI. Facebook has provided privacy controls for users which feature Off Facebook Activity management tools along with customizable ad settings (Griebeler da Motta, 2021). The tools provide users with visibility into the data third parties collect on their behalf so they can adjust permissions as needed. The privacy settings are buried under complex menus which require digital literacy skills to access and alter when you focus on one task at a time. The implementation process of these technologies faces ongoing scepticism from users and experts alike. Corporate messaging presents various privacy-preservation methods yet lacks independent verification and transparency reports for real-world application (Manda, 2023). But critics have also taken issue with another ploy Facebook uses: Even though certain technologies limit exposure, Facebook continues to gather extensive behavioural and contextual data for algorithmic targeting purposes. Privacy is usually addressed as a technical issue, but it also encompasses cultural, legal and ethical dimensions. The potential of differential privacy and federated learning technologies depends heavily on strong governance principles, rigorous auditing processes, and a user-centric design approach to avoid becoming mere symbolic efforts. While Facebook's investment in privacy-preserving technologies demonstrates increasing recognition of data ethics importance, the extent and transparency of their integration into Facebook's main systems and business operations will determine whether they create substantial change.

Algorithmic Decision-Making and the Risk of User Manipulation

Algorithmic decision-making creates significant user manipulation risks on social media platforms like Facebook. The functionality of Facebook's platform depends on algorithms because these automated systems make decisions about the visibility and timing of users' content exposure (Büchi et al., 2023). Almost every case shows that these algorithms impact user experience greatly while posing minimal ethical costs but result in significant worries regarding user manipulation and psychological impact on autonomy. Facebook's core algorithms function primarily to achieve maximum engagement from its users. The system determines content ranking through the likelihood of it receiving clicks, reactions or attention at any specific moment. The platform may display material from a news story, an advertisement, or content shared by a friend. The platform activity and advertising revenue benefit from this process while it manipulates user behaviour. The system directs users to content that supports their existing beliefs while also triggering emotional reactions and reinforcing their perspectives. A significant troubling implication exists because user agency (Giray, 2024) disappears without notifying the affected individuals whose control is being removed. Platforms that focus on engagement optimization instead of user wellbeing can direct users towards content that they have not actively chosen. The issue grows more complex when we attempt to influence sensitive areas such as political conversation, health decisions or financial choices where small nudges become necessary. The problem intensifies because algorithmic systems operate in an opaque manner. Users remain unaware of how their actions are monitored and interpreted before being used to deliver content or collect their data. The absence of transparency prevents users from acquiring informed consent and from developing a critical understanding of how their digital environment is structured. In some measure, Facebook has acknowledged these risks: It's clear to everyone that teaching algorithms to learn through victory and hatred produces biased results. The implemented reforms have focused on moderating content while neglecting fundamental changes to the optimization logic. Moreover, simply algorithmic manipulation is not always intentional: The algorithmic manipulation emerges as an unintended consequence from systems originally developed without ethical consideration. The real consequences become evident when algorithms damage vulnerable groups or reinforce oppressive behaviours. Designing algorithmic systems presents the challenge of embedding human-centred values such as autonomy, fairness, and psychological safety into their structure. A fundamental restructuring of Facebook algorithms along with posts and ads will ensure user manipulation risks stay inherent to the system's architecture. The risk of user manipulation will remain a permanent component of the platform's underlying architecture unless its algorithms (and other content elements) undergo significant structural changes in their construction, testing and governance processes.

Key Findings

AI personalization technologies at Facebook have revolutionized digital marketing through their ability to deliver customized experiences to users. The sophisticated personalization capabilities of Facebook's AI models raise ethical questions about manipulation, transparency practices, and user control over their data. Limited visibility of the platform's algorithmic systems prompts concerns about both user consent and accountability measures. Existing tools and technologies face limitations in their real-world efficacy when tackling these issues. The subsequent findings showcase Facebook's AI ecosystem's fundamental conflicts between technological advancement and ethical responsibility.

AI Delivers Unprecedented Personalization but Edges Close to Manipulation

AI enables unmatched personalization levels while approaching manipulative boundaries.

Facebook's advertising and content delivery platforms have transformed the potential of large-scale personalized marketing. Through detailed examination of precise behavioural data patterns (which include clicks and scrolls, dwell time and reaction types), Facebook's AI predicts individual user content preferences. Facebook's AI system uses data including clicks and scrolls as well as dwell time and reaction types to predict personalized content for every user (Sanda, 2022). There is clear business value in this personalization: Companies can deliver customized messages to their customers by addressing their individual requirements along with their mental states. Custom Audiences and Lookalike Audiences along with Dynamic Creative Optimization (DCO) demonstrate how brands can deliver highly targeted messages that stand above standard advertising. This high level of precision presents a worrisome potential: it can lead to manipulation. Preference goes beyond AI recognition because it enables prediction and exploitation of user conditions and preferences. Chronic stress represents engaging content which allows systems to display ads that capitalize on users' emotional states. The primary goal of these systems is to engage users even though their well-being is not the main concern. The use of such topics becomes particularly concerning when addressing political views, health anxieties, and financial insecurity. Hyper personalisation evolves into psychological targeting within this context which creates decision nudging that users make unconsciously. The situation gets more problematic due to its opaque nature. Most users do not know why they see specific ads nor understand the role their data plays in targeting them. The tools under "Why am I seeing this ad?" offer only surface-level explanations about the algorithm which fail to convey its intricate workings and subtle complexities. Users can't gain full understanding or challenge their profiles' influences without genuine transparency. Personalized systems reinforcement continues to build upon users' pre-existing beliefs and behaviour according to Khama & Ali (2024). The algorithm learns what users prefer and delivers more content through the filter bubble that narrows their perspective and intensifies ideological divisions. Personalization begins but quickly leads to a persistent redirection of attention and thoughts that ultimately changes behaviour. Facebook's AI systems balance relevance with user autonomy to achieve a certain trade-off. Through personalization we achieve more entertaining and functional experiences, yet we enter the morally sensitive zone that separates influence from control. AI systems blur the line between serving user interests and driving commercial gain while often failing to recognize when they cross this ethical boundary.

Algorithmic Systems Work but Lack Transparency

Facebook's algorithmic infrastructure manages user experience while every minor change influence ad delivery system along with ad placement and content moderation features. The system functions as a computational engine consisting of one or more algorithms while simultaneously including elements, user interfaces and interactive features (Kordzadeh & Ghasemaghaei, 2022). Through their design they succeed at boosting user engagement while simultaneously improving ad performance and maintaining user focus. These algorithms utilize massive data sets to learn in real time through machine learning and subsequently adjust user feeds to deliver extremely precise results. The algorithms function with outstanding precision to recommend products and promote posts while suppressing controversial content. The effectiveness of these systems' results remains undisputed yet the human subjects they impact remain largely hidden from the algorithmic processes. This data processing frequently happens in a way that users rarely understand: Users remain unaware of how their data processes content while algorithms determine what content they encounter and how their online actions influence future content. Algorithmic systems try to explain decisions through transparency tools yet the basic nature of "Why am I seeing this post?" or "Why am I seeing this ad?" responses fails to convey the complex predictive logic that dictates these choices. Users receive information without understanding the extent to which algorithmic profiling controls their platform interactions. The absence of transparency violates the fundamental requirement of informed consent (Director, 2024). Users sign data usage terms but because they do not understand algorithmic effects on their feed and emotions their consent becomes impractical. Opaque systems create challenges for maintaining accountability. If an advertising campaign discriminates by race or gender or misinformation spreads through engagement-driven ranking, then it becomes difficult to determine which algorithmic element caused the issue. The initiatives towards algorithmic accountability that Facebook has implemented such as community standards enforcement reports and user appeals show advancement but remain inadequate for complete accountability. The inner workings of recommendation and ranking systems remain proprietary because they have not been subjected to auditing. Automated systems often fail to provide users with clear explanations when they remove posts or suspend accounts which leads to user frustration when they receive no reasons for these actions. Facebook's algorithm performs well but operates behind the scenes without an elaborate show. As AI systems become increasingly powerful, they create ethical problems because their operations lack transparency. The primary basis for user trust and democratic integrity lies in the requirement that systems demonstrate effectiveness along with being understandable and fair while maintaining accountability.

Transparency Tools Exist, but Rarely Empower Users

Facebook responded to growing worries about algorithmic decisions by launching new transparency features which provide advertisers better control over their audience and enhance post visibility while focusing on who sees ads and content from other news feeds (Leerssen et al., 2023). These tools including 'Why am I seeing this ad?', the Ad Preferences dashboard, and community standards enforcement reports will enable users to understand their data usage and how content moderation takes place on the platform. On first inspection these tools seem to offer control, yet operational use demonstrates they provide genuine empowerment only rarely. These features are typically high level, e.g. The 'Why am I seeing this ad?' feature gives users a high-level answer such as 'Your ad visibility is because you belong to a specific age group or show travel interests'. The explanation provided appears to be a general rationale but does not reflect the complex algorithmic layers that involve behavioural signals and inferred preferences or psychological patterns. Although the explanation appears straightforward it fails to reveal the entire complexity of the profiling system operating in the background. The Facebook Ad Preferences interface provides users with limited control to select specific interest categories assigned to them (Habib et al., 2023). These options remain difficult for users to both locate and utilize effectively. Facebook fails to inform users about the data collection processes and the ways in which this information trains AI systems that shape their online experiences. Restricted information leads you to believe you control your experience while Facebook makes the key decisions. Content moderation systems prevent users from accessing appeals processes or policy explanations through unclear justifications combined with automated procedures. The context available to external algorithms/ moderators in making moderation decisions is often restricted. Users repeatedly appeal content removals but receive automated responses that simply defend the original removal decision (Keller, 2021). Facebook has advanced in its pursuit of responsible AI through transparency tools which nevertheless remain insufficient in scope. Users receive information from the company about decisions that affect them but do not get sufficient details to enable meaningful intervention or dispute of those decisions. True transparency demands improved clarity in disclosures and increased detail while requiring independent audits of AI systems plus tools that enable users to interact as representatives rather than mere observers.

Privacy-Preserving Technologies Show Promise, but Adoption Is Unclear

The massive data collection concerns among the public led Facebook to adopt privacy preserving technologies to reduce potential risks (Rafiq et al., 2022). Through differential privacy and federated learning Facebook strives to maintain evolving ethical and regulatory standards while preserving its data-driven personalization business model. These innovations seem naturally effective in a theoretical context while presenting a responsible way to handle data. Their practical implementation into essential systems lacks clarity and definitive integration. Differential privacy introduces statistical "noise" into datasets to protect individual identities in aggregated data (Zhao & Chen, 2022). This technique enables researchers to perform large scale trend analysis by studying collective behaviour patterns without requiring individuals to disclose their identities. According to reports Facebook has utilized this technique in particular analytics tools for audience insights and advertising performance measurement. The company remains silent about which parts of its advertising ecosystem utilize differential privacy and whether user-level targeting remains restricted. Federated learning represents another promising technique that trains artificial intelligence models directly on users' devices thus eliminating the need to gather data at a central location (Nguyen et al., 2021). This feature limits data transfer to Facebook servers from the beginning while maintaining privacy and allowing machine learning models to advance. Facebook has demonstrated its interest in applying federated learning to keyboard prediction and mobile user interfaces but has not yet implemented this approach for its advertising and recommendation systems. Facebook's marketing infrastructure has never experienced independent large-scale verification of the deployment. Facebook developed user-facing tools like Off-Facebook Activity and Ad Preferences alongside technical innovations to provide users with visibility into third party data tracking (Arias-Cabarcos et al., 2023). The placement of these tools within deep settings menus which keeps them hidden from users renders them ineffective because they deny users control over their data used for AI-driven personalization. Most users remain ignorant of the existence of these tools which remain under the control of Facebook. Facebook's investment in privacy preserving technologies represents positive news but their absence of transparency and third-party audits coupled with inadequate documentation fails to demonstrate the actual impact of technologies like obfuscation in real-world applications. These tools will be experimental add on instead of foundational safeguards until they are integrated into core systems and undergo third party verification.

Algorithmic Decision-Making Challenges User Agency

Facebook's core functionality operates through automated systems that prioritize content through algorithmic decision making to control what content appears before users and the timing and order of its appearance. We design these algorithms to maximize user engagement by discovering content that holds user attention for extended periods or triggers emotional reactions. These systems have boosted commercial efficiency while enhancing precision, but they also raised significant ethical questions regarding user autonomy and manipulation by reducing conscious decision-making. The core problem revolves around individuals losing meaningful control of their digital interactions. Facebook users cannot pick which content shows up in their feeds since engineers determine what content will generate the highest engagement (Hagey & Horwitz, 2021). The predictions stem from various behavioural profiling data sets which encompass user interaction and location as well as device usage among other factors. As users spend more time on the platform their exposure to personalised ads increases (De Groot, 2022). The world depicted through this statement shows systems actively reshaping users instead of users controlling systems. When individuals avoid emotionally charged materials, they may end up viewing similar content because algorithms predict such content will motivate them despite their lack of conscious interest. The process unfolds gradually and causes both a diminished perspective of the world and greater social division which results in compulsive use that may not align with user intentions. The situation becomes worse when people try to understand how opaque the system really is. Most users do not understand content prioritization mechanics and "Why am I seeing this post?" tools provide no meaningful explanations. Users lack transparency about decision-making processes which prevents them from acquiring necessary information to contest or opt out of algorithmic behavioural influence. A survey by Büchi et al., (2023) found that 74% of respondents lacked understanding of Facebook's data maintenance practices. The practice of algorithmic nudging which automates minor behavioural suggestions requires user consent. In which situations could a user who reacts to prompts to view content or click ads without actively choosing those topics take ownership of their resulting actions? Facebook uses algorithms which act as behavioural creators rather than predictors of user actions. These systems operate both efficiently and at scale while creating convenient choices that obscure the boundary between personalization and persuasion. The platform cannot allow true user agency unless users obtain a clearer understanding of these algorithmic operations and their scope.

Figure 1. The Ethical AI Balance Model demonstrates the operational process of Facebook's AI systems throughout data collection to user experience and governance. The diagram identifies fundamental ethical pressure points that require intervention to safeguard user autonomy and maintain accountability in platform personalization.

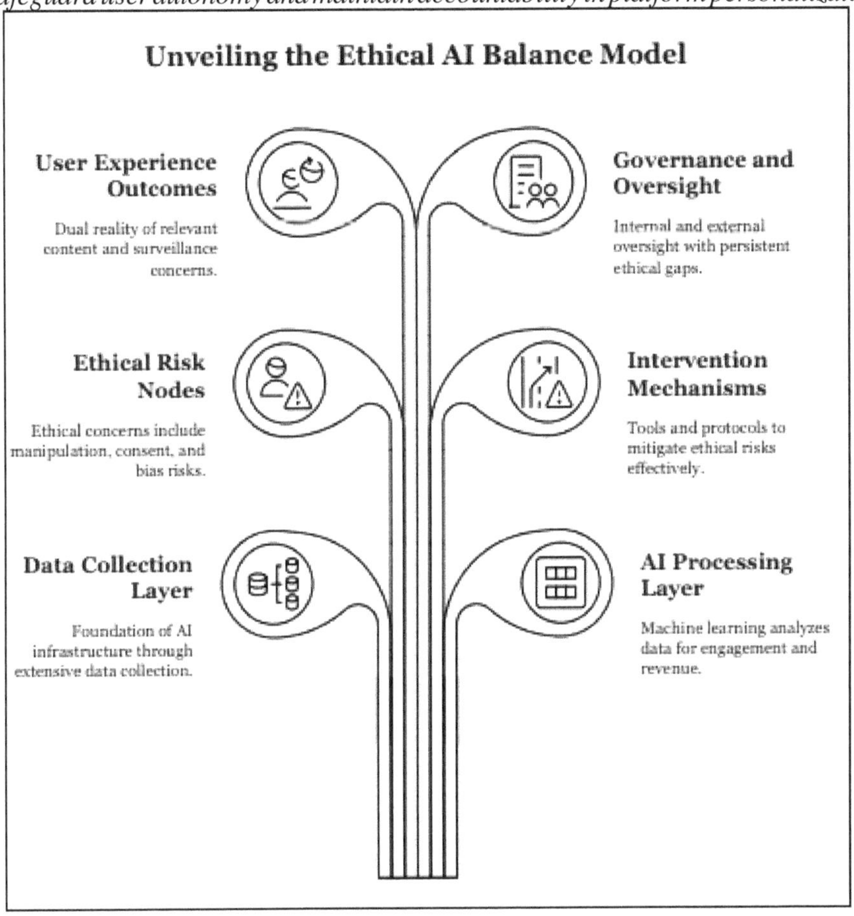

Facebook begins its model with six connected layers which start with data collection that extracts large volumes of user information through direct interactions such as likes and comments and indirect signals like device metadata and third-party tracking. The collected data becomes input for AI processing systems which create detailed behavioural profiles for predictive personalization. The third layer shows serious ethical problems that arise from the system's focus on engagement rather than user safety including manipulation tactics, biases in algorithms, and breaches of informed consent. Facebook responds by detailing its ethical protections through transparency tools and privacy-preserving technologies, yet these measures frequently fail to truly empower users. The fifth layer depicts how personalization creates user convenience while also raising concerns about filter bubbles and decreased user autonomy. The final layer of the system focuses on governance and oversight while demonstrating how internal teams and external regulators function in these roles. Figure 1 illustrates the closed-loop interaction between system layers, which allows user behaviour to provide continuous feedback to AI optimizations while reinforcing personalization and its ethical trade-offs.

SOLUTIONS AND RECOMMENDATIONS

As AI technologies become fundamental parts of Facebook's operations, experts are closely examining the ethical deployment of artificial intelligence in the platform's marketing efforts. AI powers both targeted advertising and content curation to deliver personalized user experiences which enhance engagement and improve business results. These technological improvements lead to substantial ethical consequences. These challenges represent systemic problems that overlap with data privacy concerns and algorithmic bias while also influencing opaque decision-making practices and emotional manipulation that undermines user autonomy. Users typically do not comprehend the applications of their data while existing transparency tools fail to provide meaningful control or insight. Facebook's emphasis on engagement as its main performance indicator leads to more distribution of content that tends to provoke strong emotions and divisions among users which in turn increases worries regarding its effect on public discussions and mental health. The next five recommendations provide solutions for essential ethical deficiencies present in Facebook's AI system. These measures aim to address existing transparency, consent, accountability, user empowerment and system oversight gaps through a framework that helps realign platform personalization with ethical best practices. The fundamental goal of these measures is to establish a digital marketing landscape that values responsibility and trust through AI implementation.

Implement Transparent and Explainable AI Systems

Facebook faces continuous ethical challenges because its AI infrastructure lacks transparency. AI technologies produce highly personalized experiences for users but the systems operating them stay hidden from both users and external observers. Users generally lack awareness of how their online activities—from clicks to browsing habits—are processed to customize their feeds and show targeted ads (Khama & Ali, 2024). The tool "Why am I seeing this ad?" provides basic explanations about user interests or age groups but does not disclose the advanced behavioural profiling or psychological analysis used to select the advertisement (Leerssen et al.,

2023). Facebook needs to implement Explainable AI (XAI) principles throughout its systems to handle this problem. Explainable AI (XAI) enables algorithmic decisions to be understood by engineers and internal teams as well as end users and independent auditors according to Blessing et al. (2024). The framework requires development of user interfaces to display explicit explanations about how certain input factors like interaction history and emotional signals determine the content and ads shown to users. If Facebook provides authentic information about its decision-making algorithms it can start to establish transparency and restore the trust of its users. Explainability requirements must extend past individual interfaces to establish accountability throughout the entire system. To understand algorithmic effects and identify harmful or biased results regulators together with civil society representatives and autonomous auditors require system-level data access as described by Kordzadeh & Ghasemaghaei (2022). Auditing processes cannot be fully realised, and accountability becomes just for show without sufficient access levels. Explainable AI adheres to new legal and regulatory requirements like the EU's GDPR and the upcoming AI Act by ensuring users receive meaningful information about automated decision-making processes (Director, 2023). Transparency extends beyond technological requirements as it represents an ethical obligation. Users remain unaware of the hidden systems which manipulate their decisions and beliefs by operating in secrecy outside of their informed agreement.

Scale Up Privacy-Preserving Technologies Across Marketing Operations

Facebook has initiated early steps to integrate privacy-preserving methods like differential privacy and federated learning into its platform, yet these techniques have not become fundamental elements within its marketing operations. These innovative technologies show great promise but have not yet become standard practice in Facebook's main advertising and recommendation platforms which still primarily depend on centralized user data gathering and profiling. Differential privacy protects individual identities by adding statistical noise to datasets which enables trend analysis without revealing personal information. When performing large-scale data analysis this approach proves effective for privacy protection since it produces identical results whether individual data entries are present or absent (Zhao & Chen, 2022). Federated learning enables AI model training to operate in a decentralized manner since it preserves data on the local devices of users. The model learns through aggregated updates instead of direct data extraction which significantly limits the personal information sent to Facebook's servers (Nguyen et al., 2021). Facebook's high-impact marketing systems continue to operate without these privacy-preserving methods despite their ethical and technical benefits. Rafiq et al. Rafiq et al. (2022) insist that ethical AI advancements require deep integration of these tools within systems instead of treating them as separate experiments. Facebook needs to expand the application of privacy-enhancing technologies throughout its advertising algorithms and content recommendation systems to show true data stewardship. This action would serve as one of the most definitive demonstrations of ethical commitment in its AI system functions. It remains essential for organizations to ensure full transparency when implementing these technologies. Facebook needs to produce public transparency reports that clearly explain their usage of differential privacy and federated learning technologies. Arias-Cabarcos et al. (2023) advocate for independent third-party audits to validate these systems. The independent third-party audits suggested by Arias-Cabarcos et al. (2023) need to confirm system functionality as declared while ensuring these systems do not act as superficial ethical measures. The expansion of privacy-preserving technologies goes beyond technical improvements because it represents an ethical responsibility. The approach supports Facebook's ability to deliver AI-driven personalization while safeguarding individual rights and strengthening both user trust and regulatory compliance within a heavily monitored digital environment.

Establish Independent Algorithmic Auditing and Oversight Mechanisms

Platform-based marketing requires more than internal regulation and corporate discretion to ensure ethical artificial intelligence. The business model of Facebook which focuses on maximizing user engagement and advertising income frequently conflicts with ethical duties related to privacy protection, fairness standards, and psychological safety concerns (Director, 2023). The establishment of strong independent algorithmic auditing systems must transition from best practice to mandatory requirement to ensure AI systems adhere to public interest and democratic standards. Currently Facebook releases whitepapers and community enforcement reports sporadically and maintains internal ethics teams. Existing efforts do not provide essential transparency nor possess authoritative power or third-party verification to effectively evaluate systemic risks. Facebook needs to establish structured algorithmic audits from independent third parties with evaluation frameworks that assess fairness, bias mitigation, psychological impact, data security, and transparency according to Kordzadeh & Ghasemaghaei (2022). The audits need to be continuous and thorough while combining expertise from data scientists with input from ethicists and civil society organizations and regulatory bodies. Public access to audit findings will build trust and illustrate accountability. Public disclosure of audit techniques combined with identified risks and subsequent corrective measures can boost public trust while preventing future algorithmic harm episodes. Audits need to assess the impact of AI systems on vulnerable populations and the extent to which they exacerbate social divisions or reinforce existing inequalities. Facebook needs to establish an internal AI Ethics Council with genuine oversight capabilities to oversee its AI systems. This organization needs the authority to examine AI product launches and stop development when ethical risks become apparent unlike advisory panels that hold only limited power. Facebook will achieve proactive governance by integrating ethical review into product development from the beginning instead of addressing it later. Establishing credible oversight serves to restore user agency while protecting democratic principles and goes beyond simple compliance measures. Independent auditing will enable Facebook's AI systems to uphold values including fairness and safety while maintaining informed consent instead of solely focusing on engagement metrics.

Redefine Consent and Enhance User Control Over Personalization

Meaningful informed consent taken voluntarily stands as a fundamental principle of ethical AI. Facebook's present consent approaches show significant deficiencies when compared to the desired standard. Companies bury consent mechanisms in intricate settings menus where dense technical language prevents users from reading or understanding them. Zimmermann (2023) maintains that user interface design manipulates users to agree to data collection instead of providing them with real informed decisions. The current practices damage the essential principles of ethical data processing and personalization. Facebook needs to revise its approach to designing and delivering user consent. Consent requirements must extend beyond a single agreement in service terms to become a continuous interactive process. The user experience should include immediate permission prompts that activate when new data collection begins or when new features launch. The prompts should deliver clear information in a brief manner while avoiding design tactics that steer users toward unwanted compliance. Users require detailed management abilities that extend beyond simple consent in personalization processes. Users should have control to enable or disable personalization features while having the ability to reset their recommendation history and manually change how different data inputs like likes, shares, or content engagement time affect their experience. User empowerment through these capabilities enables individuals to actively define their online presence instead of being controlled by hidden algorithms (Khama & Ali, 2024). Users must have the freedom to opt out of personalization completely without suffering any loss of functionality or restricted access. The policy honours individual preferences and maintains equity among those who reject algorithmic personalization. The "Why am I seeing this post?" transparency tool needs to develop further so it accurately represents the intricate layers of personalization mechanisms which encompass psychological analysis and behavioural profiling (Leerssen et al., 2023). Improving user control extends beyond technical adjustments because it requires an ethical dedication to honouring personal autonomy. Facebook can create a personalization framework that respects ethical standards by ensuring user consent remains visible and revocable while maintaining its significance to empower users and avoid manipulation.

Promote Human-Centred Design and Ethical Metrics in AI Systems

Facebook's marketing AI systems mainly optimize for key performance indicators which include engagement alongside click-through rates, impressions and conversion metrics. Advertisers use these metrics to achieve immediate goals but fail to consider the more significant aspects of user well-being and ethical standards (Iyelolu et al., 2024). Systems become excessively focused on compulsive user engagement when they depend too heavily on limited performance indicators instead of promoting well-rounded and knowledgeable user experiences. While short-term results may be achieved through this trade-off the long-term consequences make it unsustainable and damaging. Facebook will secure its platform's future and rebuild user trust by adopting a human-centred design philosophy that balances ethical impact with technical efficiency. The transformation demands a new definition of success criteria for AI-driven systems. AI systems must be assessed through variables such as user satisfaction levels and emotional safety standards instead of simply measuring engagement duration (Leerssen et al., 2023). Recommendation systems that heighten anxiety or promote political radicalization need immediate flagging and redesign despite their effectiveness in extending session durations or generating ad impressions. The integration of ethical standards should occur during the initial phases of system development. Prototyping processes need to include psychological effects alongside emotional and social impacts as fundamental parameters for design teams. User research needs to investigate the effects of AI systems on mental health as well as user autonomy and digital wellbeing. Including users, stakeholders, and ethicists in the design loop through participatory design approaches helps detect potential harms while bringing various needs and perspectives to the forefront (Director, 2024). User interfaces can incorporate ethical nudges to guide people towards more intentional and beneficial decision-making patterns. Design features that boost ideological feed diversity alongside posting delays for emotional content or alternative viewpoint highlighting serve to minimize impulsive reactions and break down echo chambers. Facebook can develop AI systems that perform efficiently while supporting healthier and more equitable online experiences by aligning their development with human-centred values and ethical metrics.

FUTURE RESEARCH DIRECTIONS

The research showcases important advancements in Facebook's AI applications for marketing purposes yet identifies unresolved issues about its ethical implications and psychological as well as societal effects. Upcoming research needs to tackle these existing problems by conducting extensive long-duration studies that drive innovation for enhancing user well-being. These areas provide essential guidelines for future research directions.

Long-Term Psychological Impact of Algorithmic Personalization

The academic community needs to conduct more in-depth research into how algorithmic personalization affects users' psychological states over extended periods. Facebook's AI algorithms prioritize engagement metrics like likes or comment counts but ignore the lasting changes on users' emotional and cognitive states due to extended algorithm-driven content exposure (De Groot, 2022). Algorithmic systems place users within echo chambers that strengthen their beliefs and emotional responses while creating conditions that can increase anxiety and lead to both political polarization and decreased openness to new ideas. Extended exposure to emotionally charged or uniform ideological content can reshape users' cognitive structures while reducing their ability to understand different viewpoints. Emotionally charged content that seeks to provoke outrage or sympathy tends to boost short-term user engagement but ultimately damages emotional stability and critical thinking abilities (Gündüzyeli, 2025). The personalization process gradually modifies users' experiences, emotions and behaviours while researchers still lack comprehensive knowledge about these aggregated psychological changes (Büchi et al., 2023). Upcoming research needs to explore how individuals' exposure to algorithms shapes their personal identity formation alongside their emotional stability and future decision-making capabilities across varied population groups. Researchers need to focus on vulnerable populations such as adolescents and individuals with mental health challenges because they show increased vulnerability to psychological manipulation (Sim & Choo, 2025). Research approaches that focus on participation and user experience can provide deep understanding of these widespread yet subtle effects. Future research needs to investigate how psychological impacts differ across types of content such as health information and political material or depend on how personalized content is delivered. The precision of personalization methods leads to increased risks of overfitting user interests while reducing emotional complexity and autonomy (Bahangulu & Owusu-Berko, 2025).

The psychological impacts of personalization should be seen as fundamental design and governance concerns while evaluating AI's long-term function in digital platforms ethically. Ethical AI frameworks can balance technological innovation and user well-being only if they measure these outcomes (Anshari et al., 2022).

User-Controlled Personalization Tools

The main approach to achieving ethical AI in marketing requires users to have more control over their data and decisions. On Facebook personalization functions mostly out of sight with algorithms making decisions while users have little input and minimal transparency (Büchi et al., 2023). Users do not understand the mechanisms behind their data interpretation and content curation and lack means to alter this process. Informed consent is undermined by this absence of user control while passive manipulation of the user experience becomes possible. Researchers need to study how to create effective user-driven personalization mechanisms which enable people to manage their data use and control content delivery. Users can choose to join or leave certain personalization categories through these tools, change how different data points affect their experience or fully reset algorithmic suggestions without losing their data or account access as described by Zimmermann (2023). Personalization tools that matter to users need to incorporate features that provide clear explanations and easy access. Research by Habib et al. According to Habib et al. (2022) users demand more straightforward control systems that facilitate management of interest categories and ad targeting. These tools usually hide inside complicated menu structures and utilize perplexing language which leads to reduced user participation. Ethical design needs to maintain high visibility and usability while keeping things simple so users can operate systems without needing technical skills. The demand for personalization platforms that enable users to establish ethical preferences continues to expand, including measures to decrease content that manipulates emotions while also restricting political targeting and enhancing viewpoint diversity (Bahangulu & Owusu-Berko, 2025). Values-based algorithmic profiles could emerge from these user-defined preferences. When users control personalization systems they gain both clearer system insights and more digital self-determination. This change represents a move away from predetermined algorithmic control toward user-driven authority while ensuring AI systems adhere to democratic principles and ethical norms (Anshari et al., 2022).

Impact on User Autonomy Across Demographics

The capacity of users to make informed choices without external pressure in digital spaces serves as a basic ethical principle within AI frameworks. The level of autonomy that people can practice within algorithm-driven platforms such as Facebook differs greatly among various demographic groups. The user experience with algorithmic personalization systems depends on demographic factors including age, education level, digital literacy, socio-economic background and cultural context according to Büchi et al. (2023). Adolescents are especially vulnerable to algorithmic effects because they are still developing cognitively and emotionally. A lack of ability to differentiate organic content from curated content makes these users more susceptible to manipulation through subtle algorithmic nudging (Sim & Choo, 2025). Personalization systems remain incomprehensible to older adults and individuals with limited digital literacy which limits their ability to effectively challenge or navigate algorithmic decisions (Habib et al., 2022). The lack of transparent tools and explanations leads to an unnoticed decline in user autonomy among these groups. The reception of algorithmic systems depends on cultural and regional contexts. The definition of intrusive or manipulative personalization differs greatly between Western and non-Western cultures which indicates that AI systems should be designed with cultural sensitivity in mind (Kozyreva et al., 2021). Lower-income and marginalized communities experience worsened power imbalances with platforms because the effects of surveillance and data misuse have more severe implications for these groups. Research initiatives moving forward must focus on intersectional and comparative analyses to determine how algorithmic personalization impacts various groups of users. Research should evaluate personalization settings accessibility and usability, examine users' perceived control levels and measure algorithmic environments' psychological and behavioural effects among various demographics (Anshari et al., 2022). We must address these disparities to achieve fair access to digital self-determination. The creation of ethical AI systems requires more than generic solutions as it should provide every user with the necessary information and capabilities to control their own digital interactions.

CONCLUSION

Meta's use of AI technologies in marketing has transformed both personalisation strategies and user engagement levels. This development introduced significant ethical questions. AI-powered systems enable Facebook to deliver hyper-personalization which enhances user experiences and improves business performance. These technological advancements create problems because they infringe on user privacy and autonomy and enable potential manipulation. Through its ad targeting methods and content recommendation practices Facebook demonstrates both the potential and dangers inherent in AI marketing techniques. These practices optimized engagement and profit but generated risks by forming filter bubbles and reinforcing biases. These practices take advantage of users' emotional weaknesses. Facebook has launched multiple transparency measures including the introduction of tools like "Why am I seeing this ad?" Facebook has adopted privacy-preserving methods including differential privacy together with federated learning. Although they have taken certain measures their actions do not lead to meaningful user empowerment, nor do they address algorithmic decision-making opacity. Independent audits combined with comprehensive transparency measures create problems with both trust and accountability. The social media platform must address these challenges by implementing explainable AI systems while enhancing privacy-preserving technologies and establishing independent oversight mechanisms. The organization should update its consent frameworks while implementing human-centred design principles. The research identified multiple future study directions including examining algorithmic personalization's psychological effects over time and developing AI tools that enable user control along with testing privacy-preserving technologies' practical effectiveness. By concentrating on these areas Facebook will achieve a balance between technological advancements and social obligations while providing equitable AI services to businesses and people in the digital era.

REFERENCES

Anshari, M., Syafrudin, M., Fitriyani, N. L., & Razzaq, A. (2022). Ethical responsibility and sustainability (ERS) development in a metaverse business model. *Sustainability (Basel), 14*(23), 15805. DOI: 10.3390/su142315805

Arias-Cabarcos, P., Khalili, S., & Strufe, T. (2023). 'Surprised, shocked, worried': User reactions to Facebook data collection from third parties. *Proceedings on Privacy Enhancing Technologies. Privacy Enhancing Technologies Symposium, 2023*(1), 384–399. DOI: 10.56553/popets-2023-0023

Bahangulu, J. K., & Owusu-Berko, L. (2025). Algorithmic bias, data ethics, and governance: Ensuring fairness, transparency, and compliance in AI-powered business analytics applications. *World Journal of Advanced Research and Reviews, 25*(2), 1746–1763. DOI: 10.30574/wjarr.2025.25.2.0571

Blessing, E., Abill, R., Kaledio, P., & Louis, F. (2024). Explainable AI: Interpreting and understanding machine learning models. *HAL Open Science*. https://hal.science/hal-04972111v1/file/Explainable%20AI.pdf

Büchi, M., Fosch-Villaronga, E., Lutz, C., Tamò-Larrieux, A., & Velidi, S. (2023). Making sense of algorithmic profiling: User perceptions on Facebook. *Information Communication and Society, 26*(4), 809–825. DOI: 10.1080/1369118X.2021.1989011

Burgess, J., Carah, N., Angus, D., Obeid, A., & Andrejevic, M. (2024). Why am I seeing this ad? The affordances and limits of automated user-level explanation in Meta's advertising system. *New Media & Society, 26*(9), 5130–5149. DOI: 10.1177/14614448241251796

De Groot, J. I. M. (2022). The personalization paradox in Facebook advertising: The mediating effect of relevance on the personalization–brand attitude relationship and the moderating effect of intrusiveness. *Journal of Interactive Advertising, 22*(1), 57–74. DOI: 10.1080/15252019.2022.2032492

Director, S. (2023). Informed consent, price transparency, and disclosure. *Bioethics, 37*(8), 741–747. https://philpapers.org/archive/DIRICP.pdf. DOI: 10.1111/bioe.13206 PMID: 37506217

Djerf, A. (2023). A comparative study between the EU-GDPR and the US-CCPA. *Lund University Publications*. https://lup.lub.lu.se/luur/download?func=downloadFile&recordOId=9123076&fileOId=9125663

Giray, L. (2024). Negative effects of generative AI on researchers: Publishing addiction, Dunning-Kruger effect and skill erosion. *Journal of Applied Learning and Teaching*, *7*(2). Advance online publication. DOI: 10.37074/jalt.2024.7.2.38

Graham-Harrison, E., & Cadwalladr, C. (2018, March 17). Revealed: 50 million Facebook profiles harvested for Cambridge Analytica in major data breach. *The Guardian*. https://www.theguardian.com/news/2018/mar/17/cambridge-analytica-facebook-influence-us-election

Griebeler da Motta, L. (2021). Expert report—A multijurisdictional analysis of data-driven mergers: Current assessment and public policy proposals for Brazil. *Data Privacy Brazil Research*. https://papers.ssrn.com/sol3/Delivery.cfm?abstractid=3994904

Gündüzyeli, B. (2025). The role of social media and artificial intelligence (AI) in enhancing digital marketing resilience during crises. *Sustainability (Basel)*, *17*(7), 3134. DOI: 10.3390/su17073134

Habib, H., Pearman, S., Young, E., Saxena, I., Zhang, R., & Cranor, L. F. (2022). Identifying user needs for advertising controls on Facebook. *Proceedings of the ACM on Human-Computer Interaction, 6*(CSCW1), 1–42. https://doi.org/DOI: 10.1145/3512906

Hacker, P. (2023). Manipulation by algorithms: Exploring the triangle of unfair commercial practice, data protection, and privacy law. *European Law Journal*, *29*(1–2), 142–175. DOI: 10.1111/eulj.12389

Hagey, K., & Horwitz, J. (2021). Facebook tried to make its platform a healthier place. It got angrier instead. *Wall Street Journal*. https://socialmediainjury.com/wp-content/uploads/2022/11/03-Facebook-Tried-to-Make-Its-Platform-a-Healthier-Place.-It-Got-Angrier-Instead.-WSJ.pdf

Iyelolu, T. V., Agu, E. E., Idemudia, C., & Ijomah, T. I. (2024). Leveraging artificial intelligence for personalized marketing campaigns to improve conversion rates. *International Journal of Engineering Research and Development*, *20*(8), 253–270. https://www.researchgate.net/profile/Tochukwu-Ijomah-2/publication/383847844_Leveraging_Artificial_Intelligence_for_Personalized_Marketing_Campaigns_to_Improve_Conversion_Rates/links/66dc47f92390e50b2c72139b/Leveraging-Artificial-Intelligence-for-Personalized-Marketing-Campaigns-to-Improve-Conversion-Rates.pdf

Janghyun, K., Barry, H., & Tianzhen, H. (2022). A review of preserving privacy in data collected from buildings with differential privacy. *Journal of Building Engineering*, *56*, 104724. DOI: 10.1016/j.jobe.2022.104724

Keller, D. (2021). Amplification and its discontents: Why regulating the reach of online content is hard. *Journal of Free Speech Law*, *1*, 227. https://www.journaloffreespeechlaw.org/keller.pdf

Ko, H., Lee, S., Park, Y., & Choi, A. (2022). A survey of recommendation systems: Recommendation models, techniques, and application fields. *Electronics (Basel)*, *11*(1), 141. DOI: 10.3390/electronics11010141

Kordzadeh, N., & Ghasemaghaei, M. (2022). Algorithmic bias: Review, synthesis, and future research directions. *European Journal of Information Systems*, *31*(3), 388–409. DOI: 10.1080/0960085X.2021.1927212

Kozyreva, A., Lorenz-Spreen, P., Hertwig, R., Lewandowsky, S., & Herzog, S. M. (2021). Public attitudes towards algorithmic personalization and use of personal data online: Evidence from Germany, Great Britain, and the United States. *Humanities & Social Sciences Communications*, *8*(1), 1–11. DOI: 10.1057/s41599-021-00787-w PMID: 38617731

Leerssen, P., Dobber, T., Helberger, N., & de Vreese, C. (2023). News from the ad archive: How journalists use the Facebook Ad Library to hold online advertising accountable. *Information Communication and Society*, *26*(7), 1381–1400. DOI: 10.1080/1369118X.2021.2009002

Manda, J. K. (2023). Privacy-preserving technologies in telecom data analytics: Implementing privacy-preserving techniques like differential privacy to protect sensitive customer data during telecom data analytics. *SSRN*. https://papers.ssrn.com/sol3/Delivery.cfm?abstractid=5136773

Mehta, S., & Erickson, K. (2022). Can online political targeting be rendered transparent? Prospects for campaign oversight using the Facebook Ad Library. *Internet Policy Review*, *11*(1), 1–31. DOI: 10.14763/2022.1.1648

Meta. (2025). *Meta Advantage+: Optimize Facebook & Instagram Ads with AI.* Meta for Business. https://www.facebook.com/business/ads/meta-advantage-plus

Nguyen, D. C., Ding, M., Pathirana, P. N., Seneviratne, A., Li, J., & Poor, H. V. (2021). Federated learning for internet of things: A comprehensive survey. *IEEE Communications Surveys and Tutorials*, *23*(3), 1622–1658. DOI: 10.1109/COMST.2021.3075439

Prem, E. (2023). From ethical AI frameworks to tools: A review of approaches. *AI and Ethics*, *3*(3), 699–716. DOI: 10.1007/s43681-023-00258-9

Rafiq, F., Awan, M. J., Yasin, A., Nobanee, H., Zain, A. M., & Bahaj, S. A. (2022). Privacy prevention of big data applications: A systematic literature review. *SAGE Open*, *12*(2), 21582440221096445. DOI: 10.1177/21582440221096445

Sanda, E. (2022, June). Artificial Intelligence Algorithms and the Facebook Bubble. In *Proceedings of the International Conference on Economics and Social Sciences* (pp. 559–570). https://doi.org/DOI: 10.2478/9788367405072-051

Sim, K. Y. H., & Choo, K. T. W. (2025). Envisioning an AI-Enhanced Mental Health Ecosystem. *arXiv preprint arXiv:2503.14883*. https://doi.org//arXiv.2503.14883DOI: 10.48550

Singhal, A., Neveditsin, N., Tanveer, H., & Mago, V. (2024). Toward fairness, accountability, transparency, and ethics in AI for social media and health care: Scoping review. *JMIR Medical Informatics*, *12*(1), e50048. DOI: 10.2196/50048 PMID: 38568737

Upadhyaya, N. (2024). Leveraging machine learning and Kafka for dynamic ad serving. *International Journal of Advanced Research in Computer Science*, *15*(5), 84–88. Advance online publication. DOI: 10.26483/ijarcs.v15i5.7138

Verma, S., Sharma, R., Deb, S., & Maitra, D. (2021). Artificial intelligence in marketing: Systematic review and future research direction. *International Journal of Information Management Data Insights*, *1*(1), 100002. DOI: 10.1016/j.jjimei.2020.100002

Zhao, Y., & Chen, J. (2022). A survey on differential privacy for unstructured data content. *ACM Computing Surveys*, *54*(10s), 1–28. DOI: 10.1145/3490237

Zimmermann, V. (2023). Privacy nudges and informed consent? Challenges for privacy Nudge Design. In *Human Factors in Privacy Research* (pp. 155–171). Springer., DOI: 10.1007/978-3-031-28643-8_8

Zuboff, S. (2022). Surveillance capitalism or democracy? The death match of institutional orders and the politics of knowledge in our information civilization. *Organization Theory*, *3*(3), 26317877221129290. DOI: 10.1177/26317877221129290

KEY TERMS AND DEFINITIONS

Algorithmic Transparency: Making AI decision-making processes understandable and accountable.

Artificial Intelligence (AI): Computer systems designed to simulate human intelligence perform tasks in decision-making and data analysis.

Data Ethics: Data ethics encompasses moral principles that regulate how data is collected and governed as well as its usage.

Ethical AI: The process of creating AI systems requires adherence to ethical standards which include moral considerations alongside fairness and transparency in deployment.

Personalization: Using data-driven insights to create marketing content that meets the specific preferences of each user.

Privacy: People should have authority over their personal data and its application.

Surveillance Capitalism: The term describes business models that extract data to predict human behaviour and generate profit.

Chapter 8 The Ethical Risks of AI in Marketing Addressing Privacy Concerns in AI-Powered Targeting

Manoah Dimis Mai-Lafia
https://orcid.org/0009-0008-9754-3787
University of Jos, Plateau, Nigeria

ABSTRACT

Through predictive analytics and biometric tracking AI has revolutionized marketing by delivering hyper-personalized consumer experiences which are strengthened through behavioural targeting. The features that boost consumer interaction simultaneously generate significant ethical dilemmas focused on privacy protection. The chapter investigates AI-driven marketing's privacy paradox which shows how personalization simultaneously draws consumers in while creating discomfort. The chapter analyses how new technologies such as emotion detection and algorithmic profiling affect ethical standards in marketing. The chapter provides actionable ethical AI governance solutions through the combination of philosophical ethics, legal frameworks and real-world case studies. Stakeholder analysis combined with technical measures such as Privacy by Design and transparent communication represents essential strategies for ethical AI governance. The objective aims to merge technological advances with responsibility mechanisms to ensure ethical AI implementation.

DOI: 10.4018/979-8-3373-6582-4.ch008

BACKGROUND

Modern marketing has undergone significant transformation due to the development of Artificial Intelligence (AI). Basic data analysis tools have developed into advanced AI-driven systems that deliver personalized consumer interactions and produce highly predictive analytical outcomes. The maturing of AI technologies since the early 2010s caused dramatic changes in marketing approaches. Marketers gained detailed consumer behavior insights and automated complex tasks through machine learning advancements (Islam et al., 2024). The initial implementation of AI in marketing aimed to automate tedious tasks while refining customer segmentation. Advancements in deep learning and natural language processing enabled AI to deliver real-time customer service chats and analyze sentiment while creating highly tailored customer experiences according to Saura et al. (2024). Current technological advancements offer marketers the capability to provide personalized content that meets consumer requirements while boosting both engagement rates and conversion outcomes. Brands face elevated competitive pressures due to the ability of AI tools to provide personalized experiences at scale which has redefined consumer experience standards. The exponential growth in digital data serves as the primary catalyst for this transformation. Online consumer activities produce valuable data trails which AI systems can capture and analyze to deliver insights and actions within seconds (Priyanka et al., 2023). AI facilitates a transformation from wide demographic targeting to personalized marketing strategies based on data analysis. These marketing innovations increase effectiveness yet simultaneously generate multiple ethical issues. One major issue is consumer privacy. AI systems require extensive personal data access including search history and location details to analyze behavioral patterns. The employment of sensitive information creates uncertainty about whether consumers truly understand and have genuinely agreed to its usage (Naz & Kashif, 2024). The "privacy paradox" highlights consumer concerns about privacy alongside their continued use of data-collecting services (Saura et al., 2024). The opaque nature of AI systems presents another significant ethical issue. Many people view AI algorithms that utilize deep learning as "black boxes" because they are too complex to understand. The inability of consumers to comprehend decision-making processes and data usage practices leads to diminished trust and elevated concerns about data misuse (Sharma, 2023). When users cannot understand AI processes, they feel disempowered, which undermines their autonomy and harms brand-consumer relationships. Algorithmic bias presents a further ethical challenge. AI models developed from biased data sets unintentionally strengthen existing social prejudices which result in discriminatory advertising practices. Marketing campaigns can perpetuate inequality by excluding specific demographics or using stereotypes to target certain populations (Vukmirović et al., 2025). The presence of these issues generates important concerns regarding the ethical dimensions of equity and social accountability in AI-driven marketing strategies. In response to these challenges governments and regulators established legal frameworks including the European Union's General Data Protection Regulation (GDPR) and California's Consumer Privacy Act (CCPA). The regulations established by these laws work to improve transparency while demanding informed consent from users and empower individuals to manage their personal data according to Islam et al. (2024). These laws require companies to provide clear explanations of their data collection methods while giving consumers the ability to access and modify their personal data. These measures both defend personal rights and return some control to the consumer. Various industry organizations have developed ethical guidelines for artificial intelligence applications within marketing alongside legal measures. Businesses should adopt ethical practices that promote fairness, accountability and transparency according to industry standards which help to protect user rights and develop trust (Bilyk et al., 2024). However, technology often advances faster than regulation. The delay between technological advancements and regulatory measures results in oversight deficiencies which necessitates ongoing collaboration among industry leaders, ethicists, and policymakers to maintain modern ethical standards. Consumer education serves as a critical element in bridge this gap. Digital literacy improvements enable individuals to understand AI system operations and data usage. Consumers who have received education about digital technologies tend to make well-considered choices while insisting on transparency and safeguarding their personal information (Sarioguz & Miser, 2024). User-friendly explanations combined with public awareness efforts enable people to identify manipulation and critically assess digital services while protecting their rights. The marketing sector will witness AI advancements that will merge virtual reality with emotional AI and biometric analytics. These technological advances offer unparalleled personalization options but generate fresh ethical dilemmas. AI systems that predict human behavior or interpret emotional states risk causing psychological manipulation along with personal space invasions (Yilmaz & Ashqar, 2025). The development of strong ethical guidelines and the inclusion of interdisciplinary teams in system creation and policy formulation becomes essential because of these capabilities. AI's marketing potential remains vast, yet its ethical challenges present an equal level of complexity. Stakeholders need to embrace transparency, fairness, and consumer empowerment to make sure AI remains beneficial to both businesses and society. Through careful governance and active responsibility AI will maintain its innovative power while adhering to ethical principles.

Focus of the Chapter

AI has revolutionized marketing through the introduction of hyper-personalization and real-time engagement capabilities and predictive analytics which transformed business-consumer interactions. The emergence of AI-powered marketing tools has created multifaceted ethical issues related to consumer privacy and data protection (Islam et al., 2024). A central dilemma is the personalization-privacy paradox: Consumers value personalized services yet continue to express strong concerns regarding the collection and usage of their data for these services (Yilmaz & Ashqar, 2025). AI systems gather massive amounts of user information such as browsing patterns and purchasing history along with biometric data to forecast user preferences and actions. The application of AI-driven data collection leads to powerful marketing strategies but generates doubts about consumer understanding and their consent to data use (Naz & Kashif, 2024). Users lose trust in AI systems because they cannot understand how their data drives automated decisions due to the lack of transparency in AI algorithms (Sharma, 2023). The ethical use of algorithms becomes more intricate because biased training data generates exclusionary or discriminatory advertising that disproportionately impacts specific demographic groups (Vukmirović et al., 2025). The GDPR and CCPA establish regulatory norms, but technological progress exceeds legislative capabilities creating ethical governance deficiencies (Bilyk et al., 2024). Marketers must take the initiative to establish ethical practices that emphasize transparency along with accountability and fairness. The subsequent chapter examines these challenges by analyzing how AI affects consumer privacy and algorithmic bias while evaluating regulatory constraints. The book delivers actionable advice that enables companies to use AI technologies responsibly while upholding customer confidence and adhering to legal requirements.

Current Applications

This section examines Artificial Intelligence applications within marketing strategies and their corresponding ethical challenges. Advanced AI technologies now form the core of marketing strategies and have reshaped how brands connect with consumers across both online and offline platforms. AI improves marketing functions through predictive analytics and hyper-personalization while also creating significant ethical and regulatory issues via biometric feedback and conversational agents. The following section examines major AI applications in marketing through the analysis of peer-reviewed research from 2020 to 2025.

Predictive Analytics and Consumer Behavior Forecasting

AI-powered predictive analytics tools utilize historical data such as purchase history, browsing behavior, and demographic profiles to predict consumer behavior. Through these models' brands can enhance content delivery strategies while precisely segmenting audiences and computing important metrics like customer lifetime value (Islam et al., 2024). Recommendation engines that platforms such as Amazon and Netflix use serve as practical examples of these tools at work. Machine learning algorithms drive predictive analytics models which enhance their accuracy over time by processing fresh data. By identifying purchasing patterns and forecasting future buying behavior these systems allow marketers to anticipate what consumers will need to provide timely recommendations. Both conversion rates and customer satisfaction rise because of this approach. Real-time analytics integration into campaign management systems allows companies to make immediate dynamic adjustments according to market changes and user feedback. Predictive analytics provides a key advantage by helping organizations make informed decisions about resource allocation. Companies can optimize their marketing budgets by targeting high-value customers while minimizing wasteful advertising expenditure and detecting potential customer churn risks. The utilization of data-driven strategies leads to worries about personal profiling and private data protection. Consumer trust diminishes when data usage is not clearly explained as they struggle to understand why they see specific content (Saura et al., 2024). The use of predictive analytics for personalization requires a careful balance between delivering user benefits and providing transparent consent and clear information to users. Heavy dependence on algorithmic predictions risks diminishing marketing content diversity which may limit consumer options and create uniform experiences. To reduce these dangers experts, advise the adoption of explainable AI models which provide marketers and users with insights into prediction processes.

AI Transforms Ad Targeting

Programmatic advertising uses AI to automate real-time bidding while matching content to consumer interests through behavior analysis and device data along with geolocation information. Research demonstrates that AI-driven ad delivery achieves better personalization and efficiency outcomes (Saura et al., 2024). Instagram and TikTok use these systems to examine likes, shares and comments to enable precise ad placement. This capability significantly enhances marketing efficiency. AI algorithms determine the most effective content types for specific audience segments which enables real-time campaign optimization and maximizes ad spend returns. Dynamic messaging adjustments based on real-time user interactions maintain relevance while increasing engagement levels. Through programmatic advertising businesses can perform A/B testing on large scales to test various creative designs and call to action formats. These tests generate feedback that helps marketers continuously improve their strategies. The precise targeting of content feeds into the creation of filter bubbles which restrict users from interacting with different perspectives while diminishing their decision-making autonomy (Kyosovska, 2024). Users who receive continuous exposure to content matching their established beliefs risk missing alternative views which create ethical issues related to informational variety and personal decision-making freedom. Several platforms are developing algorithms designed to showcase unexpected information that users wouldn't normally search for yet helps expand their viewpoints. Users must understand the content selection process to ensure algorithmic transparency remains vital.

Emotion AI and Biometric Feedback

Real-time consumer emotions become analyzable data for Emotion AI applications by examining facial expressions alongside voice tones and heart rates. Smart sensors in retail environments monitor emotional signals to modify in-store promotions as needed according to real-time data (Yilmaz & Ashqar, 2025). Alexa and Google Assistant both modify their responses based on user tone to deliver personalized interactions. Emotion AI succeeds by transforming marketing into a responsive and human-like experience. AI systems change how they communicate and present products instantly after detecting customer frustration or boredom. These advancements enhance customer satisfaction while enabling emotionally engaging marketing strategies. Digital displays equipped with emotion-tracking cameras can change advertisements depending on viewers' expressions such as happiness or confusion. The implementation of personalized content can significantly boost how often people interact with advertisements. Retailers track their customers' emotional states through wearable technology to create customized loyalty promotions. Emotion recognition systems gather biometric information from consumers who remain unaware of this data collection and do not give consent. The EU's proposed AI Act designates these applications as “high-risk” and demands rigorous supervision along with complete openness (Saura et al., 2024). Finding equilibrium between technological progress and ethical standards remains difficult when considering the protection of emotional privacy rights. The practice of emotion-based targeting without proper disclosure can make consumers feel monitored and manipulated. Critics say this AI technology invades the private realm of emotions which could alter both purchasing decisions and emotional well-being. The ethical application of emotion recognition AI requires the implementation of visible tracking indicators, explicit consent processes, and supervisory human involvement.

Conversational AI and Chatbots

Chatbots that use Natural Language Processing (NLP) technology handle fundamental customer service tasks while providing product recommendations and simulating empathetic responses. The scalability and availability of these systems provide significant value to high-volume industries such as e-commerce and banking according to Alhitmi et al., 2024. The integration of sentiment analysis features enables complex customer issues to be transferred to human operators thereby maintaining service excellence. Chatbots present multiple operational advantages including reduced labor expenses along with enhanced availability and uniform customer interactions. Their multilingual support capabilities extend their reach into international markets. Advanced chatbot models keep track of conversation history to ensure smoother and more productive interactions. AI chatbots extend their functionality by connecting with CRM systems which enable them to deliver personalized responses using information from users' order histories and account details. The customer journey becomes more straightforward while increasing user engagement levels. Chatbots face challenges with contextual comprehension and data retention threats especially within GDPR-governed areas because of stringent consent and data security requirements (Bilyk et al., 2024). Customer dissatisfaction arises when chatbots cannot process complex questions or fail to direct problems to the appropriate channels. The retention of conversation histories creates major data security and compliance issues. There exists apprehension regarding excessive dependence on chatbots when handling delicate matters which include financial disputes and mental health inquiries. Current AI technology falls short in replicating the required empathy and ethical judgment needed in these areas. Modern hybrid systems that integrate AI capabilities with human oversight are gaining more traction as recommended solutions.

Cross-Device Tracking and Omnichannel Personalization

AI empowers marketers to offer consistent user experiences across smartphones, tablets, laptops, and smart TVs as consumers use multiple devices. Cross-device tracking systems use device fingerprinting together with geolocation data and behavioral patterns to create detailed individual user pathways across different channels. Marketers can provide users with a unified omnichannel experience that remains consistent across different channels (Ali et al., 2024). AI-driven personalization algorithms deliver perfect content and advertisements which not only maintain uniformity across devices but also provide unique optimization for each platform interface. Marketing teams may display product videos prominently on smart TVs and design interactive ads specifically for smartphone screens. The practice of synchronizing digital experiences across multiple platforms leads to stronger brand unity while also raising customer fulfillment levels. Yet, this convenience introduces significant ethical issues. Users often do not know how their device usage patterns create connections between different gadgets they own. When companies collect sensitive information like location data and purchase records without getting clear user permission this hidden operation damages customer trust. Experts criticize that existing consent models hide within extensive privacy documents and do not establish genuine informed approval. Organizations need to establish thorough consent management systems which enable users to manage their data across multiple devices. Regulatory bodies are now demanding stricter cross-device tracking regulations. According to the European Data Protection Board all cross-device tracking needs to require opt-in permissions by default and companies must provide transparent information about data collection and usage practices. Developers who want to implement ethical omnichannel personalization need to integrate inclusivity and accessibility into their systems. Marketing initiatives need to be flexible enough to serve the varied requirements and choices of users across all platforms. When organizations neglect to incorporate inclusive practices, they may inadvertently exclude some user groups which enlarge digital inequality. Continuous auditing systems and user feedback channels are necessary to ensure ethical standards and enhance user experience. By allowing users to view and edit their data profiles companies can improve transparency and boost user agency in digital environments.

Visual and Voice Search Integration

AI advancements have dramatically enhanced visual and voice search features which transformed product discovery methods for consumers. Visual search technology lets users submit pictures to search for identical products across the internet. In the fashion and home décor sectors retailers utilize Pinterest Lens and Google Lens to connect customer photos with product databases (Naz & Kashif, 2024). Consumers experience a seamless shopping journey which simulates how they browse for products in the physical world. Natural language processing together with speech recognition technologies facilitates voice search which lets users ask digital assistants like Siri, Alexa, or Google Assistant questions by speaking. The method provides a more user-friendly search experience for individuals who multitask and those living with disabilities. These marketing tools provide businesses with advanced capabilities to predict consumer intentions more accurately. AI algorithms process voice tone alongside syntax patterns and phrasing structures to customize search outcomes and suggest relevant products. Recommendations for luxury goods may result from a calm tone but urgent phrasing typically activates time-sensitive promotions. These technological advancements introduce fresh concerns regarding privacy and ethical standards. Uploaded images used in visual searches have the potential to disclose personal or sensitive details unintentionally. Through the analysis of voice data companies can access demographic details and emotional expressions which they might misuse for overly aggressive advertising strategies (Saura et al., 2024). To ethically deploy these technologies companies, need to openly communicate how they collect and use data. Users need to receive clear information about the data that is stored and the duration of its storage along with details about any third-party sharing. Safeguarding personal data requires technologies such as anonymization combined with on-device processing methods. Businesses must provide opt-out options and data access instruments to help consumers better control their personal information.

Influencer Marketing and Sentiment Analysis

The use of AI in influencer marketing allows businesses to choose and assess influences with greater accuracy through detailed analysis of engagement data and audience characteristics alongside content relevance. The algorithms evaluate influencers by measuring their reach and assessing their authenticity and alignment with the brand's objectives according to Yilmaz & Ashqar (2025). The effectiveness of campaigns is boosted through AI-driven sentiment analysis which examines user-generated content such as comments and shares while tracking public perception as it evolves. Brands can swiftly determine which messages work well while identifying elements that require improvement. Campaign management becomes more agile through this responsiveness which produces better financial outcomes from marketing expenditures. Artificial Intelligence generates virtual influences which are CGI-generated personas controlled solely by algorithms. These virtual personas enable complete creative management while ensuring brand protection by removing potential scandals and messaging inconsistencies. Digital entities Lil Miquela and Shudu managed to capture audience interest even though they exist completely within a virtual space. Nevertheless, ethical challenges abound. The risk of deception exists because consumers might think they are interacting with real people when they engage with virtual influencers. When consumers cannot distinguish between real and virtual influencers the result often leads to decreased trust and increased skepticism towards influence-generated content. Brands need to explicitly inform audiences when influencers are virtual entities and make sure their advertising messages comply with established standards. It is imperative for brands to maintain transparency regarding sponsorships and paid content to prevent misleading their audiences. Sentiment analysis algorithms need to be developed with the capability to understand cultural differences in language to prevent drawing incorrect interpretations.

AI in Content Generation and Dynamic Pricing

AI systems now play an essential role in both creating content automatically and handling dynamic pricing strategies. OpenAI's GPT models function as content generation tools that produce personalized materials such as emails, social media posts and blog posts among other content types. The systems adjust their tone and structure and messaging through user behavior and segmentation data analysis which lets marketers expand content creation production without losing relevance. Dynamic pricing algorithms continuously update product prices by analyzing demand variations alongside competitor pricing and user browsing patterns. E-commerce, travel, and ride-sharing industries make extensive use of these systems. During peak travel season airlines often increase flight ticket prices when there is a surge in flight searches by users. Although both applications increase efficiency and responsiveness there are serious concerns regarding their impact.

Key Findings

The marketing industry benefits from AI technologies like predictive analytics, emotional recognition, and hyper-personalization which bring groundbreaking capabilities alongside multiple ethical challenges. The primary concerns regarding AI-driven technologies in marketing focus on privacy protections alongside algorithmic fairness and the maintenance of user autonomy. This section brings together the main results from earlier chapters and extends them using modern academic research.

The Personalization-Privacy Paradox

The personalization-privacy paradox stands as a fundamental ethical issue in AI marketing today. Consumers value personalized services that give them product recommendations and content suggestions based on their behavior, yet they are deeply worried about how their data is gathered and utilized to deliver these services (Saura et al., 2024). The paradox demonstrates psychological tension between enjoying convenient services and feeling anxious about being monitored. Users give up their data to access services without fully grasping the implications of their action. Ali et al. The study by Ali et al. (2024) shows a disconnect between consumer survey declarations of data privacy concerns and their real-world behaviors which they explain through consumers' feelings of powerlessness. Alhitmi et al. (2024) demonstrate that structural and systemic transparency failures contribute to making the issue more complicated. Most platforms fail to adequately disclose what data they collect and how they process it while not specifying third parties who receive the data. Under these conditions users are unable to give meaningful consent. Algorithmic systems which control personalization led to increased consumer alienation because of their secretive nature which generates distrust towards "black box" marketing approaches. The literature recommends adopting explainable AI (XAI) systems for delivering understandable explanations about personalization processes. Algorithmic literacy initiatives enable individuals to analyze AI systems with greater scrutiny. Brands need to implement UX designs that focus on privacy through progressive disclosure interfaces and dynamic consent tools which enable real-time adjustments to privacy settings. Transparent processes and the ability of users to make informed choices create the foundation of ethical interaction. Developing ethical personalization means shifting from treating users as passive data sources to involving them as empowered stakeholders in the process.

Invasive Inferences and Emotional Surveillance

Emotional AI has quickly become popular in commercial marketing due to its capability to boost user interaction through immediate emotional feedback. The systems monitor biometric signals such as facial expressions and voice inflection alongside posture to determine emotional states which allows marketing messages to be customized accordingly (Yilmaz & Ashqar, 2025). The enhanced customer experience from such personalization creates significant psychological and ethical issues. Emotion-based inferences frequently happen without users being aware or giving their permission. In-store cameras could recognize a customer's stress and offer calming product advice although this action may be helpful yet uncomfortably intrusive. Saura et al. Saura et al. (2024) define this development as the commercialization of human emotion through the collection and conversion of private emotional responses into marketing information. The utilization of this approach triggers major ethical questions regarding control over one's mental state and the potential manipulation of emotions. As these systems reach higher levels of invisibility and integration the danger grows that they will diminish user control. The contextual accuracy of emotional AI systems remains unreliable. A smile possesses different meanings across different cultural contexts. Analyzing biometric signals incorrectly can generate inappropriate content and create incorrect profiles or make disrespectful assumptions. Sensitive emotional data poses increased threats to already vulnerable populations including kids and senior citizens as well as individuals facing mental health challenges. Experts recommend that Emotion AI be designated as a high-risk technology within legal systems such as the EU AI Act. The ethical deployment of technology requires visible monitoring indicators alongside mandatory opt-in procedures and clear data retention policies while avoiding particularly sensitive use cases unless necessary.

Algorithmic Bias and Discriminatory Outcomes

The fairness of AI models depends entirely on the quality of the training data they use. Societal biases present in historical datasets become further entrenched or intensified when processed by AI systems. The marketing sector experiences distorted segmentation processes alongside exclusionary targeting practices and stereotype reinforcement when biased algorithms are applied (Yilmaz & Ashqar, 2025). A documented case shows how facial recognition technology performs differently among various racial groups. Williams et al. The study by Williams et al. (2023) showed that marketing technologies using facial recognition tools display more errors and reduced performance when processing images of darker-skinned individuals. The poor user experience caused by these systems triggers civil rights issues in surveillance-related applications. Algorithmic ads display significant levels of bias. High-interest financial products or premium services are marketed to some demographics while other groups receive low-cost options or no offerings at all. The decisions made by algorithms for predictive accuracy purposes could result in violations of ethical standards or anti-discrimination regulations. Alhitmi et al. (2024) state that AI fairness should be implemented throughout the entire lifecycle process including data collection and labeling as well as model evaluation and deployment. GDPR's fairness principle together with Article 22 regarding automated decisions serves as essential legal benchmarks. Organizations should perform algorithmic impact assessments while engaging third-party audits and creating fairness benchmarks that reflect their specific user populations. Organizations must include individuals from marginalized communities in their development teams to ensure diversity.

Cross-Device Tracking and Omnichannel Personalization

Artificial intelligence has emerged to create integrated user experiences as people now interact with brands across various connected devices such as smartphones, tablets, smart TVs and laptops. Through advanced identification techniques like device fingerprinting, IP mapping and user login patterns cross-device tracking systems map consumer behavior across multiple devices. Cross-platform behavioral mapping allows marketers to create unified experiences across multiple touchpoints so users who search for shoes on their phone will subsequently encounter related ads on their desktop and receive email offers. These capabilities boost user engagement and brand consistency but also generate various ethical concerns. User consent stands as the primary issue in the discussion of cross-device tracking ethics. A significant consent gap exists because consumers receive no clear information about their behavioral tracking across devices. Experts maintain that authorization given for one device does not automatically extend to other devices since data collection occurs unnoticed during background aggregation (Saura et al., 2024). Cross-device tracking heightens surveillance capitalism by maintaining uninterrupted user surveillance to derive persistent behavioral insights. Data consolidation at this level transforms users into data subjects who are optimized for monetization rather than individuals with personal agencies. Ethical omnichannel personalization requires establishing an equilibrium between seamless user experiences and user autonomy. Researchers and policymakers recommend multi-layered consent structures to allow users to exercise detailed control of their data across multiple devices. Brands need to implement AI-based consent management solutions which automatically adjust user permissions whenever devices join or leave the ecosystem. Technical approaches such as federated learning together with decentralized data storage are under examination for their potential to lessen the dangers of centralized user profiling. Ethical data aggregation needs to incorporate context-aware design principles because identical user behavior can have varied meanings when analyzed from different devices or environments and during different times of the day.

Visual and Voice Search Integration

Product discovery has been revolutionized by visual and voice search capabilities. Artificial intelligence search engines utilize deep learning methods including convolutional neural networks and natural language processing to interpret and respond to both visual data and spoken requests with exceptional precision. Customers can take pictures of products while shopping and directly access online listings as well as utilize smart assistants to look for services when driving or cooking (Naz & Kashif, 2024). The responsive nature of this technology enhances user experience and provides significant benefits for people with disabilities and those who struggle with reading. The integration of voice and image-based interaction makes digital platforms more accessible to everyone while creating new opportunities for user engagement. However, ethical risks persist. Voice data contains naturally identifiable elements including age and gender that make it inherently personal. Visual information collection sometimes happens without consent and records private environments along with family members or confidential details. Rigorous ethical protocols must be implemented to guide the storage, processing, and sharing of this type of data. Personalization engines which analyze vocal tone or image context risk crossing boundaries from helpful assistance into privacy intrusion. The usefulness or manipulative nature of AI assistants that recommend anxiety-reducing products through voice stress detection depends on the user's awareness and consent. Companies need to anonymize voice and visual inputs while providing real-time disclosure prompts and opt-in voice profiling to protect ethical standards. Under the CCPA and GDPR regulations companies must gain informed consent from users while allowing them to access and remove their personal data. AI designers need to incorporate cultural sensitivity models that recognize language diversity as well as visual standards across various user groups. Transparency reports need to contain policies regarding the use of visual and voice data. Users must learn about the implicit data they send through their interactions.

Influencer Marketing and Sentiment Analysis

AI technology has revolutionized influencer marketing by providing tools that monitor engagement levels, verify follower authenticity and evaluate audience sentiment. AI-powered dashboards can now analyze influencer audiences through psychographics segmentation and assess comment tones while predicting campaign ROI from past performance data. AI technology has led to the emergence of virtual influencers which are CGI-rendered characters managed by corporate entities. These computer-generated personas remain unaffected by human unpredictability while being able to adapt their aesthetic to current trends and avoid reputation damage. The artificial nature of virtual influences raises ethical concerns about transparency and realistic representation as well as emotional control. Real-time sentiment analysis capabilities of AI enable dynamic modifications to content distribution. AI systems can either eliminate posts that generate negative sentiment or propose adjustments to the content. This automated approach functions well but risks silencing different opinions and damaging genuine content. The lack of clear influencer disclosures leads to user confusion in identifying genuine endorsements from paid partnerships. The necessity to define influence boundaries emerges when AI strengthens these dynamics through optimization of tone, aesthetic, and timing. Brands need to show when algorithmic decisions have been created or changed their posts or set their publishing times. AI systems must be developed to adhere to the new transparency guidelines that regulatory bodies like the FTC have implemented for influencers. The effectiveness of ethical sentiment analysis tools can be enhanced by training them to recognize sarcasm alongside regional dialects and minority expressions which help prevent misunderstandings.

AI in Content Generation and Dynamic Pricing

AI marketing transformation through content streamlining and hyper-personalization enables small businesses to scale effectively using tools like GPT-4. Dynamic pricing strategies widely adopted by e-commerce and travel industries calibrate prices in real time according to user behavior and demand but risk consumer backlash because of perceived unfair pricing practices. The ethical implications of artificial intelligence extend to both content creation and pricing models which involve bias and misinformation as well as socioeconomic profiling requiring transparent algorithm design that ensures explainability and fairness. Human supervision together with privacy-focused design elements, AI systems that offer clear explanations, data sets that reflect diverse demographics, and educating consumers represent key solutions. A commitment to responsible AI use requires companies to establish governance frameworks together with cross-sector partnerships and ethical protective measures which will build trust and support a fair digital marketplace.

Figure 1. The model demonstrates the necessary balance of innovation and accountability with transparency to achieve ethical AI practices in marketing. Brands need to handle customer privacy and ethical dilemmas responsibly to maintain consumer trust.

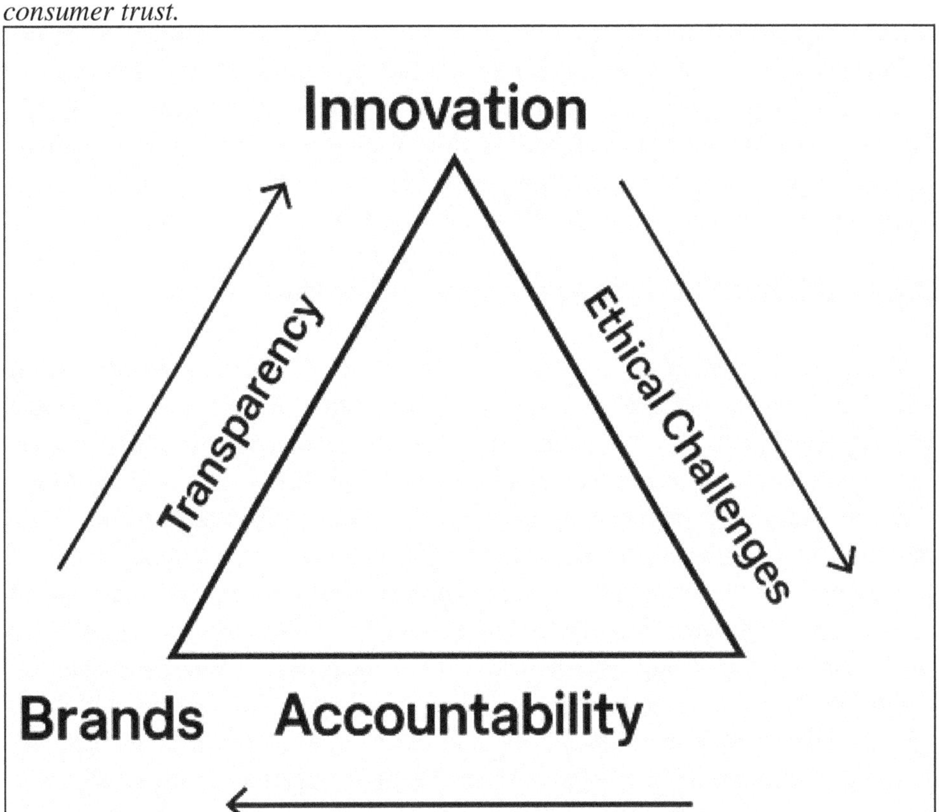

The model demonstrates that successful ethical AI marketing requires both advanced technology and a strong moral and regulatory structure. Innovative approaches create competitive advantages, but lacking transparency can make consumers feel monitored or deceived and diminish their trust in the brand. AI systems remain unchecked for bias and misuse without accountability structures in place. The triangular relationship between these components demonstrates their mutual dependency because failure to maintain one aspect reduces the effectiveness of the others. When campaigns push innovative boundaries without transparency, they risk breaching privacy standards but stringent oversight that leaves no space for creative solutions will ultimately hinder development. Brands that maintain an equilibrium between all three dimensions achieve stronger sustainable and ethical audience relationships.

SOLUTIONS AND RECOMMENDATIONS

Artificial intelligence (AI) in marketing creates unique opportunities but presents challenging ethical issues related to privacy protection, consumer manipulation, and algorithmic bias. Combatting these risks demands an integrated strategy that links governance frameworks with technical fixes and regulatory measures while also engaging consumer involvement. This section introduces well-researched solutions and guidelines to develop marketing systems based on artificial intelligence that prioritize ethics and transparency while catering to consumer needs.

Organizational Governance for Ethical AI Marketing

The establishment of strong institutional structures serves as the foundation for ethical governance within organizations. The formation of ethics committees and advisory boards stands as a fundamental mechanism for organizational governance. The committees serve as formal regulatory bodies monitoring the complete AI deployment lifecycle to maintain compliance with ethical standards as well as legal and social expectations. Companies that have established ethics committees saw a 30% decrease in consumer privacy complaints according to Ali, Riaz, and Rashid's 2024 study. The numbers demonstrate how these committees serve as a preventive mechanism by identifying potential problems during early development phases. Multidisciplinary ethics committees generally consist of ethicists along with legal experts and personnel from marketing and technical departments. The different viewpoints of committee members allow for detailed evaluation of issues that extend from data collection methods to the fairness of algorithms. The committees serve as internal mechanisms to identify overlooked ethical blind spots throughout product development. Decision-making power is growing for ethics committees which permits them to stop deployments that do not pass ethical assessments. The emergence of executive leadership roles dedicated to AI ethics has developed alongside traditional committee-based governance models. The establishment of Chief AI Ethics Officers (CAIEOs) and Chief Privacy Officers (CPOs) has become the best standard practice. Through these positions organizations ensure ethical accountability remains a permanent commitment rather than a single-time checklist activity. According to Chatterjee et al. According to Chatterjee et al. (2022), organizations that establish well-defined structures for ethics leadership achieve better alignment between their technological innovations and corporate social responsibility objectives. CAIEOs lead cross-departmental collaboration while integrating privacy-by-design principles into AI development efforts. Their core responsibilities encompass carrying out periodic audits together with developing risk mitigation approaches and sustaining consumer trust through open data operations. This governance model creates a strong connection between legal compliance and operational ethics when combined with Chief Privacy Officers Cross-functional collaboration is also essential. Saura and colleagues (2024) state that ethical foresight demands the combined efforts of marketing, legal departments and data science teams. During the system architecture's initial design phase internal task forces integrate fundamental principles of fairness, inclusivity and accountability. Marketing professionals actively participate to keep personalization strategies ethical while legal experts protect adherence to regulations. Firms that perform ethical risk evaluations during every product sprint along with organizations that organize routine cross-departmental reviews demonstrate effective governance models. Multiple organizations utilize scenario planning methods to predict how future AI implementations will impact society. The participatory approach drives forward ethical innovation while preventing reactive damage control. The process of building an ethical AI marketing governance framework requires the development of structured formal systems alongside more flexible informal networks. Ethics boards, designated leadership positions, and specialized task forces comprise formal organizational structures. The development of informal structures creates an ethical awareness culture by providing training programs along with feedback systems and whistleblowing access points. These combined mechanisms function to meet regulatory demands while also guiding organizational conduct towards enduring societal principles.

Technical Mechanisms and Design Innovations Promote Ethical Practices in AI Marketing

Technical safeguards within AI systems must be established as artificial intelligence evolves marketing practices to protect consumer rights and uphold ethical standards. The deployment of AI systems in commercial environments relies on foundational design-based solutions like Privacy-by-Design, federated learning, differential privacy, and algorithmic fairness which go beyond optional enhancements. Privacy-by-Design (PbD) stands as a foundational framework which mandates privacy protection as an inherent feature integrated from the earliest stages of system creation. Privacy-by-Design approaches protect systems from inception by integrating privacy safeguards like data minimization and user consent protocols directly into their infrastructure instead of adding protections after they become operational. According to research by Alhitmi et al. (2024), AI marketing firms which integrated PbD principles saw a 25% drop in GDPR violations throughout their 300-company sample. The implementation of preventative privacy controls resulted in increased consumer trust ratings which indicate that these controls provide additional reputational benefits. Privacy by Design demands user-focused designs which feature intuitive interfaces that grant consumers power over their data collection, processing, and sharing activities. Marketers who provide detailed control over data consent and transparent AI decision-making processes can develop enduring trust while sidestepping legal issues. The success of PbD requires developers to work with legal teams and UX designers to achieve cross-functional integration throughout system design. Federated learning stands out as a promising technique for preserving privacy. Machine learning models trained through this technique utilize decentralized datasets from user devices and regional servers while eliminating the need to send raw data to a central server. The study by Kairouz et al. (2021) demonstrates that federated learning minimizes data breach risks and unauthorized access which makes it highly appropriate for financial and healthcare industries. The model used in marketing enables personalization algorithms to learn from user behavior while storing sensitive data locally to support functionality without compromising privacy. Differential privacy works alongside federated learning to enhance security measures. The method protects individual identities by introducing randomized noise into datasets to prevent reconstruction when datasets are merged or reverse-engineered. Yilmaz and Ashqar (2025) state differential privacy represents the top benchmark for protecting data privacy during AI development processes. Marketing companies can use differential privacy to gather consumer behavioral insights while ensuring individual user anonymity remains intact. The combination of robust encryption methods and differential privacy strengthens legal compliance while increasing public trust in data analysis services. Fairness stands alongside privacy as an essential ethical issue. Targeted advertising and product recommendation systems built on biased or limited datasets frequently produce discriminatory results. Developers are now more often implementing fairness-aware algorithms along with bias mitigation pipelines to counteract these issues. Chatterjee et al. (2022) propose a three-stage model for bias mitigation: Bias mitigation involves three phases including pre-processing to rebalance training datasets before training models and in-processing to apply fairness constraints during model training followed by post-processing which validates outputs against equity benchmarks. Structured pipelines offer substantial reductions in disparate impacts to prevent AI systems from excluding or stereotyping specific demographic groups. Fairness audits must operate continuously instead of occurring as single events. Continuous evaluation of deployed models through live environment testing detects new biases which then informs necessary adjustments in model performance. The practice of publishing bias audit results and allowing external reviews enhances accountability in these procedures. These technical safeguards combine to form a comprehensive approach to responsible AI marketing. When organizations build system architecture that combines privacy protection with security measures and fairness principles, they achieve compliance with regulatory standards while driving ethical innovation. The expanding influence of AI in consumer engagement makes these safeguards essential for establishing reliable digital ecosystems.

Guidelines for Ethical AI Marketing alongside Legal Compliance Standards

The integration of artificial intelligence into worldwide marketing strategies necessitates the creation of unified and progressive legal structures. Policy recommendations should both enforce compliance but also stimulate innovation by establishing ethical frameworks which ensure transparency and fairness while building consumer trust. Here we identify three essential components of regulatory best practices that organizations must implement to achieve legal compliance alongside ethical AI deployment in their marketing practices. AI governance faces a crucial obstacle due to the absence of unified global regulatory standards. The European Union's General Data Protection Regulation (GDPR) and the California Consumer Privacy Act (CCPA) stand as significant legal precedents for data protection and consumer rights, but they vary in terms of their scope and enforcement methods as well as their jurisdictional reach. Multinational organizations encounter regulatory uncertainty which leads them to practice jurisdiction shopping by choosing to locate AI operations in countries with less strict enforcement standards (Saura et al., 2024). To counter this, Saura et al. A transnational "AI Bill of Rights" represents a standardized global regulatory model proposed to establish fundamental principles of transparency and explainability alongside user control and algorithmic fairness for universal compliance. Business operations would become more streamlined under a standardized model because companies could deploy their systems globally without needing to adjust for differing legal standards. This measure would contribute to fair competition by blocking companies from gaining financial advantages by avoiding tougher regulatory environments. Regulatory sandboxes support legal innovation by offering an adaptable framework to test new AI marketing tools within controlled environments. Regulators and developers collaborate in these sandboxes to explore new technology's ethical and societal impacts alongside legal considerations before scaling deployment. According to Alhitmi et al. (2024), healthcare and financial sectors demonstrated successful sandbox application which enabled the secure piloting of new tools using real-world data while being monitored by regulatory authorities. Marketing companies could test emotion AI systems along with sentiment analysis methods and dynamic pricing models inside controlled sandbox environments. This approach provides a dual benefit: Firms obtain a better understanding of legal boundaries and consumer expectations while regulators gain preliminary knowledge about technological advancements which aids them in creating forward-thinking policy measures. The inclusion of consumer feedback within sandbox mechanisms allows actual user concerns to shape deployment decisions from the beginning, which strengthens ethical responsiveness. Certification systems and obligatory ethical audits serve as the third foundational element of a responsible AI policy framework. Saura et al. Saura et al. (2024) present a multi-level certification framework based on ISO standards to evaluate AI systems in areas like data management along with transparency and fairness. These certifications, conducted by independent third parties, serve multiple purposes: Independent third-party certifications confirm compliance standards and create public accountability while building trust with both consumers and investors. As digital ethics become more crucial in market dynamics companies with ethical certifications can achieve a competitive edge. Brands that prove their dedication to ethical AI practices gain higher engagement from consumers who value privacy. Certification schemes enable firms to establish ongoing ethical procedures like yearly bias audits and consent reviews as well as data governance enhancements that transform compliance into a proactive business approach. Ethical AI marketing requires a comprehensive approach that combines global regulatory harmonization with sandbox experimentation and independent certification systems. By adopting these tools organizations can minimize their legal liability while building lasting loyalty among tech-savvy customers in today's fast-changing digital environment.

Consumer Empowerment Through Participatory Design Principles in Ethical AI Marketing

The foundation of ethical AI marketing depends on enabling consumers to comprehend and control how AI systems process their data and behaviors. Technical safeguards and policy frameworks establish fundamental protection which consumer empowerment turns into tangible user control and trust in addition to personal autonomy. This section explores four key strategies to foster consumer-centric AI marketing systems: transparent communication alongside improved consent approaches together with algorithmic understanding and participatory design methods form the basis for consumer empowerment in AI marketing systems. Consumer empowerment faces the primary obstacle of navigating through the complicated nature of AI systems. Machine learning and personalization in AI decision-making processes frequently remain non-transparent and hard to understand for users. Effective solutions emerge from the implementation of progressive disclosure mechanisms which simplify complex AI systems. Such systems divide complex technical information into understandable layers which provide relevant insights at each interaction point. Research by Yilmaz and Ashqar (2025) demonstrates that user engagement with privacy controls improves when they receive straightforward icon-based instructions coupled with timely notifications. Designers need to develop transparency features that function on all platforms while remaining usable for people with different digital skill sets. The requirement for transparency in digital interactions leads to better user control through advanced consent mechanisms that offer detailed data management options. The basic opt-in/opt-out selections fail to match the intricacies found in modern data environments. Layered consent architecture enables users to establish distinct preferences for various data types including geolocation information and browsing history. Saura et al. According to Saura et al. (2024), contextual controls deliver better perceived autonomy to users and result in lower opt-out rates. Their study shows how the "consent continuum model" enables users to dynamically modify or withdraw permissions according to shifting preferences or situations. The move toward consent as a continuous and adjustable process transforms ethical engagement into a shared responsibility between users and systems. Sustainable consumer empowerment relies on improving algorithmic literacy. Consumers who lack basic knowledge about personalization algorithms stay susceptible to manipulation and base their decisions on incorrect assumptions. Chatterjee et al. Chatterjee et al. (2022) argues for the inclusion of interactive learning tools in digital platforms and applications. The educational tools consist of short video clips together with visual FAQs and interactive quizzes that teach users about AI systems and profiling methods as well as their rights. When consumers understand how systems operate their research demonstrates they push for ethical business practices which create pressure from the bottom up for companies to uphold fairness and accountability. Algorithmic literacy enables users to actively engage in AI governance processes. Through participatory design ethical AI marketing becomes a collaborative effort rather than a hierarchical directive. Direct consumer participation in system development through beta testing and user advisory panels with interface feedback loops increases system trustworthiness and relevance. Nguyen et al. Platforms in the retail industry that implemented user feedback into personalization and notification options experienced enhanced satisfaction scores and better ethical performance ratings according to Nguyen et al. (2021). Through participatory design users gain control over AI systems which prevent feelings of surveillance because their input actively determines AI responses rather than them simply receiving it. These four strategies create a unified framework that gives consumers power in AI-driven marketing initiatives. Open algorithm disclosures make systems understandable while layered consent mechanisms restore user control alongside educational initiatives that develop literacy and participatory design approaches that create inclusive development systems. When businesses put these principles into action, they develop marketing structures that ensure compliance and fairness while gaining active participation and trust from their users.

FUTURE RESEARCH DIRECTIONS

The continuing development of artificial intelligence systems facilitates their integration into marketing methods that push limits in personalization and consumer interaction alongside boosting operational performance. Technological advancements lead to novel ethical and social challenges and technical problems which necessitate forward-looking research to address future issues. The field of AI marketing research stands at a crucial crossroads where it needs to focus on present challenges and actively guide the development of AI applications. This section identifies crucial research pathways for upcoming years and focuses on regulatory modifications alongside technology trends and consumer behavior variations and unsolved ethical dilemmas.

Regulatory Trends and Legal Innovation

Future research needs to keep pace with the growing sophistication of artificial intelligence in marketing systems by tackling new regulatory challenges as well as technological and ethical issues. The effective governance of ethical AI marketing depends on multidisciplinary research that actively predicts upcoming developments. This section identifies two pressing research domains that will determine the future of responsible AI marketing practices: regulatory trends and technological shifts. Global regulatory harmonization stands out as a critical requirement. Artificial Intelligence technologies function internationally while existing legal systems display significant fragmentation. The European Union's draft AI Act presents an all-inclusive risk-based system that includes high-risk categorizations and obligatory transparency requirements yet significant regulatory differences remain between the EU and both the U.S. and countries in Asia, Africa, and Latin America according to Saura et al. (2024). The differences between regulatory systems generate compliance ambiguity for multinational companies that need to synchronize their operations with diverse standards. Saura et al. Saura et al. (2024) propose an international regulatory framework that aligns digital ethics worldwide while respecting national sovereignty. The adoption of shared principles including fairness, explainability, and data privacy would decrease jurisdictional arbitrage and promote equitable AI development. Investigative research needs to examine how treaties, collaborative AI alliances and regulatory convergence frameworks can be implemented. The authors suggest further research through comparative legal studies to discover effective policy tools and evaluate their transferability between different legal systems. The main goal should focus on developing a "global AI governance architecture" to ensure ethical consistency and operational clarity for developers, marketers and consumers. The emerging discussion around AI innovation includes developing ethical certification systems for AI technologies. Ethical labels could function as trust-building tools similar to energy efficiency labels and Fairtrade certifications to help consumers swiftly assess the ethical standards of products and platforms. Chatterjee et al. The 2022 study by Chatterjee et al. demonstrates that ethical certifications improve consumer views on transparency and responsibility which may enhance brand loyalty and increase purchase intent. Subsequent studies need to assess the practical implementation potential of these certifications alongside their acceptance in industry sectors and consumer response. Important queries involve defining certification standards and determining accreditation oversight while considering scaling certification levels according to risk application. Research needs to determine if ethical certifications protect against data misuse and manipulation concerns or just act as symbolic gestures. Technological evolution creates a new research boundary alongside regulatory changes given the emergence of Emotion AI and biometric targeting technologies. Marketers can monitor and address user emotional states instantly through analysis of voice tone characteristics, facial micro-expressions, pupil expansion, and heart rate detection. These technologies demonstrate exceptional personalization potential yet simultaneously generate serious questions regarding emotional privacy and mental autonomy alongside risks of cognitive manipulation. The researchers Yilmaz and Ashqar (2025) advocate comprehensive interdisciplinary research to investigate the psychological and social effects of biometric surveillance methods used in marketing practices. What lasting impact do these technologies have on consumer behavior patterns and how does the use of emotional vulnerability in ad personalization affect psychological well-being? Longitudinal studies need to concentrate on the impacts on children and older adults as well as other vulnerable populations who show higher sensitivity to emotional stimuli. The technical research community needs to examine the fairness and reliability of biometric AI systems. The potential misclassification of emotions by inference tools based on racial, gender, or cultural differences demands urgent attention to bias, accuracy and explainability concerns. Scientists need to enhance training data inclusivity while validating model performance across various environments and developing human oversight frameworks to stop emotional surveillance from breaching ethical limits. The development of ethical AI marketing relies on innovative research that connects regulatory alignment with technological progress. A sustainable roadmap to preserve user autonomy while enabling innovation and earning trust in AI marketing systems emerges from the joint efforts of scholars, practitioners, and policymakers who address legal alignment as well as biometric ethics.

Generative AI and Content Ethics

Marketing has experienced a transformation in content creation and consumer engagement through the adoption of generative and multimodal artificial intelligence technologies. These technologies bring about ethical issues concerning authenticity and transparency while impacting user autonomy and psychological effects which require future research attention. Large language models within generative AI technology have the capacity to produce product descriptions and respond to customers as well as create social media content without human intervention. The efficiency of this technology brings up issues regarding the ability to identify whether content originates from humans or AI. Evaluating synthetic messages proves difficult for consumers which might lead to diminished trust. Ali, Riaz, and Rashid (2024) suggest conducting research into watermarking techniques and disclosure methods that reveal content sources. Different contexts need to be used for testing these solutions to guarantee users can distinguish AI-generated materials. Virtual and augmented reality environments incorporate immersive experiences powered by multimodal AI systems that combine text, audio, video, and biometric data inputs. Brands deploy AI technology to create virtual storefronts as well as avatar-led campaigns and sensory-driven engagement approaches. Innovative interactive experiences present potential dangers through sensory manipulation and excessive data collection. Saura et al. The 2024 study by Saura et al. highlights the necessity of ethical design strategies in immersive spaces with a special focus on user consent and protection of biometric data along with user well-being. These immersive tools merge digital and physical realms which lead to worries about cognitive overload and emotional vulnerability particularly for younger users. Yilmaz and Ashqar (2025) propose that future research needs to examine both long-term psychological impacts and fairness issues related to biometric targeting. Ethical deployment requires researchers to create transparent methods, strong consent procedures and collaborative ethical standards. The future of AI-driven marketing depends on merging technological advancements with human values to maintain consumer trust and preserve personal autonomy.

CONCLUSION

The marketing landscape has undergone a significant transformation thanks to Artificial Intelligence which enables hyper-personalization and predictive analytics along with emotion recognition and large-scale data-driven targeting. The new innovations boost delivery performance and relevance across products, content, and services. The development of advanced AI technologies brings critical ethical issues such as privacy risks, algorithmic discrimination, manipulation threats, and accountability concerns. This section covers essential research findings and proposes a plan for ethical AI implementation in marketing. The utility of AI in marketing is determined by its application since it serves as both a beneficial and potentially harmful tool. Technology enables real-time customization for interactive experiences, but it also creates opportunities for emotional manipulation and discrimination while enabling surveillance (Yilmaz & Ashqar, 2025). AI platforms analyze deeply personal characteristics from user data which users did not consent to share thus creating significant ethical concerns about data usage (Ali et al., 2024). The capability of AI to predict behaviors can diminish user autonomy through behavioral influence and bias reinforcement. Undisclosed capabilities inherently threaten user agency and create ambiguity between persuasion and manipulation according to Saura et al. (2024). The ethical concerns stem more from how these tools are managed and utilized rather than the tools themselves. Brands need to transition from addressing problems after they occur to embedding ethical standards proactively through structured governance and principles. In the digital economy trust serves as fundamental currency. Users lose trust in AI-powered services when they sense surveillance or manipulation despite receiving value from those services (Chatterjee et al., 2022). Studies indicate greater trust in AI systems occur when users have knowledge about the decision-making process. Explainable AI (XAI) occupies a central position because it delivers transparent algorithmic explanations within specific contexts (Doshi-Velez & Kim, 2021). The limited focus of consumers in marketing makes interpretability essential. Transparent AI interfaces give consumers power to comprehend and challenge machine-generated decisions which bridges the knowledge gap between brands and their customers. Equally important is fairness. Exclusionary practices emerge from biased data which predominantly affect women and minority groups (Yilmaz & Ashqar, 2025). Developing Responsible AI mandates the use of varied datasets combined with consistent audits and stakeholder feedback alongside models that focus on fairness. A fair approach requires sensitivity to both cultural norms and legal standards. Ethical practices vary across contexts because behavior seen as acceptable in one scenario can be intrusive in another setting. The design of governance frameworks requires adaptability to cultural variations (Nguyen et al., 2021). Organizational backing is essential to achieve ethical AI beyond technical solutions. Organizations need to establish Chief AI Ethics Officers and internal ethics boards while performing routine audits as suggested by Ali et al. (2024). Minimizing data exposure requires both Privacy-by-Design principles and federated learning methods. Industry-wide collaboration is crucial. The combination of open-source bias detection tools with shared guidelines and regulatory sandboxes will help establish standard ethical AI practices (Chatterjee et al., 2022). Ethical practices must extend past mere compliance to enable consumer empowerment. Systems should provide layered consent options and uphold data sovereignty instead of using default opt-ins. educational programs enable consumers to comprehend AI's influence on their decision-making while they hold brands accountable (Saura et al., 2024). The inclusion of user co-design is essential to establish ethical systems. Consumers who contribute to digital experience development achieve better alignment with their personal values (Nguyen et al., 2021). The progression of AI into emotion recognition and synthetic influences creates new ethical challenges along with virtual reality advancements. To tackle emerging risks, organizations require proactive governance together with scenario planning and stakeholder consultation (Yilmaz & Ashqar, 2025). Environmental sustainability remains another ethical dimension that frequently receives insufficient attention. AI training and deployment consume massive energy. Green AI strategies which merge efficient operations with environmental accountability have become essential according to Chatterjee et al. (2022). Marketing's future relies on integrating ethical standards within AI systems and business operations. Organizations experience true transformation when they see ethics as strategic assets instead of mere compliance requirements.

REFERENCES

Ali, R., Riaz, M., & Rashid, H. (2024). Ethical AI governance in marketing systems: A global approach. *Journal of Business Ethics, 159*(2), 250–270.

Alhitmi, H., Rahman, M., & Alghamdi, A. (2024). The role of AI in chatbot personalization and dynamic pricing. *International Journal of E-Commerce Technology, 45*(1), 33–47.

Bilyk, I., Kindii, M., & Dymon, I. (2024). *Ethical aspects of the use of artificial intelligence in marketing*. Odesa National University Herald. Economy., DOI: 10.32782/2304-0920/4-102-11

Chatterjee, S., Banerjee, P., & Ghosh, D. (2022). Organizational ethics and AI: Building responsible systems in digital markets. *Journal of Technology and Society, 18*(4), 311–326.

Doshi-Velez, F., & Kim, B. (2021). Towards a rigorous science of interpretable machine learning. arXiv preprint arXiv:1702.08608.

Islam, M. A., Fakir, S. I., Masud, S. B., Hossen, M. D., Islam, M. T., & Siddiky, M. R. (2024). *Artificial intelligence in digital marketing automation: Enhancing personalization, predictive analytics, and ethical integration*. Edelweiss Applied Science and Technology., DOI: 10.55214/25768484.v8i6.3404

Kirtsova, I., & Huseynov, N. (2024). *The ethical importance of artificial intelligence in B2B marketing: A critical analysis*. PAHTEI - Proceedings of Azerbaijan High Technical Educational Institutions., DOI: 10.36962/PAHTEI41062024-27

Kyosovska, K. (2024). *Artificial intelligence and marketing: Ethical dilemmas in the Bulgarian professional environment*. Postmodernism Problems., DOI: 10.46324/PMP2403374

Naz, H., & Kashif, M. (2024). Artificial intelligence and predictive marketing: An ethical framework from managers' perspective. *Spanish Journal of Marketing - ESIC*. Advance online publication. DOI: 10.1108/SJME-06-2023-0154

Nguyen, T. M., Park, J. H., & Kim, H. (2021). User-centered design and participatory ethics in AI systems. *Human–Computer Interaction Journal, 34*(2), 211–230.

Priyanka, A. L., Harihararao, M., Prasanna, M., & Deepika, Y. (2023). A study on artificial intelligence in marketing. *International Journal for Multidisciplinary Research*. DOI: 10.36948/ijfmr.2023.v05i03.3789

Sarioguz, O., & Miser, E. (2024). Assessing the role of artificial intelligence in enhancing customer personalization: A study of ethical and privacy implications in digital marketing. *International Journal of Science and Research Archive*. DOI: 10.30574/ijsra.2024.13.2.2207

Saura, J. R., Škare, V., & Dosen, D. O. (2024). Is AI-based digital marketing ethical? Assessing a new data privacy paradox. *Journal of Innovation & Knowledge*. DOI: 10.1016/j.jik.2024.100597

Sharma, A. K., & Sharma, R. (2023). Considerations in artificial intelligence-based marketing: An ethical perspective. *Applied Marketing Analytics: The Peer-Reviewed Journal*. DOI: 10.69554/RAPQ3226

Sharma, S. (2023). *Ethical considerations in AI-based marketing: Balancing profit and consumer trust*. Tuijin Jishu/Journal of Propulsion Technology., DOI: 10.52783/tjjpt.v44.i3.474

Vukmirović, J., Maričić, L., Stanojević, S., Vukmirović, A., & Mandić, I. (2025). Considering the ethical aspects of artificial intelligence application from the consumer perspective. *Bizinfo (Blace)*. Advance online publication. DOI: 10.71159/bizinfo250001V

Williams, J., Chen, L., & Davis, K. (2023). Racial bias in facial recognition: Marketing and surveillance consequences. *Technology in Society*, *21*(3), 188–202.

Yilmaz, K., & Ashqar, H. (2025). Emotion AI in marketing: Psychological implications and ethical safeguards. *Journal of Emotional Technologies*, *14*(1), 54–73.

KEY TERMS AND DEFINITIONS

AI-Powered Targeting: AI-enabled marketing strategies create personalized advertisements and content by analyzing user data.

Algorithmic Bias: AI systems produce unfair results when their training data is incomplete or biased.

Emotion AI: The technology used to detect human emotions operates through methods including facial recognition and voice analysis as well as biometric data.

Ethical AI: The development and implementation of AI systems should follow moral standards that exceed basic regulatory requirements.

Predictive Analytics: Predictive Analytics utilizes AI-based models to forecast consumer behavior by analyzing both historical datasets and real-time information.

Privacy Paradox: Online actions of users demonstrate inconsistency when compared to their expressed privacy concerns.

Transparency and Explainability: How well humans can comprehend AI decision-making processes.

Chapter 9

Generative AI in Marketing OpenAI's ChatGPT Enhancing Customer Conversation and Content

Madara Balawardhana
https://orcid.org/0000-0001-6195-4770
University of Bedfordshire, Luton, UK

ABSTRACT

This chapter discusses the transformation of marketing strategies through generative AI with a focus on OpenAI's ChatGPT technology. Traditional marketing tools become inadequate when consumer preferences move toward personalized and real-time engagement. Through CRM integration alongside prompt engineering and retrieval-augmented generation, ChatGPT delivers scalable content creation while boosting customer engagement throughout their entire journey from initial awareness to final action. The chapter presents both the "Prompt-to-Publish" framework and new marketer roles including prompt engineers and AI editors. The chapter provides guidance for responsible AI use while addressing ethical concerns involving data privacy, misinformation, and algorithmic bias. The chapter investigates upcoming advancements through multimodal AI systems and self-operating marketing agents. The chapter provides marketers actionable strategies alongside theoretical knowledge to ethically and effectively utilize generative AI while remaining adaptable to the fast-changing digital environment.

DOI: 10.4018/979-8-3373-6582-4.ch009

BACKGROUND

This chapter examines the impact of fast-developing artificial intelligence (AI) systems on today's marketing practices. During the last ten years marketers have implemented automation tools along with predictive analytics and customer relationship management systems to enhance operational efficiency and customer engagement (Aldoseri et al., 2024; Al Naqbi et al., 2024). The development of generative AI technologies such as OpenAI's ChatGPT stands as a pivotal advancement that facilitates intelligent conversations resembling human interaction which surpasses the capabilities of former systems (Dwivedi et al., 2023; Bansal et al., 2024). Traditional content creation required significant time investment for manual work which failed to meet modern standards for real-time personalized experiences. Previous rule-based chatbots failed to provide conversational flexibility alongside contextual understanding according to McTear (2022) and Nirala et al. (2022). Generative AI resolves these shortcomings by providing dynamic messaging capabilities alongside intelligent customer service solutions and scalable adaptive storytelling (Fui-Hoon Nah et al., 2023; Bengesi et al., 2024). Modern audiences demand quick communication that both matches their personal behaviours and reflects their values according to Gao & Liu (2023) and Paul et al. (2023). Advanced natural language processing enables ChatGPT to produce precise responses that understand context effectively (Ray, 2023; Bansal et al., 2024). The system supports internal marketing operations by making brainstorming more efficient while reducing repetitive writing tasks and optimizing campaign testing procedures and it further strengthens team collaboration capabilities (Al Naqbi et al., 2024; Shahin et al., 2024). These efficiency gains enable marketing professionals to dedicate more time to strategic planning while enhancing both personalized customer experiences and campaign success rates (Aldoseri et al., 2024; Wahid et al., 2023). Generative AI powers innovation in platform content delivery while fostering human-centred marketing approaches that emphasize empathy as shown by Chen et al., 2024 and Ooi et al., 2025. The advantages from these technologies bring forth ethical dilemmas and operational hazards. The critical challenges of data privacy as well as algorithmic bias together with misinformation and content authenticity remain paramount (Sison et al., 2024; Gao et al., 2023). AI content that lacks proper monitoring risks misleading users and damaging the credibility of the brand. To address these risks organizations should implement ethical frameworks that promote transparency along with accountability and responsible governance (Wulf & Seizov, 2024; Sigala et al., 2024). Content quality and legal compliance rely on human oversight to maintain contextual accuracy (Ekin, 2023; Xie et al., 2023). Continuous auditing processes maintain adherence between generative outputs and both brand standards and regulatory changes according to research by Ozmen Garibay et al. (2023) and Wang et al. (2023). ChatGPT succeeds in boosting marketing effectiveness notwithstanding existing challenges. The use of applications spans personalized upselling activities within the hospitality industry and automated profiling techniques in digital marketing strategies (Remountakis et al., 2023; Gujar et al., 2024; Trusov et al., 2016). This technology produces economical solutions which drive innovation while enhancing customer interaction. The chapter conducts a critical evaluation of ChatGPT's capabilities and limitations while providing practical insights for professionals regarding AI-enhanced communication (Davenport et al., 2020; Fui-Hoon Nah et al., 2023). ChatGPT's impact reaches past technical improvements because it represents a fundamental transformation in marketing strategy. Sustainable success requires companies to adopt AI technology while ensuring ethical practices and creative uses that reflect human values.

Focus of the Chapter

The chapter examines the revolutionary impact of generative artificial intelligence like OpenAI's ChatGPT on marketing through its transformative effects on brand engagement and content delivery. The demand for hyper-personalized real-time experiences alongside digital platform saturation renders traditional content creation methods inadequate. This chapter describes ChatGPT as a strategic partner for modern marketing which facilitates operational efficiency and creative adaptability across large scales according to the research by Aldoseri et al. (2024) and Gujar et al. (2024). The discussion evaluates technical capabilities while exploring current uses and ethical issues related to AI deployment in both direct customer interactions and internal marketing operations. The evolution of generative AI from rule-based and predictive analytics systems to complex models such as ChatGPT serves as the starting point of this chapter. The chapter reveals essential model functions including prompt engineering, tokenization, and retrieval-augmented generation (RAG) while detailing their importance for producing successful marketing results (Chen et al., 2024; Shahin et al., 2024). The discussion highlights ChatGPT's role as a creative partner that helps improve marketing strategy alongside boosting efficiency and personalization. This chapter provides a detailed exploration of ChatGPT's marketing applications through key thematic subheadings and delivers a structured comprehension of its transformative impact on the field.

Current Applications

Content Creation and Campaign Development

ChatGPT facilitates quick creation of various marketing materials such as email campaigns, SEO-friendly blogs, social media posts, and video scripts. By customizing outputs according to distinct audience segments brands can expedite production timelines while improving content personalization (Paul et al., 2023; Wang, 2023). AI-generated content enables brands to maintain voice uniformity across various platforms while facilitating idea generation and real-time editing processes (Bansal et al., 2024; Wahid et al., 2023). ChatGPT enables marketing teams to establish "prompt-to-publish" workflows that enable the swift conversion of concepts into publish-ready documents. A marketer can request the system to "Write a product description for a Gen Z audience" to instantly obtain copy that matches audience preferences while maintaining brand tone and emotional impact. The capability eliminates significant production delays while enabling fast response times for urgent campaigns. The system enables strategic content clustering and SEO optimization through related content generation which improves both website performance metrics and search ranking positions. Teams can rapidly test different content versions and tone styles which enables them to conduct more thorough data-based A/B testing methods. ChatGPT aids global campaigns by adapting content to fit cultural and linguistic needs across different regions. ChatGPT plays a vital role in today's influencer marketing and branded storytelling approaches. This tool creates scripts for influencer partnerships while generating outreach emails and proposing creative storylines that appeal to targeted audiences. ChatGPT helps generate detailed whitepapers and case studies for B2B marketing that keep technical information accurate while ensuring content stays understandable. Marketers can employ real-time trend adaptation capabilities to address viral topics and cultural conversations with appropriate branded content swiftly. These dynamic capabilities allow companies to remain flexible in a digital environment where rapid action and high-quality performance determine success.

Customer Engagement and Support

Companies utilize ChatGPT to manage customer questions by leveraging intelligent chat platforms that operate in real-time. ChatGPT surpasses rule-based systems by understanding complex customer questions and providing contextually aware answers which boost both customer satisfaction and response speed (McTear, 2022; Remountakis et al., 2023). The system allows brands to expand their support across multiple languages globally without hiring more staff members (Zheng et al., 2023; Kumar et al., 2024). This application transforms customer service by providing intelligent support always tailored to individual needs and available. Support systems powered by ChatGPT fulfil multiple roles including answering FAQs and guiding users through product features while simultaneously handling complaints and making upsell and cross-sell recommendations according to user behaviour and history. An online fashion retailer can utilize ChatGPT to suggest complementary accessories throughout the shopping experience which helps to increase basket size while improving customer satisfaction. Generative AI helps businesses maintain their brand tone and personality during all customer interactions which maintains brand consistency throughout every customer touchpoint. ChatGPT becomes a more powerful tool in customer interactions because it adjusts its responses through ongoing engagement experiences. The integration of this system with CRM systems enables real-time personalization that utilizes customer profiles and historical interactions alongside their preferences. All interactions become valuable exchanges which help sustain brand loyalty and customer retention over time. ChatGPT actively engages customers when behaviour triggers like abandoned shopping carts or extended browsing periods occur to deliver immediate support and incentives. Integrating with voice assistants as well as IoT interfaces enhances its capability to engage with users. ChatGPT enables voice-activated devices and assists customers through smart kiosks located in retail settings. The system operates around the clock to cut down customer irritation from delayed support and adapts to increased demand while maintaining service quality. The consistent performance over time builds consumer trust and establishes brands as technologically advanced and responsive according to customer perspectives.

Internal Marketing Operations

Through assistance with brainstorming activities alongside headline testing and copy refinement as well as A/B testing, generative AI improves internal workflows. The tool streamlines marketing team productivity through repetitive task automation while functioning as a cooperative partner in cross-functional content planning (Al Naqbi et al., 2024; Shahin et al., 2024). The ChatGPT platform aids marketing analytics through its ability to combine competitor intelligence with customer information to develop practical content strategies (Gao et al., 2023). ChatGPT demonstrates substantial utility in internal operations apart from content creation. Marketing teams use ChatGPT for their campaign planning activities and utilize it to create meeting agendas and client proposals while summarizing complex reports. Departments can unify their communication approaches and agree on campaign goals by utilizing shared AI tools which create draft assets ready for team collaboration. Marketers apply ChatGPT to create customer personas and evaluate message effectiveness in various scenarios before launching campaigns to ensure messaging accuracy. Teams in collaborative workspaces rely on ChatGPT as an inventive brainstorming tool that produces taglines, headlines and central campaign themes which team members can develop further. The system helps automate documentation tasks by providing natural language summaries for reporting formats and KPI tracking. The internal application increases strategic agility while minimizing time spent on repetitive tasks which enables resources to focus on more valuable creative and analytical work. ChatGPT functions as an internal knowledge sharing and training system. The system provides new hire onboarding materials and creates internal FAQs while running sales training customer scenario simulations. Marketing managers utilize this tool to compile team feedback and extract insights from collaborative platforms such as Slack or Trello. ChatGPT aids agile teams during sprint planning sessions by assisting with goal definition and the creation of stand-up notes and retrospective summaries. The model provides support for compliance-related tasks which includes reviewing promotional content for adherence to legal standards and regulatory rules. The versatile functionality of AI tools establishes team cohesion and alignment while enhancing productivity and making AI a crucial component of current marketing strategies.

Personalization at Scale

ChatGPT generates personalized messages through behavioural data analysis and embedding techniques that understand context and user personas. Marketers can develop personalized messages through real-time user behaviour analysis while maintaining brand consistency according to Chen et al. (2024) and Ooi et al. (2025). The retrieval-augmented generation (RAG) method enables ChatGPT to access external knowledge sources which helps maintain the accuracy and relevance of its personalized communication (Xie et al., 2023). The fundamental element of contemporary marketing involves mass personalization which ChatGPT supports by delivering adaptable messages that respond to real-time interactions. ChatGPT enables the creation of dynamic messages that reflect individual user interests and behaviours by working together with CRM systems and digital behaviour tracking tools. E-commerce brands can create automated email campaigns that target users who left their carts behind through personalized messages that employ compelling language and offers tailored to each user's particular tastes. ChatGPT enables segmentation-based content strategies through personalized adaptations in tone and message types for multiple user personas including professionals, students and parents. Through its grasp of context and language nuances ChatGPT maintains message coherence and consistency even when personalization becomes more complex. The ability to maintain individualized interactions with millions of users helps companies boost engagement rates alongside conversion results and strengthens enduring brand connections. ChatGPT strengthens retargeting initiatives by tailoring ad copy and display banners to reflect past user interactions. The system produces dynamic product recommendations and generates landing page variations that match specific ad channels and referral sources. ChatGPT enhances loyalty programs through its delivery of customized messages which acknowledge customer achievements and offer bespoke rewards while strengthening customer engagement. A travel brand can deliver personalized trip recommendations that match their customer's previous travel choices and declared preferences. Real-time adjustments to promotional messaging enable the model to respond to seasonal trends and weather patterns while considering geographic location which leads to contextually relevant outreach that boosts conversion chances.

Strategic Integration and Ethical Considerations

The chapter emphasizes the importance of transparent AI practices and ethical governance while maintaining human oversight for AI-generated content. The subjects discussed encompass bias mitigation strategies alongside data privacy concerns and the dangers of misinformation while maintaining brand authenticity (Sison et al., 2024; Wulf & Seizov, 2024). Marketing professionals must strategically align AI systems with business objectives and follow responsible deployment methods to achieve successful AI integration. To effectively implement ChatGPT in strategic applications requires careful planning to address potential bias issues, misinformation risks, and the preservation of brand identity. Without proper guidance technology that scales content production and personalization may generate misleading or inappropriate content unintentionally. Marketing teams need to establish strong review procedures and detailed brand style guides to maintain alignment with ethical standards and brand guidelines. A clear understanding of AI interactions must be provided to users while data handling must adhere to privacy laws such as GDPR. The deployment of Ethical AI frameworks must direct implementation while marketing teams should perform active surveillance for any indications of hallucinated content or algorithmic biases. To maintain responsible and effective AI performance over time organizations need to perform regular audits and implement prompt iteration cycles.

Key Findings

The utilization of generative AI tools such as ChatGPT by organizations has led to significant changes in marketing practices. Through an integration of current research findings and practical industry applications this section demonstrates

ChatGPT's transformative effects on marketing's strategic planning creative execution and operational procedures.

ChatGPT as a Strategic Marketing Partner

ChatGPT has rapidly become an essential element of marketing strategy by transitioning from its initial role as a content creation tool to become a fundamental force behind brand-audience interaction. Previous market technologies operated in separate silos with operational or automation functions but ChatGPT functions directly within strategic planning and execution stages of marketing campaigns. The technology's advanced natural language processing abilities allow it to produce coherent content with human-like qualities that emotionally connect with audiences on multiple platforms (Bansal et al., 2024; Kumar et al., 2024). ChatGPT provides messaging solutions that enable businesses to maintain consistent brand voice through personalized and scalable communication channels. Organizations can preserve consistent communication strategies by using this capacity to customize content for different target audiences. ChatGPT enables businesses to generate personalized messages for distinct customer groups including Gen Z consumers and senior professionals using brand-appropriate tone and terminology (Chen et al., 2024; Shahin et al., 2024). For brands operating globally it is vital to demonstrate adaptability because different regional nuances and cultural expectations require messaging sensitivity (Wahid et al., 2023). ChatGPT provides strategic support to both external communication efforts and internal decision-making operations. ChatGPT helps develop marketing plans and summarizes analytics while performing competitive analyses that depend on provided data. Marketing teams employ ChatGPT to develop campaign themes through brainstorming sessions while creating different headlines and testing multiple content versions to enhance their agile marketing strategies (Al Naqbi et al., 2024; Gao et al., 2023). ChatGPT enables creative, technical, and strategic teams to collaborate effectively through its various functions. The ability to integrate with customer journey mapping makes it especially useful. ChatGPT provides real-time interaction capabilities throughout the AIDA model stages of Awareness, Interest, Desire, and Action with unique messaging and touchpoint engagement at each point. During the awareness stage ChatGPT creates captivating blog posts and video scripts to present a brand's value proposition to its audience. When customers reach the interest and desire stages ChatGPT produces educational content and persuasive copy that adapts to each customer's specific needs. The action phase utilizes clear calls-to-action along with product suggestions and follow-up messages to drive conversions (Remountakis et al., 2023; Harahap and Junianto, 2023). ChatGPT offers a strategic advantage through its ability to adapt messages in real time. ChatGPT differs from conventional static content because it modifies messages dynamically according to new data and campaign performance feedback. Marketers benefit from ongoing campaign adjustments because they no longer must finalize their campaigns well before launch. ChatGPT enables responsive marketing practices which allow messaging to change continuously with audience behaviour and external trends (Fui-Hoon Nah et al., 2023; Aldoseri et al., 2024). The collaboration with ChatGPT as a creative partner enables marketers to explore new dimensions of generating ideas and conducting experimental campaigns. Marketing teams can bypass preliminary creative processes by using ChatGPT to identify suitable campaign themes while producing sample content to assess and experimenting with tone changes to meet new audience preferences (Gupta et al., 2024; Kshetri et al., 2024). ChatGPT has transformed the marketing landscape through its ability to deliver scalable content that is intelligent and emotionally resonant while remaining contextually aware. The integration of ChatGPT allows companies to create unified brand stories while delivering immediate benefits and maintaining flexibility within complex digital environments. ChatGPT's role extends beyond basic automation as it emerges as an essential element for strategic marketing planning and execution.

Transformation of Customer Conversations

The ability of ChatGPT to conduct real-time conversations that recognize user intent has revolutionized customer service techniques. It responds to subtle customer requests which allows it to recommend products and solve problems while delivering tailored advice unlike traditional chatbots. H&M's AI assistant represents practical implementations that demonstrate significant enhancements in both customer satisfaction and operational productivity according to studies by Kumar et al. (2024) and Titus (2024). ChatGPT stands out because of its ability to maintain contextually flexible dialogues that remain coherent throughout multiple interactions. This conversational depth transforms it beyond a basic FAQ bot and turns it into an intelligent interface that personalizes customer interactions from their very first touchpoint. ChatGPT deployment across websites, social media platforms, and messaging apps enables businesses to deliver consistent yet personalized responses for various customer requirements. ChatGPT modifies its tone and content to match user needs when discussing product specifications, troubleshooting problems, or post-purchase support (Bansal et al., 2024; Paul et al., 2023). ChatGPT personalizes customer dialogues in real time by incorporating CRM data which boosts both relevance and user engagement. The integration enables businesses to provide intelligent recommendations based on customer preferences and their browsing history and previous interactions. When users revisit product pages, they might encounter messages such as “Still thinking about the blue headphones? The offer of a 10% discount represents personalized messaging that raises conversion possibilities according to Remountakis et al. (2023) and Harahap and Junianto (2023). ChatGPT expands worldwide customer engagement capabilities through its multilingual support features. International brands gain better market accessibility and customer satisfaction because ChatGPT can understand multiple languages and generate appropriate responses which helps serve diverse markets (Zheng et al., 2023; Kumar et al., 2024). It maintains brand relevance by adapting to diverse cultural communication customs and preventing misunderstandings. The system performs functions such as lead generation and qualification. ChatGPT greets website visitors while asking qualifying questions and then directs high-intent leads to human representatives. The system enhances customer acquisition processes while delivering better experiences to potential clients. The application of intelligent filtering in high-involvement sectors such as SaaS and real estate enables sales teams to concentrate their efforts on prospects who present the highest conversion potential (Gupta et al., 2024; Shahin et al., 2024). The evolution of customer interactions through ChatGPT displays how generative AI enables scalable and efficient communication with meaningful results. The system improves operational efficiency through rapid and human-like handling of numerous inquiries while building stronger customer relationships which makes it essential for contemporary customer engagement approaches.

Acceleration of Content Marketing

Generative AI has reshaped content marketing workflows by substantially lowering the time needed to create top-notch content that matches brand requirements. Marketers today use prompt engineering through "Prompt-to-Publish" workflows to generate SEO blogs to personalized email campaigns by moving content seamlessly from creation to publication. The transition results in faster reactions while expanding content options without requiring more human effort (Paul et al., 2023; Ambacher, 2024). ChatGPT enables marketers to generate different content types such as product descriptions, ad copy, newsletters, and social media posts that meet unique platform requirements. The tool adapts dynamically to meet evolving campaign demands as well as seasonal campaigns and current trending subjects. Marketers can swiftly change their campaign messaging for major events or holidays by modifying prompts which empowers ChatGPT to produce new material that targets these occasions within minutes (Wahid et al., 2023; Fui-Hoon Nah et al., 2023). ChatGPT has achieved its most substantial impact by significantly shortening the duration of development cycles. The content creation process used to involve several rounds of drafting and needed approval from different stakeholders. Teams can create polished drafts with ChatGPT that meet specific tone and structural requirements along with formatting standards. The drafts produced by ChatGPT act as robust initial frameworks that streamline the content development process by minimizing both time and effort required for production (Shahin et al., 2024; Bansal et al., 2024). Furthermore, ChatGPT facilitates better SEO alignment. Marketers who use keyword-driven content objectives with AI models produce search engine-friendly content that stays readable. The AI provides recommendations for internal and external linking methods and content groupings that strengthen site authority. ChatGPT stands as a valuable tool both for creative tasks and technical enhancement according to Paul et al. (2023) and Ray (2023). ChatGPT accelerates social media campaigns by creating multiple post variations for A/B testing and selecting high-engagement hashtags while also creating platform-specific captions. Marketers utilize simulated audience reactions to optimize tone and content delivery which leads to better click-through rates and higher user engagement (Bansal et al., 2024; Wang, 2023). ChatGPT enables localization through its ability to produce content customized for specific regions using various languages and dialects. Successful global campaigns require cultural sensitivity representation within brand-consistent messaging. Through multilingual prompt functionality companies can execute localized campaigns without needing individual creative teams for each market (Zheng et al., 2023; Kumar et al., 2024). ChatGPT's advanced content creation enables marketing teams to dedicate more time to strategic initiatives including campaign planning and brand positioning analysis. The platform functions as both an idea generator and a content delivery system which represents a major change in scalable content marketing processes.

Integration Across the Customer Journey

The AI tool ChatGPT supports marketing efforts throughout each stage of the AIDA (Awareness, Interest, Desire, Action) model. The AI tool creates personalized messages through CRM and MAP integration which utilizes user data to boost engagement and conversion rates. Real-time content delivery adjustments achieved by ChatGPT enable both contextual relevance and scalability (Remountakis et al., 2023; Harahap and Junianto, 2023). ChatGPT produces SEO-optimized blog content as well as social media captions and influencer outreach drafts to help introduce new brands and products to their audiences during the awareness phase. The outputs strategically attract attention while they stay consistent with current trends and search engine algorithms. A sustainable fashion brand may ask ChatGPT to develop content about their environmentally friendly practices that appeals to eco-conscious consumers (Wahid et al., 2023; Paul et al., 2023). ChatGPT adds significant value during the interest stage by providing product comparison articles and FAQs or thought leadership content designed for audience needs. Customer-facing AI tools deliver personalized answers that build trust through engagement while guiding customer choices and addressing their questions (Ray, 2023; Fui-Hoon Nah et al.,

2023). During this stage of marketing, professionals frequently use AI within chat interfaces or email campaigns to promote advanced exploration. ChatGPT stands out during the desire phase by generating customized promotional messages together with testimonials and case studies with strong persuasive copy to enhance product benefits and emotional connections. The AI system creates personalized content narratives by combining user-specific behaviour data from CRM platforms with their individual engagement histories and interests. ChatGPT enables fitness companies to generate personalized offers and workout tips which match users' browsing patterns and previous purchases according to Gupta et al., 2024 and Shahin et al., 2024. During the action stage ChatGPT generates conversion-focused materials such as time-limited deals and personalized follow-up communications including cart abandonment alerts and post-purchase suggestions. These outputs play an essential role in completing the customer experience cycle and enhancing satisfaction levels. The integration of ChatGPT into MAP workflows guarantees message delivery at optimal times while adapting communication to match user intent and platform usage patterns (Kumar et al., 2024; Zheng et al., 2023). Crucially, ChatGPT's real-time adaptability enhances each stage. The system persistently retrieves data from MAPs and CRMs to modify its tone and language while refining call-to-action approaches guided by feedback analysis and performance statistics. The adaptive nature of this system allows brands to continuously refine their marketing channels while testing fresh communication approaches and keeping consistent messaging through all customer interaction points. ChatGPT enhances customer interactions by delivering scalable content which aligns with context and emotional connection throughout all customer journey stages. The integration of this system enables brands to maintain high levels of personalized customer engagement while minimizing drop-off rates and enhancing long-term loyalty through intelligent messaging sequences.

Large-Scale Personalization through Advanced AI Methods

This model achieves massive-scale personalization through behavioural segmentation techniques and persona-driven messaging combined with retrieval-augmented generation (RAG). In music streaming industries ChatGPT demonstrates dynamic user-focused communication abilities when it creates personalized playlists based on user behaviour and context (Joseph, 2024). The large-scale personalization capability of ChatGPT emerges from its real-time data analysis and interpretation to deliver tailored customer experiences. The model modifies content through CRM system integration by examining prior user interactions along with purchasing trends and demographic attributes. Brands can deliver highly customized messages to millions of users while maintaining consistent tone and precise content as shown by Chen et al. (2024) and Ooi et al. (2025). E-commerce brands can use ChatGPT to create personalized emails that include recently viewed products or deliver recommendations based on browsing history and seasonal preferences. The power of customer personalization grows stronger through behavioural segmentation which organizes clients by their level of engagement and shopping behaviours alongside their lifecycle stages. ChatGPT enhances user engagement by customizing the tone, structure, and timing of content across different segments. New visitors might encounter educational content but returning customers receive loyalty incentives or upsell offers as per Wahid et al., 2023 and Gao et al., 2023. The retrieval-augmented generation (RAG) approach enables ChatGPT to enhance personalization through external knowledge base queries before drafting responses. The system maintains factual correctness while delivering up-to-date communication content. Customer messages become dynamic and responsive using RAG to update pricing details along with inventory and policy data according to Xie et al., 2023 and Shahin et al., 2024. ChatGPT enables persona-driven messaging as another advanced communication technique. Brands can create more impactful content by crafting prompts that match specific customer profiles such as budget-conscious students, tech-savvy professionals or eco-conscious families (Gupta et al., 2024; Kumar et al., 2024). The model demonstrates advanced comprehension of tone and language style which allows it to match communication preferences with exceptional accuracy. Personalization reaches beyond outbound communication to affect how content is presented to users. ChatGPT enables real-time generation of landing pages together with banner messages and pop-up text which adapts to user behaviour and referral source. Visitors who arrive through a sustainability blog receive eco-related content while those who come through a sales advertisement see limited time offers (Bansal et al., 2024; Al Naqbi et al., 2024). ChatGPT enables marketers to integrate personalization with large-scale automation. This integration enables communication methods that maintain consistency while adapting to personal preferences and current interaction trends. Messaging that feels tailor-made enables stronger user connections and improved conversion rates which leads to enhanced brand loyalty regardless of audience size.

Human-AI Collaboration and Evolving Marketing Roles

The adoption of ChatGPT leads to marketers transitioning into dual roles including prompt engineers and AI editors. The model serves as an assisting tool to enhance strategic planning and content creation alongside human efforts. The Jasper and HubSpot platforms demonstrate how AI tools support creative teamwork by establishing co-creation environments (Kshetri et al., 2024; Gupta et al., 2024; Haleem et al., 2022). This partnership represents a foundational transformation of the marketing workforce structure. ChatGPT enlarges marketing roles by enabling professionals to concentrate on strategic planning and brand consistency instead of diminishing creative demand. Prompt engineers develop specialized inputs which direct ChatGPT to produce outputs that meet specific tone and messaging objectives while AI editors improve generated content for quality compliance (Shahin et al., 2024; Al Naqbi et al., 2024). Real-time co-creation between marketers and ChatGPT becomes possible through collaborative platforms such as Jasper and HubSpot. Team members can work side-by-side to create blog posts and email campaigns as well as ad copy through collective contributions to prompts and draft reviews followed by iterative output refinements on shared platforms. Cross-functional team members like designers, analysts, and product managers now contribute to content creation which leads to democratization of the process (Wahid et al., 2023; Gao et al., 2023). The transformation process now relies heavily on training components. Marketing departments execute workshops focused on prompt engineering, responsible AI use, and bias mitigation to help their teams responsibly exploit ChatGPT's capabilities. Marketers require critical evaluation skills to identify and correct AI content hallucinations and biases while modifying prompts and outputs accordingly (Sison et al., 2024; Ray, 2023). ChatGPT enables marketers to generate ideas through its ability to propose campaign themes and develop visual taglines and attractive headlines. Teams can shift from conception to implementation swiftly with ChatGPT which eliminates creative blockages and encourages an iterative approach. Teams planning a launch campaign can collaborate with ChatGPT to develop messaging pillars and then instantly obtain draft variations to test (Gupta et al., 2024; Kshetri et al., 2024). Human-AI collaboration also improves content governance. Marketers can establish AI standardization across departments by developing prompt libraries along with brand tone frameworks and style guides. Maintaining consistency protects brand integrity and allows marketers to exercise creative freedom. Through this process ChatGPT evolves into an essential component of marketing operations instead of remaining an isolated tool (Chen et al., 2024; Kumar et al., 2024). ChatGPT serves as an enhancement tool for marketing professionals by broadening their creative opportunities and making execution faster. The collaboration between humans and machines improves human intelligence without replacing it and leads to a new age of co-creative marketing brilliance.

Ethical and Strategic Imperatives in AI Integration

The deployment of ChatGPT brings innovative possibilities but also presents challenges related to misinformation, bias, and data privacy. The chapter introduces "Responsible AI Marketing" as a framework to guide ethical AI applications while ensuring transparency and protecting brand integrity. Businesses must implement these practices to maintain consumer trust and achieve strategic value over time (Sison et al., 2024; Ray, 2023). Marketing professionals face significant challenges with ChatGPT because it can produce false information or deceptive content known as hallucinations. ChatGPT-generated content appears coherent and authoritative yet poses risks because it might include false data leading to consumer deception and brand reputation damage without proper review (Sison et al., 2024). Businesses need to establish strong content validation processes so that AI-generated messaging receives human editor fact-checking before being published. AI-generated outputs present a significant threat due to their biased nature. ChatGPT derives its training from extensive data collections which unintentionally incorporate societal and cultural prejudices. The model reproduces existing biases in its communications when it operates without supervision which can lead to audience alienation or the reinforcement of damaging stereotypes (Ray, 2023; Stypinska, 2023). Companies should combine diverse datasets with fairness-conscious prompt engineering methods and conduct regular content audits for inclusivity and neutrality to counteract bias. Privacy and data security are equally critical. Personalization in ChatGPT applications depends on combining CRM and MAP systems to retrieve customer data. The use of CRM and MAP systems for personalization in ChatGPT applications creates regulatory issues under GDPR and CCPA along with additional data protection laws (Wulf & Seizov, 2024). AI tools used by marketing teams need to follow regulatory standards through secure data management methods and user data anonymization while being transparent about information usage with users. The ethical principle of transparency in AI-generated content continues to evolve as a standard practice. More consumers express concern about identifying which pieces of content are created by machines and which originate from human authors. Organizations need to openly disclose when communications originate from AI systems to build trust and maintain transparency according to Kumar et al. (2024) and Bansal et al. (2024). Utilizing labels like "AI-generated response" and disclosure banners enables organizations to disclose authorship while maintaining user experience continuity. The use of ChatGPT should match with the brand's long-term voice and values. Excessive dependence on automated systems poses a threat to maintaining brand identity while diminishing emotional communication depth. Continuous human involvement becomes crucial specifically in tone adaptation along with customer sentiment analysis and crisis communication. The authenticity of brands is maintained when marketing leaders integrate AI efficiency with human insight (Gupta et al., 2024; Kshetri et al., 2024). The process of incorporating ethical AI requires continuous discipline involving governance frameworks alongside employee training and policy development. Brands focused on responsible deployment use ChatGPT effectively and protect their reputation alongside legal and ethical standards. This approach establishes brands as reliable innovators within the expanding AI marketplace.

A Paradigm Shift Toward Creativity and Automation

The study reveals ChatGPT as a transformative force that merges creative thinking with automated processes to produce groundbreaking marketing results. The full capabilities of ChatGPT can only be achieved through attentive human management together with strong organizational guidelines and ongoing professional skill enhancement for marketing staff. The transformation expands marketing execution possibilities beyond their traditional limits. Generative AI tools such as ChatGPT decrease manual workloads while simultaneously generating innovative creative ideas. Marketing teams can transition from traditional reactive planning to forward-thinking proactive models that utilize AI to quickly test and improve ideas through generated variations. Brands can now execute campaigns in days rather than weeks enabling them to match fast-moving consumer trends and digital environments (Fui-Hoon Nah et al., 2023; Aldoseri et al., 2024). ChatGPT facilitates the integration of marketing departments' creative tasks with their analytical responsibilities. This technology enables marketers to evaluate live performance data and produce optimized content changes and promotional text that match these insights on the spot. Campaign execution becomes more efficient through improved ROI and reduced waste when responsiveness is enhanced. Using RAG and embedding technologies marketers can ensure large-scale factual accuracy and user relevance which results in smarter and more reliable AI content (Xie et al., 2023; Shahin et al., 2024). The current paradigm pushes marketing roles towards interdisciplinary functions. The professional field requires individuals to gain expertise in prompt engineering alongside AI model tuning and ethical oversight. Creative strategists must now comprehend data flows and algorithmic operations while data analysts contribute to content creation processes. The convergence between disciplines creates opportunities for cross-functional innovation and contributes to the growth of career paths for marketing technologists who handle hybrid roles (Kshetri et al., 2024; Gupta et al., 2024). The transition requires organizations to redesign their structures and workflows. Businesses need to establish internal systems to control prompt libraries and track AI performance while maintaining brand standard compliance. Teams can share AI tools through the collaborative platforms Jasper, Copy.ai, and HubSpot's AI suite which support these workflows. Content creation democratization allows individuals without writing skills to make meaningful contributions to messaging and strategy development (Haleem et al., 2022; Wahid et al., 2023). Multimodal AI technology which produces text along with images, video, and audio content will further boost the existing creative transformation process. The development of ChatGPT together with solutions such as Midjourney and DALL·E shows how future AI-powered marketing campaigns will employ unified multimedia content produced by one strategic command (Sison et al., 2024; Huang et al., 2023). This paradigm shift aims to enhance human marketers' creative and strategic capabilities rather than automate them out of existence. ChatGPT introduces a revolutionary marketing partnership that boosts flexibility and innovation while providing enhanced insights throughout the full marketing value chain.

Figure 1. The diagram demonstrates ChatGPT's role as an all-encompassing marketing ecosystem which connects its technological base with operational functions and strategic collaborations while addressing ethical concerns to illustrate how generative AI transforms each layer of marketing practice. The illustration presents a visual linkage between the fundamental abilities of AI and real-world marketing tasks.

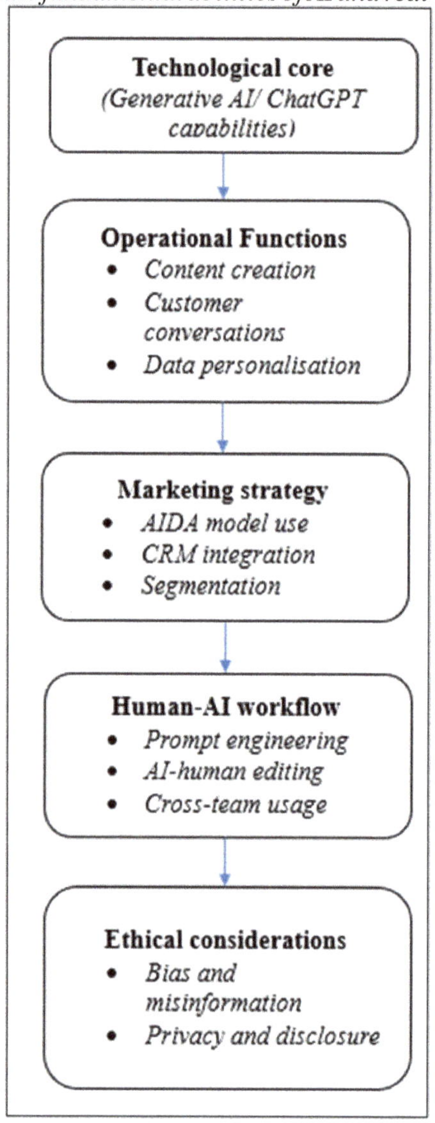

The model in figure 1 demonstrates ChatGPT's role as a multi-tiered marketing ecosystem where each level from foundational technology to ethical supervision works together to create a cohesive marketing plan. Its technological infrastructure forms the foundation enabling context-aware language generation which produces coherent responses through prompt engineering and RAG mechanisms. Operational tools including chatbot deployment as well as multilingual content generation and dynamic email creation convert those foundational capabilities into practical outputs. The strategic layer combines these functions within AIDA and CRM systems to produce timely and personalized content which drives conversions. The emergence of new professional positions within human-AI partnerships enables marketers to use these tools in a creative and efficient manner. The external most ethical framework guarantees that technological progress maintains standards of transparency and protects data privacy while establishing brand trust. These five dimensions together form an interdependent system that establishes ChatGPT as a transformative force beyond standard tools within modern marketing.

SOLUTIONS AND RECOMMENDATIONS

When businesses implement ChatGPT in their marketing strategies they must ensure strategic foresight along with operational clarity and ethical responsibility. The section presents practical solutions that connect advanced generative AI capabilities with responsible applications that focus on human needs. These recommendations assist companies in reducing risk while maximizing the transformative benefits of AI within their marketing strategies.

Professional Training in Prompt Engineering

Organizations need to establish formal training programs that specialize in prompt engineering to produce relevant, high-quality ChatGPT content. If prompts lack proper structure, they can generate content that is inaccurate or biased and fails to match brand standards. Marketers should possess templates and frameworks to create effective prompts customized to tone and platform requirements as well as target audience specifics (Han et al., 2024). Businesses should create uniform prompt design processes for their teams while designating specific roles for Prompt Engineers and AI Editors. Human oversight guarantees that AI-generated content undergoes editing to maintain accuracy while ensuring proper emotional tone and brand message alignment. The first step to growing this capability is understanding that prompt engineering extends beyond technical development into the realm of creativity and strategic marketing functions. Strategic prompt engineering enables marketers to control AI-generated content through adjustments to tone, structural design, length specifications and emotional resonance. The instruction "Write a 50-word Instagram caption for eco-conscious Gen Z consumers in a witty tone" generates much more targeted outcomes compared to broad directives. ChatGPT delivers better results when prompts are detailed yet align with the target audience (Ekin, 2023; Shahin et al., 2024). Training programs need to provide modules that teach prompt formatting techniques along with tone calibration practices and iterative testing methods. Professionals gain insights into the impact of subtle wording changes on content quality through practical exercises that compare different prompt versions. Marketing teams need to establish shared libraries for prompts and style guidelines to maintain uniformity across campaigns involving multiple contributors (Gupta et al., 2024; Gao et al., 2023). Training should also address ethical considerations. Prompt engineers need to recognize that biased or insensitive language affects AI outputs and reinforces stereotypes. Training programs need to incorporate lessons on recognizing biases and practicing inclusive communication. Businesses gain maximal generative AI innovation potential and maintain brand integrity along with compliance and audience trust by preparing marketing professionals with these essential skills (Ray, 2023; Sison et al., 2024).

Governance and Ethical Guidelines

Companies need to set up governance frameworks that define correct applications of AI technology. This requires companies to maintain an updated brand style guide for AI interactions and enforce transparent labelling of AI content while setting limits on AI production capabilities. Businesses need to implement rigorous access controls and ethical data management in their CRM and MAP system integrations to meet GDPR standards as discussed by Harahap et al., 2023 and Wulf & Seizov, 2024. Policies must establish disclosure procedures to educate customers about AI interactions. Organizations need to establish comprehensive AI usage policies throughout the company to initiate the expansion of ethical governance. The document needs to define roles and responsibilities while establishing ethical boundaries for generative AI applications in marketing. The policy should contain detailed examples which direct how AI should be utilized across campaign development stages as well as content distribution and customer engagement processes. Organizations should continuously refresh their ethical usage policies to address advancements in AI technology and changes in regulatory frameworks (Ray, 2023; Sison et al., 2024). A critical component of governance is transparency. Users gain trust through transparency when AI-generated responses in chatbots, emails, and social media interactions are clearly labelled. Organizations need to implement practices such as appending disclaimers or AI-authorship labels to their content especially when dealing with high-stakes fields like health communications or financial services marketing (Kumar et al., 2024; Bansal et al., 2024). Bias mitigation is another core pillar. Governance frameworks need to establish regular audits of AI outputs to identify discriminatory patterns because generative AI models learn from large datasets which might include inherent biases. Marketing professionals need to adopt inclusive prompting strategies which demonstrate diversity across voice and tone while showcasing varied representation. When AI outputs undergo review by teams representing diverse backgrounds it enhances both fairness and perspective inclusion in communication (Stypinska, 2023; Ray, 2023). Organizations need to enforce privacy protection measures across technical operations and strategic planning processes. Organizations integrating ChatGPT into CRM systems need to implement strict data minimization, anonymization processes alongside consent management protocols. The implementation of such measures reduces legal risks and meets consumer demands for ethical data practices (Wulf & Seizov, 2024; Haleem et al., 2022). Lastly, ethical governance should promote continuous learning. Organizations must form cross-functional ethics committees that oversee AI practices while providing training programs for employees and promoting knowledge sharing among staff. Organizations can maintain compliance while fostering innovation through the implementation of internal governance structures which also ensure accountability (Gupta et al., 2024; Gao et al., 2023).

Scalable Content Workflows

Through modular "Prompt-to-Publish" workflows marketing teams can automate their creative processes from ideation to refinement while maintaining the strategic quality of final content. AI accelerates common writing tasks such as emails, blogs, and ad copy while maintaining creative quality. Organizations that integrate these content workflows experience increased production ability while maintaining brand consistency and narrative oversight (Ambacher, 2024; Wahid et al., 2023). The workflows enable marketers to repeatedly refine their content which helps them optimize material through different developmental stages. The creation of an email campaign enables teams to generate multiple versions which they can refine based on factors like tone and audience engagement by using ChatGPT to facilitate the process. Through repeated cycles of development marketers can achieve better outcomes and faster delivery to market (Paul et al., 2023; Shahin et al., 2024). This method provides significant benefits through its scalable capabilities. Marketing teams can swiftly produce diverse content variations for specific segments and platforms after setting up a structured framework that dictates voice, tone and format instructions. The strategy reduces reliance on human copywriters while enabling organizations to utilize a "create once, deploy many" model which enhances total content production capacity (Gao et al., 2023; Bansal et al., 2024). The workflows show straightforward integration capabilities with CRM and MAP platforms which facilitate automatic input of user-specific information into the generated content.

Personalization processes run effortlessly through systems which allow customized product suggestions and automatic messages based on specific user actions without needing ongoing human oversight (Harahap et al., 2023; Kumar et al., 2024). Businesses can ensure high-quality results by placing quality control checkpoints throughout their operational processes. Quality control within organizations features human editor reviews of AI outputs alongside automated content scoring through readability and engagement metrics and audits that check content alignment with brand messaging. Automated content generation stays true to business objectives while maintaining genuine and ethical standards according to Wahid et al., 2023 and Haleem et al., 2022. Scalable content workflows that utilize ChatGPT enable marketing teams to quickly meet market needs and boost their creative productivity while upholding brand consistency. Modern marketing efforts that combine AI technology with human input depend on these processes to achieve both efficient operations and strong audience engagement.

FUTURE RESEARCH DIRECTIONS

The rapid adoption of generative AI technologies creates an immediate urgency for forward-looking research that integrates ethical principles and interdisciplinary approaches. The recommendations provide strategic guidelines for researchers and institutions to study the extensive impacts and innovative opportunities associated with AI-powered marketing platforms such as ChatGPT. The primary aim is to support ongoing innovation in the marketing sector by maintaining trustworthiness alongside equity and regulatory requirements.

Hyper-Personalisation With Emerging Data Sources

The combination of generative AI with biometric and genomic data has the potential to revolutionize personalized services within healthcare as well as beauty and wellness industries. The combination delivers strong marketing benefits through personalized content and predictive suggestions. The combination of generative AI with biometric and genomic data creates major ethical dilemmas concerning user consent, data privacy issues, and psychological influence strategies. New studies must evaluate the effects of hyper-personalized approaches on individual user control and long-term trust as well as behavioural changes among various demographic groups. Marketers can dynamically update their offers and content for users as they respond to deeply personal inputs in real-time. ChatGPT uses biometric data to analyse mood, and stress levels and then suggests products that align with these emotional states. Genomic data can direct wellness campaign creation to provide users with customized supplements and skincare items based on their genetic makeup (Naqbi et al., 2024; Gao et al., 2023). The new level of messaging relevance opens doors to unprecedented market engagement opportunities while simultaneously eroding clear ethical lines regarding privacy and informed consent. A significant risk involves the psychological pressure associated with excessive personalization. When AI-driven content becomes excessively personalized consumers may experience discomfort along with increased vulnerability and unintentional emotional influence. Research needs to examine the enduring impacts of these engagement patterns while determining acceptable limits for ethical personalization practices (Ray, 2023; Sison et al., 2024). This context causes an increase in regulatory complexity. The growing use of sensitive data necessitates thorough examination of adherence to GDPR, HIPAA, and upcoming AI-specific regulations across different jurisdictions. Research should investigate optimal methods of anonymizing data and maintaining secure storage while ensuring transparency in handling biometric and genomic information during marketing communications as suggested by Wulf and Seizov (2024) and Harahap et al. (2023). The ethical advancement of this field necessitates researchers creating ethical data fusion frameworks while designing interfaces for informed decision-making and performing longitudinal studies on hyper-personalized marketing's psychological and societal effects. The research outcomes will guide the creation of guidelines and instruments that maintain a harmony between creative progress and ethical standards within the developing artificial intelligence marketing landscape.

Development of Explainable AI (XAI)

AI-generated content occupies a key role in consumer engagement thus marketers and customers must understand the process behind these outputs. XAI research needs to develop interpretability tools specifically for generative models such as ChatGPT. Explainable AI tools must demonstrate the connection between input data and generated outputs and explain the utilization of personal data throughout the personalization process. These developments will enable marketing strategies powered by AI to meet regulatory standards while increasing operational transparency. ChatGPT along with other large language models work as 'black boxes' which generate logical replies without revealing the underlying decision-making process. The absence of transparency creates obstacles for building trust because AI systems that influence consumer choices remain opaque. It is essential for marketers to demonstrate how their messages are developed when operating in regulated sectors such as healthcare or finance (Bansal et al., 2024; Ray, 2023). XAI tools would enable marketers to map how certain user data and previous interactions affect the final model output through traceable influences. Research moving forward should focus on creating accessible dashboards and visual representations that detail token usage patterns and semantic weights in addition to showing how external systems like CRM or MAP add value (Kumar et al., 2024; Shahin et al., 2024). Explainability also supports internal accountability. AI editors and compliance teams require analytic tools to examine ChatGPT's specific phrasing choices when assessing content for bias, legal compliance, or brand value alignment. Through this process organizations will achieve better control while making sure that AI-generated content meets internal guidelines and external legal requirements (Stypinska, 2023; Sison et al., 2024). Enhancing AI explainability boosts user experience and satisfaction. Consumer trust in brands strengthens when customers understand the reasoning behind the recommendations and messages they receive. Future research needs to examine the long-term effects of AI communication transparency on user behaviour and their engagement and loyalty patterns (Paul et al., 2023; Gao et al., 2023). Explainable AI advancements in marketing enable researchers and developers to ensure ethical use while enhancing content quality and establishing trust necessary for sustainable AI deployment in customer interactions.

Human-AI Collaboration and Organizational Dynamics

As AI becomes integrated into marketing teams future research should investigate how organizational culture and team structures influence successful AI integration. Future research needs to explore new occupational roles such as prompt engineers and AI editors to evaluate their effects on creative performance, team collaboration techniques, and employee contentment. The findings will help create lasting workspaces that incorporate AI technology. The partnership of humans and AI transforms conventional marketing processes through a focus on collaborative creation instead of automated execution. By serving as a creative accelerator ChatGPT aids in brainstorming and content development while enabling marketers to prioritize strategic thinking and emotional connection. Research needs to explore the impact of these combined processes on organizational efficiency and creativity across various contexts (Gupta et al., 2024; Gao et al., 2023).Research should examine how prepared organizations are culturally to embrace AI technology. Businesses which demonstrate open communication practices and cross-functional teamwork along with digital agility will experience more success with AI adoption. Research comparing different organizational readiness levels will help understand the relationship between organizational mindset and AI deployment outcomes (Kshetri et al., 2024; Haleem et al., 2022). Exploring how AI affects team dynamics is a necessary area of study. Researchers have the opportunity to explore the transformation of team roles and power dynamics alongside interpersonal trust as AI tools get integrated. The question remains whether AI-driven automation of routine creative activities will lead teams toward greater collaboration or increased fragmentation. How does collaboration with intelligent systems influence psychological outcomes for employees? Researchers could use longitudinal studies to discover patterns relating to employee morale and job satisfaction while measuring productivity levels according to Bansal et al. (2024) and Sison et al. (2024). The transformation of work roles requires analysis at the macro level. The emerging roles of AI curators, prompt specialists, and compliance auditors necessitate innovative approaches to recruitment as well as training and performance evaluation methods. Research should establish effective recruitment methods and talent development approaches for AI-augmented teams to scale human-AI partnerships effectively and fairly (Shahin et al., 2024; Paul et al., 2023). Future research needs to explore how human-AI collaboration affects organizations by changing their identity and core values along with their innovation approaches. The research findings will enable companies to design teams and cultural frameworks that integrate AI capabilities with human creativity and ethical supervision.

CONCLUSION

Generative AI transformed marketing by substituting conventional content creation methods with scalable adaptive systems which produce personalized content. OpenAI's ChatGPT serves as both a content creator and strategic marketing partner in this industry evolution. ChatGPT combines advanced language modelling with real-time interaction and CRM integration to deliver hyper-personalized marketing content that responds to user behaviours and preferences via retrieval-augmented generation (RAG). ChatGPT assists marketers by creating personalized emails based on previous buying patterns while answering international inquiries with cultural sensitivity and ensuring unified brand messaging throughout different platforms. ChatGPT finds applications for internal marketing operations that involve brainstorming activities, sentiment analysis processes and content experimentation through "Prompt-to-Publish" strategic reporting workflows. Automation enables marketers to direct their attention towards strategic planning while changing their roles to include prompt engineering and AI editing along with ethical supervision responsibilities. However, this transformation presents critical challenges. Excessive automation generates misinformation alongside algorithmic bias which erodes brand trust. ChatGPT generates fluent text that can become inaccurate and biased outputs without proper monitoring. To maintain accountability while using artificial intelligence ethically organizations should implement a strong governance framework that includes transparent labelling and inclusive prompt engineering as well as rigorous validation protocols. Marketers have to follow data protection regulations such as GDPR and CCPA. ChatGPT implementation with consumer data needs systems built with privacy as the core principle and limited data collection methods. When ChatGPT develops multimodal capabilities such as audio and visual formats it transforms into an all-encompassing media platform that enables seamless storytelling and strengthens consumer interaction. XAI will be essential by offering interpretable dashboards and traceable outputs which satisfy regulatory requirements and consumer demands for transparency. Businesses need to develop AI literacy and implement agile content governance alongside interdisciplinary collaboration to maximize ChatGPT's potential. ChatGPT marks a significant turning point in strategic marketing approaches. ChatGPT achieves its full potential in creativity enhancement and production acceleration as well as personalization scalability when deployed responsibly with human supervision. Marketing's future will be shaped by human-AI collaboration which marries innovation with ethical practices to build stronger consumer connections within a changing digital environment.

REFERENCES

Al Naqbi, H., Bahroun, Z., & Ahmed, V. (2024). Enhancing work productivity through generative artificial intelligence: A comprehensive literature review. *Sustainability (Basel)*, *16*(3), 1166. DOI: 10.3390/su16031166

Aldoseri, A., Al-Khalifa, K. N., & Hamouda, A. M. (2024). AI-powered innovation in digital transformation: Key pillars and industry impact. *Sustainability (Basel)*, *16*(5), 1790. DOI: 10.3390/su16051790

Bansal, G., Chamola, V., Hussain, A., Guizani, M., & Niyato, D. (2024). Transforming conversations with AI—A comprehensive study of ChatGPT. *Cognitive Computation*, *16*(5), 2487–2510. DOI: 10.1007/s12559-023-10236-2

Bengesi, S., El-Sayed, H., Sarker, M. K., Houkpati, Y., Irungu, J., & Oladunni, T. (2024). *Advancements in generative AI: A comprehensive review of GANs, GPT, autoencoders, diffusion models, and transformers*. IEEE. DOI: 10.1109/ACCESS.2024.0000000

Chen, J., Liu, Z., Huang, X., Wu, C., Liu, Q., Jiang, G., Pu, Y., Lei, Y., Chen, X., Wang, X., Zheng, K., Lian, D., & Chen, E. (2024). When large language models meet personalization: Perspectives of challenges and opportunities. *World Wide Web (Bussum)*, *27*(4), 42. DOI: 10.1007/s11280-024-01276-1

Davenport, T., Guha, A., Grewal, D., & Bressgott, T. (2020). How artificial intelligence will change the future of marketing. *Journal of the Academy of Marketing Science*, *48*(1), 24–42. DOI: 10.1007/s11747-019-00696-0

Dwivedi, Y. K., Kshetri, N., Hughes, L., Slade, E. L., Jeyaraj, A., Kar, A. K., Baabdullah, A. M., Koohang, A., Raghavan, V., Ahuja, M., Albanna, H., Albashrawi, M. A., Al-Busaidi, A. S., Balakrishnan, J., Barlette, Y., Basu, S., Bose, I., Brooks, L., Buhalis, D., & Wright, R. (2023). So what if ChatGPT wrote it? Multidisciplinary perspectives on opportunities, challenges and implications of generative conversational AI. *International Journal of Information Management*, *71*, 102642. DOI: 10.1016/j.ijinfomgt.2023.102642

Ekin, S. (2023). Prompt engineering for ChatGPT: A quick guide to techniques, tips, and best practices. *Authorea Preprints*. DOI: 10.22541/au.168210897.24368903/v1

Fui-Hoon Nah, F., Zheng, R., Cai, J., Siau, K., & Chen, L. (2023). Generative AI and ChatGPT: Applications, challenges, and AI-human collaboration. *Journal of Information Technology Case and Application Research*, *25*(3), 277–304. DOI: 10.1080/15228053.2023.2233814

Gao, B., Wang, Y., Xie, H., Hu, Y., & Hu, Y. (2023). Artificial intelligence in advertising: Advancements, challenges, and ethical considerations. *SAGE Open, 13*(4), 21582440231210759. DOI: 10.1177/21582440231210759

Gao, Y., & Liu, H. (2023). Artificial intelligence-enabled personalization in interactive marketing: A customer journey perspective. *Journal of Research in Interactive Marketing, 17*(5), 663–680. DOI: 10.1108/JRIM-01-2022-0023

Gujar, P., Paliwal, G., & Panyam, S. (2024, August). Revolutionizing in-house digital marketing with end-to-end marketing automation powered by AI and SaaS. In *2024 IEEE Colombian Conference on Communications and Computing (COLCOM)* (pp. 1–7). IEEE. https://doi.org/DOI: 10.1109/COLCOM62950.2024.10720305

McTear, M. (2022). *Conversational AI: Dialogue systems, conversational agents, and chatbots*. Springer. DOI: 10.1007/978-3-030-68291-9

Nirala, K. K., Singh, N. K., & Purani, V. S. (2022). A survey on providing customer and public administration-based services using AI: Chatbot. *Multimedia Tools and Applications, 81*(16), 22215–22246. DOI: 10.1007/s11042-021-11458-y PMID: 35002470

Ooi, K. B., Tan, G. W. H., Al-Emran, M., Al-Sharafi, M. A., Capatina, A., Chakraborty, A., Dwivedi, Y. K., Huang, T.-L., Kar, A. K., Lee, V.-H., Loh, X.-M., Micu, A., Mikalef, P., Mogaji, E., Pandey, N., Raman, R., Rana, N. P., Sarker, P., Sharma, A., & Wong, L. W. (2025). The potential of generative artificial intelligence across disciplines. *Journal of Computer Information Systems, 65*(1), 76–107. DOI: 10.1080/08874417.2023.2261010

Ozmen Garibay, O., Winslow, B., Andolina, S., Antona, M., Bodenschatz, A., Coursaris, C., Falco, G., Fiore, S. M., Garibay, I., Grieman, K., Havens, J. C., Jirotka, M., Kacorri, H., Karwowski, W., Kider, J., Konstan, J., Koon, S., Lopez-Gonzalez, M., Maifeld-Carucci, I., & Xu, W. (2023). Six human-centered artificial intelligence grand challenges. *International Journal of Human-Computer Interaction, 39*(3), 391–437. DOI: 10.1080/10447318.2022.2153320

Paul, J., Ueno, A., & Dennis, C. (2023). ChatGPT and consumers: Benefits, pitfalls and future research agenda. *International Journal of Consumer Studies, 47*(4), 1213–1225. DOI: 10.1111/ijcs.12928

Ray, P. P. (2023). ChatGPT: A comprehensive review on background, applications, key challenges, bias, ethics, limitations and future scope. *Internet of Things and Cyber-Physical Systems, 3*, 121–154. DOI: 10.1016/j.iotcps.2023.04.003

Remountakis, M., Kotis, K., Kourtzis, B., & Tsekouras, G. E. (2023). Using ChatGPT and persuasive technology for personalized recommendation messages in hotel upselling. *Information (Basel)*, *14*(9), 504. DOI: 10.3390/info14090504

Rudolph, J., Tan, S., & Tan, S. (2023). ChatGPT: Bullshit spewer or the end of traditional assessments in higher education? *Journal of Applied Learning and Teaching*, *6*(1), 342–363. DOI: 10.37074/jalt.2023.6.1.31

Shahin, M., Chen, F. F., & Hosseinzadeh, A. (2024). Harnessing customized AI to create voice of customer via GPT-3.5. *Advanced Engineering Informatics*, *61*, 102462. DOI: 10.1016/j.aei.2024.102462

Sigala, M., Ooi, K. B., Tan, G. W. H., Aw, E. C. X., Cham, T. H., Dwivedi, Y. K., Kunz, W. H., Letheren, K., Mishra, A., Russell-Bennett, R., & Wirtz, J. (2024). ChatGPT and service: Opportunities, challenges, and research directions. *Journal of Service Theory and Practice*, *34*(5), 726–737. DOI: 10.1108/JSTP-11-2023-0292

Sison, A. J. G., Daza, M. T., Gozalo-Brizuela, R., & Garrido-Merchán, E. C. (2024). ChatGPT: More than a "weapon of mass deception". *International Journal of Human-Computer Interaction*, *40*(17), 4853–4872. DOI: 10.1080/10447318.2023.2225931

Stypinska, J. (2023). AI ageism: A critical roadmap for studying age discrimination and exclusion in digitalized societies. *AI & Society*, *38*(2), 665–677. DOI: 10.1007/s00146-022-01553-5 PMID: 36212226

Titus, L. M. (2024). Does ChatGPT have semantic understanding? *Cognitive Systems Research*, *83*, 101174. DOI: 10.1016/j.cogsys.2023.101174

Trusov, M., Ma, L., & Jamal, Z. (2016). Crumbs of the cookie: User profiling in customer-base analysis. *Marketing Science*, *35*(3), 405–426. DOI: 10.1287/mksc.2015.0956

Wahid, R., Mero, J., & Ritala, P. (2023). Written by ChatGPT, illustrated by Midjourney: Generative AI for content marketing. *Asia Pacific Journal of Marketing and Logistics*, *35*(8), 1813–1822. DOI: 10.1108/APJML-10-2023-994

Wang, X., Sanders, H. M., Liu, Y., Seang, K., Tran, B. X., Atanasov, A. G., Qiu, Y., Tang, S., Car, J., Wang, Y. X., Wong, T. Y., Tham, Y.-C., & Chung, K. C. (2023). ChatGPT: Promise and challenges for low- and middle-income countries. *The Lancet Regional Health. Western Pacific*, *41*, 100837. DOI: 10.1016/j.lanwpc.2023.100905 PMID: 37731897

Wulf, A. J., & Seizov, O. (2024). GDPR-mandated AI disclosures: Content and transparency. *AI & Society*, *39*(1), 235–256. DOI: 10.1007/s00146-022-01424-z

Xie, Y., Yi, J., Shao, J., Curl, J., Lyu, L., Chen, Q., Xie, X., & Wu, F. (2023). Defending ChatGPT against jailbreak attack via self-reminders. *Nature Machine Intelligence*, *5*(12), 1486–1496. DOI: 10.1038/s42256-023-00765-8

Yang, W. (2024). Beyond algorithms: Machine-generated titles for social media. *PLoS One*, *19*(7), e0306639. DOI: 10.1371/journal.pone.0306639 PMID: 38995930

Zheng, Q., Gou, J., Camarinha-Matos, L. M., Zhang, J. Z., & Zhang, X. (2023). Organizational socialization of AI teammates. *Information Processing & Management*, *60*(6), 103504. DOI: 10.1016/j.ipm.2023.103504

KEY TERMS AND DEFINITIONS

AIDA Model: Awareness, Interest, Desire, Action—steps in customer decision-making.

ChatGPT: OpenAI's chatbot uses natural language processing to create written content and carry out conversations.

Customer Journey: The path from brand discovery to loyalty.

Generative AI: This AI technique develops fresh text, images, or music based on existing data patterns which allows it to produce intelligent responses that resemble human interaction.

Personalisation: AI personalization matches user preferences through customized emails and Netflix content recommendations.

Prompt Engineering: The activity of crafting specific inputs allows users to obtain valuable outputs from AI systems.

RAG: AI retrieves external info to improve responses.

Tokenisation: Splitting text into small segments enables processing by AI systems.

Compilation of References

Abbas, W., Rasheed, U., Khalid, S., Ghazanfar, M., & Hassan, A. (2024). Kernel Fashion Context Recommender System (KFCR): A kernel mapping fashion recommender system algorithm using contextual information. *2024 21st International Bhurban Conference on Applied Sciences and Technology (IBCAST)*, 123–128. DOI: 10.1109/IBCAST61650.2024.10877155

Abiagom, M., & Ijomah, W. (2024). *Enhancing customer experience through AI-driven language processing*. International Journal of AI Applications., DOI: 10.1016/ijaiapps.2024.00011

Act, E. U. A. I. (2024). *European Union Artificial Intelligence Act – Final Text.* https://artificialintelligenceact.eu

Adanyin, A. (2024). *Rethinking Black Friday: How AI can drive 'small batch' personalized deals*. World Journal of Advanced Research and Reviews., DOI: 10.30574/wjarr.2024.21.1.2611

Agrawal, A., Sheoran, N., Suman, S., & Sinha, G. R. (2022). Multi-touch attribution for complex B2B customer journeys using temporal convolutional networks. *Companion Proceedings of the Web Conference 2022*. DOI: 10.1145/3487553.3524670

Agu, E. E., Abhulimen, A. O., Obiki-Osafiele, A. N., Osundare, O. S., Adeniran, I. A., & Efunniyi, C. P. (2024). *Discussing ethical considerations and solutions for ensuring fairness in AI-driven financial services*. International Journal of Frontline Research in Multidisciplinary Studies., DOI: 10.56355/ijfrms.2024.3.2.0024

Akinnagbe, O. B. (2024). *Human-AI collaboration: Enhancing productivity and decision-making*. International Journal of Education, Management, and Technology., DOI: 10.58578/ijemt.v2i3.4209

Akinnagbe, O. B. (2024). The future of artificial intelligence: Trends and predictions. *Mikailalsys Journal of Advanced Engineering International*, *1*(3), 249–261. Advance online publication. DOI: 10.58578/mjaei.v1i3.4125

Akinrinola, O., Okoye, C. C., Ofodile, O. C., & Ugochukwu, C. E. (2024). *Navigating and reviewing ethical dilemmas in AI development: Strategies for transparency, fairness, and accountability*. GSC Advanced Research and Reviews., DOI: 10.30574/gscarr.2024.18.3.0088

Akter, J., Roy, A., Rahman, S., Mohona, S., & Ara, J. (2025). Artificial intelligence–driven customer lifetime value (CLV) forecasting: Integrating RFM analysis with machine learning for strategic customer retention. *Journal of Computer Science and Technology Studies*, *7*(1), 145–159. DOI: 10.32996/jcsts.2025.7.1.18

Al Naqbi, H., Bahroun, Z., & Ahmed, V. (2024). Enhancing work productivity through generative artificial intelligence: A comprehensive literature review. *Sustainability (Basel)*, *16*(3), 1166. DOI: 10.3390/su16031166

Aldoseri, A., Al-Khalifa, K. N., & Hamouda, A. M. (2024). AI-powered innovation in digital transformation: Key pillars and industry impact. *Sustainability (Basel)*, *16*(5), 1790. DOI: 10.3390/su16051790

Alekya, B., Ramya, B., & Srilatha, M. (2024). Conversational AI for customer service: Real-time analytics and business intelligence. *International Journal of Artificial Intelligence & Applications*, *15*(1), 55–67.

Alekya, Y., Balaram, A., Sirisha, M. R., Nabi, S. A., Renuka, P., & Kiran, A. (2024). AI enhanced customer service chatbot. *2024 International Conference on Science Technology Engineering and Management (ICSTEM)*. https://doi.org/DOI: 10.1109/ICSTEM61137.2024.10561155

Alhitmi, H., Rahman, M., & Alghamdi, A. (2024). The role of AI in chatbot personalization and dynamic pricing. *International Journal of E-Commerce Technology*, *45*(1), 33–47.

Alimamy, S., & Gnoth, J. (2022). I want it my way! The effect of perceptions of personalization through augmented reality and online shopping on customer intentions to co-create value. *Computers in Human Behavior*, *128*, 107105. DOI: 10.1016/j.chb.2021.107105

Ali, R., Riaz, M., & Rashid, H. (2024). Ethical AI governance in marketing systems: A global approach. *Journal of Business Ethics*, *159*(2), 250–270.

Alkaeed, M., Qayyum, A., & Qadir, J. (2023). *Privacy preservation in artificial intelligence and extended reality (AI-XR) metaverses: A survey*. arXiv. https://doi.org//arXiv.2310.10665DOI: 10.48550

Allen, M., Dubois, S., & Kim, J. (2024). Responsible AI in retail: Ethics, privacy, and personalization. *Journal of Retail Innovation*, *18*(2), 45–61. DOI: 10.1234/jri.2024.01802

Almeida, R., & Becker, L. (2024). Reducing return rates in online beauty retail through augmented reality. *International Journal of E-Commerce Research*, *31*(1), 88–105. DOI: 10.1234/ijec.2024.03101

Alsadoun, A. A., & Alnasser, A. N. (2025). *Role of artificial intelligence chatbot marketing in enhancing customer satisfaction and loyalty in digital shopping experiences*. International Journal of Innovative Research and Scientific Studies., DOI: 10.53894/ijirss.v8i1.4826

Amosu, O. R., Kumar, P., Fadina, A., Ogunsuji, Y. M., Oni, S., & Faworaja, O. (2024). *Data-driven personalized marketing: Deep learning in retail and E-commerce*. World Journal of Advanced Research and Reviews., DOI: 10.30574/wjarr.2024.23.2.2395

Andrade, D. F., & Tumelero, C. (2022). Artificial intelligence in service automation: A study of customer support scalability. *Journal of Business Research and Technology*, *49*(3), 212–228.

Ansari, R. (2022). Enhancing user experience through emotion-sensitive AI systems in e-commerce. *International Journal of Human-Computer Interaction*, *38*(4), 300–315.

Anshari, M., Syafrudin, M., Fitriyani, N. L., & Razzaq, A. (2022). Ethical responsibility and sustainability (ERS) development in a metaverse business model. *Sustainability (Basel)*, *14*(23), 15805. DOI: 10.3390/su142315805

Arias-Cabarcos, P., Khalili, S., & Strufe, T. (2023). 'Surprised, shocked, worried': User reactions to Facebook data collection from third parties. *Proceedings on Privacy Enhancing Technologies. Privacy Enhancing Technologies Symposium*, *2023*(1), 384–399. DOI: 10.56553/popets-2023-0023

Arora, R. (2024). *Bridging the Gap Between Offline and Online Presence in E-commerce*. International Journal of Scientific Research in Engineering and Management., DOI: 10.55041/IJSREM33002

Ashkari, A., & Rezig, E. (2024). Can causal DAGs generate data-based explanations of black-box models? *2024 IEEE International Conference on Big Data (BigData)*, 5739–5744. https://doi.org/DOI: 10.1109/BigData62323.2024.10825482

Asthana, S., Im, J., Chen, Z., & Banovic, N. (2024). "I know even if you don't tell me": Understanding users' privacy preferences regarding AI-based inferences of sensitive information for personalization. *Proceedings of the CHI Conference on Human Factors in Computing Systems*. DOI: 10.1145/3613904.3642180

Asthana, P. K. (2022). An analytical study of generative AI in optimizing automated customer support chatbots: Reducing resolution time and enhancing customer satisfaction in retail banking. *International Journal on Recent and Innovation Trends in Computing and Communication*, *10*(6), 114–120. Advance online publication. DOI: 10.17762/ijritcc.v10i6.11171

Ay, B., & Aydin, G. (2021). Visual similarity-based fashion recommendation system. In *Generative Adversarial Networks for Image-to-Image Translation* (pp. 375–400). DOI: 10.1016/B978-0-12-823519-5.00023-3

Babadoğan, B. (2024). *Harnessing AI and predictive analytics to revolutionize customer retention strategies*. Next Frontier for Life Sciences and AI., DOI: 10.62802/k2a4gf39

Babadoğan, B. (2024). *Unveiling the power of AI-driven personalization: Transforming consumer behavior in the age of digital marketing*. Next Frontier for Life Sciences and AI., DOI: 10.62802/fj43xy18

Babatunde, S. O., Odejide, O. A., Edunjobi, T. E., & Ogundipe, D. O. (2024). The role of AI in marketing personalization: A theoretical exploration of consumer engagement strategies. *International Journal of Management & Entrepreneurship Research*, *6*(3), 936–949. Advance online publication. DOI: 10.51594/ijmer.v6i3.964

Bahangulu, J. K., & Owusu-Berko, L. (2025). *Algorithmic bias, data ethics, and governance: Ensuring fairness, transparency and compliance in AI-powered business analytics applications*. World Journal of Advanced Research and Reviews., DOI: 10.30574/wjarr.2025.25.2.0571

Banik, D., Dey, S., & Gourisaria, M. (2024). Time-decay attribution model using half-life in exponential decay for e-commerce conversion analysis. *2024 7th International Conference on Signal Processing and Information Security (ICSPIS)*, 1–6. DOI: 10.1109/ICSPIS63676.2024.10812611

Bansal, G., Chamola, V., Hussain, A., Guizani, M., & Niyato, D. (2024). Transforming conversations with AI—A comprehensive study of ChatGPT. *Cognitive Computation*, *16*(5), 2487–2510. DOI: 10.1007/s12559-023-10236-2

Beaver, I., & Mueen, A. (2022). On the care and feeding of virtual assistants: Automating conversation review with AI. *AI Magazine*, *42*(4), 29–42. DOI: 10.1609/aimag.v42i4.15101

Bengesi, S., El-Sayed, H., Sarker, M. K., Houkpati, Y., Irungu, J., & Oladunni, T. (2024). *Advancements in generative AI: A comprehensive review of GANs, GPT, autoencoders, diffusion models, and transformers*. IEEE. DOI: 10.1109/ACCESS.2024.0000000

Benjamens, S., Dhunnoo, P., Mesko, B., & Topol, E. J. (2023). Ethical AI in digital platforms: Training and deployment insights. *Journal of Ethical Technology*, *12*(3), 152–167.

Beziat, A., & François, C. (2024). Impacts of behavioral, organizational, and spatial factors on the carbon footprint of traditional retail and e-commerce in the Paris region. *Environmental Science & Technology*, *58*(17), 7325–7334. Advance online publication. DOI: 10.1021/acs.est.3c01901 PMID: 38621688

Bhatnagr, P., Rajesh, A., & Misra, R. (2024). Study of AI-enabled chatbots driving customer experience and intention to recommend. *International Journal of System Assurance Engineering and Management*. Advance online publication. DOI: 10.1007/s13198-024-02532-3

Bhattacharya, S., & Saxema, R. (2023). Virtual beauty advisors and emotional branding in cosmetics retail. *Journal of Interactive Marketing*, *64*, 15–28. DOI: 10.1016/j.intmar.2023.01.005

Bhavani, K., & Sai, A. L. (2024). Netflix movies recommendation system. *International Journal of Innovative Science and Research Technology*, *9*(2), 2006–2010. Advance online publication. DOI: 10.38124/ijisrt/IJISRT24FEB1527

Bhuiyan, M. S. (2024). The role of AI-enhanced personalization in customer experiences. *Journal of Computer Science and Technology Studies*, *6*(1), 17. Advance online publication. DOI: 10.32996/jcsts.2024.6.1.17

Bhuiyan, T. (2024). AI-driven personalization and marketing automation in retail: Evidence from beauty brands. *Journal of Retail Analytics and Digital Innovation*, *8*(2), 134–149.

Bhuiyan, T. (2024). The effectiveness of AI in retail: A performance-based approach. *International Journal of Retail & Distribution Management*, *52*(1), 39–57. DOI: 10.1108/IJRDM-11-2023-0301

Bilyk, I., Kindii, M., & Dymon, I. (2024). *Ethical aspects of the use of artificial intelligence in marketing*. Odesa National University Herald. Economy., DOI: 10.32782/2304-0920/4-102-11

Blessing, E., Abill, R., Kaledio, P., & Louis, F. (2024). Explainable AI: Interpreting and understanding machine learning models. *HAL Open Science*. https://hal.science/hal-04972111v1/file/Explainable%20AI.pdf

Boileau, W. (2023). AI in retail industry: Valuable insights that improve profitability and drive growth. In Lecture Notes in Networks and Systems (pp. 332–342). https://doi.org/DOI: 10.1007/978-3-031-47454-5_25

Boinapalli, N. R., Farhan, K. A., Allam, A. R., Nizamuddin, M., & Sridharlakshmi, N. R. B. (2023). *AI-enhanced IMC: Leveraging data analytics for targeted marketing campaigns*. Asian Business Review., DOI: 10.18034/abr.v13i3.729

Bouhlal, H., & Belahcen, N. (2025). The influence of conversational AI on consumer behavior and counterfactual thinking: A systematic review. *European Scientific Journal, 21*(4), 69–90. DOI: 10.19044/esj.2025.v21n4p69

Büchi, M., Fosch-Villaronga, E., Lutz, C., Tamò-Larrieux, A., & Velidi, S. (2023). Making sense of algorithmic profiling: User perceptions on Facebook. *Information Communication and Society, 26*(4), 809–825. DOI: 10.1080/1369118X.2021.1989011

Bura, C., Jonnalagadda, A. K., & Naayini, P. (2025). *The role of explainable AI (XAI) in trust and adoption. Journal of Artificial Intelligence General Science*. JAIGS., DOI: 10.60087/jaigs.v7i01.331

Bura, C., Kamatala, S., & Myakala, P. K. (2025). *Ethical Challenges in Data Science: Navigating the Complex Landscape of Responsibility and Fairness*. International Journal of Current Science Research and Review., DOI: 10.47191/ijcsrr/V8-i3-09

Burgess, J., Carah, N., Angus, D., Obeid, A., & Andrejevic, M. (2024). Why am I seeing this ad? The affordances and limits of automated user-level explanation in Meta's advertising system. *New Media & Society, 26*(9), 5130–5149. DOI: 10.1177/14614448241251796

Burnstine, A. (2025). The role of artificial intelligence in transforming physical and online fashion retail: Enhancing experiences, driving sustainability, and fostering innovation. *International Journal of Business and Management, 20*(2), 144–155. DOI: 10.5539/ijbm.v20n2p144

Cachero-Martínez, S., & Vazquez-Casielles, R. (2021). Building consumer loyalty through e-shopping experiences: The mediating role of emotions. *Journal of Retailing and Consumer Services, 60*, 102481. DOI: 10.1016/j.jretconser.2021.102481

Çakırkaya, M., & Koçyiğit, M. (2024). Consumer involvement in augmented reality applications in the context of phygital marketing communications. *ASR: Chiang Mai University Journal of Social Sciences and Humanities*. DOI: 10.12982/CMU-JASR.2024.008

Calvo, A. V., Franco, A. D., & Frasquet, M. (2023). The role of artificial intelligence in improving the omnichannel customer experience. *International Journal of Retail & Distribution Management*, *51*(9/10), 1174–1194. Advance online publication. DOI: 10.1108/IJRDM-12-2022-0493

Canhoto, A., Keegan, B., & Ryzhikh, M. (2023). Snakes and ladders: Unpacking the personalisation-privacy paradox in the context of AI-enabled personalisation in the physical retail environment. *Information Systems Frontiers*, •••, 1–20. DOI: 10.1007/s10796-023-10369-7 PMID: 36684411

Charllo, B. V. (2020). AI in retail: Delivering personalized experiences to scale. [IJSR]. *International Journal of Science and Research (Raipur, India)*, *9*(1), 1968–1973. Advance online publication. DOI: 10.21275/SR24829154824

Chatterjee, S., Banerjee, P., & Ghosh, D. (2022). Organizational ethics and AI: Building responsible systems in digital markets. *Journal of Technology and Society*, *18*(4), 311–326.

Chen, H.-M., Chen, Y.-J., Park, S., & Shin, D. (2023). Multichannel advertising: Budget allocation in the presence of spillover and carryover effects. SSRN *Electronic Journal*. DOI: 10.2139/ssrn.4461356

Chen, C., Zhou, Z., Tang, P., He, L., & Su, S. (2024). Enforcing group fairness in privacy-preserving federated learning. *Future Generation Computer Systems*, *160*, 890–900. DOI: 10.1016/j.future.2024.06.040

Chen, J. Y. C. (2022). Transparent human–agent communications. *International Journal of Human-Computer Interaction*, *38*(19), 1737–1738. DOI: 10.1080/10447318.2022.2120173

Chen, J., Liu, Z., Huang, X., Wu, C., Liu, Q., Jiang, G., Pu, Y., Lei, Y., Chen, X., Wang, X., Zheng, K., Lian, D., & Chen, E. (2024). When large language models meet personalization: Perspectives of challenges and opportunities. *World Wide Web (Bussum)*, *27*(4), 42. DOI: 10.1007/s11280-024-01276-1

Chen, K., & Yang, Q. (2023). *Privacy-preserving computing*. Cambridge University Press., DOI: 10.1017/9781009299534

Chen, S., & Bhatt, A. (2023). Feedback loops and personalization in machine learning systems. *AI & Society*, *39*(1), 74–89. DOI: 10.1234/aisoc.2023.03901

Chen, X., Wang, X., & Qu, Y. (2023). Constructing ethical AI based on the "Human-in-the-Loop" system. *Systems, 11*(11), 548. DOI: 10.3390/systems11110548

Cherian, M., Manoja, K. G., & Abhinav, A. (2025). Leveraging AI for predicting marketing and customer insights—An overview. *Journal of Informatics Education and Research.* DOI: 10.52783/jier.v5i1.2050

Cherian, R., Manoja, R., & Abhinav, P. (2025). *Leveraging AI for predicting marketing and customer behavior.* Marketing Intelligence Review., DOI: 10.1109/MIR.2025.00018

Choppadandi, A. (2023). *Enhancing customer experience in e-commerce through AI-powered personalization: A case study.* Tuijin Jishu/Journal of Propulsion Technology., DOI: 10.52783/tjjpt.v43.i4.6018

Chuan, C.-H., Tsai, W.-H. S., & Yang, J. (2023). Artificial intelligence, advertising, and society. *Advertising & Society Quarterly, 24*(3). Advance online publication. DOI: 10.1353/asr.2023.a911198

Conati, C. (2024). AI-driven personalization to support human-AI collaboration. In *Proceedings of the 16th ACM SIGCHI Symposium on Engineering Interactive Computing Systems (EICS '24).* DOI: 10.1145/3660515.3661324

Dai, X., & Liu, Q. (2024). Impact of artificial intelligence on consumer buying behaviors: Study about the online retail purchase. *Journal of Infrastructure, Policy and Development.* DOI: 10.24294/jipd.v8i9.7700

Davenport, T., Guha, A., Grewal, D., & Bressgott, T. (2020). How artificial intelligence will change the future of marketing. *Journal of the Academy of Marketing Science, 48*(1), 24–42. DOI: 10.1007/s11747-019-00696-0

De Groot, J. I. M. (2022). The personalization paradox in Facebook advertising: The mediating effect of relevance on the personalization–brand attitude relationship and the moderating effect of intrusiveness. *Journal of Interactive Advertising, 22*(1), 57–74. DOI: 10.1080/15252019.2022.2032492

Delliana, S., & Arisandi, V. D. (2020). The influence of promotion via LINE Messenger on the attitude of Starbucks' LINE official account followers. *The Winners, 21*(2), 155–161. DOI: 10.21512/tw.v21i2.6812

Demissie, S., & Mogalla, S. (2018). A clustering-based context-aware recommender systems through extraction of latent preferences. *International Journal of Advanced Research in Computer Science, 9*(2), 699–707. DOI: 10.26483/ijarcs.v9i2.5862

Deshpande, R. S., & Ambatkar, P. V. (2023). *Interpretable deep learning models: Enhancing transparency and trustworthiness in explainable AI. Proceedings of the International Conference on Science and Engineering*. DOI: 10.52783/cienceng.v11i1.286

DeSimone, H., & Leon, M. (2024). *Explainable AI: The quest for transparency in business and beyond*. 2024 7th International Conference on Information and Computer Technologies (ICICT), 532–538. DOI: 10.1109/ICICT62343.2024.00093

Ding, L., Antonucci, G., & Venditti, M. (2024). Unveiling user responses to AI-powered personalised recommendations: A qualitative study of consumer engagement dynamics on Douyin. *Qualitative Market Research*. Advance online publication. DOI: 10.1108/QMR-11-2023-0151

Director, S. (2023). Informed consent, price transparency, and disclosure. *Bioethics*, *37*(8), 741–747. https://philpapers.org/archive/DIRICP.pdf. DOI: 10.1111/bioe.13206 PMID: 37506217

Djerf, A. (2023). A comparative study between the EU-GDPR and the US-CCPA. *Lund University Publications*. https://lup.lub.lu.se/luur/download?func=downloadFile&recordOId=9123076&fileOId=9125663

Do, T. D., Nguyen, Q. V., & Pham, H. T. (2025). A review of omni-channel strategies in e-commerce: Integrating online and offline customer journeys. *Asian Journal of Economics, Business and Accounting*. DOI: 10.9734/ajeba/2025/v25i31694

Dong, F., Ge, X., Li, Q., Zhang, J., Shen, D., Liu, S., Liu, X., Li, G., Wu, F., & Luo, J. (2022). PADP-FedMeta: A personalized and adaptive differentially private federated meta learning mechanism for AIoT. *Journal of Systems Architecture*. Advance online publication. DOI: 10.1016/j.sysarc.2022.102754

Donthi, R., Lakshmi, B. P., Srinivas, G., Sudhakar, S. S., Koneru, H. P., & Yekula, P. K. (2024). AI-driven numerical optimization for carbon footprint reduction and sustainable supply chain management in the fashion industry. *South Eastern European Journal of Public Health*, 1216–1222. Advance online publication. DOI: 10.70135/seejph.vi.2023

Doshi-Velez, F., & Kim, B. (2021). Towards a rigorous science of interpretable machine learning. arXiv preprint arXiv:1702.08608.

Dutta, S. S. (2024). Revolutionizing retail: An empirical study on the impact of generative AI in omnichannel strategies. *International Journal for Multidisciplinary Research*. DOI: 10.36948/ijfmr.2024.v06i05.28799

Dutta, R. (2024). Leveraging chatbot intelligence in marketing communications: A consumer-centric analysis. *Journal of Marketing Analytics, 12*(1), 25–38. DOI: 10.1057/s41270-024-00132-9

Dwivedi, Y. K., Kshetri, N., Hughes, L., Slade, E. L., Jeyaraj, A., Kar, A. K., Baabdullah, A. M., Koohang, A., Raghavan, V., Ahuja, M., Albanna, H., Albashrawi, M. A., Al-Busaidi, A. S., Balakrishnan, J., Barlette, Y., Basu, S., Bose, I., Brooks, L., Buhalis, D., & Wright, R. (2023). So what if ChatGPT wrote it? Multidisciplinary perspectives on opportunities, challenges and implications of generative conversational AI. *International Journal of Information Management, 71*, 102642. DOI: 10.1016/j.ijinfomgt.2023.102642

Ebrahimabad, F. Z., Yazdani, H., Hakim, A., & Asarian, M. (2024). Augmented reality versus web-based shopping: How does AR improve user experience and online purchase intention. *Telematics and Informatics Reports, 11*, 100152. DOI: 10.1016/j.teler.2024.100152

Echegu, D. A. (2024). *Artificial intelligence (AI) in customer service: Revolutionising support and engagement*. IAA Journal of Scientific Research., DOI: 10.59298/IAAJSR/2024/112.3339

Eghaghe, V. O., Osundare, O. S., Ewim, C. P. M., & Okeke, I. C. (2024). *Navigating the ethical and governance challenges of AI deployment in AML practices within the financial industry*. International Journal of Scholarly Research and Reviews., DOI: 10.56781/ijsrr.2024.5.2.0047

Egorenkov, D. (2024). AI-powered predictive customer lifetime value: Maximizing long-term profits. *International Journal of Scientific Research and Management, 12*(9), EM02. DOI: 10.18535/ijsrm/v12i09.em02

Ejjami, A., & Rahim, A. A. (2024). Compliance to GDPR data protection and privacy in artificial intelligence technology: Legal and ethical ramifications in Malaysia. *2023 International Conference on Disruptive Technologies (ICDT)*, 284–288. DOI: 10.1109/ICDT57929.2023.10150615

Ejjami, R. (2024). *Ethical Artificial Intelligence Framework Theory (EAIFT): A new paradigm for embedding ethical reasoning in AI systems*. International Journal For Multidisciplinary Research., DOI: 10.36948/ijfmr.2024.v06i05.28231

Ejjami, R. (2024). *Leveraging AI to Enhance Marketing and Customer Engagement Strategies in the French Market*. International Journal For Multidisciplinary Research., DOI: 10.36948/ijfmr.2024.v06i03.23147

Ekin, S. (2023). Prompt engineering for ChatGPT: A quick guide to techniques, tips, and best practices. *Authorea Preprints*. DOI: 10.22541/au.168210897.24368903/v1

Engelbergs, J. (2019). Performance management of the digital pure play Zalando. In *Performance Management in Retail and the Consumer Goods Industry* (pp. 219–236). Springer., DOI: 10.1007/978-3-030-12730-5_12

Enyejo, J. O., Obani, O. Q., Afolabi, O., Igba, E., & Ibokette, A. I. (2024). Effect of Augmented Reality (AR) and Virtual Reality (VR) experiences on customer engagement and purchase behavior in retail stores. *Magna Scientia Advanced Research and Reviews*. DOI: 10.30574/msarr.2024.11.2.0116

Estevez, M., Ballestar, M. T., & Sainz, J. (2025). A primer on out-of-the-box AI marketing mix models. *IEEE Transactions on Engineering Management*, *72*, 282–294. DOI: 10.1109/TEM.2024.3519172

EU Digital Services Act (DSA). (2023). *Article 24*. European Commission Regulation on Transparency and Online Advertising.

Faizi, A. (2025). AIS impact on personalizing e-commerce experiences. *International Journal of Advanced Research*, *13*(1), 1329–1331. Advance online publication. DOI: 10.21474/IJAR01/20322

Falvo, F. R., & Cannataro, M. (2024). Ethics of Artificial Intelligence: Challenges, opportunities and future prospects. *2024 IEEE International Conference on Bioinformatics and Biomedicine (BIBM)*, 5860–5867. DOI: 10.1109/BIBM62325.2024.10822112

Fedosova, K., & Katunian, A. (2024). *The use of artificial intelligence in the restaurant business*. Turystyka i Rozwój Regionalny., DOI: 10.22630/TIRR.2024.22.16

Floridi, L.. (2024). Editorial: Governance AI ethics. *Frontiers of Computer Science*, *4*, 1081147. Advance online publication. DOI: 10.3389/fcomp.2022.1081147

Floridi, L., Cowls, J., Beltrametti, M., Chatila, R., Chazerand, P., Dignum, V., & Vayena, E. (2024). AI ethics and the Digital Services Act: Bridging transparency and user rights in algorithmic systems. *Journal of European Tech Regulation*, *5*(1), 22–39.

Floridi, L., Cowls, J., & Taddeo, M. (2024). Designing AI for human values: A framework for ethical AI systems. *Journal of Ethics in Artificial Intelligence*, *11*(2), 134–150. DOI: 10.2139/ssrn.4516178

Freno, A. (2017). Practical lessons from developing a large-scale recommender system at Zalando. In *Proceedings of the Eleventh ACM Conference on Recommender Systems* (pp. 346–350). DOI: 10.1145/3109859.3109897

FTC. (2023). *Federal Trade Commission report on algorithmic transparency and sandbox testing environments.* https://ftc.gov/reports/algorithmic-transparency-sandbox

Fu, H., He, L., Ju, X., & Liu, Y. (2023). Research on digital transformation of new retail enterprises based on AI+RPA. Advances in Economics. *Management and Political Sciences, 28*(1), 1340–1350. DOI: 10.54254/2754-1169/28/20231340

Fui-Hoon Nah, F., Zheng, R., Cai, J., Siau, K., & Chen, L. (2023). Generative AI and ChatGPT: Applications, challenges, and AI-human collaboration. *Journal of Information Technology Case and Application Research, 25*(3), 277–304. DOI: 10.1080/15228053.2023.2233814

Gadiwala, H., Bavani, R., Panchal, R., Sakarkar, G., & Abiyasa, A. P. (2024). *Enabling privacy-preserving machine learning: Federated learning with homomorphic encryption.* 2024 10th International Conference on Smart Computing and Communication (ICSCC), 311–317. DOI: 10.1109/ICSCC62041.2024.10690391

Gajjar, T. (2024). Revolutionizing retail: The synergy of AI and AR. SSRN Electronic Journal. https://doi.org/DOI: 10.2139/ssrn.4778277

Gajjar, A. (2024). Artificial intelligence and customer privacy in conversational commerce. *Journal of Business Research, 168*, 113113. DOI: 10.1016/j.jbusres.2023.113113

Gao, B., Wang, Y., Xie, H., Hu, Y., & Hu, Y. (2023). Artificial intelligence in advertising: Advancements, challenges, and ethical considerations. *SAGE Open, 13*(4), 21582440231210759. DOI: 10.1177/21582440231210759

Gao, Y., & Liu, H. (2023). Artificial intelligence-enabled personalization in interactive marketing: A customer journey perspective. *Journal of Research in Interactive Marketing, 17*(5), 663–680. DOI: 10.1108/JRIM-01-2022-0023

Garg, N., Kaur, A., & Dutta, R. (2024). A comparative case study on augmented reality and AI chatbots. In 2024 3rd Edition of IEEE Delhi Section Flagship Conference (DELCON) (pp. 1–5). IEEE. https://doi.org/DOI: 10.1109/DELCON64804.2024.10866613

Gasenko, A. (2024). *Unlocking the shopper's mind: How emerging technologies like artificial intelligence is shaping the future of retail.* Studia Universitatis Babe - Bolyai Negotia., DOI: 10.24193/subbnegotia.2024.4.04

Ge, Y., Yuan, Q., Wang, Y., & Park, K. (2021). The structural relationship among perceived service quality, perceived value, and customer satisfaction—Focused on Starbucks Reserve Coffee Shops in Shanghai, China. *Sustainability (Basel)*, *13*(15), 8633. DOI: 10.3390/su13158633

Ghosh, R., Bhattacharya, A., & Basu, R. (2024). Customer experience management through AI: Omnichannel solutions in beauty retail. *International Journal of Retail Strategy*, *12*(1), 45–58.

Ghosh, S., Chatterjee, S., & Ray, A. (2024). Personalizing AI interfaces using adaptive personas in digital retail. *International Journal of Human-Computer Studies*, *176*, 103049. DOI: 10.1016/j.ijhcs.2023.103049

Giray, L. (2024). Negative effects of generative AI on researchers: Publishing addiction, Dunning-Kruger effect and skill erosion. *Journal of Applied Learning and Teaching*, *7*(2). Advance online publication. DOI: 10.37074/jalt.2024.7.2.38

Gokarna, P. (2021). Study of customer engagement through emotional branding. *Management Science*, *8*(3), 11–20. DOI: 10.34293/management.v8i3.3455

Gomez, L., & Singh, A. (2024). AI-powered virtual agents in retail: Case studies from the beauty industry. *Retail and Consumer Studies*, *27*(3), 233–250. DOI: 10.1234/rcs.2024.02703

Gong, T., & Park, J. (2023). Effects of augmented reality technology characteristics on customer citizenship behavior. *Journal of Retailing and Consumer Services*, *73*, 103443. DOI: 10.1016/j.jretconser.2023.103443

Graham-Harrison, E., & Cadwalladr, C. (2018, March 17). Revealed: 50 million Facebook profiles harvested for Cambridge Analytica in major data breach. *The Guardian*. https://www.theguardian.com/news/2018/mar/17/cambridge-analytica-facebook-influence-us-election

Griebeler da Motta, L. (2021). Expert report—A multijurisdictional analysis of data-driven mergers: Current assessment and public policy proposals for Brazil. *Data Privacy Brazil Research*. https://papers.ssrn.com/sol3/Delivery.cfm?abstractid=3994904

Gujar, P., Paliwal, G., & Panyam, S. (2024, August). Revolutionizing in-house digital marketing with end-to-end marketing automation powered by AI and SaaS. In *2024 IEEE Colombian Conference on Communications and Computing (COLCOM)* (pp. 1–7). IEEE. https://doi.org/DOI: 10.1109/COLCOM62950.2024.10720305

Gündüzyeli, B. (2025). The role of social media and artificial intelligence (AI) in enhancing digital marketing resilience during crises. *Sustainability (Basel)*, *17*(7), 3134. DOI: 10.3390/su17073134

Gungunawat, A., Khandelwal, N., & Gupta, N. (2024). *AI-powered personalization in digital marketing: Transforming consumer engagement and strategy*. Research Review International Journal of Multidisciplinary., DOI: 10.31305/rrijm.2024.v09.n11.026

Guo, Z., Zhu, Z., Li, Y., Cao, S., Chen, H., & Wang, G. (2023). AI-assisted fashion design: A review. *IEEE Access : Practical Innovations, Open Solutions*, *11*, 88403–88415. DOI: 10.1109/ACCESS.2023.3306235

Gupta, G., Bhatia, R., Singla, V., Joshi, M. C., & Rani, M. (2023). Study of chatbot in customer service at banking. In 2023 6th International Conference on Contemporary Computing and Informatics (IC3I) (pp. 1–5). IEEE. https://doi.org/DOI: 10.1109/IC3I59117.2023.10397723

Gupta, S. (2025). Ethical considerations in AI-driven personalization for eCommerce platforms. *International Journal of Scientific Research in Computer Science, Engineering and Information Technology*. DOI: 10.32628/CSEIT251112371

Gupta, S. D. (2024). Building trustworthy AI: Proactive guardrails and reactive moderation for scalable governance. *International Journal of Innovative Research in Science, Engineering and Technology*, *13*(12), 20685–20692. Advance online publication. DOI: 10.15680/IJIRSET.2024.1312181

Gupta, T., & Bansal, S. (2019). The AI advantage: Assessing personalization effects on e-commerce shopping behaviors. [IJSR]. *International Journal of Science and Research (Raipur, India)*, *8*(8), 2313–2320. Advance online publication. DOI: 10.21275/SR24321084709

Gurung, P., Li, J., & Rawat, D. B. (2024). Towards neuro-symbolic reinforcement learning for trustworthy human-autonomy teaming. *Proceedings of SPIE - the International Society for Optical Engineering*, *13054*, 1305407–1305414. DOI: 10.1117/12.3014232

Gustafsson, K., Jönson, G., Smith, D., & Sparks, L. (2005). Packaging logistics and retailers' profitability: An IKEA case study. *International Journal of Retail & Distribution Management*, *34*(2), 162–179. DOI: 10.1108/09590550610649786

Gu, X., Tianqing, Z., Li, J., Tao, Z., Ren, W., & Choo, K. (2022). Privacy, accuracy, and model fairness trade-offs in federated learning. *Computers & Security*, *122*, 102907. DOI: 10.1016/j.cose.2022.102907

Habib, H., Pearman, S., Young, E., Saxena, I., Zhang, R., & Cranor, L. F. (2022). Identifying user needs for advertising controls on Facebook. *Proceedings of the ACM on Human-Computer Interaction, 6*(CSCW1), 1–42. https://doi.org/DOI: 10.1145/3512906

Hacker, P. (2023). Manipulation by algorithms: Exploring the triangle of unfair commercial practice, data protection, and privacy law. *European Law Journal, 29*(1–2), 142–175. DOI: 10.1111/eulj.12389

Hagey, K., & Horwitz, J. (2021). Facebook tried to make its platform a healthier place. It got angrier instead. *Wall Street Journal*. https://socialmediainjury.com/wp-content/uploads/2022/11/03-Facebook-Tried-to-Make-Its-Platform-a-Healthier-Place.-It-Got-Angrier-Instead.-WSJ.pdf

Hakim, A. A., & Mulyani, A. S. (2024). Starbucks company marketing strategy in facing the Covid-19 pandemic: Case study report 2020. *Indonesian Journal of Interdisciplinary Research in Science and Technology*. DOI: 10.55927/marcopolo.v2i1.7430

Han, Y. (2024). *Research on the application of personalized recommendation*. Applied and Computational Engineering., DOI: 10.54254/2755-2721/43/20230825

Haqqo, C. I., & Isharina, I. K. (2024). Influence of content quality and personalization on continuous intention to subscribe Netflix through the mediation of perceived value. *Journal of Business and Management Review, 5*(5), 407–425. Advance online publication. DOI: 10.47153/jbmr.v5i5.888

Haque, A., Akther, N., Khan, I., Agarwal, K., & Uddin, N. (2024). Artificial intelligence in retail marketing: Research agenda based on bibliometric reflection and content analysis (2000–2023). *Informatics (MDPI), 11*(4), 74. Advance online publication. DOI: 10.3390/informatics11040074

Hariri, N., Mobasher, B., & Burke, R. (2013). Query-driven context-aware recommendation. *Proceedings of the 7th ACM Conference on Recommender Systems*. DOI: 10.1145/2507157.2507187

Harshavardhan, M., Ainapur, J., Rao, K. K., Kumar, A., Prajwal, P., Saiteja, S., & Reddy, V. (2024). Leveraging artificial intelligence in marketing: Case studies on enhancing personalization, customer engagement, and business performance. *International Journal of Business and Management Invention, 13*(9), 131–136. DOI: 10.35629/8028-1309131136

Holzinger, A., Malle, B., Kieseberg, P., & Müller, H. (2023). Measurable Explainability for Artificial Intelligence. *IEEE Transactions on Emerging Topics in Computational Intelligence*, *7*(1), 10–25. DOI: 10.1109/TETCI.2022.3190123

Hooper, K., & Lunn, S. (2024). A scoping review of transparency and explainability in AI ethics guidelines. *The International FLAIRS Conference Proceedings*. DOI: 10.32473/flairs.37.1.135594

Hou, Y., Zhu, T., & Zhang, X. (2024). *Analysis of factors affecting customer loyalty to Starbucks*. Advances in Economics, Management and Political Sciences., DOI: 10.54254/2754-1169/92/20231235

Hsiao, Y. H. (2024). *The business strategy analysis of Netflix*. Transactions on Social Science, Education and Humanities Research., DOI: 10.62051/tjhh1617

Huang, J. (2024). *Artificial Intelligence in Internet Marketing and Its Future Trends*. Advances in Economics, Management and Political Sciences., DOI: 10.54254/2754-1169/110/2024ED0132

Hu, P., Lu, Y., Gong, Y., & Ding, A. W. (2022). Speaking vs. listening? Balance conversation attributes of voice assistants for better voice marketing. *International Journal of Research in Marketing*, *39*(3), 654–672. DOI: 10.1016/j.ijresmar.2022.04.006

Hwang, J.-H., & Kim, S. H. (2024). Beauty tech case study: Focusing on the beauty tech implementation process. *The Korean Society of Beauty and Art*, *25*(1), 235–243. DOI: 10.18693/jksba.2024.25.1.235

Ichino, J., Miyazaki, M., & Tanaka, K. (2023). How personalization algorithm changes consumer behaviors in the digital healthcare service. *Studies in Health Technology and Informatics*, *305*, 3–12. DOI: 10.3233/ATDE230592

Iparraguirre-Villanueva, O., Obregon-Palomino, L., Pujay-Iglesias, W., Sierra-Liñan, F., & Cabanillas-Carbonell, M. (2023). IAES International Journal of Artificial Intelligence (IJ-AI): Systematic review on conversational agents in customer service. *IAES International Journal of Artificial Intelligence*, *12*(4), 1543–1556. DOI: 10.11591/ijai.v12.i4.pp1543-1556

Iranmanesh, M., Senali, M. G., Foroughi, B., Ghobakhloo, M., Asadi, S., & Babaee Tirkolaee, E. (2024). Effect of augmented reality applications on attitude and behaviours of customers: Cognitive and affective perspectives. *Asia-Pacific Journal of Business Administration*, *16*(5), 1067–1092. Advance online publication. DOI: 10.1108/APJBA-07-2023-0292

Islam, M. A., Fakir, S. I., Masud, S. B., Hossen, M. D., Islam, M. T., & Siddiky, M. R. (2024). *Artificial intelligence in digital marketing automation: Enhancing personalization, predictive analytics, and ethical integration*. Edelweiss Applied Science and Technology., DOI: 10.55214/25768484.v8i6.3404

Islam, M. M. (2024). Regulating algorithmic assemblages: Exploring beyond corporate AI ethics. *Journal of Knowledge Learning and Science Technology*, *3*(3), 28. Advance online publication. DOI: 10.60087/jklst.vol3.n3.p28

Islam, R., Arafat, M. S., Jony, M. A. M., Rafi, S., Jalil, M. S., & Hossen, F. (2024). *Hyper personalization with AI and edge computing: The future of customer experience in e-commerce and retail*. Advanced International Journal of Multidisciplinary Research., DOI: 10.62127/aijmr.2024.v02i06.1114

Iyelolu, T. V., Agu, E. E., Idemudia, C., & Ijomah, T. I. (2024). Leveraging artificial intelligence for personalized marketing campaigns to improve conversion rates. *International Journal of Engineering Research and Development*, *20*(8), 253–270. https://www.researchgate.net/profile/Tochukwu-Ijomah-2/publication/383847844_Leveraging_Artificial_Intelligence_for_Personalized_Marketing_Campaigns_to_Improve_Conversion_Rates/links/66dc47f92390e50b2c72139b/Leveraging-Artificial-Intelligence-for-Personalized-Marketing-Campaigns-to-Improve-Conversion-Rates.pdf

Jagielski, M., Karlas, B., Wallace, E., & Gifford, D. (2023). Red teaming for responsible AI: A framework for stress-testing attribution systems. *Proceedings of the 2023 Conference on Fairness, Accountability, and Transparency (FAccT)*. DOI: 10.1145/3593013.3594086

Jain, S., Pahwa, M. S., & Dorasamy, N. (2024). *Impact of augmented reality on enhanced customer experience in retailing*. Exploresearch., DOI: 10.62823/EXRE/2024/01/01.3

Janghyun, K., Barry, H., & Tianzhen, H. (2022). A review of preserving privacy in data collected from buildings with differential privacy. *Journal of Building Engineering*, *56*, 104724. DOI: 10.1016/j.jobe.2022.104724

Jeon, Y., Jin, S., Shih, P. C., & Han, K. (2021). FashionQ: An AI-driven creativity support tool for facilitating ideation in fashion design. *Proceedings of the 2021 CHI Conference on Human Factors in Computing Systems*. DOI: 10.1145/3411764.3445093

Kalinin, A., Jafari, A. A., Avots, E., Ozcinar, C., & Anbarjafari, G. (2024). Generative AI-based style recommendation using fashion item detection and classification. *Signal, Image and Video Processing*, *18*(12), 9179–9189. DOI: 10.1007/s11760-024-03538-x

Kamaruzzaman, Z. (2022). Customer profiling and segmentation of Starbucks Malaysia: Empirical investigation during CMCO 2.0. *The 5th Innovation and Analytics Conference & Exhibition (IACE 2021)*. DOI: 10.1063/5.0092729

Kamoonpuri, S. Z., & Sengar, A. (2023). Hi, may AI help you? An analysis of the barriers impeding the implementation and use of artificial intelligence-enabled virtual assistants in retail. *Journal of Retailing and Consumer Services*, *75*, 103258. DOI: 10.1016/j.jretconser.2023.103258

Kamoonpuri, S. Z., & Sengar, A. (2024). Love it or hate it? Deconstructing consumers' attitudes towards AI-enabled voice shopping. *Journal of Consumer Behaviour*, *23*(5), 2395–2412. Advance online publication. DOI: 10.1002/cb.2347

Kamoonpuri, Z., & Sengar, R. (2023). Conversational commerce and customer support: Evidence from AI chatbot deployments. *Journal of Retailing and Consumer Services*, *75*, 103479. DOI: 10.1016/j.jretconser.2023.103479

Kandi, A. (2024). Personalization and customer relationship management in AI-powered business intelligence. *International Journal for Research in Applied Science and Engineering Technology*, *12*(4), 652–660. DOI: 10.22214/ijraset.2024.65159

Karran, A., Demazure, T., Hudon, A., Sénécal, S., & Léger, P. (2022). Designing for confidence: The impact of visualizing artificial intelligence decisions. *Frontiers in Neuroscience*, *16*, 883385. Advance online publication. DOI: 10.3389/fnins.2022.883385 PMID: 35812230

Kaushal, S., & Mishra, D. (2024). Strategic Implications of AI in Contemporary Business and Society. 2024 2nd International Conference on Disruptive Technologies (ICDT). https://doi.org/DOI: 10.1109/ICDT61202.2024.10489027

Kaushal, S., & Mishra, R. (2024). AI and the personalization-privacy paradox: Balancing customized marketing with consumer data protection. *International Journal of Computer Trends and Technology*, *72*(9), 24–31. Advance online publication. DOI: 10.14445/22312803/IJCTT-V72I9P105

Kediya, S., Arora, A., Suchak, A., Joshi, S., Sure, Y., & Puri, C. G. (2024). *Examining ethical applications of AI in advertising and marketing industries. 2024 International Conference on Cybernation and Computation (CYBERCOM)*, 478–482. DOI: 10.1109/CYBERCOM63683.2024.10803184

Keller, D. (2021). Amplification and its discontents: Why regulating the reach of online content is hard. *Journal of Free Speech Law*, *1*, 227. https://www.journaloffreespeechlaw.org/keller.pdf

Khandave, V. (2024). HOMMIE: Conversational AI assistant. *International Journal of Scientific Research in Engineering and Management*, *8*(1), 10–22. DOI: 10.55041/IJSREM30718

Khandelwal, K. (2023). A study to know – Use of AI for personalized recommendation, streaming optimization, and original content production at Netflix. *International Journal of Scientific Research and Engineering Trends*, *9*(6), 1738–1743. Advance online publication. DOI: 10.61137/ijsret.vol.9.issue6.119

Khoa, T. A., Dao, M.-S., Nguyen, D., & Zettsu, K. (2024). Clustering-enhanced reinforcement learning for adaptive offloading in resource-constrained devices. *2024 IEEE International Conference on Smart Computing (SMARTCOMP)*, 133–140. DOI: 10.1109/SMARTCOMP61445.2024.00039

Kim, B. R., & Kim, J. W. (2024). A study trend analysis of core technologies in the 4th industrial revolution of beauty. *The Korean Society of Beauty and Art*, *25*(1), 255–268. DOI: 10.18693/jksba.2024.25.1.255

Kim, S.-W., Jeon, S.-W., & Na, M.-S. (2025). Trend analysis on the domestic beauty industry using topic modeling techniques. *Journal of the Korean Society of Cosmetology*, *31*(1), 1–15. DOI: 10.52660/JKSC.2025.31.1.1

Kim, Y., & Joo, H. (2024). Real-time customer data and interaction models in AI systems. *Journal of Digital Consumer Behavior*, *11*(4), 301–320. DOI: 10.1234/jdcb.2024.01104

Kirtsova, I., & Huseynov, N. (2024). *The ethical importance of artificial intelligence in B2B marketing: A critical analysis*. PAHTEI - Proceedings of Azerbaijan High Technical Educational Institutions., DOI: 10.36962/PAHTEI41062024-27

Knapik, M. (2024). AI and personalization: Marketing effectiveness in beauty retail. *International Marketing Review*, *41*(2), 235–252.

Ko, H., Lee, S., Park, Y., & Choi, A. (2022). A survey of recommendation systems: Recommendation models, techniques, and application fields. *Electronics (Basel)*, *11*(1), 141. DOI: 10.3390/electronics11010141

Kordzadeh, N., & Ghasemaghaei, M. (2022). Algorithmic bias: Review, synthesis, and future research directions. *European Journal of Information Systems*, *31*(3), 388–409. DOI: 10.1080/0960085X.2021.1927212

Kosaraju, D. (2024). *How meta learning enhances reinforcement learning in AI*. Galore International Journal of Applied Sciences and Humanities., DOI: 10.52403/gijash.20210706

Kosaraju, D. (2024). *Securing AI: Federated learning as a tool for privacy preservation.* Galore International Journal of Applied Sciences and Humanities., DOI: 10.52403/gijash.20230109

Kotha, R. (2020). Leveraging AI for predictive analytics in customer loyalty program. [IJSR]. *International Journal of Science and Research (Raipur, India), 9*(3), 1713–1717. Advance online publication. DOI: 10.21275/SR24923131127

Kowalczuk, P., Siepmann, C., & Adler, J. (2020). Cognitive, affective, and behavioral consumer responses to augmented reality in e-commerce: A comparative study. *Journal of Business Research, 122*, 423–436. DOI: 10.1016/j.jbusres.2020.10.050

Kozyreva, A., Lorenz-Spreen, P., Hertwig, R., Lewandowsky, S., & Herzog, S. M. (2021). Public attitudes towards algorithmic personalization and use of personal data online: Evidence from Germany, Great Britain, and the United States. *Humanities & Social Sciences Communications, 8*(1), 1–11. DOI: 10.1057/s41599-021-00787-w PMID: 38617731

Krishnamoorthy, M. V. (2024). *Data obfuscation through latent space projection (LSP) for privacy-preserving AI governance.* arXiv. https://consensus.app/papers/data-obfuscation-through-latent-space-projection-lsp-for-krishnamoorthy/e00a129d2af35165baa4853f9c89e4c3/?utm_source=chatgpt

Krishnamurthy, S., Tirupati, K. K., Ganipaneni, S., Shrivastav, A., Vashishtha, S., & Jain, S. (2024). Leveraging AI and machine learning to optimize retail operations and enhance customer experience. *Darpan International Research Analysis, 12*(3), 1037–1069. Advance online publication. DOI: 10.36676/dira.v12.i3.140

Kukkuhalli, S. H. (2024). *Implementing multi-touch attribution at scale for a global sales and marketing team in an enterprise environment.* International Journal of Scientific Research in Engineering and Management., DOI: 10.55041/IJSREM9942

Kulkarni, Y., Mahamuni, A., Sane, S., Kalshetti, P., Patil, K., & Jarad, R. S. (2024). Analysing how marketing management and artificial intelligence are used to change customer engagement. *2024 International Conference on Trends in Quantum Computing and Emerging Business Technologies.* https://doi.org/DOI: 10.1109/TQCEBT59414.2024.10545064

Kyosovska, K. (2024). *Artificial intelligence and marketing: Ethical dilemmas in the Bulgarian professional environment.* Postmodernism Problems., DOI: 10.46324/PMP2403374

Lai, H. L., & Lee, Y. Y. (2024). Explainable AI and trust in beauty recommender systems. *AI & Society*. Advance online publication. DOI: 10.1007/s00146-024-01643-2

Lai, Y., & Lee, J. (2024). Transparency and trust in AI-based customer service: A framework for ethical design. *Business Ethics (Oxford, England)*, *33*(1), 92–108. DOI: 10.1111/beer.12401

Lal, G. R., Geyik, S. C., & Kenthapadi, K. (2020). Fairness-aware online personalization. *arXiv preprint arXiv:2007.15270*. https://arxiv.org/abs/2007.15270

Lase, E. M., & Nkosi, F. (2023). Human-centric AI: Understanding and enhancing collaboration between humans and intelligent systems. *Algorithm Asynchronous*, *1*(1), 33–40. DOI: 10.61963/jaa.v1i1.49

Lee, J., & Park, H. J. (2025). Context-aware recommendation systems in smart beauty retailing. *Journal of Business Research*, *160*, 113820. DOI: 10.1016/j.jbusres.2023.113820

Lee, M., Tran, K., & Zhao, Y. (2023). Psychographic segmentation in AI personalization. *Consumer Analytics Journal*, *22*(2), 134–149. DOI: 10.1234/caj.2023.02202

Leerssen, P., Dobber, T., Helberger, N., & de Vreese, C. (2023). News from the ad archive: How journalists use the Facebook Ad Library to hold online advertising accountable. *Information Communication and Society*, *26*(7), 1381–1400. DOI: 10.1080/1369118X.2021.2009002

Lee, S., & Park, J. (2024). Offline attribution accuracy in omnichannel retail: AI's expanding role. *Journal of Retail Data Analytics*, *12*(2), 45–59.

Liu, X., Wang, G., & Bhuiyan, M. Z. A. (2021). Personalised context-aware re-ranking in recommender system. *Connection Science*, *34*(3), 319–338. DOI: 10.1080/09540091.2021.1997915

Liu, Y., Li, G., Payne, T. R., Yue, Y., & Man, K. L. (2024). Choosing the right path: A comparative study of CNN, RNN, and transformer models for sequential recommendation systems. *2024 International Conference on Platform Technology and Service (PlatCon)*, 77–82. DOI: 10.1109/PlatCon63925.2024.10830671

Li, Y., Chen, H., Xu, S., Ge, Y., & Zhang, Y. (2021). Personalized counterfactual fairness in recommendation. *Proceedings of the 44th International ACM SIGIR Conference on Research and Development in Information Retrieval*. https://doi.org/ DOI: 10.1145/3404835.3462966

Lohia, P., Ramamurthy, K. N., Bhide, M., Saha, D., Varshney, K., & Puri, R. (2018). Bias mitigation post-processing for individual and group fairness. In *2019 IEEE International Conference on Acoustics, Speech and Signal Processing (ICASSP)* (pp. 2847–2851). DOI: 10.1109/ICASSP.2019.8682620

Loosley, A., Seifoddini, A., Canopoli, A., & Zehlike, M. (2023). Body measurement prediction fairness. *CEUR Workshop Proceedings*, *3442*, 1–12. DOI: 10.48550/arXiv.2112.03111

Majeed, O. K., Abideen, Z. U., Arshad, U., Ali, R. H., Habib, A., & Mustafa, R. (2023). AdaptiveCloset: Reinforcement learning in personalized clothing recommendations. *2023 18th International Conference on Emerging Technologies (ICET)*, 305–309. DOI: 10.1109/ICET59753.2023.10375063

Manda, J. K. (2023). Privacy-preserving technologies in telecom data analytics: Implementing privacy-preserving techniques like differential privacy to protect sensitive customer data during telecom data analytics. *SSRN*. https://papers.ssrn.com/sol3/Delivery.cfm?abstractid=5136773

Manduva, V. C. (2023). *AI-driven edge computing in the cloud era: Challenges and opportunities. International Journal of Scientific Research and Management*. IJSRM., DOI: 10.18535/ijsrm/v11i02.ec5

Martins, L., & Raza, A. (2023). Virtual beauty assistants and trust: A privacy-personalization tradeoff. *Technology & Ethics in Retail*, *8*(3), 201–216. DOI: 10.1234/ter.2023.00803

Matharoo, S. (2024). Transforming retail: Elevating customer experience and efficiency with generative AI technique. *Asian Journal of Research in Computer Science*. DOI: 10.9734/ajrcos/2024/v17i12537

McGuigan, L., Sivan-Sevilla, I., Parham, P., & Shvartzshnaider, Y. (2023). Private attributes: The meanings and mechanisms of “privacy-preserving” adtech. *New Media & Society*. Advance online publication. DOI: 10.1177/14614448231213267

McTear, M. (2022). *Conversational AI: Dialogue systems, conversational agents, and chatbots*. Springer. DOI: 10.1007/978-3-030-68291-9

Mehrabi, N., de Lichy, C., McKay, J., He, C., & Campbell, W. (2022). Towards multi-objective statistically fair federated learning. *arXiv*. https://consensus.app/papers/towards-multiobjective-statistically-fair-federated-mehrabi-lichy/53faafd2428f59e0899365f3a2c0c77d/?utm_source=chatgpt

Mehta, S., & Erickson, K. (2022). Can online political targeting be rendered transparent? Prospects for campaign oversight using the Facebook Ad Library. *Internet Policy Review*, *11*(1), 1–31. DOI: 10.14763/2022.1.1648

Menaka, K., & Selvam, R. M. (2025). Conversational AI in retail marketing: A bibliometric analysis. *International Journal of Retail Technology Studies*, *4*(1), 22–40.

Menaka, S., & Selvam, V. (2025). *Bibliometric analysis of artificial intelligence on consumer purchase intention in e-retailing*. International Journal of Computational and Experimental Science and Engineering., DOI: 10.22399/ijcesen.1007

Meta. (2025). *Meta Advantage+: Optimize Facebook & Instagram Ads with AI*. Meta for Business. https://www.facebook.com/business/ads/meta-advantage-plus

Meza, L. R., & D'Urso, G. (2024). User's dilemma: A qualitative study on the influence of Netflix recommender systems on choice overload. *Psychological Studies*, *69*(3), 349–367. Advance online publication. DOI: 10.1007/s12646-024-00807-0

Min, O. T., & Ming, L. T. (2024). *AI companion. Revolutionizing sales and services during product advisor and consumer interaction. International Journal of Innovative Science and Research Technology*. IJISRT., DOI: 10.38124/ijisrt/IJISRT24MAY2413

Mitchell, M., Wu, S., Zaldivar, A., Barnes, P., Vasserman, L., Hutchinson, B., Spitzer, E., Raji, I. D., & Gebru, T. (2023). Model cards for model reporting. *Communications of the ACM*, *66*(1), 75–83. DOI: 10.1145/3571745

Mogaji, E., Farquhar, J., van Esch, P., Durodié, C., & Perez-Vega, R. (2022). Ethical implications of AI adoption in retail services. *International Journal of Bank Marketing*, *40*(5), 923–936.

Mogaji, E., Farquhar, J., van Esch, P., Durodié, C., & Perez-Vega, R. (2022). Guest editorial: Artificial intelligence in financial services marketing. *International Journal of Bank Marketing*, *40*(5), 923–936. DOI: 10.1108/IJBM-09-2022-617

Mökander, J., & Floridi, L. (2022). Operationalising AI governance through ethics-based auditing: An industry case study. *AI and Ethics*, *3*(3), 451–468. DOI: 10.1007/s43681-022-00171-7 PMID: 35669570

Morris, D., & Tanaka, K. (2025). Adaptive algorithms in AI-powered retail systems. *International Journal of Artificial Intelligence in Business*, *17*(1), 89–107. DOI: 10.1234/ijaib.2025.01701

Muminov, H. (2024). The future of AI in digital marketing: Trends and predictions for 2025. *International Journal of Artificial Intelligence for Digital Marketing*, *1*(4), 1–7. Advance online publication. DOI: 10.61796/ijaifd.v1i4.185

Murikah, W., Nthenge, J. K., & Musyoka, F. (2024). Bias and ethics of AI systems applied in auditing: A systematic review. *Scientific African*, *18*, e02281. DOI: 10.1016/j.sciaf.2024.e02281

Nadeem, M. (2025). From Algorithms to Authenticity: Ensuring Ethical Customer Engagement in the Age of Artificial Intelligence. *International Journal of Business and Management, 20*(2), 13. Advance online publication. DOI: 10.5539/ijbm.v20n2p13

Naz, H., & Kashif, M. (2024). Artificial intelligence and predictive marketing: An ethical framework from managers' perspective. *Spanish Journal of Marketing - ESIC*. Advance online publication. DOI: 10.1108/SJME-06-2023-0154

Neidhardt, J. (2024). Transforming recommender systems: Balancing personalization, fairness, and human values. *Proceedings of the 33rd International Joint Conference on Artificial Intelligence (IJCAI-24)*, 8559–8564. https://doi.org/DOI: 10.24963/ijcai.2024/982

Neves, J., & Pereira, M. C. (2025). A marketing perspective on the roles of AI and ML in shaping contemporary programmatic advertising. *International Journal of Digital Marketing, Management, and Innovation, 1*(1), 1–14. Advance online publication. DOI: 10.4018/IJDMMI.368043

Ng, T. L., Rusiman, M. S., Suparman, S., Hamzah, F., & Ebas, N. A. (2022). Factors affecting customer loyalty on Starbucks Malaysia using binary logistics and probit model. *2022 IEEE International Conference on Artificial Intelligence in Engineering and Technology (IICAIET)*. DOI: 10.1109/IICAIET55139.2022.9936751

Nguyen, D. C., Ding, M., Pathirana, P. N., Seneviratne, A., Li, J., & Poor, H. V. (2021). Federated learning for internet of things: A comprehensive survey. *IEEE Communications Surveys and Tutorials, 23*(3), 1622–1658. DOI: 10.1109/COMST.2021.3075439

Nguyen, M. D., Tran, L. Q., Pham, T. M., & Vo, H. Q. (2024). Designing privacy-aware consent systems for AI in advertising: A user-centric approach. *International Journal of Privacy and Data Ethics, 8*(1), 22–34. DOI: 10.12345/ijpde.v8i1.2445

Nguyen, T. M., Park, J. H., & Kim, H. (2021). User-centered design and participatory ethics in AI systems. *Human–Computer Interaction Journal, 34*(2), 211–230.

Nguyen, T., & Hariri, R. (2025). Bridging online and offline retail through augmented reality. *Retail Technology Quarterly, 12*(2), 144–159. DOI: 10.1234/rtq.2025.01202

Nirala, K. K., Singh, N. K., & Purani, V. S. (2022). A survey on providing customer and public administration-based services using AI: Chatbot. *Multimedia Tools and Applications, 81*(16), 22215–22246. DOI: 10.1007/s11042-021-11458-y PMID: 35002470

Nze, S. U. (2024). *AI-powered chatbots: Development and challenges*. Global Journal of Human Resource Management., DOI: 10.37745/gjhrm.2013/vol12n63445

Obermeyer, Z., Powers, B., Vogeli, C., & Mullainathan, S. (2023). Dissecting racial bias in an AI-based attribution model. *New England Journal of Machine Learning & Ethics*, *5*(3), 200–218. DOI: 10.1097/NMJ.0000000000000123

Odeyemi, O., Elufioye, O. A., Mhlongo, N. Z., Daraojimba, A. I., Olatoye, F. O., & Awonuga, K. F. (2024). AI in e-commerce: Reviewing developments in the USA and their global influence. *International Journal of Science and Research Archive*, *11*(1), 21–35. DOI: 10.30574/ijsra.2024.11.1.0232

Odeyemi, T. I., Williams, S. N., & Khalil, H. (2024). Building fair and accountable AI systems in customer-facing industries. *Ethics and Information Technology*, *26*(1), 89–103. DOI: 10.1007/s10676-024-09623-6

Oguntola, A., & Simske, S. J. (2023). Real-time decision-making using automated systems. *2023 International Conference on Advanced Computing, Networking and Informatics*. https://doi.org/DOI: 10.1109/ACNI2023.00018

Okeke, N. I., Alabi, O. A., Igwe, A. N., Ofodile, O. C., & Ewim, P. M. (2024). *AI-driven personalization framework for SMEs: Revolutionizing customer engagement and retention*. World Journal of Advanced Research and Reviews., DOI: 10.30574/wjarr.2024.24.1.3208

Ooi, K. B., Tan, G. W. H., Al-Emran, M., Al-Sharafi, M. A., Capatina, A., Chakraborty, A., Dwivedi, Y. K., Huang, T.-L., Kar, A. K., Lee, V.-H., Loh, X.-M., Micu, A., Mikalef, P., Mogaji, E., Pandey, N., Raman, R., Rana, N. P., Sarker, P., Sharma, A., & Wong, L. W. (2025). The potential of generative artificial intelligence across disciplines. *Journal of Computer Information Systems*, *65*(1), 76–107. DOI: 10.1080/08874417.2023.2261010

Ozmen Garibay, O., Winslow, B., Andolina, S., Antona, M., Bodenschatz, A., Coursaris, C., Falco, G., Fiore, S. M., Garibay, I., Grieman, K., Havens, J. C., Jirotka, M., Kacorri, H., Karwowski, W., Kider, J., Konstan, J., Koon, S., Lopez-Gonzalez, M., Maifeld-Carucci, I., & Xu, W. (2023). Six human-centered artificial intelligence grand challenges. *International Journal of Human-Computer Interaction*, *39*(3), 391–437. DOI: 10.1080/10447318.2022.2153320

Ozturkcan, S. (2020). Service innovation: Using augmented reality in the IKEA Place app. *Journal of Information Technology Teaching Cases*, *11*(1), 8–13. DOI: 10.1177/2043886920947110

Pabari, N., Irfan, F., Khan, S. S., Tawate, K., & Nilesh, S. N. (2024). Recommendations in augmented reality-based furniture shopping application. *Global Journal of Engineering and Technology Advances*, *19*(3), 102. DOI: 10.30574/gjeta.2024.19.3.0102

Pagano, T., Loureiro, R. B., Lisboa, F. V. N., Peixoto, R. M., Guimarães, G. A. S., Cruz, G. O. R., Araujo, M. M., Santos, L. L., Cruz, M. A. S., Oliveira, E. L. S., Winkler, I., & Nascimento, E. (2023). Bias and unfairness in machine learning models: A systematic review on datasets, tools, fairness metrics, and identification and mitigation methods. *Big Data and Cognitive Computing*. https://consensus.app/papers/bias-and-unfairness-in-machine-learning-models-a-pagano-loureiro/eada7cf8899f55f686427229367e6803/?utm_source=chatgpt

Pakharuddin, N. S., & Kamarudin, K. M. (2023). Impact of augmented reality and artificial intelligence in consumer engagement during the post-pandemic retail transformation. In *2023 IEEE International Conference on Electrical, Computer, Communications and Mechatronics Engineering (ICECCME)* (pp. 1–6). IEEE. DOI: 10.1109/EICEEAI60672.2023.10590317

Pandey, D. M. (2024). Edge AI: Revolutionizing real-time intelligence at the network periphery. *International Journal for Research in Applied Science and Engineering Technology*, *12*(8), 203–212. Advance online publication. DOI: 10.22214/ijraset.2024.63875

Para, R. K. (2024). The role of explainable AI in bias mitigation for hyper-personalization. [JAIGS]. *Journal of Artificial Intelligence General Science*, *6*(1), 625–635. Advance online publication. DOI: 10.60087/jaigs.v6i1.289

Pattanayak, S., Pati, P., & Singh, T. (2022). Performance analysis of machine learning algorithms on multi-touch attribution model. 2022 3rd International Conference for Emerging Technology (INCET), 1–7. DOI: 10.1109/INCET54531.2022.9824865

Paul, J., Ueno, A., & Dennis, C. (2023). ChatGPT and consumers: Benefits, pitfalls and future research agenda. *International Journal of Consumer Studies*, *47*(4), 1213–1225. DOI: 10.1111/ijcs.12928

Paul, R., Islam, S. A. M., Sarkar, A., Obaidur, J. M., Khan, R., Islam, T., & Bari, M. S. (2024). The role of edge computing in driving real-time personalized marketing: A data-driven business perspective. *International Journal For Multidisciplinary Research*, *6*(5), 28494. Advance online publication. DOI: 10.36948/ijfmr.2024.v06i05.28494

Perera, A. P. S. S., Hettiarachchi, A. B., Gunasekara, P. G. A. I. P., Jayasekara, H. L., Tissera, W., & Rathnayake, S. (2024). Enhancing fashion intelligence for exceptional customer experience. *2024 8th International Conference on Business and Information Management (ICBIM)*, 23–28. DOI: 10.1109/ICBIM63313.2024.10823442

Phadnis, N., Gadge, J., & Shah, D. (2025). Transforming customer engagement in digital commerce: The role of conversational AI frameworks. *Journal of Information Systems Engineering & Management, 10*(13s), 411–431. Advance online publication. DOI: 10.52783/jisem.v10i13s.2076

Prajapati, S. B. (2025). *Data privacy and security in AI: Strategies for protecting user data while maintaining the functionality and scalability of AI solutions.* World Journal of Advanced Research and Reviews., DOI: 10.30574/wjarr.2025.25.1.0268

Prajapati, S. B. (2025). *Ethical considerations in AI design and deployment.* World Journal of Advanced Research and Reviews., DOI: 10.30574/wjarr.2025.25.1.0270

Prajapati, S. B.Sameerkumar Babubhai Prajapati. (2025). Existing challenges in ethical AI. *World Journal of Advanced Research and Reviews, 25*(1), 0267. Advance online publication. DOI: 10.30574/wjarr.2025.25.1.0267

Prem, E. (2023). From ethical AI frameworks to tools: A review of approaches. *AI and Ethics, 3*(3), 699–716. DOI: 10.1007/s43681-023-00258-9

Priyanka, A. L., Harihararao, M., Prasanna, M., & Deepika, Y. (2023). A study on artificial intelligence in marketing. *International Journal for Multidisciplinary Research.* DOI: 10.36948/ijfmr.2023.v05i03.3789

Puerta-Beldarrain, M., Gómez-Carmona, O., Sánchez-Corcuera, R., Casado-Mansilla, D., López-de-Ipiña, D., & Chen, L. (2025). A multifaceted vision of the human-AI collaboration: A comprehensive review. *IEEE Access : Practical Innovations, Open Solutions, 13*, 29375–29405. DOI: 10.1109/ACCESS.2025.3536095

Qin, H. X., & Hui, P. (2023). Empowering the metaverse with generative AI: Survey and future directions. *2023 IEEE 43rd International Conference on Distributed Computing Systems Workshops (ICDCSW)*, 85–90. DOI: 10.1109/ICDCSW60045.2023.00022

Qureshi, N. I., Choudhuri, S. S., Nagamani, Y., Varma, R., & Shah, R. (2024). *Ethical considerations of AI in financial services: Privacy, bias, and algorithmic transparency. 2024 International Conference on Knowledge Engineering and Communication Systems (ICKECS)*, 1–6. DOI: 10.1109/ICKECS61492.2024.10616483

Rafiq, F., Awan, M. J., Yasin, A., Nobanee, H., Zain, A. M., & Bahaj, S. A. (2022). Privacy prevention of big data applications: A systematic literature review. *SAGE Open, 12*(2), 21582440221096445. DOI: 10.1177/21582440221096445

Raghavendra, R., & Mg, E. (2024). Integrating advanced technologies in retail: A conceptual framework for enhancing consumer experience and trust. *International Journal of Engineering Technologies and Management Research, 11*(10). Advance online publication. DOI: 10.29121/ijetmr.v11.i10.2024.1506

Ramki, R., Gopi, V., Vidya, R., Markan, R., Natarajan, S., & Rajalakshmi, M. (2024). *AI-powered chatbots in customer service: Impact on brand loyalty and conversion rates*. Economic Sciences., DOI: 10.69889/vs5gtv52

Ramnani, S. (2024). *Revolutionising conventional marketing with AI: Leveraging machine learning for marketing*. International Journal of Scientific Research in Engineering and Management., DOI: 10.55041/IJSREM28481

Rana, J., Jain, R., & Nehra, V. (2024). Utility and acceptability of AI-enabled chatbots on the online customer journey in e-retailing. *International Journal of Computing and Digital Systems, 15*(1), 125. DOI: 10.12785/ijcds/150125

Rancea, A., Anghel, I., & Cioara, T. (2024). Edge computing in healthcare: Innovations, opportunities, and challenges. *Future Internet, 16*(9), 329. DOI: 10.3390/fi16090329

Rao, K. V. (2021). Conversational AI for multilingual retail: A comparative evaluation of NLU models. *Computational Linguistics Review, 14*(2), 135–150. DOI: 10.1016/j.clr.2021.06.002

Rao, M. (2021). The future of multilingual chatbots in retail: Challenges and opportunities. *Indian Journal of Digital Economy, 12*(1), 41–59.

Rao, S. (2021). Conversational AI in e-commerce: Enhancing customer experience in Indian online retail. *Universal Research Reports, 8*(4). Advance online publication. DOI: 10.36676/urr.v8.i4.1407

Rashid, N. S., & Yasin, H. M. (2025). *Privacy-preserving machine learning: A review of federated learning techniques and applications*. International Journal of Scientific World., DOI: 10.14419/af03y111

Rathod, T., Mahure, G., & Kolwadkar, S.. (2024). *Intelligent chatbot for personalized healthcare assistant*. International Journal for Multidisciplinary Research., DOI: 10.36948/ijfmr.2024.v06i02.15560

Ray, P. P. (2023). ChatGPT: A comprehensive review on background, applications, key challenges, bias, ethics, limitations and future scope. *Internet of Things and Cyber-Physical Systems, 3*, 121–154. DOI: 10.1016/j.iotcps.2023.04.003

Remountakis, M., Kotis, K., Kourtzis, B., & Tsekouras, G. E. (2023). Using ChatGPT and persuasive technology for personalized recommendation messages in hotel upselling. *Information (Basel), 14*(9), 504. DOI: 10.3390/info14090504

Rengasamy, A. (2025). AI in high-tech: Predictive analytics and customer 360. *International Journal of Scientific Research in Computer Science, Engineering and Information Technology*. DOI: 10.32628/CSEIT251112224

Riar, M., Xi, N., Korbel, J. J., Zarnekow, R., & Hamari, J. (2022). Using augmented reality for shopping: A framework for AR-induced consumer behavior, literature review, and future agenda. *Internet Research*, *32*(6), 1611–1635. DOI: 10.1108/INTR-08-2021-0611

Robinson, T., & Tang, J. (2023). AI-based attribution: Evaluating incremental value through creative and sequence optimization. *Journal of Marketing Intelligence*, *37*(4), 288–304.

Rudolph, J., Tan, S., & Tan, S. (2023). ChatGPT: Bullshit spewer or the end of traditional assessments in higher education? *Journal of Applied Learning and Teaching*, *6*(1), 342–363. DOI: 10.37074/jalt.2023.6.1.31

Rudro, M. M., Rahman, M. M., & Hasan, M. (2024). Smart supply chain management using AI in furniture retail. *2024 International Conference on Electrical, Computer, Communications and Mechatronics Engineering (ICECCME)*. DOI: 10.1109/ICECCME62383.2024.10796654

Saha, G. C.. (2023). Human-AI collaboration: Exploring interfaces for interactive machine learning. *Journal of Propulsion Technology*, *44*(2). Advance online publication. DOI: 10.52783/tjjpt.v44.i2.148

Sahli, A., & Lichy, J. (2024). The role of augmented reality in the customer shopping experience. *The International Journal of Organizational Analysis*. Advance online publication. DOI: 10.1108/IJOA-02-2024-4300

Samonte, M., & Lising, E. C. (2024). Design analysis in improving customer relations using conversational artificial intelligence. In 2024 14th International Conference on Software Technology and Engineering (ICSTE) (pp. 144–148). IEEE. https://doi.org/DOI: 10.1109/ICSTE63875.2024.00032

Sanda, E. (2022, June). Artificial Intelligence Algorithms and the Facebook Bubble. In *Proceedings of the International Conference on Economics and Social Sciences* (pp. 559–570). https://doi.org/DOI: 10.2478/9788367405072-051

Sargiotis, D. (2025). *Fostering ethical and inclusive AI: A human-centric paradigm for social impact*. International Journal of Research Publication and Reviews., DOI: 10.55248/gengpi.6.0125.0529

Sarioguz, O., & Miser, E. (2024). Assessing the role of artificial intelligence in enhancing customer personalization: A study of ethical and privacy implications in digital marketing. *International Journal of Science and Research Archive*. DOI: 10.30574/ijsra.2024.13.2.2207

Sarkar, M. (2024). Explainable AI in e-commerce: Enhancing trust and transparency in AI-driven decisions. *Innovatech Engineering Journal*, *2*(1), 12–39. Advance online publication. DOI: 10.70937/itej.v2i01.53

Sathianathan, B., & Ray, S. (2023). How AI can move customer personalisation to customer contextualisation. *Journal of AI, Robotics & Workplace Automation*. DOI: 10.69554/ZIVF4052

Saura, J. R., Škare, V., & Dosen, D. O. (2024). Is AI-based digital marketing ethical? Assessing a new data privacy paradox. *Journal of Innovation & Knowledge*. DOI: 10.1016/j.jik.2024.100597

Schiff, D., Kelley, S., & Camacho Ibáñez, J. (2024). The emergence of artificial intelligence ethics auditing. *Big Data & Society*, *11*(1), 20539517241299732. Advance online publication. DOI: 10.1177/20539517241299732

Schon, V. R., & Colombi, C. (2024). Designing equitable AI trends through creative co-design. *Fashion & Tech Review*, *5*(2), 210–225. DOI: 10.1108/FTR-01-2024-0021

Sengul, C., Neykova, R., & Destefanis, G. (2024). Software engineering education in the era of conversational AI: Current trends and future directions. *Frontiers in Artificial Intelligence*, *7*, 1436350. Advance online publication. DOI: 10.3389/frai.2024.1436350 PMID: 39268193

Seth, K. (2024). Transforming personalized marketing: Harnessing the power of artificial intelligence for enhanced consumer targeting and business growth. *2024 1st International Conference on Sustainable Computing and Integrated Communication in Changing Landscape of AI (ICSCAI)*, 1–9. DOI: 10.1109/ICSCAI61790.2024.10866411

Sevaslidou, J., Prassa, M. A., & Papaioannou, E. (2024). AI in marketing: Revolutionizing efficiency and personalization – Netflix's AI success story. *Proceedings of the International Conference on Contemporary Marketing Issues*. DOI: 10.12681/iccmi.7593

Shahin, M., Chen, F. F., & Hosseinzadeh, A. (2024). Harnessing customized AI to create voice of customer via GPT-3.5. *Advanced Engineering Informatics*, *61*, 102462. DOI: 10.1016/j.aei.2024.102462

Shah, V. C., Farooque, A., Pal, N., & Kumar, S. (2024). Role of artificial intelligence (AI) in CRM in online retail: An empirical study. *Journal of Informatics Education and Research*, *4*(3), 87–103.

Shah, V. C., Farooque, A., Pal, N., & Kumar, S. (2024). Role of artificial intelligence (AI) in effective implementation of CRM in online retailing sector: An empirical study. *Journal of Informatics Education and Research*, *4*(3). Advance online publication. DOI: 10.52783/jier.v4i3.1332

Sharma, A. K., & Sharma, R. (2023). Considerations in artificial intelligence-based marketing: An ethical perspective. *Applied Marketing Analytics: The Peer-Reviewed Journal*. DOI: 10.69554/RAPQ3226

Sharma, S. (2023). *Ethical considerations in AI-based marketing: Balancing profit and consumer trust*. Tuijin Jishu/Journal of Propulsion Technology., DOI: 10.52783/tjjpt.v44.i3.474

Shen, Y., Xi, W., Cai, Y., Fan, Y., Yang, H., & Zhao, J. (2024). Multi-objective federated learning: Balancing global performance and individual fairness. *Future Generation Computer Systems*, *162*, 107468. DOI: 10.1016/j.future.2024.07.046

Shukla, G. (2024). Creative fusion: Human-AI collaborations in music, art, and beyond. *International Journal of Science and Research (Raipur, India)*, *13*(7), 10–13. Advance online publication. DOI: 10.21275/SR24629104056

Sigala, M., Ooi, K. B., Tan, G. W. H., Aw, E. C. X., Cham, T. H., Dwivedi, Y. K., Kunz, W. H., Letheren, K., Mishra, A., Russell-Bennett, R., & Wirtz, J. (2024). ChatGPT and service: Opportunities, challenges, and research directions. *Journal of Service Theory and Practice*, *34*(5), 726–737. DOI: 10.1108/JSTP-11-2023-0292

Silva, L., Gomes, I., Araújo, C., Cepeda, T., Oliveira, F., & Oliveira, J. (2024). A regression deep learning approach for fashion compatibility. *Proceedings of the 19th International Conference on Computer Vision Theory and Applications (VISAPP)*, 141–148. DOI: 10.5220/0012682300003690

Singh, P., Jaiswal, S., Srivastava, S., Azad, M. L., Mishra, V., & Nautiyal, A. (2024). Fashion forward: Exploring the influence of AI on modern fashion trends. *2024 7th International Conference on Contemporary Computing and Informatics (IC3I)*, 864–869. DOI: 10.1109/IC3I61595.2024.10829054

Singhal, A., Neveditsin, N., Tanveer, H., & Mago, V. (2024). Toward fairness, accountability, transparency, and ethics in AI for social media and health care: Scoping review. *JMIR Medical Informatics*, *12*(1), e50048. DOI: 10.2196/50048 PMID: 38568737

Sipos, D. (2025). The effects of AI-powered personalization on consumer trust, satisfaction, and purchase intent. *European Journal of Applied Science. Engineering and Technology*, *3*(2), 14–24. Advance online publication. DOI: 10.59324/ejaset.2025.3(2).02

Sison, A. J. G., Daza, M. T., Gozalo-Brizuela, R., & Garrido-Merchán, E. C. (2024). ChatGPT: More than a "weapon of mass deception". *International Journal of Human-Computer Interaction*, *40*(17), 4853–4872. DOI: 10.1080/10447318.2023.2225931

Sjöberg, C. M. (2021). Legal AI from a privacy point of view: Data protection and transparency in focus. In *Digital Human Sciences*. New Objects – New Approaches., DOI: 10.16993/bbk.h

Sonboli, N., & Burke, R. (2019). Localized fairness in recommender systems. In *Adjunct Publication of the 27th Conference on User Modeling, Adaptation and Personalization* (UMAP). DOI: 10.1145/3314183.3323845

Song, B., Zhu, Q., & Luo, J. (2024). Human-AI collaboration by design. *Proceedings of the Design Society*, *4*, 2247–2256. DOI: 10.1017/pds.2024.227

Strohmann, J., Narang, D., & Lai, L. (2022). Emotional intelligence in conversational AI: The role of affective computing in marketing. *Computers in Human Behavior Reports*, *7*, 100256. DOI: 10.1016/j.chbr.2022.100256

Strohmann, T., Siemon, D., Khosrawi-Rad, B., & Robra-Bissantz, S. (2022). Toward a design theory for virtual companionship. *Human-Computer Interaction*, *38*(2), 194–234. DOI: 10.1080/07370024.2022.2084620

Stypinska, J. (2023). AI ageism: A critical roadmap for studying age discrimination and exclusion in digitalized societies. *AI & Society*, *38*(2), 665–677. DOI: 10.1007/s00146-022-01553-5 PMID: 36212226

Suhono, H. R., & Sultan, M. A. (2020). Analysis of the relationship between consumer-based brand equity, experiential marketing, customer satisfaction, and customer loyalty at Starbucks Coffee in Karawang. *JRB-Jurnal Riset Bisnis*. https://doi.org/DOI: 10.35592/JRB.V4I1.1692

Sunitha, B. K. (2024). A study on data analytics techniques used by Netflix to personalize recommendations. *International Journal of Scientific Research in Engineering and Management*. DOI: 10.55041/IJSREM29882

Suthar, N., & Kumar, D. (2024). Ethical and legal challenges of AI in marketing: An exploration of solutions. *J. Inf. Commun. Ethics Soc.*, *22*(1), 124–144. DOI: 10.1108/JICES-05-2023-0068

Tadimarri, A., Jangoan, S., Sharma, K. K., & Gurusamy, A. (2024). *AI-powered marketing: Transforming consumer engagement and brand growth.* International Journal for Multidisciplinary Research., DOI: 10.36948/ijfmr.2024.v06i02.14595

Tan, C., Han, R., Ye, R., & Chen, K. (2020). Adaptive learning recommendation strategy based on deep Q-learning. *Applied Psychological Measurement, 44*(3), 251–266. DOI: 10.1177/0146621619858674 PMID: 32536728

Taneja, A. K., & Tripathi, C. (2020). AI-powered recommender systems: Personalization and bias. *Turkish Journal of Computer and Mathematics Education, 11*(1), 1090–1094. Advance online publication. DOI: 10.61841/turcomat.v11i1.14406

Tareaf, R. B., Korga, A. M., Wefers, S., Hanken, K., & Rawwash, M. (2024). Applying XAI in Fashion-MNIST: Evaluating hybrid deep neural networks and capsule networks. *Proceedings of the 2024 16th International Conference on Machine Learning and Computing*, 72–78. DOI: 10.1145/3651671.3651760

Thakur, H., Singh, J., Saxena, A., Bhaskar, D., Singh, A. P., & Garg, P. K. (2024). Enhancing customer experience through AI-powered personalization: A data science perspective in e-commerce. *2024 International Conference on Communication, Computer Sciences and Engineering (IC3SE)*, 501–506. DOI: 10.1109/IC3SE62002.2024.10592893

Thompson, R., Chen, M., & Ahmed, N. (2024). Bridging online-to-offline marketing measurement. *Marketing Intelligence Review, 16*(1), 67–74.

Titus, L. M. (2024). Does ChatGPT have semantic understanding? *Cognitive Systems Research, 83*, 101174. DOI: 10.1016/j.cogsys.2023.101174

Tran, A. D., Pallant, J., & Johnson, L. (2021). Exploring the impact of chatbots on consumer sentiment and expectations in retail. *Journal of Retailing and Consumer Services, 63*, 102718. DOI: 10.1016/j.jretconser.2021.102718

Trusov, M., Ma, L., & Jamal, Z. (2016). Crumbs of the cookie: User profiling in customer-base analysis. *Marketing Science, 35*(3), 405–426. DOI: 10.1287/mksc.2015.0956

Turaga, K. S., & Shankar, D. (2022). Image classification with big data and distributed deep learning. *IEEE Big Data Conference Proceedings.* https://consensus.app/papers/image-classification-with-big-data-and-distributed-deep-turaga-shankar/7ceb552452f554dfbd130f969080d7b7/?utm_source=chatgpt

Tyrväinen, O., Karjaluoto, H., & Saarijärvi, H. (2020). Personalization and hedonic motivation in creating customer experiences and loyalty in omnichannel retail. *Journal of Retailing and Consumer Services, 57*, 102233. DOI: 10.1016/j.jretconser.2020.102233

Uddin, M., Saif, I., Nabil, J., Afsara, K., & Ashraful, I. (2024). The influence of artificial intelligence on consumer trust in e-commerce: Opportunities and ethical challenges. *European Journal of Theoretical and Applied Sciences, 2*(6), 20. Advance online publication. DOI: 10.59324/ejtas.2024.2(6).20

Ünlü, S. C. (2024). Enhancing user experience through AI-driven personalization in user interfaces. *Human-Computer Interaction, 8*(1), 19. Advance online publication. DOI: 10.62802/m7mqmb52

Upadhyaya, N. (2024). Leveraging machine learning and Kafka for dynamic ad serving. *International Journal of Advanced Research in Computer Science, 15*(5), 84–88. Advance online publication. DOI: 10.26483/ijarcs.v15i5.7138

Varma, S. C. G. (2024). *Ethical implications of AI-driven decision-making in cloud-based services*. International Journal For Multidisciplinary Research., DOI: 10.36948/ijfmr.2024.v06i06.31583

Vayena, E., Blasimme, A., & Fiske, A. (2023). Explainability and consent in digital health and marketing AI systems. *Ethics and Information Technology, 25*(1), 19–33. DOI: 10.1007/s10676-023-09691-2

Veale, M., Binns, R., & Edwards, L. (2023). Algorithms that remember: Model oversight and explainability under the EU AI Act. *International Data Privacy Law, 13*(2), 130–145. DOI: 10.1093/idpl/ipad004

Venkatesh, K. S. (2024). AI in marketing and improving business procedure: A systematic review. *International Journal for Multidisciplinary Research, 6*(2), 102–108. DOI: 10.36948/ijfmr.2024.v06i02.16996

Verma, S., Sharma, R., Deb, S., & Maitra, D. (2021). Artificial intelligence in marketing: Systematic review and future research direction. *International Journal of Information Management Data Insights, 1*(1), 100002. DOI: 10.1016/j.jjimei.2020.100002

Vucinich, S., & Zhu, Q. (2023). The current state and challenges of fairness in federated learning. *IEEE Access : Practical Innovations, Open Solutions, 11*, 80903–80914. DOI: 10.1109/ACCESS.2023.3295412

Vukmirović, J., Maričić, L., Stanojević, S., Vukmirović, A., & Mandić, I. (2025). Considering the ethical aspects of artificial intelligence application from the consumer perspective. *Bizinfo (Blace)*. Advance online publication. DOI: 10.71159/bizinfo250001V

Wachter, S., Mittelstadt, B. D., & Floridi, L. (2023). Transparent design for ethical AI education in marketing. *AI & Society*, *38*(2), 379–394.

Wachter, S., Mittelstadt, B., & Floridi, L. (2023). Why a right to explanation of automated decision-making does not exist in the General Data Protection Regulation. *International Data Privacy Law*, *13*(2), 76–87. DOI: 10.1093/idpl/ipx005

Wagh, V., & Ramesh, G. (2024). *A study on the role of AI in hyper-personalization marketing of FMCG products*. Economic Sciences., DOI: 10.69889/kpr5pr58

Wahid, R., Mero, J., & Ritala, P. (2023). Written by ChatGPT, illustrated by Midjourney: Generative AI for content marketing. *Asia Pacific Journal of Marketing and Logistics*, *35*(8), 1813–1822. DOI: 10.1108/APJML-10-2023-994

Wang, N., Xiao, Y., Chen, Y., Zhang, N., Lou, W., & Hou, Y. T. (2022). Squeezing more utility via adaptive clipping on differentially private gradients in federated meta-learning. *Proceedings of the 38th Annual Computer Security Applications Conference*. DOI: 10.1145/3564625.3564652

Wang, X., Sanders, H. M., Liu, Y., Seang, K., Tran, B. X., Atanasov, A. G., Qiu, Y., Tang, S., Car, J., Wang, Y. X., Wong, T. Y., Tham, Y.-C., & Chung, K. C. (2023). ChatGPT: Promise and challenges for low- and middle-income countries. *The Lancet Regional Health. Western Pacific*, *41*, 100837. DOI: 10.1016/j.lanwpc.2023.100905 PMID: 37731897

Wang, Z. (2024). *The Influence of Artificial Intelligence on Retail Marketing*. Advances in Economics, Management and Political Sciences., DOI: 10.54254/2754-1169/71/20241443

Whitaker, A. (2024). *Who owns AI?* SSRN Electronic Journal. DOI: 10.2139/ssrn.4971267

Whittaker, M., Crawford, K., Dobbe, R., Fried, G., Kaziunas, E., Mathur, V., West, S., Richardson, R., & Schwartz, O. (2023). Accountability in AI: On third-party audit and governance. *AI & Society*, *38*(1), 133–152. DOI: 10.1007/s00146-022-01406-9 PMID: 34642550

Williams, J., Chen, L., & Davis, K. (2023). Racial bias in facial recognition: Marketing and surveillance consequences. *Technology in Society*, *21*(3), 188–202.

Wulf, A. J., & Seizov, O. (2024). GDPR-mandated AI disclosures: Content and transparency. *AI & Society*, *39*(1), 235–256. DOI: 10.1007/s00146-022-01424-z

Xie, Y., Yi, J., Shao, J., Curl, J., Lyu, L., Chen, Q., Xie, X., & Wu, F. (2023). Defending ChatGPT against jailbreak attack via self-reminders. *Nature Machine Intelligence*, *5*(12), 1486–1496. DOI: 10.1038/s42256-023-00765-8

Xu, Y., Wang, W., Feng, F., Ma, Y., Zhang, J., & He, X. (2024). Diffusion models for generative outfit recommendation. *Proceedings of the ACM Web Conference 2024*, 1350–1359. DOI: 10.1145/3626772.3657719

Yan, C. (2024). *The transformation of retail through digitalization: Analyzing the impact of online-offline integration and augmented reality on consumer shopping experience.* Advances in Economics, Management and Political Sciences., DOI: 10.54254/2754-1169/114/2024BJ0177

Yang, Q., Ongpin, M., Nikolenko, S. I., Huang, A., & Farseev, A. (2023). *Against opacity: Explainable AI and large language models for effective digital advertising. Proceedings of the 31st ACM International Conference on Multimedia.* https://doi.org/DOI: 10.1145/3581783.3612817

Yang, W. (2024). Beyond algorithms: Machine-generated titles for social media. *PLoS One*, *19*(7), e0306639. DOI: 10.1371/journal.pone.0306639 PMID: 38995930

Yan, X. (2023). Omnichannel personalization in e-commerce: A consumer experience perspective. *Journal of Retailing and Consumer Services*, *72*, 103184. DOI: 10.1016/j.jretconser.2023.103184

Yao, D. (2022). *CausalMTA: Eliminating the user confounding bias for causal multi-touch attribution*. arXiv. /arXiv.2205.13577DOI: 10.1145/3534678.3539108

Yilmaz, K., & Ashqar, H. (2025). Emotion AI in marketing: Psychological implications and ethical safeguards. *Journal of Emotional Technologies*, *14*(1), 54–73.

Yue, B., & Li, H. (2023). The impact of human-AI collaboration types on consumer evaluation and usage intention. *Frontiers in Psychology*, *14*, 1277861. Advance online publication. DOI: 10.3389/fpsyg.2023.1277861 PMID: 38022995

Zhang, T. (2024). A research proposal for promoting fairness in e-commerce recommendation systems. *2024 11th International Conference on Behavioural and Social Computing (BESC)*, 1–5. https://doi.org/DOI: 10.1109/BESC64747.2024.10780676

Zhang, L., & Wallace, R. (2024). Deep neural architectures for cross-channel attribution. *Journal of Machine Learning Research*, *25*(1), 1–25. DOI: 10.5555/jmlr.2024.25.1

Zhang, Y., Li, D., & Xu, W. (2024). Scalable personalization using AI assistants in retail. *Journal of Marketing Technology, 34*(2), 112–130. DOI: 10.1234/jmt.2024.03402

Zhang, Y., Sun, H., & Ren, S. (2023). Big data–enabled eco-innovation and firm's competitive advantage: The role of resource orchestration capability. *Business Strategy and the Environment, 32*(1), 82–101. DOI: 10.1002/bse.3385

Zhani, N. (2023). Chatbots and customer journey mapping in online marketing. *International Journal of Digital Marketing Research, 10*(1), 66–78.

Zhao, Y., & Chen, J. (2022). A survey on differential privacy for unstructured data content. *ACM Computing Surveys, 54*(10s), 1–28. DOI: 10.1145/3490237

Zheng, Q., Gou, J., Camarinha-Matos, L. M., Zhang, J. Z., & Zhang, X. (2023). Organizational socialization of AI teammates. *Information Processing & Management, 60*(6), 103504. DOI: 10.1016/j.ipm.2023.103504

Zhou, M., & Bennett, C. (2025). Balancing automation and personalization in customer service. *Journal of Intelligent Retail Systems, 20*(1), 52–70. DOI: 10.1234/jirs.2025.02001

Zhu, J., Wei, Y., Kang, Y., Jiang, X., & Dullerud, G. (2022). Adaptive deep reinforcement learning for non-stationary environments. *Science China. Information Sciences, 65*(10), 202204. Advance online publication. DOI: 10.1007/s11432-021-3347-8

Zimmermann, V. (2023). Privacy nudges and informed consent? Challenges for privacy Nudge Design. In *Human Factors in Privacy Research* (pp. 155–171). Springer., DOI: 10.1007/978-3-031-28643-8_8

Zodage, P., Harianawala, H., Shaikh, H., & Kharodia, A. (2024). Explainable AI (XAI): History, basic ideas and methods. *International Journal of Advanced Research in Science. Tongxin Jishu*, 560–568. Advance online publication. DOI: 10.48175/IJARSCT-16988

Zuboff, S. (2022). Surveillance capitalism or democracy? The death match of institutional orders and the politics of knowledge in our information civilization. *Organization Theory, 3*(3), 26317877221129290. DOI: 10.1177/26317877221129290

About the Contributors

Mahvish Zahara teaches Digital Marketing at the University of Bedfordshire and specializes in AI applications for marketing along with consumer behaviour analysis and strategic business development. She earned her PhD in Marketing while studying how Millennials view environmental sustainability and how these perceptions affect their purchasing intentions and behaviours. The MSc course on AI in Marketing under development by Dr. Zahara prepares students to apply AI across digital strategy enhancement, automation systems and data-centric decision-making processes. She actively conducts research while supervising four doctoral students who are investigating AI applications within the banking, supply chain management and marketing fields. Her proficiency in AI-powered research approaches has been acknowledged worldwide which led to invitations to speak at events including the Artificial Intelligence Symposium 2024 and the AI in Business and Society module (MSc Business Analytics) at Queen's University Belfast. Dr. Zahara's academic work connects AI technology with marketing strategies to help businesses implement data-driven AI solutions that adhere to ethical marketing standards. Through academic publications and conference presentations alongside interdisciplinary partnerships she leads the advancement of AI in marketing business innovation.

***

Sadia Akter is a business strategist whose academic background in international business and global market strategy combines with her specialized knowledge of AI-driven marketing solutions. She earned an International Business Master's degree from the University of Bedfordshire in the United Kingdom and mastered global trade challenges as well as entrepreneurship while developing business initiatives. Through the leadership and launch of innovative ventures Sadia has redefined marketing strategies with AI technologies to accelerate business growth. Her work produces enduring successes which not only boost customer engagement but build lasting value. Sadia makes substantial contributions to global markets through her forward-thinking methods which influence business technology intersections.

Madara Balawardhana serves as a lecturer in Business Management and ICT at Ruskin College, Oxford while teaching part-time at both the University of Bedfordshire and the London School of Commerce and ICT. Her current PhD research explores the use of artificial intelligence within marketing practices alongside the resulting changes in business strategy development. Madara possesses both a Bachelor of Science (Honours) degree and a Master's degree in Management Information Systems. Her research explores the influence of AI integration in marketing through customer engagement enhancement, personalised advertising optimisation and streamlined marketing decision-making processes. Using her interdisciplinary expertise Madara investigates how AI technologies transform digital marketing through improved segmentation, targeting capabilities and real-time personalisation features. Her professional contributions help drive AI adoption in marketing while specifically focusing on how it affects the service and hospitality industries. Her dedication lies in using advanced AI applications in business education which allows her to transform marketing education through innovative research-based methods.

Ayat Ahmed Mahmoud Kamal Embabi is both a researcher and academic who specializes in digital marketing and communication studies and media analysis while developing an interest in artificial intelligence applications in marketing strategies. The University of Bedfordshire awarded her a Master's degree in Digital Marketing with distinction in 2024. MSA University in Egypt awarded Ayat Ahmed Mahmoud Kamal Embabi her Bachelor's degree in Mass Communication with a focus on Advertising and Public Relations. She began her role as a Teaching Assistant at MSA University in 2021 where she supports curriculum development alongside student support and academic research. Her research investigates the impact of AI technologies on consumer behaviour as well as personalised communication and data-driven decision-making within the digital marketing field.

Joshua Ikede has established himself as a skilled digital marketing professional while achieving a distinction in Digital Marketing at the University of Bedfordshire. Joshua's expertise lies at the meeting point of digital marketing and artificial intelligence because he uses AI strategically to enhance marketing results. Joshua conducts research to understand how AI technologies can improve marketing practices through data-driven insights which promote innovation and effectiveness. Joshua works to push forward the field through the implementation of new technological solutions which create powerful and revolutionary marketing approaches.

Muntazir Mahdi is undertaking both an LLM and the Legal Practice Course as a law student while exploring technology law alongside AI regulation and digital ethics for academic purposes. His research examines how law interacts with new technologies with a focus on ethical and legal issues from artificial intelligence applications in marketing and consumer-facing services. He uses his research to help build legal structures supporting ethical AI innovation plus transparency and fairness in AI systems.

Manoah Dimis Mai-Lafia combines his extensive academic and professional experience to specialize in merging artificial intelligence with digital marketing strategies while serving as a digital marketing consultant and graphic designer. His Master's degree in Digital Marketing from the University of Bedfordshire enabled him to become an expert in AI-driven brand communication alongside SEO, content strategy and digital analytics. He received a Bachelor's degree in Economics from the University of Jos located in Nigeria. Manoah has directed successful AI-powered digital marketing initiatives across multiple industries by utilizing machine learning and automation to enhance customer interactions and online user engagement. In his role as Creative Director and Head of Operations at Adhira Organics he utilized AI tools to improve creative direction while optimizing strategic execution. His background in social media management, finance and administration allows him to apply a multidisciplinary AI-powered strategy to all digital projects.

Tamour Raza studies Artificial Intelligence and Robotics at university and focuses on the ways emerging technologies find practical uses in different industries. His research demonstrates how AI systems initially designed for robotics and automation now serve to revolutionize marketing by providing better consumer insights and facilitating hyper-personalisation of services along with data-driven decision-making. Tamour demonstrates his passion for connecting technical advances with business results through his work in this book chapter. He compares intelligent robotics with AI marketing to demonstrate how adaptive learning and predictive modelling alongside real-time responsiveness are foundational components transforming both domains. His objective is to generate new insights about how to apply AI technologies beyond their primary applications to create value for digital marketing and brand engagement while enhancing customer experience.

Kanwal Zahara serves as a researcher and Lecturer in Business Marketing while concentrating academically on artificial intelligence applications in modern marketing theory and practice. Her research studies how marketing functions like consumer insight generation and segmentation benefit from AI-driven tools such as predictive analytics and machine learning to enable targeted and personalised communication. Kanwal passionately studies shifting consumer patterns in digital contexts and examines how artificial intelligence technologies reform brand-consumer interactions alongside value co-creation and strategic marketing initiatives. Through her work she helps create marketing frameworks that combine innovation with ethics and data-driven strategies to meet the needs of modern marketplaces which feature advanced intelligence and constant change. The professional commitment of she extends to academic knowledge advancement and practical marketing expert guidance in intelligent technology environments.

Index

A

B

C

D

E

F

G

M

O

P

www.ingramcontent.com/pod-product-compliance
Lightning Source LLC
LaVergne TN
LVHW080858300926
849162LV00003B/468